A NEW SHORT GRAMMAR

OF THE

GREEK TESTAMENT

A NEW SHORT GRAMMAR

OF THE

GREEK TESTAMENT

*For Students Familiar with the
Elements of Greek*

PARTS I, III AND IV

BY

A. T. ROBERTSON, A.M., D.D., LL.D., Litt.D.,

PART II

BY

W. HERSEY DAVIS, A.M., Th.D., D.D.,

BAKER BOOK HOUSE
Grand Rapids, Michigan

5-15-78 M.

ISBN: 0-8010-7656-0

PHOTOLITHOPRINTED BY CUSHING - MALLOY, INC.
ANN ARBOR, MICHIGAN, UNITED STATES OF AMERICA
1977

To

THE MEMORY OF

JAMES HOPE MOULTON

BRILLIANT PIONEER IN THE

SCIENTIFIC GRAMMAR OF

THE GREEK NEW TESTAMENT

PREFACE TO THE NINTH EDITION

It was October, 1908, that the First Edition of the *Short Grammar of the Greek New Testament* came from the press of A. C. Armstrong and Son. It was an experiment and struck out on a new line. The author believed that there was a real need for a book for students who knew the elements of Greek and yet who were not able to cope with the larger and more difficult grammars, a book that would be a real introduction to the author's *Grammar of the Greek New Testament in the Light of Historical Research* which did not actually see the light till July, 1914, but on which the author was already at work steadily. In a way, the *Short Grammar* was a by-product of the long years of work on the large one. It was struck off at white heat, so to speak, to meet a definite need.

But it had to take note of the new philological discoveries. Comparative philology had revolutionized the study of language as to cases, tenses, voices, modes, prepositions, what not. The papyri had shown that the Greek New Testament was not in a peculiar "Biblical" language, but in the full stream of the κοινή.

And the book had to be brief and cheap enough to find general use. So it was launched.

In these twenty-three years the book has been the text-book in innumerable schools all over the world. When Doran took over the house of Armstrong, already Hodder and Stoughton had published it in Britain. Four translations followed in quick succession (Italian in 1910, French in 1911, German in 1911, Dutch in 1912). And this is the Ninth Edition for America and Britian.

This time the book has been completely rewritten. My gifted colleague, Dr. W. Hersey Davis, has done Part II Accidence. He has given the actual forms used in the New Testament and the κοινή and no others, a great convenience in a school grammar. He has also made the paradigms full enough so that the student will not need any of the classical grammars to help him. But this is not a "Beginner's Grammar" like that useful one by Dr. Davis (*A Beginner's Grammar of the Greek New Testament*). It is still a book for students familiar with the elements of Greek and designed as an introduction to the larger grammar.

The book has been tested by teachers for twenty odd years. Many suggestions from them have helped to make this Edition what it is as it now goes forth upon a new career.

The plates of this volume have been paid for by the Seminary Publication Fund in order to reduce the price for students.

I appreciate the skill and courtesy of Mr. Joseph S. Dickson of Louisville, Ky., the compositor who put this volume in type.

A. T. ROBERTSON

PREFACE TO THE TENTH EDITION

No grammar of the Greek New Testament has had so many editions and so many translations since its first appearance in 1908. This fact is proof of the need of such a book in harmony with modern philological knowledge (comparative philology) and the new discoveries concerning the κοινή (the papyri and inscriptions). Not all students care for this type of grammar and some prefer the traditional type. This grammar meets the definite need of those who do desire to be introduced to the new linguistic learning. Corrections of *errata* have been made in the text where practicable. There is given a list of *Corrigenda* in addition. Many thanks are given to

Rev. Joseph Nordenhaug, Ph. D., of Oslo, Norway;

Rev. C. J. Allen, Ph. D., of Fairmont, N. C.;

Rev. Prof. V. F. Pottle, of Philadelphia, Pa.;

Rev. L. M. Polhill, Th. M., of Forsythe, Ga.;

for verifying references.

Louisville, Ky. A. T. ROBERTSON
October, 1933

TABLE OF CONTENTS

PART I.   INTRODUCTION

PART II.   ACCIDENCE

PART III.   THE BUILDING OF WORDS

PART IV.   SYNTAX

A BRIEF BIBLIOGRAPHY

Abbott, E. A., Johannine Vocabulary (1905).

Abbott, E. A., Johannine Grammar (1906).

Abbott-Smith, G., A Manual Greek Lexicon of the New Testament. 2 ed. (1923).

Abel, F. M., Grammaire du grec biblique suivi d'un choix de papyrus (1927).

Allen, H. F., The Infinitive in Polybius Compared with the Infinitive in Biblical Greek (1907).

Blass-Debrunner, Grammatik des neutestamentlichen Griechisch. Sechste durchgesehene und vermehrte Auflage (1931).

Blass-Thackeray, Grammar of New Testament Greek. 2d ed. (1905).

Boisacq, Dictionnaire étymol. de la langue grecque (1916).

Bonhöffer, A., Epiktet und das N. T. (1911).

Brugmann-Thumb, Griechische Grammatik. 4 Auflage (1913).

Buck, C. D., Introduction to the Study of the Greek Dialects (1910).

Burton, E. D., Syntax of the Moods and Tenses of the New Testament. 3rd ed. (1909).

Buttmann-Thayer, A Grammar of the New Testament Greek (1880).

Cadbury, H. J., The Style and Literary Method of Luke (1920).

Claflin, Edith, Syntax of Boeotian Dialect Inscriptions (1905).

Clyde, J., Greek Syntax (1876).

Conybeare and Stock, Selections from the Septuagint with Grammar (1905).

Cremer, H., Biblico-Theological Lexicon of N. T. Greek. 4th Engl. ed. (1892).

Cremer, H., Biblisch-theologisches Wörterbuch (1902).

Crönert, W., Memoria Graeca Herculanensis (1903).

Curtius, G., Greek Etymology (1886).

Dalman, G., Grammatik des jüdisch-palästinischen Aramäisch. 2d ed. (1905).

Dalman, G., The Words of Jesus. Engl. ed. (1902).

Dana, H. E.-Mantey, J. R., A Manual Grammar of the Greek New Testament (1927).

Davis, W. Hersey, A Beginner's Grammar of the Greek New Testament. 4th ed. (1928).

Deissmann, A., Bibelstudien (1895).

Deissmann, A., Neue Bibelstudien (1897).

Deissmann-Grieve, Bible Studies (1901).

Deissmann, Licht vom Osten. 4 Aufl. (1923).

Deissmann-Strachan, Light from the Ancient East. 4th ed. (1927).

Delbrück, B., Grundriss der vergleich. Grammatik d. indog. sprachen. Syntax Bde III-V (1893, 1897, 1900).

Dieterich, K., Untersuchungen zur Geschichte der Sprache von der hellen. Zeit (1898).

Ebeling, H., Griechisch-deutsches Wörterbuch zum Neuen Testament (1913).

Gersdorf, C. G., Beiträge zur Sprachcharakteristik der Schriftsteller des N. T. (1816).

Gildersleeve, B. L., and Miller, C. W. E., Syntax of Classical Greek. Part I (1900), Part II (1911).

Giles, P., A Short Manual of Comparative Philology. 2 ed. (1901).

Goodwin, W. W., Syntax of the Moods and Tenses of the Greek Verb. 2 ed. (1890).

Green, S. G., Handbook to the Grammar of the Greek N. T. Rev. ed. (1904).

Gregory, C. R., Prolegomena to Tischendorf (Vol. III, 1894).

Grimm-Thayer, A Greek-English Lexicon of the N. T. (1887).

Hadley and Allen, Greek Grammar (1895).

Harper and Weidner, Introductory New Testament Greek Method (1888).

Hatch, E., Essays in Biblical Greek (1892).

Hatch, W. H. P., Beginner's New Testament Greek Book (1905).

Havers, W., Untersuchungen zur Kasussyntax der indog. Sprachen (1911).

Hayes, D. A., Greek Culture and the New Testament (1925).

Heine, G., Synonomik des neutestam. Griechisch (1898).

Heinrici, K. F., Der literarische Charakter der neut. Schriften (1908).

Helbing, R., Grammatik der Septuaginta. Laut-und Wortlehre (1907).

Hobart, W. K., The Medical Language of Luke (1882).

Hoole, C. H., The Classical Element in the N. T. (1888).

Horn, R. C., The Use of the Subjunctive and the Optative Moods in the Non-literary Papyri (1926).

Jannaris, A. N., A Historical Greek Grammar (1897).

Kennedy, H. A. A., Sources of N. T. Greek (1895).

Kretschmer, P., Die Einl. in die Geschichte der griech. Sprache (1906).

Kühner-Blass, Ausführliche Grammatik der griechischen Sprache. Formenlehre. 3 Aufl. I Teil (1890). II Teil (1892).

Kühner-Gerth, Ausf. Gramm. Satzlehre. 3 Aufl. I Teil (1898). Teil II (1904).

Kuhring, W., De praepositionum Graecarum in chartis Aegyptiacis usu (1906).

Laughlin, T. C., The Solecisms of the Apocalypse (1902).

Liddell and Scott, Greek-English Lexicon. 8th ed. 1882). New (9th) Ed. by H. S. Jones (1925—).

Machen, J. G., New Testament Greek for Beginners (1923).

Mayser, E., Grammatik der griech. Papyri aus der Ptolemäerzeit. I Laut—und Wortlehre (1906). Satzlehre II.1. (1926).

Meecham, H. G., Light from Ancient Letters (1923).

Meillet, A., Introduction à l'étude comparative des langues indoeuropéennes. 4th ed. (1915).

Meisterhans-Schwyzer, Grammatik der attischen Inschriften. 3 Aufl. (1900).

Milligan, G., The Greek Papyri with Special Reference to Their Value for N. T. Study (1912).

Milligan, G., Selections from the Greek Papyri (1910).

Milligan, G., Here and There among the Papyri (1922).

Monro, D. B., Homeric Grammar. 2 ed. (1891).

Moulton, J. H., A Grammar of New Testament Greek. Vol. I. Prolegomena (1906). 3rd ed. (1908). Vol. II Accidence and Word Formation. Finished by W. F. Howard (1929).

Moulton-Dieterich, Einleitung in die Sprache des N. T. (1911).

Moulton, J. H., From Egyptian Rubbish Heaps (1916).

Moulton and Milligan, The Vocabulary of the Greek Testament Illustrated from the Papyri and Other Non-literary Sources (1914-29). In one volume (1930).

Moulton, W. F., and Geden, A. S., A Concordance to the Greek Testament (1897).

Mutzbauer, C., Die Grundbedeutung des Konjunktivs und Optativs und ihre Entwick. in Griech. (1908).

Nachmanson, E., Laute und Formen der Magnetischen Inschriften (1904).

Nachmanson, E., Beiträge zur Kenntnis der altgriech. Volkssprache (1910).

Nägeli, T., Der Wortschatz des Apostels Paulus (1905).

Nestle, E., Novum Testamentum Graece. 9 Aufl. (1927).

Norden, E., Agnostos Theos, Untersuchungen zur Formgeschichte religiöser Rede (1913).

Papyri (various publications as Oxyrhynchus, etc.).

Pernot, H., Études sur la langue des Evangiles (1927).

Preisigke, F., Wörterbuch der griechischen Papyrusurkunden mit Einschluss der griechischen Inschriften, etc. Vollendet von Emil Kiessling (1914-1927).

Prellwitz, Etym. Wörterbuch d. griech. Sprache. 2 Aufl. (1905).

Preuschen-Bauer, Griechisch-Deutsches Wörterbuch zu den Schriften des N. T. (1928).

Psichari, J., Essai sur le grec de la Septante (1908).

Radermacher, L., Neutestamentliche Grammatik. Das Griechische des N. T. im Zusammenhang mit der Volkssprache. 2 Aufl. (1925).

Radermacher, L., Besonderheiten der Koine-Syntax (Wien. Stud. 31, 1909).

Regard, P. F., La phrase nominale dans la langue du Nouveau Testament (1919).

Reinhold, H., De Graecitate Patrum, etc. (1898).

Robertson, A. T., A Short Grammar of the Greek New Testament (1908. 8th ed. 1928). 9th ed. wholly rewritten with help of W. H. Davis (1931).

Robertson-Bonaccorsi, Breve Grammatica del Nuovo Testamento greco (1910).

Robertson-Grosheide, Beknopte Grammatica op het Grieksche Nieuwe Testament (1912).

Robertson-Montet, Grammaire du grec du Nouveau Testament (1911).

Robertson-Stocks, Kurzgefasste Grammatik des Neutestamentlichen Griechisch (1911).

Robertson, A. T., A Grammar of the Greek New Testament in the Light of Historical Research. 1914. 4th ed. 1923. Pages 1540.

Robertson, A. T., New Testament Grammar after Thirty Years (pp. 82-92 of Festgabe für Adolph Deissmann, 1927).

Robertson, A. T., An Introduction to the Textual Criticism of the N. T. 2 ed. (1928).

Robertson, A. T., The Minister and His Greek N. T. 2 ed. (1924).

Robertson, A. T., Word Pictures in the N. T. 6 vols. (I to III 1930, IV 1931).

Robertson-Davis, A New Short Grammar of the Greek Testament (1931).

Rossberg, C., De praepos. Graecarum in chartis Aegyptiis Ptol. aetatis usu (1909).

Rouffiac, J., Recherches sur les caractères du grec dans le N. T. après les inscriptions de Priène (1911).

Rutherford, W. G., The New Phrynichus (1881).

Sacco, G., La Koinè del Nuovo Testamento e la transmissione del Sacro Testo (1928).

Schanz, M., Beiträge zur histor. Syntax d. griech. Sprache 1822ff.)

Schmid, W., Der Atticismus in seinen Hauptvertretern. 4 Bde (1887-1897).

Schmidt, W., De Flavii Josephi elocutione (1894).

Schulze, W., Graeca Latina (1901).

Schweizer, E., Grammatik der pergamenischen Inschriften (1898).

Sharp, G., Remarks on the Definitive Article in the Greek of the N. T. (1803).

Sharp, D. S., Epictetus and the New Testament (1914).

Simcox, W. H., The Language of the N. T. (1890).

Simonson, W. H., A. Greek Grammar. 2 vols. (1903, 1908).

Slotty, F., Der Gebrauch des Konjunktivs und Optativs in den griechischen Dialekten (1915f).

Smyth, H. W., The Greek Dialects (1894).

Smyth, H. W., A Greek Grammar for Schools and Colleges (1916).

Solmsen, F., Beiträge zur griech. Wortforschung (1909).

Sophocles, E. A., A Greek Lexicon of the Roman and Byzantine Period (1888).

Souter, A., A Pocket Lexicon to the Greek N. T. (1916).

Souter, A., Novum Testamentum Graece (1910). The Revisers' Text.

Stahl, J. M., Kritisch-historische Syntax des griech. Verbums der Klass. Zeit (1907).

Streeter, B. H., The Four Gospels. 2 ed. (1927).

Swete, H. B., Introduction to the O. T. in Greek. 2 ed. (1914).

Thackeray, H. St. John, A Grammar of the O. T. in Greek. Vol. I. Accidence (1909).

Theimer, A., Beiträge zur Kenntnis des Sprachgebr. im N. T. (1896).

Thieme, G., Die Inschriften von Magnesia am Mäander und das N. T. (1906).

Thomson, P., The Greek Tenses in the N. T. (1895).

Thumb, A., Die griech. Sprache im Zeitalter des Hellenismus (1901).

Thumb, A., Handbuch der neugriech. Volkssprache. 2 Aufl. (1910).

Thumb (A.)-Angus (S.), Handbook of the Modern Greek Vernacular (1912).

Tischendorf, C., Novum Testamentum Graece. Editio octava critica major. 2 vols. (1869-1872). Bd III. Prolegomena. C. R. Gregory (1894).

Trench, R. C., Synonyms of the N. T. 11 ed. (1890). Deutsche Ausgabe von Werner (1907).

Vander Meulen, Jacob, Familiar Talks with Students of the Greek New Testament (1931).

Viereck, P., Sermo Graecus et. (1888).

Viteau, J., Étude sur le grec du N. T. I Le Verbe (1893). II Le Sujet (1896).

Völker, F., Syntax de griech. Papyri. I. Der Artikel (1903).

Votaw, C. W., The Use of the Infinitive in Biblical Greek (1896).

Wackernagel, J., Die hellenistiche Gemeinsprache (1905. Teil I. Abt. viii im Kult. d. Gegenwart).

Waldis, J., Sprache und Stil der grossen griech. Inschrift (1920).

Wessely, C., Die lat. Elemente in d. Gräcität d. ägypt. pap. (1902).

Westcott (B. F.) and Hort (F. J. A.), The New Testament in the Original Greek. Many eds. Vol. II. Appendix (1881).

Wilke, C. G., Die nt Rhetorik (1843).

Wilke-Grimm, Clavis N. T. Philogica. 4 Aufl. (1903).
Translated by J. H. Thayer (1887).

Williams, C. B., The Participle in the Book of Acts (1908).

Winer, G. B., Grammatik des nt. Sprachidioms. 7 Aufl. (1867).

Winer-Masson, A Grammar of the N. T. Greek (1859).

Winer-Moulton (W. F.), A Treatise of the Grammar of N. T. Greek. 3rd ed. (1882).

Winer-Thayer (J. H.), A Grammar of the Idiom of the N. T. (1869). Various eds.

Winer-Schmiedel (P. W.), Winer's Grammatik des neut. Sprachidioms. 8 Aufl. (1894—II.2, 1898). Never finished.

Witkowski, St., Epistulae privatae Graecae. 2 Aufl. (1911).

Wright, J., A Comparative Grammar of the Greek Language (1912).

Zarncke, E., Die Entstehung der griech. Literatursprachen (1890).

PART I

INTRODUCTION

CHAPTER I

THE FAMILY OF LANGUAGES TO WHICH THE GREEK BELONGS

1. *The Origin of Language.*

The languages of men probably go back to a common origin, but that origin is lost to modern men. The late Alfredo Trombetti of Rome (*The Unity of Origin of Language*) claimed to be able to prove this to be a fact.

2. *Three Stages in the History of Language.*

Grammatical students find three stages in the history of language (Isolating, Agglutinative, Inflectional). The isolating tongues, like Chinese, Burmese, etc., have no inflection and depend on position in the sentence and tone of voice for clearness. Agglutinative tongues like Hungarian and Turkish employ various prefixes, infixes, and suffixes to express relations of words with each other. The inflectional languages use stem and endings which no longer exist separately. All language was originally pictographic as is seen in the Egyptian hieroglyphs.

3. *Two Great Inflectional Families.*

(a) The Semitic family includes the Arabic, Aramaic, Assyrian, Sumerian, Babylonian, Canaanite (Phoenician), Ethiopic (Abyssinian), Hebrew, Sabaean, Syriac. These languages have a tri-literal root, consonantal writing, small use of moods and tenses, many internal changes in inflection. The Assyrian and Babylonian are ideographic and syllabic and written from left to right. The Arabic, Aramaic and Hebrew are alphabetic and written from right to left.

(b) The Indo-Germanic Family is much the largest. Giles (*Manual of Comparative Philology*, pp. 7 – 23) greatly prefers Indo-Germanic to Indo-European, Aryan, or Indo-Keltic. Not all the languages of India can be included and Armenian is neither Indian nor European. The term Indo-Germanic takes in all the inflectional languages except the Semitic from Northeast India to Western Europe. Giles finds eight groups in the Indo-Germanic Family.

(1) *The Aryan Group.*

Here belong the Sanskrit, the oldest member (Vedas 1500 B. C.) known to us and the most helpful for the study of Greek words and forms. The Sanskrit as a spoken language died out before the Christian era. The Prakit, Pali, Hindi, and modern Gipsy dialect come from it.

The Iranian dialects (Zend in which the Persian sacred books are written, 1100 B. C.; old Persian, language of the old inscriptions from 520 B. C. on).

(2) *The Armenian.* Called by Herodotus an offshoot of the Phrygian. Inscriptions in the Phrygian language still exist. The New Testament is translated into Armenian.

(3) *Greek.*

Numerous dialects with long history. Pelasgians, Achaeans, Dorians, Aeolians, Ionians, these followed each other. The Ionic was the base of the old Attic which finally became the literary language of Athens. But there were numerous minor subdivisions like the Arcadian, Boeotian, Northwest, Thessalian, etc. (Robertson, *Grammar*, p. 16; Buck, *Introduction to the Study of the Greek Dialects*).

(4) *Albanian.*

No literature earlier than seventeenth century. Language of Illyria.

(5) *Latin* and kindred Italian dialects (Oscan, Umbrian, etc.). The modern Romance languages (French, Italian, Provencal, Spanish, Portuguese, Rumanian, Rhaeto-Romanic) all come from Latin. Vast literature and many inscriptions.

(6) *Keltic.*

The old Gaulish of Caesar's time, Welsh, Cornish, Breton, Manx, Irish, Scotch Gaelic, all belong here.

(7) *Germanic or Teutonic.*

Here are three great branches (Gothic; Scandinavian, including Danish, Icelandic, Norwegian, Swedish, the Runic inscriptions going back to the third century A. D.; the West Germanic dialects: Anglo-Saxon, Frisian, Old Saxon or Low German, Old High German, Old Low Franconian from which come Dutch and Flemish). Our modern English is a combination of Anglo-Saxon with Norman-French.

(8) *The Baltic-Slavonic Group.*

Slavonic proper (Old Bulgarian, Russian, Servo-Croatian, Slovenian, Bohemian, Polish, Sorabian or Wendish) and the Baltic group (Old Prussian, Lettic, Lithuanian).

4. *The Original Indo-Germanic Tongue.*

There was, no doubt, an original language from which all the eight Indo-Germanic families of languages sprang. Brugmann calls it *Ur und Grundsprache*, "original and ground speech." Kretschmer considers it a necessary hypothesis. It is interesting to trace some common words through the Indo-Germanic languages where the original root has survived with various phonetic changes. Take *father*, for instance: Sanskrit *pitr*, perhaps from *pa* to protect, Greek πατήρ, Latin *pater*, Danish *vader*, Swedish *fader*, Anglo-Saxon *faeder*, German *vater*, even French *père*. So *mother* is Sanskrit *matr*, from *ma* to measure, Greek μήτηρ, Latin *mater*, old Slavonic *mati*, Swedish *moder*, Danish *moeder*, Anglo-Saxon *modor*, Old English *moder*, German *mutter*, even French *mère*. These examples can be multiplied indefinitely by consulting Skeat's *Etymological Dictionary*. This philological kinship and history is not guess-work. It may be well to give a sample of

Grimm's law of the permutation of consonants as found in Smyth's Greek Grammar, p. 1:

π = f	τ = th	β = p	δ = t
πατήρ	τρεῖς	τύρβη	δύο
father	three	thorp	two
γ = c(k)	φ = b	θ = d	χ =g
ἀγρός	φέρω	θύρα	χήν
acre	bear	door	goose

There are, besides these cognate words, a great number of derived words in English like geometry (γεωμετρία), Theatre (θέατρον), mystery (μυστήριον).

5. *Relation of the Greek to the Other Members of the Indo-Germanic Family.*

Precisely as French, Italian, Portuguese, Spanish are all descendants of the Latin, so Sanskrit, Zend, Greek, Latin, Gothic are all children of the original Indo-Germanic tongue. But Greek does not come from Sanskrit nor Latin from Greek. Somewhere at some time in the remote past there was a breaking up of the Indo-Germanic stock. The different branches went their several ways, but retained much of the original linguistic stock common to all or to various members of the family. The Sanskrit grammar (say Whitney's *Sanskrit Grammar*) is peculiarly illuminating for the study of the Greek which is further along the road. So Latin Grammar is very helpful for the Greek and Greek for Latin and both for the study of Anglo-Saxon and English, French, and German. The science of comparative philology has thrown a flood of light upon the scientific grammar of the Greek tongue. The old method is not true to the facts in the explanation of cases, tenses, modes, voices, prepositions, article, or any thing. An excellent book on this subject is Wright's *Comparative Grammar of the Greek Language* (1912).

CHAPTER II

THE GREEK ANCESTRY OF THE KOINH

6. *The Unity of the Greek Language.*

From the earliest fragments of the pre-Homeric Greek to the latest modern Greek newspaper there is unity and identity of essential vocabulary and idiom. There is less difficulty to the modern Greek in reading Homer than to a modern American or Englishman in reading King Alfred's Chronicles. Even Shakespeare, still more Chaucer, causes the modern reader to search diligently in the glossary for the meaning of the antique words and idioms. It used to be the fashion for some teachers of classical Attic to speak patronizingly of the Greek of Paul or of John as a degenerated *patois*. But that is a conception that has passed away with the new knowledge. The historical method of linguistic study treats a language as a whole. A grammar so made includes all the facts and finds out the rules from the facts. It does not select a few facts to illustrate arbitrary rules and consider all the rest as exceptions. The problem for the student of the Greek New Testament is to find out precisely where the New Testament comes in the long stream of the Greek language which is still flowing (a live, not a dead language). Professor Herbert Weir Smyth, Professor of Greek in Harvard University, said of my *Grammar of the Greek New Testament in the Light of Historical Research*: "Its primary distinction lies in the fact that it is the only work that attempts to survey the language of a single book of Ancient Greek literature from the point of view of the history of Greek speech as a whole." That certainly is the aim of that work and Dr. Smyth is in hearty sympathy with that method of studying Greek grammar.

7. *Periods in the History of the Language.*

There are various ways of dividing the long life of the Greek tongue. Much remains to be learned about the primitive Greek before Homer. The Mycenaean Age from 1500 to 1000 B. C. covers this period in which the obscure origin of the Greek language takes root in the Cretan civilization. The age of the Dialects runs from 1000 B. C. to 300 B. C., from Homer to Alexander's conquest of the oriental world and a bit beyond. The age of the κοινή is roughly from 300 B. C. after Alexander's death to 330 A. D. the time when the seat of government was set up in Constantinople instead of Rome. During this period Greek was a *Weltsprache*, the language of the Mediterranean world, a language common (κοινή) to all instead of just a dialect. From 330 to 1453 (the year when the Turks captured Constantinople) may be called Byzantine Greek. Modern Greek runs from 1453 to the present day. Here we have over three thousand years of known history for this marvellous tongue which includes the richest treasures of all time. But greater than Homer, than Aeschylus, than Sophocles, than Herodotus, than Thucydides, than Plato, than Aristotle is the New Testament and it is written in the κοινή which is a worthy vehicle for the greatest of all books.

8. *The Dialects.*

Strabo called the Greeks and their dialects Ionic, Doric, and Aeolic (everything not Ionic or Doric), but not so Herodotus or Thucydides. Buck (*Greek Dialects*, p. 8) roughly divides the dialects thus:

West Greek Division.
   (1) Northwest Greek: Phocian, Locrian, Elean, etc.
   (2) Doric: Laconian, Corinthian, Argolic, Cretan, etc.

East Greek Division.
   (1) Attic–Ionic.
   (2) Aeolic: Lesbian, Thessalian, Boeotian.
   (3) Arcado–Cyprian or Achaean.

The numerous mountains and vales and islands kept the people separate in clans and dialects. These dialectical differences are preserved in the vast number of inscriptions preserved in Greece, the islands, and Asia Minor. The various political leagues gave rise to several larger divisions overlapping or overleaping the geographical boundaries like the Attic κοινή under the Athenian Empire in the fifth century B. C., the Doric κοινή in the fourth century B. C., the Northwest κοινή under the Aeolian League in the third century B. C., all this before the κοινή caused by Alexander's victories (B. C. 334 on) spread over the Mediterranean world. But the Attic was the language of Thucydides, Aeschylus, Sophocles, Plato, Aristotle, Demosthenes, and this literary Attic became the model for modern students of Greek culture. But before the time of Alexander, no one dialect dominated all of Greek life and thought.

9. *Literary and Vernacular.*

Unfortunately we do not possess literary remains of all these Greek dialects except in the inscriptions. We do have books in the Epic (Homer), the Ionic (Herodotus), the Attic like Thucydides, the Doric like Theocritus, the Aeolic like Sappho. The inscriptions are usually in the vernacular, though sometimes in the literary style (official documents, decrees, etc.). But in all well developed languages there is always the vernacular style spoken by the people in everyday life and the literary style employed in writing books. The literary style is more stilted and fixed, less flexible and changeable than the vernacular.

10. *Vernacular Attic the Ancestor of the Vernacular κοινή.*

The Macedonians under Philip, the father of Alexander, used the Attic κοινή. The Ionic dialect first gave way before the Attic, though Ionic peculiarities are occasionally found in later times. "It is this Attic, already well-nigh established in Ionic territory, and in some respects modified by Ionic, that the Macedonians took up and spread, and which is henceforth termed the κοινή or, more specifically, the Attic κοινή" (Buck, *Greek Dialects*, p. 157). But it is vernacular Attic that Alexander and his army carried over the world, not the literary Attic. A fairly clear idea of this Vernacular Attic can be obtained from inscriptions (Meisterhans-Schwyzer, *Grammatik der Attischen Inschriften.* 3 Auflage. 1900). In this later vernacular Attic we have the immediate background of the vernacular κοινή seen in such forms as γίνομαι, the sparing use of the optative, the disappearance of the dual, the limited use of the superlative. There was developed also a literary κοινή seen in such writers as Polybius, Josephus, Plutarch.

11. *The Influence of the Other Dialects in the* κοινή.

It was not a mixture of the Attic with the other dialects. Just as Ionic and Aeolic had left traces on the Attic when it triumphed over them, so each of the chief dialects left deposits here and there in the κοινή. So then it is not surprising to see in the New Testament the Ionic σπείρης (Acts 27:1), the Boeotian-Aeolic εἴχοσαν (John 15:22,24), the Arcadian-Doric ἀφέωνται (Lu. 5:20), the Northwest Greek ἔγνωκαν (John 17:7) and the accusative in –ες like τέσσαρες (for–ας) in some New Testament manuscripts and τοὺς πράκτορες in a papyrus of 1 A. D. (B. G. U. 350).

12. *Modern Greek and the* κοινή.

The Modern Greek Vernacular carries on the tradition of the Attic Vernacular through the κοινή Vernacular and the Byzantine Vernacular. Tendencies seen in the κοινή Vernacular have become normal in the Modern Greek Vernacular, like the disappearance of the optative and the infinitive. Fortunately we have a first-class grammar of the Modern Greek Vernacular by which one can readily judge the development of the language (*Handbook of the Modern Greek Vernacular* by Albert Thumb. Translated by S. Angus. 1912.)

13. *Atticism Not the* κοινή.

There continued through the κοινή a school of writers who tried to preserve or to revive the literary Attic, writers like Dionysius of Halicarnassus, Dio Chrysostom, Lucian, Aelian.

There are teachers today who consider nothing but literary Attic to be first-class Greek. There were once Purists who held that the Greek of the New Testament had to be the finest literary Attic since it was inspired. On the other hand some Hebraists held the New Testament to be in a language of the Holy Ghost unlike any Greek ever written before, a sort of pious jargon or Jewish-Greek. Both were wrong. It is far better than either of these extremes. It is written in the κοινή, the language of the Graeco-Roman world in the first century A. D.

CHAPTER III

CHARACTERISTICS OF THE VERNACULAR KOINH.

14. *Simplification.*

The language of business called for shorter sentences than the complicated and involved periods of the Attic historians and orators. The chief monuments of this eminently practical form of Greek appear in the thousands of papyri from various points in Egypt (Fayum, Oxyrhynchus, etc). There is already a vast number of these documents gathered in Oxford, London, Berlin, Paris, and now made available by careful editions which still continue to come from the press as a result of the researches of Grenfell and Hunt and many others. Edwin Mayser of Stuttgart has discussed the grammar of the papyri (*Grammatik der griech. Papyri. Laut–und Wortlehre*, 1906; *Satzlehre*,1926) and so has Albert Thumb(*Die griechische Sprache im Zeitalter des Hellenismus*, 1901). Fr. Preisigke has produced a lexicon of the papyri (*Wörterbuch der griechischen Papyrusurkunden*, 1927). It was Adolph Deissmann (then of Heidelberg, now of Berlin) who first called the attention of scholars to the fact that the Greek of the papyri resembled closely the Greek of the New Testament in his *Bible Studies* (1901. First German edition, *Bibelstudien*, 1895). This was followed by his *Light from the Ancient East* (1910. German ed. 1908. 4th English ed. 1927). It was the late James Hope Moulton who first began the formal application of the new light from the papyri to the Greek New Testament (*Prolegomena to a Grammar of New Testament Greek*, 1906. 3rd ed. 1908). These papyri include scraps from the junk-pile, trash baskets of Egypt, some of them used as wrapping for mummies, some dumped in piles and preserved under the dry sand of Egypt. The scraps preserve for us the actual life of the day and include letters of all sorts, duns, contracts, receipts, proclamations, anything, everything. Two popular books that will help one get this point of view are Moulton's *From Egyptian Rubbish Heaps* (1916) and Meecham's *Light from Anc. Letters* (1923).

15. *Universality.*

The very fact that the κοινή was a world speech and meant to be understood by merchants, travellers, statesmen, soldiers all over the Graeco-Roman world had a compelling influence toward uniformity in vocabulary, forms and syntax. Dialectical peculiarities would be sloughed off of necessity to a large extent. A glance through Buck's *Greek Dialects* will show one the numerous diversities in the Greek during the Age of the Dialects. To this day in England a Cornishman and a Yorkshireman have difficulty in understanding one another. The conquests of Alexander had a levelling influence very much like the modern newspaper, radio, and "talkies." It was a providential circumstance that Paul could carry the message of Christ in one language and be understood wherever he went. Those who held on to their local language as in Lycaonia, Palestine, Egypt, Italy would know Greek. So Paul wrote to the church in Rome in Greek.

16. *Provincialism.*

And yet local pecularities were to a certain extent inevitable. Inscriptions show local influence on the κοινή in Phrygia, Palestine, Egypt in particular. Dieterich notes in Asia Minor the use of εἶμαι for εἰμί, τίς for ὅστις, θέλω rather than the future tense. But Thumb (*Griechische Sprache*, p. 27) holds that most of the so-called Alexandrian peculiarities like εἶχαν, ἤλθοσαν, γέγοναν, ἑώρακες are general throughout the κοινή.

17. *New Meanings to Old Words.*

This was inevitable with the clash of new ideas as men commingled from all parts of the world. We have that going

on constantly today in English. Dictionaries come out with
new editions every ten years to keep up with the procession.
So δαιμόνιον for demon or evil spirit, ἐκκλησία church, ἐρωτάω
to beg, ὀψώνιον for wages, παιδεύω to chastise. Christianity arose in the very century when the κοινή reached its
height as a world speech. It made its contribution of new
meanings to old words, like σωτήρ Saviour.

18.   New Words.

But new ideas sometimes require new words. Electricity
under Edison's magic hand has made almost a book of new
words about light, heat, power, refrigeration, radio, "movies."
Dr. W. Hersey Davis has found over three thousand words
in the papyri of the first century A. D. not in any Greek lexicon.
A complete lexicon of the κοινή of the first century A. D.
would be a boon to the student of the Greek New Testament.
But many appear first in the κοινή like βαπτισμός, μαθητεύω,
υἱοθεσία (cf. Robertson, *Grammar*, p. 65).

19.   Changes in Forms.

For a full discussion of this subject the student may be
referred to Chapter VI Orthography and Phonetics, Chapter
VII Declensions and Chapter VIII Conjugation of the Verb
in my large Grammar and to the corresponding chapters in
this Grammar by Dr. Davis (Chapters V to VII). A few of
them may be briefly summarised here. The μι–verbs are
becoming ω–verbs steadily. There is an increase in the
number of verbs in ίζω. We find –τωσαν instead of –ντων
in the imperative plural. Forms like ἔσχα (second aorist
tense with first aorist endings) are common. The periphrastic
imperfect is frequent. There is confusion in the use of –άω
and –έω verbs. The dual has vanished. The third declension sometimes has forms like νύκταν in the accusative singular
as though in the first. Contraction is sometimes absent
as in ὀρέων. The use of ὃς ἐάν for ὃς ἄν is noticeable. There is
frequent absence of the augment.

20. *Changes in Syntax.*

The nominative absolute is very common. Failure to make words in apposition agree in case is frequent. The accusative case occurs often with verbs that can use other cases. Prepositions are used with fewer cases than formerly. New prepositions are abundant. Compound words are very frequent. The optative mood is fast vanishing. The use of ἵνα is driving out the infinitive. The use of εἰς is slowly displacing ἐν till in Modern Greek ἐν has disappeared. Originally ἐν alone was used and either with the locative or the accusative. Finally only εἰς is used though only with the accusative. The two words mean the same thing. The superlative adjective is usually elative, not a true superlative. The passive voice is driving out the middle. The future participle is decreasing in use. These can serve as a picture of the changes going on in the κοινή which have reached a culmination in the Modern Greek.

CHAPTER IV

SPECIAL FEATURES OF THE GREEK NEW TESTA-MENT

21. *Written to Meet Definite Needs.*

This greatest of all books is not an artificial production or a literary performance. There is variety; but each book had its origin in actual need. The Gospels are explained by Luke in his Preface (1:1-4). He made use of the many treatises already written and consulted eye-witnesses of the Master and made his contribution to preserve the record of what Jesus said and did. Luke carried on the story in the Acts as his second contribution to the story of what Jesus began to do and teach (Acts 1:1). The Epistles or Letters as Deissmann prefers to call them were written either to individuals or churches to meet actual emergencies and to apply the principles of Christ to the problems of their time. In so doing the writers met the problems of our time also. The amazing thing about these occasional epistles is their adaptability to life today. The epistles to churches were read in public meeting (Col. 4:16) and were passed on from church to church. The first collections were the Epistles of Paul (then the other Epistles) and then the Four Gospels. The Revelation of John stands to itself, but it is from a time of crisis and adopts the method of earlier Jewish apocalypses. In a sense they were all tracts, or pamphlets, for the time that met actual needs with the power of the Holy Spirit so that they are of supreme worth for all time.

22. *Written by Men Conscious of a Great Mission and Message.*

There are personal details in the Epistles, but they are not trivial. The writers all reveal the leadership of the Holy Spirit. The men who write are conscious of dealing with the beginning of a great enterprise, the gospel of God in Christ. They show passion and restraint and consider themselves the bond-slaves of the Lord Jesus Christ and count it a joy and a glory to struggle and to suffer for him.

23. *In the Vernacular κοινή in the Main.*

There was the literary κοινή, but these men for the most part, as shown by the papyri, employed the language of everyday life. They preached in this language and they wrote in it. Some of them were men of the schools and so with culture, particularly Luke, Paul, and the author of Hebrews. Luke in his Preface uses the literary κοινή in a way worthy of Polybius or any historian, but he does not go on in that style. Paul in his moments of great passion and elevation, like 1 Corinthians 13 and 15 and Romans 8, rises to the noblest eloquence, but in the main his language is that of eagerness and zeal and often with a rush of tangled sentences. The Epistle to the Hebrews is more like a literary production in its marshalling of arguments than any book in the New Testament.

24. *With Individual Peculiarities.*

Style is the man, certainly the mark of the man, and it varies with changes in the man's age and progress. There is no New Testament style. Each writer is himself and his vocabulary suits his special message. The Vernacular κοινή is plain in Mark's gospel. The Apostle Paul shows all this in his four groups of Epistles. Each group has a slightly different vocabulary from the other, a thing observed in the various groups of the writings of Milton and Shakespeare. The two most striking variations in style appear in First and Second Peter on the one hand and in the Gospel and the Apocalypse of John on the other. Certainly the same man who wrote First Peter had a different amanuensis (or none) when he wrote 2 Peter and so we argue about Revelation as compared with the Gospel of John. Many modern scholars refuse to believe that the same man could have written 1 and 2 Peter or John's Gospel and the Apocalypse. It is a bit interesting that Peter and John are the two disciples called "unlearned and ignorant" (ἀγράμματοι καὶ ἰδιῶται) by the Sanhedrin (Acts 4:13). Perhaps that fact throws some light on these divergences. But it is a matter for gratitude that the writers of the New Testament are so individual.

25. *Some Semitic Influence.*

There is not so much as the old Hebraists thought who explained every idiosyncrasy as a Hebraism. Some even called it a special language of the Holy Ghost, unlike anything before or since, a sort of Hebrew-Greek jargon. That is untrue, but we do not need to go to the other extreme and deny any Semitic influence at all. All the writers except Luke were Jews who spoke Aramaic as well as the Greek κοινή. They could read Hebrew also and were familiar with the Septuagint which is full of translation Hebraisms, put into the Greek vernacular κοινή by men who knew Hebrew better than they did Greek. Mark frequently quotes the Aramaic words used by Jesus who spoke now Aramaic, now κοινή as the occasion demanded, like ταλειθά, κούμ (5:41). Paul used now Greek, now Aramaic in Jerusalem. Luke, the Greek Christian, shows many Hebraisms in his Gospel as a result of reading the Septuagint and in chapters 1 and 2 numerous Aramaisms from the oral or written sources for the infancy narratives. It would have been strange if these men in their day and time had shown no traces of their Semitic environment including many proper names.

26. *And Some Latin Influence.*

In particular words for money like δηνάριον, for government like κῆνσος and κολωνία, for military terms like κεντυρίων and λεγιών. Mark's Gospel has more than any other and it is possible that Mark wrote in Rome. But Latin was the language of the government in Palestine as elsewhere. The Latin influence is mainly in the vocabulary.

27. *The Christian Addition.*

It is not large in the vocabulary. All but some fifty words of the whole New Testament have been found in the κοινή or the older Greek. Some of these fifty may yet turn up. Some of these words like, ἀντίχριστος, εὐαγγελιστής, ψευδαπόστολοι, naturally spring out of the Christian work. But old words took on new meanings, for Christianity brought new ideas into the world. The Christians did not hesitate to take words used in the hated Emperor-cult and use them for Christ (υἱὸς θεοῦ, κύριος, σωτήρ, βασιλεύς). The language of life on earth was made to tell the story of the kingdom of heaven.

PART II

ACCIDENCE

CHAPTER V

WRITING AND SOUNDS

28. The Greek alphabet contained in the κοινή period twenty-four letters.

Form		Greek Name	English Transliteration	
Α	α	ἄλφα	alpha	a
Β	β	βῆτα	beta	b
Γ	γ	γάμμα	gamma	g
Δ	δ	δέλτα	delta	d
Ε	ε	εῖ, ἔ(ἒ ψιλόν)	epsilon	e
Ζ	ζ	ζῆτα	zeta	z
Η	η	ἦτα	eta	e
Θ	θ	θῆτα	theta	th
Ι	ι	ἰῶτα	iota	i
Κ	κ	κάππα	kappa	c (k)
Λ	λ	λά(μ)βδα	lambda	l
Μ	μ	μῦ	mu	m
Ν	ν	νῦ	nu	n
Ξ	ξ	ξεῖ	xi	x
Ο	ο	οὖ, ὄ(ὂ μικρόν)	omicron	o
Π	π	πεῖ	pi	p
Ρ	ρ	ῥῶ	rho	r
Σ	s σ	σίγμα	sigma	s
Τ	τ	ταῦ	tau	t
Υ	υ	ὖ(ὒ ψιλόν)	upsilon	y (u)
Φ	φ	φεῖ	phi	ph
Χ	χ	χεῖ	chi	ch (kh)
Ψ	ψ	ψεῖ	psi	ps
Ω	ω	ὦ(ὦ μέγα)	omega	o

a. Only since 403 B. C. has the Greek alphabet regularly had twenty-four letters. The letters of the Greek alphabet

came chiefly from Phoenicia. The alphabet as given above
was the result of a law passed (403 B. C.) in Attica prescribing
the use of the Ionic alphabet in the schools. In an earlier
period there were: (1) ϝ, *vau* or digamma (so called from its
shape); in the alphabet it came after ε, and was pronounced
like w; and (2) Ϙ, Koppa, which corresponds to the Latin Q,
came after π. Before the adoption of the Ionic alphabet,
E represented ε, η, and the spurious ει (32a); O represented
o, ω, and the spurious ου (32a); and H was used for the rough
breathing.

b. The forms (capitals) of the letters in the first column
represented in printing the forms generally used in inscriptions from IV B. C. In the second column are the forms (found
in modern books) developed by early printers from the forms
of the letters found in "cursive" or "minuscule" MSS. Of
sigma the form ς is written only at the end of a word, as
στάσις; but in some books it is found at the end of a preposition or adverb compounded with another word, as προσφέρω.
In early printed books the compendia ϛ = στ, ȣ = ου are found.

c. In the third column the names (in Greek) of the letters
in parentheses are late, some as late as the Middle Ages.
Byzantine grammarians wrote ἒ ψιλόν, "simple ε,"
ὖ ψιλόν, "simple υ," to distinguish these letters from αι and οι,
which had come to be pronounced like ε and υ. For like
reasons o was called ὂ μικρόν, "small o", to distinguish it
from ω, "large o", ὦ μέγα.

d. In the last column are the equivalents in contemporary
Latin, except the letters in parentheses, which are found in
transliterations of many modern writers.

e. In pre-Ionic and in old Attic (before 403 B. C.) H was
used to express the sound *h*; but when the symbol H came to
be used to represent the sound ē, it was halved, thus ⊢ and ⊣,
and the first half (⊢) was used as the *spiritus asper* (the sound
h). The Alexandrian grammarians introduced the second
half (⊣) to represent the *spiritus lenis*, to emphasize the absence of aspiration. From these fragments (⊢ and ⊣) came

respectively the later signs ' and ' which are called rough and smooth breathing.

f.   At first the Greeks wrote from right to left (probably Phoenician influence).   Later they wrote alternately from right to left, and from left to right.   This alternate method was called βουστροφηδόν, "as oxen turn at the plow."

Vowels and Diphthongs.

29.   In the Κοινή period, as in the Attic, there were seven vowel symbols: α, ε, η, ι, ο, υ, ω.   Of these ε and ο are short; η and ω, long; α, ι, υ are sometimes short and sometimes long.

30.   The vowels are also classified as *open* or *close* according as the mouth is more or less open in pronouncing them.   The traditional classification is:

Open vowels, α, ε, η, ο, ω.
Close vowels, ι, υ.

But see under Pronunciation.

31.   Sometimes ι and υ are called semi-vowels, because there were consonants of the sound *w* and *y* which correspond to the vowels ι and υ and show their presence in some words as ι and υ.   The forms of many words are due to the former presence of the ι– and υ–consonants.   The ι–consonant in the development of the Greek language only remained as the second element of tautosyllabic diphthongs, as λείπω; in all other positions it either disappeared or became some other sound.   The υ–consonant remained not only as the second element of diphthongs but also in other positions, until a late period, but was lost in Attic.

a.   Initial ι–consonant became the rough breathing, as in ἧπαρ *liver*, Lat. *jecur*.   Between vowels it disappeared, as in τιμα(y)ω, φιλε(y)ω.   After consonants it underwent various changes.

b.   Initial υ–consonant disappeared in Attic, as in οἶκος for ϝοῖκος, Lat. *vicus*.   Intervocalic υ–consonant (ϝ) disappeared in Attic and Ionic, as in βασιλέως, βασιλῆος, Cypr. βασιλῆϝος.

In combination with consonants it may disappear or show
its presence by certain changes.

32.   A Diphthong is two vowel sounds fused into one, the
second of which is ι or υ.   The dipthongs are αι, ει οι, υι; ᾳ,
ῃ, ῳ; αυ, ευ, ου, ηυ.

a.   ει and ου are called *genuine* diphthongs when they
are a combination of ε +ι, and ο +υ, as in λείπω, γένει,
(for γενεσι, loc. sing.), ἀκολουθέω, σπουδή.   They (ει, ου) are
called spurious when they come from the contraction of
ε +ε, ε +ο, ο +ο, ο +ε or from compensatory lengthening; as
φιλεῖτε, δηλοῦτε, θείς (for θεντς), ἄρχουσι (for ἄρχοντσι).

b.   All diphthongs, whether spurious or genuine, are theo-
retically long; but final αι and οι are considered short except
in the optative.

c.   When ι or υ does not form a diphthong with the preceding vowel, two dots, called *diaeresis*, is written over it;
as προΐστασθαι, ἰσχύϊ, διϋλίζειν.

33.   Every initial vowel or diphthong is marked with either
the smooth (’) or rough (‘) breathing (28, 6) as ἄγω, αἴρω,
ὑπό, εὑρίσκω, Ἑλλάς.   Initial υ is always written with
the rough breathing.   Breathings are written over small
letters and before capitals, and placed over the second vowel
of a diphthong.   In compounds the rough breathing is not
written, as προορίζω (πρό + ὁρίζω).

a.   Initial ρ is now marked with the rough breathing, as
ῥῆμα.   In some texts medial ρρ is written ῥρ as ἄῤῥητος.
It is questioned whether ῥ was breathed in 1 A.D.

b.   The rough breathing occurs sometimes where it is not
usual in the older Greek, as ἀφίδω (Phil. 2:23) due to analogy.
Some MSS. read ἀφελπίζοντες in Lu.   6:35 (Cf. ἀφηλπικώς in
Hermas).   Westcott and Hort accept ἐφ’ ‘ελπίδι in Rom.
8:20, and good MSS. give οὐχ ὀλίγος in Acts 12:18.   Such
examples are found occasionally in the earlier vernacular
and are common in the papyri.   The breathings were not
written in the MSS. till long after New Testament times,

except when the aspiration showed in the consonant, as καθ᾽ ἡμέραν. At this period of the language there was an increase in aspiration, though in Modern Greek the reverse is seen, for the aspiration is not pronounced. Compare the confusion as to *h* in the usage of the English cockney.

34. The *consonants* are commonly divided into stops (or mutes), spirants, liquids, nasals, and compound consonants (or double consonants).

They may be divided into two groups according to the tension or slackness of the vocal cords.

a. Voiced (vocal cords tense): β, γ, δ, λ, ρ (not with rough breathing); σ (before β); μ, ν, γ (before κ, γ, χ, ξ); ϛ.

b. Voiceless (vocal cords slack); π, κ, τ; φ, χ, θ; σ; ψ, ξ.

35. The stops (or mutes) are of three classes (according to the part of the mouth active in articulation), and of three orders (according to the presence or absence of voice, and aspiration);

a. Divided according to class:

Labial	π	β	φ
Palatal or guttural	κ	γ	χ
Lingual or dental	τ	δ	θ

Stops of the same class are called *cognate*.

b. Divided according to order:

Smooth or Breathed	Middle or Voiced	Rough or Aspirate
π	β	φ
κ	γ	χ
τ	δ	θ

Stops of the same order are called *co-ordinate*.

The rough breathing (᾽) is an aspirate.

36. The only spirant represented in the Greek alphabet is σ, s (also called a sibilant). The labial spirant of early Greek, ϝ (digamma sounded as *w*), is obsolete in the κοινή. Another spirant was the *y*- sound (see 31 and a) of the ι- consonant, which under certain conditions is represented by ϛ, as in ϛύμη, Skr. *yusam*, Lat. *jus*.

37. There are three *nasals*, μ (labial), ν (dental), and γ (nasal *ng*) before the palatals κ, γ, χ, and ξ.

38. The liquids are λ and ρ. Sometimes μ and ν are classed as liquids.

39. The compound consonants are ζ, ξ, and ψ. The digraph ξ is written for κσ, γσ, χσ; ψ for πσ, βσ, φσ. The digraph ξ is not written for κs in compounds of ἐκ(ἐξ) as ἐκσῶσαι in Acts 27:39, but some editors write ἐξῶσαι. ζ here represents a combination of σδ (δσ in primitive Greek) or δy (y = ι- consonant).

40. Besides the ordinary vowels, other sounds could in primitive Greek form syllables by themselves. These sounds are the liquids and nasals λ, ρ, μ, and ν. Especially, when by certain changes in a word (particularly the loss of a preceding vowel) they came to stand between two consonants, did they perform the function of vowels. These sounds are called *sonant* liquids and nasals, and in most grammars are written with a small circle underneath. In English, as far as ordinary pronunciation is concerned, *fathom, smitten, brittle*, may as well be written *fathm, smitn, britl*; for there would be no difference in sound.

a. Sonant λ became αλ or λα, as ἔσταλμαι for ἐστλμαι (pres. στέλλω), ἐκλάπην for ἐκλπην (pres. κλέπτω).

b. Sonant ρ became αρ or ρα, as ἔσπαρμαι for ἐσπρμαι (pres. σπείρω), loc. plu. πατράσι for πατρσι (nom. πατήρ).

c. Sonant μ became α, as ἁπλόος for σμπλοος, πόδα for ποδμ.

d. Sonant ν became α, as in loc. plu. φρασί for φρνσι (nom. plu. φρένες), acc. plu. πόδας for ποδνς.

41. *Pronunciation.*

In many respects it is not certain what exactly was the Ancient Greek pronunciation. The pronunciation of Ancient Greek varied with time and place. For the classical period we can only approximate the true pronunciation. The pronunciation of Greek in the Κοινή period is a difficult problem. It is quite evident that pronunciation had considerably changed since the classical period. The changes taking place in the κοινή period had begun in the classical period. The final effect of these changes going on in the κοινή period is seen in Modern Greek. The Boeotian dialect probably modified the pronunciation of the vowels more than any other Greek dialect.

Only a brief summary of the pronunciation of Greek in the κοινή period can be given.

a. *Vowels.* The distinction between long and short in vowels was disappearing. This change was due probably to the change of accent from pitch to stress. There was in the κοινή no practical difference between ω and o under the accent.

α was pronounced somewhat like *a* in father, but not so open. Sometimes it seems to approach an *e*– sound.

ε was getting the sound of *e* in met. ε and αι were being pronounced alike.

The sound of η is approaching the sound of ι.

ι was practically the sound of *i* in machine.

There was little difference in sound, if any, between o, ω, and ου They were sounded nearly like our oo (not a diphthongal sound).

υ was generally sounded like the German *u*, but was progressively passing into an *i*– sound (as in machine).

The diphthongs were generally monophthongs in pronunciation.

αι and ε seem to be pronounced alike.

ει and ι seem from confusion in writing to have identical pronunciation.

οι seems to be approaching υ in pronunciation. Its sound was nearly the German ü.

υι was generally sounded like üy, but it was beginning to change to the sound of ι.

The diphthongs ᾳ and ῳ had the same sound as α and ω. The sound of ῃ was nearly that of η, and both were approaching identity with ι.

The pronunciation of αυ and ευ was respectively *ah–oo* and *eh–oo* spoken rapidly. But a tendency to pronounce υ as a consonant is apparent in the Κοινή period:– αυ = *av* or *af*; ευ =*ev* or *ef*; this change was complete by the time the mass of MSS. was written. ηυ was nearly like ευ. ου was sounded nearly like our *oo*, or *u* in *full*.

The blending of vowels and diphthongs into the ι sound is called *itacism*. Even in Attica in i / B.C. there is evidence that ει=ι, η=ι, υ=ι, υι=υ, οι=ι. In i/A. D. itacism was levelling the vowel. Thus ει, ι, η, ῃ, υ, υι, οι, were frequently written one for the other.

b. *Consonants*.

(1) The Stops or Mutes. π, κ, and τ were pronounced nearly as *p*, *k*, and *t* in English.   β, γ, and δ had in Attic a sound nearly equivalent to our *b*, *g*, and *d*.   During the Κοινή period they were in a process of change. β was being pronounced as *v* (labiodental) as well as *b*.   γ was beginning to have a sound nearly equal to *y* (before *e* and *i* sounds).   δ was beginning to be sounded like *th* in *the*.   The pronunciation of the rough mutes was, φ = f; χ = ch as in Scotch *loch*, German *ich*; θ =th.

(2) The Spirant σ was sounded as sharp *s* (as in *hiss*); but before voiced consonants it was probably sounded like our soft *z*.   For this *z* sound ζ is often written, as ζμύρνα, ζβέννυμι. ζ was practically equal to our *z* (as in *zeal*). ξ and ψ are simply compounds.

(3) The liquids λ and ρ were virtually identical with our *l* and *r*.

(4) The nasals μ and ν were practically identical with our *m* and *n*.   The nasal γ (before κ, γ, χ and ξ) was nearly like our *ng*.

(5) In the use of the *h*-sound (rough breathing) there was a steady decrease. But this tendency to de-aspiration was not uniform.

42.   In the matter of spelling in the uncial MSS. of the New Testament the usual principles of external evidence

do not easily apply. Scribes would have difference of opinion
about spelling. So Aleph prefers ι rather than ει, while B
is fond of ει and not ι. Moreover a scribe was under constant temptation to correct the spelling in his document by
the spelling of his day. It is hard to be sure that a fourth
century document gives us the first century spelling. Then
again the scribe was not always a competent judge and could
also fall a victim to itacism and confuse vowels and diphthongs that were at that time pronounced alike. Thus ει,
ι, η, ῃ, υ, υι, οι, could be confused, and ε and αι, ο and ω.
Many forms in –εια were shortened to –ια as λογία, ἐριθία.

a. Final ν of συν is usually retained as in συνπάσχω.
With ἐν the ν is generally assimilated, as in ἐμβάλλω.

b. As to the use of double consonants the MSS. differ as
ἀρραβών or ἀραβών (2 Cor. 1:22). κράβαττος is spelt also
κράβατος.

Vowel Change.

43. Ablaut or Vowel Gradation is the quantitative and the
qualitative differences in the vocalic elements of related words,
which were caused by sound-laws in the Indo-germanic stock
before it split into separate languages; as λείπω, λέλοιπα,
ἔλιπον; δαίμων, δαίμονα. By analogy and other causes these
changes occur in historical Greek. This is especially true
of quantitative gradation.

When the vocalic element is changed in its quantity only,
the change is called *quantitative*; when the vocalic element is
changed in nature or quality, the change is called *qualitative*.

44. Quantitative Vowel Gradation is either the lengthening of a short vowel, or the shortening of a long vowel, in the
formation and inflection of words. Thus fut. δηλώσω, pres.
δηλόω; φιλήσω, φιλέω; νικήσω, νικάω; φόρος, φέρω.

After ε, ι, and ρ the long of α is long α, as fut. ἐάσω pres.
ἐάω.

a. Attic generally shows η for an original α. This final
η became generalized in nouns of the first declension, when it
was not preceded by ε, ι, or ρ.

b. The dialects frequently show variations in vowels of the same word.

45. A variety of quantitative vowel gradation is the exchange of quantity between two vowels (sometimes called transfer of quantity). Thus βασιλῆος becomes βασιλέως, βασιλῆα becomes βασιλέα.

46. Qualitative Vowel Gradation is the change of a vowel or diphthong into another vowel or diphthong of a different sound. It is similar to the change in English *give, gave, given*; *swim, swam, swum*; *sing, sang, sung*; *bear, bare, born*.

a. This variation has been divided into *strong* and *weak* grades (including the expulsion of a vowel, or the first vowel of a diphthong). When λ, ρ, μ, or ν formed an unpronounceable combination due to the expulsion of a vowel, a vowel sound was developed (40), as πατράσι for πατρσι.

47. A table of the most important vowel grades is:

Strong Grades		Weak Grades
1.	**2.**	
Series ε	ο	— or α
ἐ–γέν–ετο	γέ–γον–α	γί–γν–ομαι
κλέπ–τω	κέ–κλοφ–α	ἐ–κλάπ–ην
τρέπ–ω	τροπ–ή	ἐ–τράπ–ην
Series ει	οι	ι
λείπ–ω	λέ–λοιπ–α	ἔ–λιπ–ον
πείθ–ω	πέ–ποιθ–α	πισ–τός
		(for πιθ–τος)
Series ευ	ου	υ
φεύγ–ω		ἔ–φυγ–ον
ἐλεύ–σομαι	ἐλ–ήλουθ–α	ἤλυθ–ον
(= ἐλευθ–σομαι)		
Series η	ω	α
ῥήγ–νυμαι	ἔ῾ρ–ρωγ–α	ῥαγ–ῆναι
Series ᾱ	ω	α
Doric φα–μί	φω–νή	φα–μέν

N. In the substantives there was a quantitative-qualitative gradation in stems in $-μων$, $-μορ$, $-μν$; $-μην$, $-μεν$, $-μν$; $-τωρ$, $-τορ$, $τρ$; $-τηρ$, $-τερ$, $-τρ$. What is sometime called syncope (dropping of short vowel between two consonants, as in $πατρός$) is actually the weak grade of vowel gradation. But other kinds of syncopation occur.

48. *Formative lengthening* is the term given to the change of a short vowel to its corresponding long vowel in vowel gradation especially.

49. *Compensatory lengthening* is the name given to the lengthening of a short vowel to make up for the omission of one or more consonants.

a. The short vowels $α$, $ι$, $υ$ are lengthened to long $ᾱ$, $ῑ$, $ῡ$; as $μέλας$ for $μελανς$; $ἱστᾱς$ for $ἱσταντς$; $ἔκρῑνα$ for $ἐκρινσα$; $δεικνύς$ for $δεικνυντς$.

b. $ε$ is lengthened to $ει$ (spurious diphthong); as $θείς$ for $θεντς$; $ἔμεινα$ for $ἐμενσα$.

c. $ο$ is lengthened to $ου$ (spurious diphthong); as in loc. plu. $λύουσι$ for $λυοντσι$; $δούς$ for $δοντς$; in acc. plu. masc $τούς$ for $τονς$.

d. $-νy$ and $-ρy$ first became $-νν$ and $-ρρ$, then one of the consonants was dropped and compensatory lengthening of the preceding $ε$, $ι$, or $υ$, took place; as $κτείνω$ for $κτενyω$; $κλίνω$ for $κλινyω$; $φθείρω$ for $φθερyω$.

e. In the first aorist ($σ-$ aorist) of verbs with stems in $λ$, $ν$, or $ρ$ the $α$ of the stem becomes $η$, except when preceded by $ι$ or $ρ$; as $ἔφηνα$ for $ἐφανσα$; but $ἐπίκρᾱνα$ for $ἐπικρανσα$. In N. T. $-αίνω$ and $-αίρω$ have $-ᾱνα$ and $-ᾱρα$.

50. Long vowels were sometimes shortened before long vowels, as $βασιλέων$ from $βασιλήων$ (Hom.) from $βασιληϝων$.

51. *Prothesis.*

Sometimes a short vowel was prefixed to a word beginning with Indo-ger. $ρ +$ a vowel; as in $ἐρυθρός$, Lat. *ruber*, Eng. *red*; $ὀρέγω$, Lat. rego.

a. In the $κοινή$ prothesis is sometimes found in words beginning with $σ$.

b. ἐχθές, not χθές, is the regular form in the κοινή. It is doubtful whether ἐ in ἐθέλω is prothetic. The New Testament, as well as the κοινή, has only θέλω and ἤθελον.

52. *Contraction of Vowels.*

Two concurrent vowels of different syllables, or a vowel and a diphthong, may be united by contraction in a long vowel or a diphthong.

a. Two vowels which naturally form a diphthong (32) unite in that diphthong, as γένει from γενε–ι from γενεσι.

b. Two like vowels (short or long) unite to form the common long vowel, as pres. subj. φιλῆτε from φιλε–ητε. But ε ε and o o form the spurious diphthongs ει and ου.

c. When two vowels which cannot form a genuine diphthong come together, one is assimilated to the other.

(1) An o–sound prevails over a preceding or following a– or e– sound, as τιμῶμεν; from τιμάομεν; φιλῶσι from φιλέωσι. But εο and οε form the spurious diphthong ου, as γένους from γένεος.

(2) When α, ε, or η come together the first (in order) prevails over the second; as γένη from γένεα; ἐτίμα from ἐτίμαε.

d. A single vowel is absorbed before a diphthong beginning with the same vowel, as φιλεῖ from φιλέει.

e. A single vowel generally contracts with the first vowel of a diphthong not beginning with the same vowel; if ι is the second vowel of the diphthong, it becomes subscript (unpronounced if written on line as in MSS). Thus νικᾷ from νικάει.

f. The spurious diphthong ει and ου contract like simple ε and o, as in pres. inf. τιμᾶν from τιμάειν. But W. H. prefer the form τιμᾷν.

g. In contracts of the first and second declensions ε or o before α or any long vowel or diphthong is apparently absorbed, as χρυσᾶ from χρυσεα.

53. Table of contractions arranged according to the nature of the first vowel:

$a + a = \bar{a}$

$a + a\iota = a\iota$

$a + \dot{a} = \dot{a}$

$a + \epsilon = \bar{a}$

$a + \begin{cases} \text{g.} & \epsilon\iota = \dot{a} \\ \text{sp.} & \epsilon\iota = \bar{a} \end{cases}$
(See 52f)

$a + \eta = \bar{a}$

$a + \dot{\eta} = \dot{a}$

$a + \iota = a\iota$

$\bar{a} + \iota = \dot{a}$

$a + o = \omega$

$a + o\iota = \dot{\omega}$

$a + ov = \omega$ (See 52f)

$a + \omega = \omega$

$\epsilon + a = \eta$ or $\bar{a}$

$\epsilon + a\iota = \eta$ or $a\iota$

$\epsilon + \epsilon = \epsilon\iota$ (spurious)

$\epsilon + \iota = \epsilon\iota$

$\epsilon + \eta = \eta$

$\epsilon + \epsilon\iota = \epsilon\iota$

$\epsilon + o = ov$ (spurious)

$\epsilon + o\iota = o\iota$

$\epsilon + ov = ov$

$\epsilon + v = \epsilon v$

$\epsilon + \omega = \omega$

$\epsilon + \dot{\omega} = \dot{\omega}$

$\eta + \epsilon = \eta$

$\eta + \begin{cases} \text{g.} & \epsilon\iota = \eta \\ \text{sp.} & \epsilon\iota = \eta \end{cases}$
(See 52f.)

$\eta + \iota = \dot{\eta}$

$\eta + o\iota = \dot{\omega}$

$\iota + \iota = \bar{\iota}$

$o + a = \omega$
    or $= a$ (See 52 g.)

$o + \epsilon = ov$ (spurious)

$o + \begin{cases} \text{g.} & \epsilon\iota = o\iota \\ \text{sp.} & \epsilon\iota = ov \end{cases}$
(See 52f).

$o + \eta = \omega$

$o + \dot{\eta} = \dot{\omega}$
    or $= o\iota$

$o + \iota = o\iota$

$o + o = ov$ (spurious)

$o + \dot{o}\iota = o\iota$

$o + ov = ov$

$o + \omega = \omega$

$o + \dot{\omega} = \dot{\omega}$

Also the contraction of

$\iota + \epsilon\iota = \epsilon\iota$ or ι

occurs in the κοινή, as in πεῖν or πῖν for πιεῖν.

54. *Elision* is the dropping of a short final vowel when the next word begins with a vowel. In printed Greek an apostrophe (') marks the omission. In the κοινή it is not so common as in Attic. Its frequent occurrence is in prepositions, conjunctions, and adverbs. Dr. Hort gives the rule for the best New Testament uncial MSS thus: "Elision takes place habitually and without variation before pronouns and

particles; also before nouns in combinations of frequent occurrence, as ἀπ᾽ ἀρχῆς, κατ᾽ οἶκον. In other cases there is much diversity, and occasional variation." The prepositions περί and πρό are not elided.

55. Crasis is the contraction of a vowel or diphthong at the end of a word with one at the beginning of the following word. In printed Greek a coronis (') is placed over the contracted syllable. Crasis is rare in the New Testament; and, except for τοὖνομα, (for τὸ ὄνομα), τοὐναντίον and ταὐτά, is confined to combinations with καί, especially before ἐγώ, ἄν, ἐκεῖνος, ἐκεῖ. Thus κἀγώ, κἀμέ, κἀκεῖ, κἀκεῖνος, κἄν.

Consonant Change.

56.   Double consonants.

a.   The κοινή has almost exclusively σσ where Attic had ττ. There are a few instances of ττ in the N. T., as κρείττων, ἐλάττων, etc.

In primitive Greek σσ (ττ) arose from κυ or χυ, and sometimes from τυ and θυ (see 69).

b.   As to ρρ and ρσ, both forms occur in θαρσέω, θαρρέω, and ἄρσην. and ἄρρην New Attic has ρρ for Old Attic ρσ.

c.   In the N. T. initial ρ, when a simple vowel is placed before it in inflection or in composition, may or may not be doubled, as ἔρριψαν, ἐριμμένοι.

d.   θθ and φφ occur in words of Semitic origin, as Μαθθαῖος, ἐφφαθά.

57.   Mutes (stops) before Mutes.

A labial mute (π,β, φ) or a palatal mute (κ, γ, χ) before a lingual mute (τ, δ, θ) becomes co-ordinate (of the same order) with the lingual mute (35b).

a.   βτ and φτ become ππ; thus τέτριπται for τετριβται, γέγραπται for γεγραφται. γτ and χτ become κτ; thus τέτακται for τεταγται.

b.   πδ and φδ become βδ; thus from ἑπτά comes ἕβδομος; κδ becomes γδ, as ὄγδοος, ὀκτώ.

c.   πθ and βθ become φθ; thus ἐλείφθην for ἐλειπθην, ἐλήμφθην for ἐλημβθην.

κθ and γθ become χθ; thus διωχθήσονται for διωκθησονται, ἤχθην for ἤγθην.

The κ of ἐκ in composition generally remains unchanged.

58. A lingual mute (stop) before another lingual mute becomes σ; thus πέπεισται for πεπειθται, ἐπείσθην for ἐπειθθην, ψεύστης from ψευδτης.

N. The ττ developed by κy and χy sometimes remained in words inherited from the Attic. See 56, (a).

59. *Mutes (stops) before μ.*

a. Before μ a labial mute (π, β, φ) becomes μ; thus λέλειμμαι for λελειπμαι, τέτριμμαι for τετριβμαι, γέγραμμαι for γεγραφμαι.

b. Before μ a palatal mute (κ, χ) becomes γ, and γ before μ remains; thus δεδίωγμαι for δεδιωκμαι, τετάραγμαι for τεταραχμαι.

N. In noun suffixes κ and χ may remain, as ἀκμή.

c. Before μ a lingual mute (τ, δ, θ) becomes, by analogy σ; thus πέπεισμαι for πεπειθμαι. But τέτμημαι (τέμνω).

60. *Consonants before ν.*

a. β before ν becomes μ; as ἀμνός for ἀβνος, σεμνός for σεβνος (σέβομαι).

b. γιγνώσκω and γίγνομαι, because of the pronunciation of medial γν, became γινώσκω and γίνομαι.

c. λν becomes λλ in ὄλλυμι from ὄλνυμι.

61. *Nu (ν) before consonants.*

a. ν before a labial mute (π, β, φ) may become μ; as ἐμπίπτω, ἐμβλέπω, ἔμφοβος.

b. ν before a palatal mute (κ, γ, χ) or ξ may become γ-nasal; as συγγενής, etc.

N. There was a growing practice in the κοινή of non-assimilation.

c. ν before μ may become μ, as in ἐμμένω.

d. ν before λ may be assimilated, as ἐλλογάω.

N. In the case of ν of ἐν and σύν in composition non-assimilation is according to Westcott and Hort the usual practice in the best New Testament uncial MSS. before π, ψ, β, φ, κ, γ, χ; ζ, σ; λ, μ.

e. ν before σ may be dropped, as συστροφή.

N. ν before σ in inflection is dropped, and the preceding vowel lengthened. (ε to ει, and ο to ου).

62. *Consonants before σ.*

a. Before σ a labial mute (π, β, φ) forms ψ; as fut. λάμψω from λαμπσω, γράψω from γραφσω.

b. Before σ a palatal mute (κ, γ, χ) forms ξ; as fut. διώξω from διωκσω, ἄξω from ἀγσω, ἕξω from ἐχσω.

c. Before σ a lingual mute is assimilated (σσ) and one σ is dropped; as fut. ἐλεύσομαι from ἐλευθσομαι.

d. ντ, νδ and νθ, before σ are, through assimilation, dropped and the preceding vowel lengthened (by compensation) as θείς from θεντς; ἄρχουσι from ἀρχοντσι.

63. *Sigma (σ) before consonants.*

In inflection σ between two consonants is dropped when the first consonant was not a nasal and the second not ϝ or *y*, as in perf. pass. ἤγγελθε for ἤγγελσθε (but this form does not occur in N. T.).

a. ἐξ (ἐκς) drops σ in composition; as ἐκπίπτω.

b. When two sigmas are brought together in inflection, one sigma is dropped; as γένεσι, for γενεσσι, τελέσαι for τελεσσαι.

64. *Disappearance of σ.*

In primitive Greek σ became the aspirate *h* (‘) initially before vowels and medially between vowels, and then in the latter case disappeared altogether.

a. Initially: as ἅλς (Lat. *sal*), ἑπτά (Lat. *septem*).

N. But the *h* (the rough breathing ‘) disappeared when the next syllable or the next but one began with an aspirate, as ἔχω.

b. Medially (between vowels): as gen. γένους from γενεσος, as φέρῃ from φερεσαι, as ἐφέρου from ἐφερεσο.

65. Initial σy became the rough breathing (‘), as in ὕμνος.

66. Initial σϝ became the rough breathing (‘), as in ἡδύς (Lat. *suavis*), ὅς (Lat. *suus*).

67. The ι– consonant (designated *y*) following consonants give rise to various changes.

a. πγ became ππ; as in πτύω from πγυγω; as in κλέπτω.

b. λγ became λλ, as in ἄλλος (Lat. *alius*), στέλλω, μέλλω.

c. The combination αγγ, αργ, ογγ, οργ became (through joining the palatalized element with the vowel) αιν, αιρ, οιν, οιρ; as βαίνω from βανγω; φαίνω; χαίρω; μοῖρα from μοργα.

N. The combination αϝγ became αι, as καίω from καιϝω from καϝγω; as also κλαίω. εϝγ became ει, as ὀξεῖα > ὀξεϝγα.

d. The combinations εγγ, εργ, ιγγ, ιργ, υγγ, υργ became ειν, ειρ, ιν, ιρ, υν, υρ, as κτείνω from (κτεννω) κτενγω; ἐγείρω from (ἐγερρω) ἐγεργω; κλίνγω; κρίνω; πλύνω.

68. The combinations κγ and χγ became in Attic ττ and in other dialects σσ, as φυλάσσω (Attic φυλάττω) from φυλακγω; ταράσσω (Attic ταράττω) from ταραχγω.

69. In most dialects δγ and γγ after vowels became ζ, as ἐλπίζω from ἐλπιδγω; σφάζω from σφαγγω.

70. The combinations τγ and θγ after long vowels, diphthongs, and consonants, and between vowels (= σσ simplified to σ) became σ, as fem. πᾶσα from παντγα; δόξα from δοκσα from δοκτγα; μέσος from μεθγος.

N. The presents of verbs in –γω, the comparative in –γων, and feminines in –γα, made from lingual (τ, θ) stems were formed on the analogy of σσ(ττ) from κγ and χγ (67) formations: as μέλισσα (μέλιττα) from μελιτγα; κρείσσων from κρατγων (ει probably came from ἀμείνων).

71. *Aspiration.*

Aspirates (θ, φ, χ and the *spiritus asper* ') become de-aspirated when the next syllable or the next but one begins with an aspirate.

a. In reduplication an initial rough mute (φ, χ, θ) is made the cognate smooth mute (π, κ, τ); as τίθημι from θιθημι; τέθνηκα from θεθνηκα; πεφώτισμαι from φεφωτισμαι; κεχώρισμαι from χεχωρισμαι.

b. In the aorist passive the roots θε and θυ of τίθημι and θύω are changed to τε and τυ before θ of the ending, as ἐτέθην, from ἐθεθην, ἐτύθην from ἐθύθην.

c. In the first aorist passive imperative –θι of the personal ending becomes —τι after θ of the tense stem (θε), as λύθητι from λυθηθι.

d. There is de-aspiration in some words, which is sometimes called transfer of aspiration.

(1) θρίξ (with supposed root θριχ), gen. τριχός from θριχος.

(2) τρέφω (supposed root θρεφ), fut. θρέψω, perf. τέθραμμαι; τρέχω (supposed root θρεχ), fut. θρέξομαι.

e. Generally (see b) in the first aorist passive (and some other forms) two rough mutes remained unchanged, as ἐχύθην.

f. The rough breathing often disappears when followed by a rough mute in next syllable (or next but one), as ἔχω from ἔχω from σεχω.

72. When a smooth mute (π, κ, τ) is brought before the rough breathing (an aspirate), by elision or in forming compounds, it becomes a cognate rough mute (φ, χ, θ). Thus ἀφ' ὧν from ἀπ' ὧν; ἀφίημι from ἀπ' ἵημι.

73. When an aspirate disappeared before σκ it was transferred to the last consonant; as πάσχω from παθσκω.

74. *Metathesis.*

A consonant is sometimes transposed in a word; as in τίκτω from τιτκω.

There is metathesis of aspiration in the κοινή, due probably to Ionic influence, as χιτών, κιθών; χύτρα, κύθρα.

75. Variation between λ and ρ often occurs: as κεφαλαργία besides κεφαλαλγία; this way by dissimilation. But in the κοινή is found ἦρθα for ἦλθα, etc.

76. The combinations μρ and νρ medially became μβρ and νδρ, as in μεσημβρία and gen. ἀνδρός (ἀνήρ).

77. Any vowel may stand at the end of a Greek word, but the only consonants allowed to stand at the end of a genuine Greek word are ν, ρ, and σ (including ξ and ψ). All other consonants are dropped; thus σωματ becomes σῶμα; μελιτ becomes μέλι, etc.

a. The proclitics ἐκ(ἐξ) and οὐκ(οὐχ) are only apparent exceptions since they are pronounced with the following word.

b. Of course foreign (to Greek) names in the N. T. do not

regularly conform to this principle, but otherwise, as Ἀβραάμ, Ἰακώβ, etc.

78. Movable ν (ν ἐφελκυστικόν, *dragging after*).

ν may be added to words ending in –σι; to the third person singular in –ε, and to ἐστί.

It is said that ν was appended to these words, in the classical period, only when they were followed by a word beginning with a vowel. But this statement is not strictly true for the classical writers.

During the κοινή period ν was indiscriminately added to the words above. So also in the N. T.

N. Sometimes ν is added to other forms besides those named above; such is called irrational ν.

79. Final –ς in οὕτως is found before consonants and vowels indiscriminately. Westcott and Hort print οὕτω only ten times.

80. ἐκ is written before consonants, ἐξ before vowels; thus ἐκ μέρους, ἐξ αὐτῶν.

81. οὐκ is used before the smooth breathing and οὐχ before the rough breathing, as οὐκ αὐτός, οὐχ εὑρίσκω.

82. A Greek word has as many syllables as it has separate vowels or diphthongs; as ἀ-λή-θει-α.

83. The last syllable of a word is called the *ultima*; the syllable next to the last is called the *penult*; the one before the penult is called the *antepenult*.

84. The rules for dividing a word at the end of a line, based on ancient tradition and generally observed in MSS., are these:

a. A single consonant standing between two vowels is connected with the second vowel; as ἄ-γω, λι-θά-ζω.

b. The largest group of consonants that can begin a word must begin the new line (or in syllabification belongs to the second vowel); or the new line (or syllable) may begin with a group formed by a mute with μ or ν, or by the group of μν; thus μι-κρόν, πρά-γμα-τος, λι-μνή, ἔ-θνος.

c. A group that cannot begin a word is divided; as ἐλ-πίς, πράσ-σω, ἄρ-μα.

d. Compounds with prepositions and δυσ- are divided into their original parts; as εἰσ–ἐρχομαι, δυσ–φημία.

85. For purposes of accent, a syllable containing a short vowel is short and one containing a long vowel or diphthong is long. See 29 and 32.

a. Both syllables in ἄρτος, in θεός, are short.

b. Both syllables in χώρα are long. The penult in πλοῖον is long.

86. *Accent.*

In classical Greek voice—pitch, musical accent, was the original value of accent. The *acute* accent was the rising inflection of the voice. The *grave* was a falling inflection of the voice. The *circumflex* was the rising and falling of the voice on a long syllable. But about the first century A. D. the pitch accent, the musical accent, developed into pure stress. It may safely be assumed that the N. T. MSS. when first read were pronounced with stress accent.

a. The signs of the accents are the inventions of early grammarians who attempted to preserve the pronunciation of the classical language. Aristophanes of Byzantium in the third century B. C. is credited by tradition with the written signs of accent as a system. The record of ancient accentuation is imperfect.

b. The early N. T. uncial MSS. have no accents. The late MSS. have the system of accent with which Greek is now written. As far as the evidence goes, the N. T. does not seem to vary greatly in accent from the earlier Greek.

87. There are three kinds of accent in Greek:

a. The *acute* ('), as λόγος.

b. The *grave* (`), as αὐτὸς ἔλεγεν.

c. The *circumflex* (ˆ), as δοῦλος.

88. No accent can stand farther back than the third syllable from the end of a word.

a. The acute may stand on the ultima, the penult, or the antepenult; as ἀδελφός, πιστεύω, ἄνθρωπος. It may stand over long or short vowels and diphthongs.

N.   But if the ultima is short and the penult long, and the penult has an accent, it must be the circumflex; as δῶρον.

b.   The *grave* stands only on the last syllable (the ultima). When the acute falls on the last syllable (ultima) of a word and when the word as it comes in a sentence is not followed by an enclitic or a mark of punctuation, the acute accent is changed to grave; as αὐτὸς ἐγίνωσκεν, but ἐγίνωσκεν αὐτός.

The grave may stand over long or short vowels and diphthongs.

N.   According to the theory of the ancients the grave belongs to every syllable not accented with the acute or circumflex.

c.   The circumflex may stand on the ultima or the penult; as γῆ, ὁδοῦ, δῶρον, τοῦτο.

The circumflex only stands over long vowels and diphthongs.

N.   The circumflex denoted the combination of the acute and the grave; thus ˆ = ΄ ` .

89.   Words are named according to their accents:

a.   Oxytone, when acute is on ultima; ἀδελφός.

b.   Paroxytone, when acute is on penult; φίλος, εἰρήνη.

c.   Proparoxytone, when acute is on the antepenult; ἄνθρωπος, ἀπόστολος.

d.   Perispomenon, when circumflex is on the ultima; φωνῇ, ὁδοῦ, γῆ.

e.   Properispomenon, when circumflex is on the penult; δῶρον, πλοῖον.

f.   Barytone, when the last syllable has no accent. All paroxytones, proparoxytones, and properispomena are barytone.

90.   When a word is accented as far back as the quantity of the ultima permits (93), it is said to have *recessive* accent.

N.   Final –ξ and –ψ after a short vowel, prevents the acute from standing on the antepenult; but circumflex is written if long penult is accented, thus λαῖλαψ.

91.   The sign of accent stands over the vowel of the accented syllable.   In the case of diphthongs the accent stands over the

second vowel; as φεύγω, δοῦλος. When ᾳ, ῃ, and ῳ are written with capitals, ι stands on the line and the accent is written before the first vowel; as Ἀιδης (ᾅδης). In early MSS. ι subscript is written on the line, and often so written in the papyri.

92. The acute and grave follow the breathing when both belong to the same vowel, as ὅλος, ὤν; but the circumflex is written above the breathing, as ἦγον. When they belong to a capital letter they are written before it, as Ἕλλην,Ἦγε.

93. *Rules of Accentuation.*

With regard to the place of accent as determined by quantity (of vowel-sounds) the following (94—98) is a summary of the rules.

94. The antepenult, if accented, takes the acute only; ἀλήθεια. But it cannot take an accent if the ultima is long; so ἀληθείᾳ.

N. Genitives in –εως and εων of substantives with nom. in –ις and –υς allow the acute on the antepenult.

95. An accented penult takes the circumflex accent when it is long and the ultima short, as δῶρον, τοῦτο. In all other cases, if accented, it takes the acute, as δώρων, τούτων, λόγος.

N. Final –αι and –οι are counted short in determining accent, as ἄνθρωποι, γλῶσσαι, τιμῆσαι (aor. act. inf); but not so, when final in *optatives* (as παιδεύσαι, βασιλεύοι) and in old locative terminations (as οἴκοι).

96. An accented ultima, if short, has the acute, as ἀδελφός; if long, it has either the acute or the circumflex, as ἡγεμών, φωνῆς.

N. An oxytone (acute on ultima) changes its acute to grave before other words in the same sentence, as τὸν καλὸν ἄνθρωπον. See 88, b. But a final acute is not changed to a grave: (1) when an oxytone is followed by an enclitic (102); (2) in the interrogative τίς, τί; (3) when a mark of punctuation immediately follows. Modern usage differs when a comma follows an oxytone.

97. The rules may be briefly stated thus:

A. A word with a short ultima, if accented

a. on the ultima, has the acute, as θεός.

b. on a short penult, has the acute, as λόγος.

c. on a long penult, has the circumflex, as δῶρον, πλοῖον.

d. on the antepenult, has the acute, as ἀπόστολος.

B. If the ultima is long, the acute cannot stand on the antepenult, nor the circumflex on the penult. A word with a long ultima, if accented

a. on the ultima, has either the acute or the circumflex, ἡγεμών, καλῶς.

b. on the penult, has the acute, as δώρων, λέγων.

98. *Accent of contracted syllables.*

Since accentuation existed long before the contraction of vowels or later modifications, the accentuation of contracted syllables follows the earlier conditions.

A. If either of the syllables to be contracted has an accent, the contracted syllable receives an accent:

a. A contracted antepenult receives the acute, as τιμαόμενος becomes τιμώμενος.

b. A contracted penult receives the acute when the ultima is long, as τιμαόντων becomes τιμώντων; when the ultima is short, it receives the circumflex, as τιμάομεν becomes τιμῶμεν.

c. A contracted ultima receives the acute if the uncontracted form had the acute on the ultima, as ἑσταώς; becomes ἑστώς; if the uncontracted form had the acute on the penult, it receives the circumflex, as τιμάω becomes τιμῶ.

B. If neither of the uncontracted syllables had an accent, the contracted syllable has no accent, as ἐνίκαε became ἐνίκα.

99. In crasis the accent of the first word is ignored, as κἀγώ for καὶ ἐγώ.

100. In elision oxytone prepositions and conjunctions lose their accent, as ἀπ' ἀρχῆς, ἀλλ' ὅ.

101. *Proclitics.*

A few monosyllabic words link themselves so closely to a following word as not to have a separate accent. They are called *proclitics*.

A. They are:

a. The forms ὁ, ἡ, οἱ, αἱ of the definite article.

b. The prepositions εἰς, ἐν, ἐκ, (and ἐξ).

c. The conjunctions εἰ and ὡς.

d. The negative adverb οὐ (with οὐκ and οὐχ).

B. A proclitic sometimes receives an acute accent, thus:

a. When followed by an enclitic, as εἴ τις βάλλει.

b. οὐ at the end of a sentence, as ἔξεστιν δοῦναι ἢ οὔ; also when it stands alone, as ὁ δέ φησι Οὔ.

102. *Enclitics.*

Some words join themselves so closely with a preceding word as to lose their accent under specific conditions. They are called enclitics.

A. They are:

a. The indefinite pron. τὶς in all its forms.

b. The personal pron. forms μοῦ, μοί, μέ, and (except when emphatic) σοῦ, σοί, σέ.

c. The present ind. of εἰμί (except second sing. εἶ); and φημί, φησί, φασί.

d. The particles γέ, τέ, and δε (not written separately).

e. The indefinite adverbs ποτέ, πού, περ, πω, πως. But περ, πω, πως are not written separately.

B. Enclitics lose their accent when the preceding word is

a. oxytone (which keeps its acute), as καί φησι; καλόν μοι.

b. perispomenon (which keeps its accent), ἀδελφῶν σου, ὑμῶν τινες.

N. But according to some editors a dissyllabic enclitic retains its accent, as ὑμῶν τινές etc.

c. a paroxytone; a monosyllabic enclitic loses its accent, as λόγος μου; but a dissyllabic enclitic retains its accent, as εἰς κώμην τινά.

C. Enclitics incline their accent, the preceding word receiving an acute accent on its ultima, when the preceding word is
a. proparoxytone, as ἄνθρωπός τις, ἄνθρωποί τινες.
b. properispomenon, as εἶπέν τις, προσῆλθάν τινες.
c. a proclitic, as εἴ τις λέγει. But a dissyllabic enclitic retains its accent.

D. Enclitics retain their accent,
a. if they begin a sentence, τινὲς δὲ ἐξ αὐτῶν εἶπεν.
b. if dissyllables after paroxytone (see B, c above).
c. if dissyllables after a perispomenon, according to some editors (See B, b above).
d. after an elided vowel, as ἀλλ' εἰσίν.
e. if dissyllables after a proclitic, as οὐκ εἰσίν.
f. when they are emphatic.

E. If two or more enclitics occur together, each one receives the accent of the preceding, the last being unaccented, as εἴ τίς τί μοί φησιν. (But μοῦ and σοῦ throw an acute on a preceding word and receive an acute from a following enclitic). But editors differ in practice as to this rule.

F. ἐστί(ν) is written ἔστι(ν);
a. at the beginning of a sentence.
b. after οὐκ, μή, εἰ, ὡς, καί, ἀλλά, and τοῦτο.
c. when it means *exists* or *is possible*.

G. The enclitic form of the first and second personal pronouns is not used after oxytone prepositions, except in πρός με

(πρὸς ἐμέ, Acts 22:8, is rare; in Matt. 3:14 some MSS. have πρόσ μέ.)

103. Our present system of punctuation is purely modern. Punctuation is the result of interpretation. The ancients were without our modern convenience in this respect. Greek MSS. had the words written together. For full discussion see Robertson's *Grammar in Light of Historical Research,* pp. 241-245.

Modern marks of punctuation: The *comma* and *period* have the same forms as in English.

The *colon,* a point above the line (·), takes the place alike of our colon and semicolon.

The mark of interrogation (;) is the same as our semicolon, as δῶμεν; *shall we give?*

The dash and parenthesis are used in modern texts.

CHAPTER VI

INFLECTION OF NOUNS AND PRONOUNS: DECLENSIONS

INTRODUCTORY REMARKS

104. *The Parts of Speech* in Greek, as generally in other languages, are substantives, adjectives, pronouns, verbs, adverbs, prepositions, conjunctions, and particles.

105. The *root* of a word is that part which remains after taking away, in comparison with kindred words, all formative elements (prefixes, suffixes, etc.); as ἀνα–δείκ–νυ–μι, *to show forth*; δίκ–η, *the way pointed out, right*; δίκ–αιος, *a man evidently seeking the right way*. Clearly δικ is the root. The root expresses the most general and elementary idea of a word.

106. The *stem* of a word is that part which is common to all forms of the word that carries the permanent meaning or idea. Thus δωρο– is the stem of δῶρον, *gift*; δω– is the root; ρο– is the suffix; and ν is the inflectional ending (case-ending). Most stems come from roots by the addition of suffixes or prefixes, or both.

a. Sometimes the root and the stem are the same; as πούς, gen. ποδός, *foot*; ἰχθύς, gen. ἰχθύ–ος *fish*; φα–μέν *we say*.

b. The stem is often modified in form or changed in vowel; thus ἀνήρ has the stems, ἀνερ– and ἀνδρ–; the stem of φεύγ–ο–μεν is φευγ–, of ἔ–φυγ–ο–ν it is φυγ–.

107. *Inflection* is a change in the form of a word, consisting in the addition of suffixes or prefixes to the *stem*, to express its different relations to other words. Thus to the stem δωρο– is added ν = δῶρον, *gift*; to the stem λιπ are added the prefix ἐ and the suffix –μεν with the thematic vowel ο = ἐλίπομεν, *we left*.

108.   Every inflected word has *two parts*: (1) the stem, the fundamental part, and (2) the inflective part called *endings*, which are added to the stem to form cases, persons, numbers, tenses, etc.

109.   The inflection of substantives, adjectives, participles, and pronouns is called *declension*. The inflection of verbs is called *conjugation*.

110.   *Declension* then has to do with variations of number, gender, and case.

111.   *Number.*   In pre-Attic-Greek three numbers are found, *singular*, *dual*, and *plural*.   The dual speaks of two, or a pair. But the dual is not used in the New Testament, only the singular and plural.   The only dual form that occurs in the LXX and the N. T. is δύο for all the cases (as genitive in 1 Tim. 5:19), save δυσί(ν) (Lu. 16:13) for the dative - locative— instrumental, a plural form found in Aristotle, Polybius, etc. In the papyri δύω, δυῶν, δυεῖν occasionally appear along with δυσί(ν).   Ἄμφω, *both*, does not appear in the New Testament, but ἀμφότεροι appears fourteen times (Matt. 9:17, etc.) and sometimes apparently for more than *two* (Acts 19:16).   The dual was never used largely in the Greek.   It never won a foothold in the Aeolic and the New Ionic, and its use in the Attic was limited.   It is nearly gone in the late Attic inscriptions, while in the κοινή it is sporadic and constantly vanishing in the inscriptions and papyri.   In the modern Greek it is no longer used.   The development of the dual was probably due to a logical effort to distinguish pairs, as the two eyes, etc.   The Sanskrit employed it as did the Hebrew, but Latin had only *duo* and *ambo*.

112.   *Gender.*   There are three *genders*: the *masculine*, the *feminine*, and the *neuter*.

113.   Natural Gender.   Any noun used for a male is masculine, and any noun used for a female is feminine.   Thus ὁ υἱός, son; ἡ γυνή, woman.

N.   Diminutives in –ιον (neuter) and other words are exceptions.   Thus τὸ παιδίον, *little child*; τὸ τέκνον, *child*.

114. Some nouns are either masculine or feminine, and said to be of *common* gender; as ὁ παῖς, *boy*, ἡ παῖς, *girl*; ὁ or ἡ ὄνος, *ass*; ὁ θεός, *god*, ἡ θεός, *goddess*.

115. There are some names of animals which are applied to either sex under one gender; as ἡ ἀλώπηξ, *fox* (male or female) (Luke 13:32). These words are called *epicene*.

116. *Grammatical Gender.* Many names of things are masculine or feminine. Why nouns that have no natural gender are not always neuter we cannot tell. But it seems probable that grammatical gender grew out of natural gender distinctions through the habit of personification of inanimate things. No absolute rule can be laid down for the guidance of modern students, though the presence of the Greek article with substantives shows how the word in question was used; as ὁ λόγος, *the word*; ἡ φωνή, *the voice*; τὸ ἔργον, *the work*.

117. All the older Indo-European languages have three genders, but the Sanskrit has no gender for the personal pronoun, nor has the Greek except αὐτός when used as the third personal pronoun. Delbrueck thinks that originally all masculine nouns of the *a*– declension were feminine, and all the feminine nouns of the *o*– declension were masculine.

118. The termination of a word will often be a guide to the gender, as is shown under the several declensions and word-formation, but often the gender must be learned by observation. Yet the following rules are of general application for determining gender of sexless objects:

a. The names of *winds, months,* and most *rivers* are masculine.

b. Most names of *countries, islands, towns,* and *trees* are feminine. Most abstract substantives denoting a *quality, state,* or *action* are feminine.

c. Diminutives in –ιον are neuter, even when designating males or females (see above). Also *verbal substantives, indeclinable nouns* generally, *quoted words* and *expressions,* and the names of *fruits* are neuter.

d. Any word can be treated as neuter in Greek. The noun Ἄγαρ (Gal. 4:25) is not used as neuter with τό mistakenly by Paul. He treats the name as a word. In Rom. 11:4 Paul uses τῇ βάαλ rather than the frequent τῷ βάαλ of the LXX, perhaps because of the idea of αἰσχύνη attributed to Baal (so Burkitt).

Cases

119. There are *eight* cases (appearing under *five* case-forms): *Nominative, Genitive, Ablative, Dative, Locative, Instrumental, Accusative* and *Vocative.*

120. All the cases except the nominative and vocative (called *direct* cases) are called oblique cases; the nominative is regarded as the upright case. Strictly speaking, so far as the form goes, the vocative is not a case.

121. Briefly, the nominative is the *naming case,* case of subject; the genitive is the *specifying case,* case of "kind"; the ablative is the *whence* case, case of origin or separation; the dative is the case of *personal interest;* the locative is the *in* case; the instrumental is the case of *means* or *association;* the accusative is the case of *extension* (whether of thought or verbal action); the vocative is the case of *address.*

It is difficult, not to say impossible, to give intelligibly an historical explanation of the forms of the cases apart from the syntax of the cases. A short history of the case forms and the cases is given under Syntax.

122. It is now a commonplace in comparative philology that in Greek the usual seven (eight with the vocative) Indo-European cases are present, though in a badly mutilated condition *as to form.*

123. *Case-Endings.* The generalized case-endings in the κοινή Period are

Vowel Stems	Consonant Stems
ā and o	(including close vowels ι and υ)
(Vowel Declension)	(Consonant Declension)

Singular

	Masc. and Fem.	Neut.	Masc. and Fem.	Neut.
N.	–s or none	–ν	–s or none	none
G.	–s or ιο		–os	
Ab.	–s or ιο		–os	
D.	–αι		(ι)	
L.	(–ι) } αι		ι } ι	
I.	(–α)		(ι)	
A.	–ν	–ν	–ν or –ă	none
V.	none	–ν	none or like nom.	none

Plural

	Masc. and Fem.	Neut.	Masc. and Fem.	Neut.
N.	–ι	–α	–ες	–α
G.	–ων		–ων	
Ab.	–ων		–ων	
D.	(–οις)		(–σι)	
L.	(–οις) } –ις		–σι } –σι	
I.	–οις,(–αις)		(–σι)	
A.	–νς	–α	–νς, –ăς	–α
V.	like nominative		like nominative	

Singular

124. In the nominative of masculine and feminine singular of stems ending in o, ι (ει), υ (ευ), and of stems ending in mutes (consonant) the original case-ending was –s. Possibly root nouns originally made the case in –s. Thus οἶκος, πόλις. ἰχθύς, βοῦς, σάρξ, βασιλεύς, παῖς.

125. In all other stems, –α, –ya–, –ν–, –ρ–, –s–, the nominative is simply the stem-ending. (A short vowel before ν, ρ, s is lengthened). Thus χώρα, φέρουσα (φεροντya), ποιμήν, πατήρ. When ā– stems became masculine they added –s; thus νεανίας.

126. There are two original case-endings for the genitive singular in the Indo-European language, *-es, -os, -s* (probably ablaut-variants of one suffix), and *-sjo* (*so*).   The genitive (*sjo, so*) was formed after the analogy of the genitive of the demonstrative pronoun *tosjo* = τοῖο, *toso* = τοῦ.   The letter *j*=*y*. Such forms as λύκοιο, λύκοο, λύκου occur in Homer.   *-os, -s* are found in the consonant and *a-* stems; *ιο(ο)* in the *o* stems.

127.   In the parent language the ablative singular had no case-ending proper to itself, except in *o-* stems which had *-ed* and *-od*; in other stems the genitive and ablative had the same endings.   In Greek the presence of the *ed, od* ending is found only in a few adverbs; as Delph. ϝοίκω, *domo*; Cret. τῶ-δε, *hence*. This ending was preserved in Sanskrit, yugat (abl. of yugam, *a yoke*) and Old Latin, meritod (=later Lat. merito *deservedly*), facilumed (=later Lat. facillime, *easily, well*).   Probably the Greek adverbs in *-ως* are so to be explained; as ὡς, ἑτέρως, *otherwise*.

128.   In the dative singular the original case-ending was *-αι*, for all stems, which is preserved in infinitives in *-αι*, as δοῦναι.   In the *o-* and *a-* stems, the forms χώρᾳ and λόγῳ resulted from contraction with *-αι*.   For the consonantal (and *ι* and *υ*) stems see below.

129.   The original locative ending for most stems was *-ι*. It is preserved in some old forms, as οἴκοι, *at home*.   Θηβαι-γενής, *born in Thebes*.   In the *o-* and *a-* stems the *-ι* contracted with the stem to ōι(ωι) and *-āι*, as λόγῳ, χώρᾳ.   In the consonantal (and *ι* and *υ*) stems it is regular.

130.   The original instrumental case ending in the singular is most probably—*a*, seen in λάθρα (λάθρη, Hom.), and ἐπισχερώ (Hom.) *in a row*. *-a* also occurs in adverbs like ἅμα and παρά.

N.   In the *o-* and *a-* stems the *-a* combined with the stem vowel into *-ō* (*-ω*) and *-ā*.

131.   It is readily seen that in *o-* and *a-* stems the boundary line between the forms of the dat., loc., and instr. became obliterated, thus:

Dat. $\chi\omega\rho\bar{a} + a\iota = \chi\omega\rho a\iota = \chi\dot{\omega}\rho\dot{q}$

Loc. $\chi\omega\rho\bar{a} + \iota = \chi\omega\rho a\iota = \chi\dot{\omega}\rho\dot{q}$

Ins. $\chi\omega\rho\bar{a} + a = \chi\omega\rho a = \chi\dot{\omega}\rho a$

These resultant forms were finally pronounced alike and then written alike in the dative form. So also with the *o*– stems, as

Dat. $\lambda o\gamma o + a\iota = \lambda o\gamma\bar{o}\iota = \lambda o\gamma\omega\iota = \lambda\dot{o}\gamma\omega$

Loc. $\lambda o\gamma o + \iota = \lambda o\gamma\bar{o}\iota = \lambda o\gamma\omega\iota = \lambda\dot{o}\gamma\omega$

Ins. $\lambda o\gamma o + a = \lambda o\gamma\bar{o} = \lambda o\gamma\omega = \lambda\dot{o}\gamma\omega$

In the Table of Case-Endings it seems from analogy that $-\iota$ is simply added to the stem-ending in both vowel and consonant stems to form the dat., loc., and inst. singular. In the vowel stems the loc. and inst. appear in the dat. form; and in the consonant stems the dat. and inst. appear under the loc. form.

132. In the accusative singular $-\nu$ (*m* Ind-E.) remained after a vowel or became $-\breve{a}$ (sonant ν or m) after a consonant.

133. The masculine and feminine vocative has no special case ending.

134. In the neuter the case-ending of nominative, accusative, and vocative is $-\nu$ (orig. *m*, Indo-E.) in the *o*– stems. All other neuters have the bare stem-ending.

Plural

135. The original Ind-E. nom. plural case-ending of the masculine and feminine was *es* (–ες Greek) for all stems. In Greek it survives in the consonant stems as –ες, in Latin as –*es*. But the nominative (–οι) of *o*– stems became generalized after the analogy of the nom. of the demonstrative pronouns, as τοί. Then the nominative (αι) of *a*– stems was re-formed after the analogy of the –οι of *o*– stems.

136. The original Ind-E. genitive plural case-ending seems to be *ōm* (or *ŏm*), ων in Greek, for all stems. In primitive Greek the genitive of *a*– stems seems to be remodeled on the gen. of the demonstrative pronoun, as τάων, θεάων.

137. The special ablative plural case-ending disappeared early in proethnic Greek, the genitive form taking over the function of the ablative. This was doubtless due to the analogy of the use of the genitive singular (q. v.)

138. The original dative plural case-ending in the Indo-E. contained both *bh*– and *m*–, but with what vowels it is not certain. In proethnic Greek this ending had ceased to be used at all; and the dative meaning was expressed by the locative in –σι and instrumental in –οις (and –αις). The dative, however, in Latin preserves sometimes its own original ending (*bhyas* in Sanskrit) as in *dea-bus, capitibus*.

139. The original locative case-ending in the Indo-E. seems probably to have been –*s*. In Greek it seems that –ι from analogy of the singular was added. Thus the locative ending had come to be in primitive Greek –σι for all stems, as θύρασι, 'Αθήνησι, λύκοισι, ποιμέσι, etc. In the ο– stems the ending –οι–σι came either from the pronouns or from the nominative plural. The form –αισι of the α– stems was formed on the analogy of –οισι of the ο– stems. Forms in –οισι and –αισι began to disappear by beginning of the fourth century B. C. The endings –εσσι and –σσι are found in Homer. The locative ending –σι is used in the consonant stems (including ι and υ) also for the dative and instrumental.

140. The original Indo-E. instrumental case-ending was –*bhis* (and probably –*mis*), except for ο– stems which have –*ois* (Greek –οισ). Homer uses the instrumental plural φιν (in Sanskrit –*bhis*), possibly seen in ἀμ–φίς, in such forms as κεφαλῆ–φιν. On the analogy of –οις of the ο– stems there was formed –αις of the α– stems. In the vowel stems (α and ο) –οις and –αις are used for the dative and locative.

N. The old associative plural has no examples left. In primitive Greek it completely blended with the instrumental.

141. The masculine and feminine accusative plural case-ending in Indo-E. was –*ns* or *ns* (sonant *n* + s) according as the stem ended in a vowel or a consonant. In Greek, sonant *n* = α. Cret. λύκονς = Att., Ion., and Dor. λύκους;

Cret. τιμάνς = Att., Ion., and Dor. τιμᾶς; Cret. πόλινς = Ion. πόλῑς. πατέρας is from πατερνς. Then the ending –ους is made from –ονς; the ν is dropped before –ς and the ο has compensative lengthening. And the acc. plu. ending –ας of the third declension comes from –νς (sonant ν).

142. The neuter nominative accusative, and vocative plural ending, –α, probably had its origin in a feminine collective singular. ᾰ is probably an ablaut variation of ᾱ. It seems that in the primitive language certain feminine collective singulars were felt to be no longer singulars but plurals. For example δένδρα would mean something like "treedom," then the individual objects of "treedom", *trees*. This may be the origin in Greek and Sanskrit of the use whereby a neuter plural subject may have a singular verb.

Some General Rules for the accent of Nouns (Subst. and Adj.).

143. Nouns (subst. and adj.) in the oblique cases keep the accent on the same syllable as in the nom. sing. if the quantity of the ultima permits; otherwise the accent is forced forward to the following syllable by the rules of accent, on which also the kind of accent depends. Thus nom. εἰρήνη, gen. εἰρήνης; nom. ἄνθρωπος, gen. ἀνθρώπου, acc. ἄνθρωπον; nom. σῶμα, gen. σώματος.

144. Oxytones of the first and second declensions are perispomena in the gen., abl., loc., inst., and dat. of all numbers. Thus φωνή, φωνῆς, φωνῇ, φωνῶν, φωναῖς; ὁδός, ὁδοῦ, ὁδῷ, ὁδῶν, ὁδοῖς.

145. Monosyllabic words of the third declension usually accent the ultima in the gen., abl., loc., inst., and dat. of all numbers, the acute in the singular and loc., inst., and dat. plural, but the circumflex in the gen. and abl. plural. Thus νύξ, νυκτός, νυκτί, νυκτῶν, νυξί.

N. But in some words the gen.-abl. plural is not accented on the ultima; as ὁ, ἡ παῖς, παίδων; τὸ οὖς [ὤτων]; τὸ φῶς, φώτων; in πᾶς the masc. and neut. plural of the gen., abl., loc., inst., dat. are not accented on the ultima, as πάντων, πᾶσι. Monosyllabic participles in the masc. and neut., always accent the first syllable, as ὤν, ὄντος, ὄντων, etc.

146.   The genitive plural in substantives of the first declension always has the circumflex accent on the ultima, since –ῶν comes from –έων from –ήων, from –άων.

N.   But the feminine genitive plural of adjectives and participles, whose masc. nom. sing. ends in –ος, has the same accent and form as the masculine; as of ἴδιος gen. plural for all genders is ἰδίων; of λεγόμενος gen. plu. for all genders is λεγομένων.

147.   Some vocatives have a recessive accent; as ἄδελφε (but ἀδελφέ in W. H.) from ἀδελφός; πάτερ from πατήρ; ἄνερ from ἀνήρ.   These forms probably indicate the original enclitic (or unaccented) character of the vocative where it did not begin a sentence.

148.   *Declensions.* [1]   There are three declensions of nouns (both substantives and adjectives) [2] in Greek:

The First, or α– declension, with stems ending in ᾱ–.

The Second, or ο– declension, with stems ending in –ο.

The Third, or consonant declension, with stems ending in a consonant or the semi-vowels (ι and υ).

149.   It is only since the seventeenth century A. D. that grammarians distinguish for convenience three declensions in Greek.   The older grammars had ten or more.   In Sanskrit Whitney finds five declensions, as in Latin, but says: "There is nothing absolute in this arrangement; it is merely believed to be open to as few objections as any other."   The threefold division has beside for the sake of convenience the justification that the first and second declensions have vowel stems and differ in one having ᾱ– and the other ο– stems, and the third has consonant or semi-vowel stems.   Also the genitive singular of the third declension always has the suffix –ος.

150   The first and second declension are sometimes called the *vowel* declension, as opposed to the third or *consonant* declension.

---

1.   Square brackets [ ] denote that no model of the form within occurs in the New Testament.

2.   The term noun includes according to ancient usage, both substantive and adjective.   Cf. Plato's Cratylus.

DECLENSION OF SUBSTANTIVES

First Declension

152. This declension contains words ending originally (1) in ᾱ, masculine and feminine; and (2) in ια (ya), feminine. ᾱ became η in primitive Attic and Ionic and remained ᾱ in Ionic, but returned to ᾱ in Attic after ε, ι, ρ, (except when an original ϝ intervened, as Attic κόρη, Arcad. κόρϝᾱ). The nominative singular of feminines ends in –ᾱ, –ᾰ, or –η; the nominative singular of masculines adds –ς to the ending—α or –η, and ends in –ᾱς or –ης. The words in this declension are usually feminine. There are no neuters.

153. The union of the case-ending with the stem exhibits the forms in the following table:

	Fem. Sing.	Masc. Sing.	Masc. and Fem. Plural
Nom.	–ᾱ or –ᾰ, –η	–ᾱς, –ης	–αι
Gen. } Ab.	–ᾱς or ης, –ης	(–ου, –α), (–ου)[1]	–ῶν (for –ά –ων)
D. } L. } I.	–ᾳ or –ῃ, –ῃ	–ᾳ –ῃ	–αις
A.	–ᾱν or –ᾰν, –ην	–ᾱν –ην	–ᾱς
V.	–ᾱ or –ᾰ, –η	–ᾱ –ᾰ or –η	–αι

1. See §156a.

154. Feminines in –ᾱ, –η, –ᾰ.

Singular

	χώρα *land*	φωνή *voice*	ἀσθένεια *weakness*	μάχαιρα *sword*	γλῶσσα *tongue*
N. V.	χώρα	φωνή	ἀσθένεια	μάχαιρα	γλῶσσα
G. Ab.	χώρας	φωνῆς	ἀσθενείας	μαχαίρης	γλώσσης
D. L. I.	χώρᾳ	φωνῇ	ἀσθενείᾳ	μαχαίρῃ	γλώσσῃ
A.	χώραν	φωνήν	ἀσθένειαν	μάχαιραν	γλῶσσαν

Plural

N. V.	χῶραι	φωναί	ἀσθένειαι	μάχαιραι	γλῶσσαι
G. Ab.	χωρῶν	φωνῶν	ἀσθενειῶν	μαχαιρῶν	γλωσσῶν
D. L. I.	χώραις	φωναῖς	ἀσθενείαις	μαχαίραις	γλώσσαις
A.	χώρας	φωνάς	ἀσθενείας	μαχαίρας	γλώσσας

155. There are two classes of feminines; those that have long α or η, and those that have short α, in the nominative singular.

a. If the nominative singular has long α, long α is retained throughout the singular; as in χώρα (above). If the nominative singular has η, η is retained throughout the singular; as in φωνή (above).

b. If the nominative singular has short α, the accusative and vocative singular have also short α; the genitive, ablative, dative, locative, and instrumental singular have long α after ε or ι, otherwise η; as in ἀσθένεια, γλῶσσα, (§154).

c. The Attic rule that nouns ending in α *pure* (that is after ε, ι, or ρ) retain α throughout the singular, is modified in the κοινή. Substantives in –ρᾰ and participles in –υῖα usually have the genitive and ablative singular in –ης, and the dative, locative, and instrumental in –ῃ. μαχαίρης, –ῃ are found in WH all nine places where the cases occur. WH read also πρῴρης (Acts 27:30), σπείρης (Acts 10:1; 21:31; 27:1), πλημμύρης (Luke 6:48). In Acts 5:2 is found συνειδυίης. These forms became normal in the papyri from i/B. C.; cf. ἀρούρης, B. U. G. 101, 22; μοίρης, P. Lond. I p. 134, 58 etc; εἰδυίης is common after i/B. C.

d. πρύμνα is found in Acts 27:41, and πτέρναν in John 13:18. In older Greek both πρύμνα and πρύμνη were used.

156. Masculines in ας and ης.

Singular

A.	νεανίας	μαθητής	προφήτης
	young man	*disciple*	*prophet*
N.	νεανίας	μαθητής	προφήτης
G. Ab.	νεανίου	μαθητοῦ	προφήτου
D. L. I.	νεανίᾳ	μαθητῇ	προφήτῃ
A.	νεανίαν	μαθητήν	προφήτην
V.	νεανία	μαθητά	προφῆτα

Plural

N. V.	[νεανίαι]	μαθηταί	προφῆται
G. Ab.	[νεανιῶν]	μαθητῶν	προφητῶν
D. L. I.	νεανίαις	μαθηταῖς	προφήταις
A.	[νεανίας]	μαθητάς	προφήτας

Singular

B.	Ἡρῴδης	βορρᾶς
	Herod	*north wind*

N.	Ἡρῴδης	βορρᾶς
G. Ab.	Ἡρῴδου	βορρᾶ
D. L. I.	Ἡρῴδῃ	βορρᾷ
A.	Ἡρῴδην	βορρᾶν
V.	Ἡρῴδη	βορρᾶ

a. The gen. sing. ending ου– is taken from the gen. sing. of the second declension. The Doric gen. sing. ending –α came from the contraction of αο (from ασο).

b. In general, Greek names in –ας after ε or ι have gen. sing. in –ου; but those in –ᾶς and –ας not preceded by ε or ι have –α in the gen. sing. There are exceptions.

c. Nominatives in –ας (pure) have vocative sing. in α (long); those in –της have –α (short); all others generally have –η. Voc. ᾅδη is found in 1 Cor. 15:55 in Aleph ᶜ A** K L M P etc.

157. *Contracts of the First Declension.*

Contract substantives are infrequent in the N. T. They have the circumflex accent on the ultima in all the cases; μνᾶ (for μναα), *mina*, is, except for accent, declined like χώρα; γῆ (for γεα or γαα), *earth*, and συκῆ (for συκεα), *fig tree*, are except for accent declined like φωνή. The proper name Ἑρμῆς (for Ἑρμέας) is except for accent declined like Ἡρῴδης.

Second Declension

158. Words of this declension have stems in –ο. They are principally masculine and neuter with a few feminines. The masculine and feminine nominative singular ends in –ος, the neuter nom. sing. in –ον The feminines are declined like the masculines. The neuters differ from the masculines only in the nom. and vocative sing. (ending in –ον) and in the nom. voc., and acc. plu. (ending in –α).

159. The union of the case-ending with the stem exhibits the forms in the following table:

| | Singular | | Plural | |
	Masc. and Fem.	Neut.	Masc. and Fem.	Neut.
N.	–ος	–ον	–οι	–ᾰ
G. Ab.	–ου		–ων	
D. L. I.	–ῳ		–οις	
A.	–ον	–ον	–ους	–ᾰ
V.	–ε	–ον	–οι	–ᾰ

160.

	Singular			
	νόμος	ἄνθρωπος	ὁδός	δῶρον
	law	man	way	gift
N.	νόμος	ἄνθρωπος	ὁδός	δῶρον
G. Ab.	νόμου	ἀνθρώπου	ὁδοῦ	δώρου
D. L. I.	νόμῳ	ἀνθρώπῳ	ὁδῷ	δώρῳ
A.	νόμον	ἄνθρωπον	ὁδόν	δῶρον
V.	νόμε	ἄνθρωπε		δῶρον

	Plural			
N.	νόμοι	ἄνθρωποι	ὁδοί	δῶρα
G. Ab.	νόμων	ἀνθρώπων	ὁδῶν	δώρων
D. L. I.	νόμοις	ἀνθρώποις	ὁδοῖς	δώροις
A.	νόμους	ἀνθρώπους	ὁδούς	δῶρα
V.	νόμοι	ἄνθρωποι		δῶρα

a. With one or two exceptions θεός is used as the vocative in the N.T.; but θεέ is the form nearly always found in the LXX.

b. The voc. of ἀδελφός is in Attic ἄδελφε, but in the κοινή it is ἀδελφέ. (In Modern Greek it generally is ἀδερφέ, but ἄδεφλε in Pontic.) Westcott and Hort write ἀδελφέ.

161. *Contracts of the Second Declension.*

In the κοινή stems in –εο and –οο did not regularly contract according to the Attic norm (see contract adjectives).

The declension of ὀστοῦν (ὀστέον) *bone,* the only substantive of this class in the New T., is:

	Sing.		Plural
N.	ὀστοῦν		[ὀστᾶ]
G. Ab.	[ὀστοῦ, ὀστέου]		ὀστέων, [ὀστῶν]
D. L. I.	[ὀστῷ]		[ὀστέοις, ὀστοῖς]
A.	[ὀστοῦν]		ὀστέα

a. The attic norm of these words may be seen in the masculine and neuter of the contract adjectives of the second declension (§209).

b. Moeris writes: ὀστοῦν Ἀττικοί, ὀστέον Ἕλληνες. Two words, νοῦς and πλοῦς, which in Attic originally belonged to this class, are found in the third declension, declined like βοῦς. It seems that ὄρνεον (for Attic ὄρνις) is always uncontracted. See P. Ryl. 98a, 9 (II), πᾶν ὄρνεον.

162. "Attic" Declension.

a. This declension is called "Attic" because a few words in Attic (but not in other dialects) had undergone a change of quantity in their vowels: –ως was substituted for final –ος, and a preceding long vowel shortened, as νεώς and λεώς from νηός and ληός; these two words are replaced in the κοινή by the Doric ναός and λαός. A few words have a consonant before –ως.

b. In the N. T. and the κοινή generally this class is nearly gone. νεώς survives only in the compound νεωκόρος (Acts 19:35). The adjective ἵλεως occurs only in the nom. sing. in the phrase ἵλεώς σοι (Matt. 16:22) and in Heb. 8:12. Although the LXX and the papyri show ἡ ἅλως frequently, it is not found in the N. T.; ἡ ἅλων takes its place.

c. According to WH Ἀπολλώς has the following forms:

N. Ἀπολλώς.

G. Ab. Ἀπολλώ (1 Cor. 1:12; 16:12).

A. { Ἀπολλώ (Acts 19:1).
{ Ἀπολλών (1 Cor. 4:6, Tit. 3:13).

d.   The same fluctuation in the accusative (–ω, ων–) occurs in the Attic.

e.   The best MSS. have τὴν Κῶ in Acts 21:1, not Κῶν.

f.   In classical Greek there are no neuter substantives belonging to this class.   The reading ἀνώγεων in Mk. 14:15 and Luke 22:12 had no warrant in the κοινή or Attic; the true reading is ἀνάγαιον.

163.   Heteroclisis and Metaplasm.

A. In Gender. Fluctuations between the neuter and masculine of the second declension occur:

βάτος varies between the masc. (Mk. 12:26) and the fem. (Luke 20:37).

δεῖπνον is the usual form; but in some MSS. it is masculine.

δεσμός has the plural δεσμά in Luke 8:29, Ac. 16:26, and 20:23, but οἱ δεσμοί in Ph. 1:13.

ζυγός is regularly masc. in the κοινή.

θεμέλιος is masculine except in Ac. 16:26 where the acc. plu. is τὰ θεμέλια.

λιμός is certainly fem. in Luke 15:14 and Ac. 11:28; but indeterminate in other instances.

στάδιον has acc. plu. σταδίους in Lu. 24:13 and John 6:19 (but Aleph* D have στάδια)..

B. In Declensions.

a. The First and Second Declensions.

The chief variations between the first and second declensions is in compounds in –αρχης and –αρχος (Attic). In the N. T., forms in –αρχης are greatly in the majority. There is no variation in χιλίαρχος.

θεά seems to be in the κοινή the regular fem. of θεός, as θεᾶς in Ac. 19:27, but usual Attic form τὴν θεόν occurs in Ac. 19:37.

b. Fluctuations between the First or Second and Third Declensions.

ἔλεος is always neuter in the N. T.

δάκρυον has an old dat. plu. of the third decl., δάκρυσιν (Luke 7:38,44) from the old δάκρυ.

ζῆλος varies between masc. (sec. decl.) and neuter (third

decl.), as ζῆλον (acc.) in 2 Cor. 7:11 and τὸ ζῆλος in 2 Cor. 9:2.

ἦχος is masc. (sec. decl.) in Heb. 12:19, but loc. third decl. (masc. or fem.) in Luke 21:25.

Λύστρα has acc. sing. Λύστραν in Ac. 14:6, but loc. Λύστροις in Ac. 14:8.

νῖκος (τὸ) prevails (as 1 Cor. 15:54f.) over the earlier νίκη (1 Jno. 5:4).

πλοῦτος varies between the sec. and third declensions.

σάββατον has a dat.-loc.-inst. form σάββασιν as in Mk. 1:21, etc.

Third Declension

164. This declension includes all stems ending in consonants or the semi-vowels ι and υ.

165. In this declension it is important to know the stem which may usually be formed by dropping –ος of the genitive singular.

166. The nominative singular of masculine and feminine stems which do not end in ν, ρ, σ, or οντ is formed by adding ς.

A labial mute (π, β, φ) + ς becomes ψ; as λιβς = λίψ; σκολοπς = σκόλοψ.

A palatal (κ, γ, χ) + ς becomes ξ; as σαρκς = σάρξ; μαστιγς = μάστιξ.

A lingual (τ, δ, θ) + ς becomes σσ at first and then finally ς; as χαριτς =χάρις; ἐλπιδς = ἐλπίς. So ἱμάς from stem in ἱμαντ.

167. The nominative singular of masculine and feminine stems ending in ν, ρ, and ς is formed by simply lengthening the stem vowel, if short; as stem ποιμεν becomes ποιμήν; ἡγεμον becomes ἡγεμών. Of course if the vowel of the stem-ending is long, the nominative is simply like the stem; as stem σωτηρ, nominative σωτήρ; stem αἰων–, nominative αἰών.

168. The nominative singular of masculine stems in οντ is formed by dropping τ (§77) and lengthening ο to ω: as stem λεοντ–, nom. λεών. But ὀδούς (stem ὀδοντ–) is formed like the nom. of participles in –ους.

169. Neuters have in the nominative, voc., and acc. the bare stem-ending; final τ and other consonants which can-

not stand at the end of word (§77) are dropped: γένος, ἄστυ, μέλι (stem μελιτ), σῶμα (stem σωματ), γάλα (stem γαλακτ).

170 The accusative singular of masculines and feminines which end in a consonant has α [α = ν = m (sonant m)]; those ending in ι or υ have ν (Indo-Eu. m).

N. The N. T. generally conforms to the rule that barytones of two syllables with stems in -ιτ and ιδ have acc. sing. in -ιν. See 176 C, e.

171. Because the nom. singular of stems ending in -ιτ, -ιδ, -ιθ regularly fell together with the nominative of the ι-stems; new formations in the acc. singular early arose: thus πόλις : πόλιν :: χάρις : χάριν.

a. In consequence the acc. sing. of barytone stems of two syllables ending in -ιτ, -ιδ, -ιθ is formed by dropping the lingual and adding ν; as nom. χάρις, acc. χάριν.

b. But in oxytone stems the case is formed regularly; as nom. ἐλπίς, acc. ἐλπίδα.

172. The vocative singular of masculines and feminines is either like the nominative, or the simple stem.

a. Like the nominative are:

   (a) Those with stems ending in a labial or palatal mute (§35), as κῆρυξ.

   (b) Oxytone stems ending in a liquid, as ποιμήν. But πατήρ has πάτερ, and ἀνήρ has ἄνερ, but with change of accent.

b. The simple stem. In the Attic this was the usual form of the vocative, as βοῦ (βοῦς), πόλι (πόλις).

   (a) Barytone stems in -ν, ρ, ι, and ντ, and stems in -ιδ have the simple stem in the vocative; as δαῖμον (δαίμων), ῥῆτορ (ῥήτωρ), παῖ (παῖς, gen. παιδός).

c. In the Koine the tendency is for the vocative to be the same as the nominative in form, as θύγατηρ (Mark. 5:34), πατήρ (John 17:21), ἡ παῖς (Luke 8:54).

d. The vocative plural is always the same as the nominative.

173. The dative, locative, and instrumental plural add

σι to the stem (see case-endings), with necessary euphonic changes in the case of—

a. Stems in –ντ–, which drop ντ and lengthen (§49, c.) the preceding vowel (if short); ἄρχων (stem ἀρχοντ), ἄρχουσι; ἱμάς (stem ἱμαντ), ἱμᾶσι.

b. Stems in –ον and –εν, which seem simply to drop ν without lengthening the preceding vowel; ποιμήν (stem ποιμεν), ποιμέσι; ἡγεμών (stem ἡγεμον), ἡγεμόσι.

N. Actually ν is not dropped. Stems in –ον and –εν originally had weak or strong stems in the different cases (ablaut or vowel gradation). The dat., loc., and inst. plural had (after syncretism) the weak grade, and ν stood between two consonants, as ποιμνσι and ἡγεμνσι, and should have become vocalic (that is vocalic ν = α) as in Skt. rajasu (–asu from –nsu represents the original locative). The –α– (= vocalic ν) was preserved in φρασί for φρνσι (Pindar, Attic Inscript. vi/B. C.); the later φρεσί took its ε from the nom. φρένες. Thus instead of ποιμάσι, ἡγεμάσι, with –α– (vocalic ν), the stem vowel (ε and ο) was borrowed and the forms ποιμέσι and ἡγεμόσι appear.

174. a. The acc. sing. in –αν (ν in addition to α) is frequently found in various N. T. MSS. It is also found in early dialects, inscriptions, and the papyri. Examples are χεῖραν (Jno. 20:25), ἀστέραν (Matt. 2:10), τρίχαν (Matt. 5:36), σάρκαν (Jno. 6:54), ἄρσεναν (Rev. 12:13).

b. ν is also found added to the acc. sing. –η or –ῆ of nominatives in –ης: examples are ἀσφαλῆν (Heb. 6:19), ὑγιῆν (Jno. 5:11), συγγενῆν (Rom. 16:11), ποδήρην (Rev. 1:13). Such forms occur in the papyri and the LXX. Even in the Attic are found τριήρην and Δημοσθένην (frequently such accusatives of proper names of the third declension).

c. The acc. plu. in –ες occurs in many N. T. MSS. (also in LXX and papyri), especially in τέσσαρες.

175. Monosyllabic stems of the third declension generally have the accent on the ultima (the case-ending) in the gen. abl., and dat. loc., inst., of both numbers. In the gen. abl. plural ὦν has the circumflex: thus σάρξ, σαρκός etc.; νύξ, νυκτός, νυκτῶν, νυξί.

N. But φῶς, παῖς, οὖς are accented in the gen. plu. thus φώτων, παίδων, ὤτων. In the masculine and neuter plural πᾶς does not have the accent on the ultima but on the penult.

176. Stems ending in Mutes.

A. Stems in a Labial Mute (π, β, φ).

Singular

Stem	"Αραψ 'Αραβ– *an Arabian*	λαῖλαψ λαιλαπ– *storm*
N.	["Αραψ]	λαῖλαψ
G. Ab.	["Αραβος]	λαίλαπος
D. L. I.	["Αραβι]	λαίλαπι
A.	"Αραβα	λαίλαπα

Plural

N.	"Αραβες	[λαίλαπες]
G. Ab.	['Αράβων]	λαιλάπων
D. L. I.	["Αραψι]	[λαίλαψι]
A.	["Αραβας]	[λαίλαπας]

N. Only seven nouns with stems in a labial mute occur in the N. T. They are Αἰθίοψ, –οπος, ὁ, *Ethiopian*; "Αραψ, –αβος, ὁ, *Arabian*; κώνωψ, –ωπος, ὁ, *gnat*; λαῖλαψ, –απος, ἡ, *storm*; λίψ, λιβός, ὁ, *SW. wind*; μώλωψ, –ωπος, ὁ, *wound*; σκόλοψ, –οπος, ὁ, *stake*.

B. Stems in a Palatal Mute (κ, γ, χ).

Singular

Stem	σάρξ (ἡ) σαρκ– *flesh*	σάλπιγξ (ἡ) σαλπιγγ– *trumpet*	θρίξ (ἡ) θριχ–, τριχ– *hair*
N.	σάρξ	σάλπιγξ	θρίξ
G. Abl.	σαρκός	σάλπιγγος	τριχός
D. L. I.	σαρκί	σάλπιγγι	τριχί
A.	σάρκα	σάλπιγγα	τρίχα

Plural

N.	σάρκες	σάλπιγγες	τρίχες
G. Ab.	σαρκῶν	σαλπίγγων	τριχῶν
D. L. I.	σαρξί(ν)	σάλπιγξι(ν)	θριξί(ν)
A.	σάρκας	σάλπιγγας	τρίχας

a. For the change in aspirates in θρίξ, τριχός, see § 71, d, (1).

b. The nom. plu. and the oblique cases of γυνή, *woman* are from the stem γυναικ-, as γυνή, γυναικός, γυναικί, γυναῖκα, γυναῖκες, γυναικῶν, γυναιξί(ν), γυναῖκας. The vocative γύναι occurs; final κ of stem was dropped. The accent follows the rule of mono-syllables.

c. ὄρνιξ, *fowl*, with stem in ὀρνιχ- occurs in some MSS. in Lk. 13:34. It occurs (ὄρνιξι) in the papyri.

C. Stems in a Lingual (or Dental) Mute (τ, δ, θ).

Masculine and Feminine
Singular

	κυριότης (ἡ)	χάρις (ἡ)	ἐλπίς (ἡ)
Stem	κυριοτητ–	χαριτ–	ἐλπιδ–
	lordship	grace	hope
N.	κυριότης	χάρις	ἐλπίς
G. Ab.	κυριότητος	χάριτος	ἐλπίδος
D. L. I.	κυριότητι	χάριτι	ἐλπίδι
A.	κυριότητα	χάριν	ἐλπίδα

Plural

N.	κυριότητες	χάριτες	ἐλπίδες
G. Ab.	[κυριοτήτων]	χαρίτων	ἐλπίδων
D. L. I.	[κυριότησι]	χάρισι(ν)	ἐλπίσι(ν)
A.	[κυριότητας]	χάριτας	ἐλπίδας

a. Likewise are declined stems in –αδ– and –υδ–: λαμπάς, λαμπάδος, etc.; χλαμύς, χλαμύδος, etc.

b. One stem in –θ occurs, ὄρνις (stem ὀρνιθ–), *fowl*. It only occurs in the nominative in Matt. 23:37, and Luke 13:34 (W. H.). But the variant in Luke 13:34, ὄρνιξ (a Doric form, stem ὀρνιχ-) has a strong claim. ὄρνιθα, (acc.) and ὄρνιξ occur in adjoining clauses in Papyri P. S. I. 569, 3f. (253-52 B. C.).

c. γόης (ὁ) occurs in nom. plu. γόητες (2 Tim. 3:13).

d. κλείς (κλειδ–) has in the acc. sing. κλεῖδα (Lk. 11:52) as well as the Attic κλεῖν (Rev. 3:7; 20:1); and in the acc. plu. ‚κλεῖδας (Matt. 16:19) as well as κλεῖς (Rev. 1:18).

e. The acc. sing. of χάρις is commonly χάριν (about forty times), but χάριτα is found in Ac. 24:27. See 170 N.

f. The nom. form πούς, *foot*, is difficult to account for. It is regular in the nom. plu. and oblique cases, in which the stem is ποδ–.

177. Stems in –ντ–. Substantives with stems in –ντ– call for a separate treatment from the simple –τ– stems, (1) because –σ– in the case-ending of dat. loc. and instr. produces phonetic changes (§49, c; 62, d) unlike the changes in the simple –ν or –τ stems, and (2) because –ντ– was used originally in forming participles, and the substantives in –ντ– were originally participles. In the nominative –s was original; the nom. ἄρχων is a new formation. λέων (λεοντ–) was originally a –ν stem, but from analogy came to be declined like the –ντ– stems.

178.   ἄρχων (ὁ)
     Stem   ἀρχοντ–
                              ruler

	Singular	Plural
N.	ἄρχων	ἄρχοντες
G. Ab.	ἄρχοντος	ἀρχόντων
D. L. I.	ἄρχοντι	ἄρχουσι(ν)
A.	ἄρχοντα	ἄρχοντας

N. ὀδούς (ὀδοντ–), declined like διδούς (§214, f), and ἱμάς (ἱμαντ–) declined like στάς (§§214, A, 211 C. a), do not occur in all cases in the N. T. They are the only substantives of their type found in the N. T.

179. Neuter stems in –τ and –ασ (which have passed to –τ stems). No satisfactory explanation has been given of the origin of neuters in –ματ–.

a. Neuters with nom. in –ας (stem –ασ–) are declined after the analogy of stems in –ματ–. Two substantives in the N. T. show definite traces of the original declension of stems in –ασ. γῆρας (γηρασ) has the dat. loc. ins. γήρει in Luke 1:36. The regular forms as γῆρας, γήρως, γήρᾳ occur in papyri. The gen. γήρους occurs in 1 Clem. 63:3, and dat. γήρᾳ in 1 Clem. 10:7.

Both forms of the gen., γήρως, γήρους, and both forms of the dat., γήρᾳ and γήρει are found in the‾LXX. κρέας has the acc. plu. in κρέα in Rom. 14:21 and 1 Cor. 8:13; also in the LXX, Jus. Dial. 22:6, 9. In papyri gen. sing. is κρέως.

b. The dat. loc. inst. sing. of stems in –ασ was properly αι (γήραι); but –ᾳ is often found and is possibly after the analogy of stems in –α (of first declension).

180.   Singular

	σῶμα (τό)	πέρας (τό)
Stem	σωματ– body	περασ–, περατ– end
N.	σῶμα	πέρας
G. Ab.	σώματος	[πέρατος]
D. L. I.	σώματι	[πέρατι]
A.	σῶμα	πέρας

Plural

N.	σώματα	πέρατα
G. Ab.	σωμάτων	περάτων
D. L. I.	σώμασι(ν)	πέρασι(ν)
A.	σώματα	πέρατα

N. Like σῶμα are declined all neuters with nom. in –μα, which are very numerous in the N. T. Like πέρας are declined τέρας, wonder, portent; κέρας, horn.

181. Two words survive of an old declension of neuter substantives which consisted of the blending of two stems, –ωρ, –αρ and sonant ν (= α), the latter, except in nom. and acc. singular, form the gen., abl., dat., loc., inst. singular and all the cases in the plural after the analogy of stems in μπρ.

a. ὕδωρ (τό), water, and φρέαρ (τό), well. Sing. N. and A. ὕδωρ, Gen.=Abl. ὕδατος, D. L. I. ὕδατι, Plu. N. and A. ὕδατα, G.= Abl. ὑδάτων, D. L. I. ὕδασι(ν).

b. φρέαρ occurs only in the nom., accusative, and genitive (φρέατος).

c. ὄναρ (τό), dream, found only in the accusative in the N. T., originally belongs to this class. In Attic it occurs only in the nom. and acc.

182. A few neuter substantives with $-\tau$ in the gen., abl., dat., loc., ins. cases sing. and all cases of the plural have nominative (and acc.) sing. in a different stem according to which they were originally declined:

a. φῶς, *light*, belonged to the $-\epsilon\sigma$, $-o\sigma$, stems. Homer has φάος, gen. φάους. In the N. T. and Attic the other (not nom. and acc. sing.) cases were formed after the analogy of the dental stems, gen. φωτός etc., nom. plu. φῶτα.

b. οὖς, *ear*, also belonged to the $-\epsilon\sigma$, $-o\sigma$, stems; the Doric and Ionic have ὦς. In the N. T. and Attic the other (not nom. and acc. sing.) cases were formed from ὦς after the analogy of the dental stems, gen. [ὠτός] etc., nom. plu. ὦτα.

c. The nom. γόνυ belonged to an old υ declension. It early came to have its other (not nom. and acc. sing.) cases on the analogy of dental stems.

d. The nom. (and acc.) of γάλα (τό), *milk*, is the mere stem because κτ of the stem γαλακτ– (gen. γάλακτος) can not stand at the end of a word. Other cases are regular.

e. Likewise the nom. (and acc.) μέλι, *honey*, is the simple stem; $-\tau$ of the stem μελιτ (gen. μέλιτος) can not end a word. Other cases are regular.

f. The new form ἅλας (τό), *salt*, has in the N. T. practically driven out the old form ἅλς (ὁ). Except the nom. and acc. of ἅλας, gen. [ἅλατος], the form ἅλατι (dat., loc., ins.) alone occurs. In the margin of W H (Mk. 9:49) the form ἁλί from ἅλς occurs, and the acc. ἅλα occurs in the text of Mk. 9:50.

In the Ptolemaic papyri of iii / B. C· τὸ ἅλας appears, but forms from ἅλς preponderate.

183. Stems Ending in a Liquid (λ, ρ).

The only word, ἅλς, with stem ending in λ has been treated in § 182f. In the nom. $-s$ is added to stem ἁλ–.

184. Stems in $-\rho-$ (from §§ 184 to 186).

a. Originally stems in $-\tau\eta\rho$, $-\tau\omega\rho$, $-\eta\rho$ had vowel gradation in the different cases:

Strong	Middle	Weak
$-\tau\eta\rho$	$-\tau\epsilon\rho$	$-\tau\rho$
$-\tau\omega\rho$	$-\tau o\rho$	$-\tau\rho$
$-\eta\rho$	$-\epsilon\rho$	$-\rho$

In the weak grades the vowel disappeared and when a consonant of a case-ending immediately followed $-\tau\rho$ or $-\rho$, then ρ became vocalic. $-\rho\alpha-$ in $\pi\alpha\tau\rho\acute{\alpha}\sigma\iota\,(\nu)$, $\dot{\alpha}\nu\delta\rho\acute{\alpha}\sigma\iota\,(\nu)$, etc., represents vocalic ρ (§ 40, b).

b. Vowel gradation early began to be levelled out. Of most (except the relationship-nouns noted below) words ending in $-\tau\eta\rho$, $-\eta-$ of the nominative was levelled out into all the cases, as $\sigma\omega\tau\acute{\eta}\rho$, $\sigma\omega\tau\hat{\eta}\rho os$, etc. But $\dot{\alpha}\sigma\tau\acute{\eta}\rho$ and $\dot{\alpha}\acute{\eta}\rho$ generalized the middle grade $-\tau\epsilon\rho$ and $-\epsilon\rho$ in all the oblique cases and nom. plural, as $\dot{\alpha}\sigma\tau\acute{\eta}\rho$, $\dot{\alpha}\sigma\tau\acute{\epsilon}\rho os$, etc.; $\dot{\alpha}\acute{\eta}\rho$, $\dot{\alpha}\acute{\epsilon}\rho os$, etc.

c. Nouns ending in $-\tau\omega\rho$ generalized the middle grade $-\tau o\rho$ in all the oblique cases and the nom. plural.

d. More survivals of original vowel gradation (ablaut) are shown in the relationship nouns than in any other type or class of stem. When nouns show considerable survivals of vowel gradation in inflection, the inflection is sometimes called "strong".

185. Liquid Stems showing considerable vowel gradation:

Singular

	$\pi\alpha\tau\acute{\eta}\rho$ (ὁ)	$\mu\acute{\eta}\tau\eta\rho$ (ἡ)	$\theta\upsilon\gamma\acute{\alpha}\tau\eta\rho$ (ἡ)	$\dot{\alpha}\nu\acute{\eta}\rho$ (ὁ)
Stem	$\pi\alpha\tau\epsilon\rho-$	$\mu\eta\tau\epsilon\rho-$	$\theta\upsilon\gamma\alpha\tau\epsilon\rho-$	$\dot{\alpha}\nu\epsilon\rho-$
	father	mother	daughter	man
N.	$\pi\alpha\tau\acute{\eta}\rho$	$\mu\acute{\eta}\tau\eta\rho$	$\theta\upsilon\gamma\acute{\alpha}\tau\eta\rho$	$\dot{\alpha}\nu\acute{\eta}\rho$
G. Ab.	$\pi\alpha\tau\rho\acute{os}$	$\mu\eta\tau\rho\acute{os}$	$\theta\upsilon\gamma\alpha\tau\rho\acute{os}$	$\dot{\alpha}\nu\delta\rho\acute{os}$
D. L. I.	$\pi\alpha\tau\rho\acute{\iota}$	$\mu\eta\tau\rho\acute{\iota}$	$\theta\upsilon\gamma\alpha\tau\rho\acute{\iota}$	$\dot{\alpha}\nu\delta\rho\acute{\iota}$
A.	$\pi\alpha\tau\acute{\epsilon}\rho\alpha$	$\mu\eta\tau\acute{\epsilon}\rho\alpha$	$\theta\upsilon\gamma\alpha\tau\acute{\epsilon}\rho\alpha$	$\ddot{\alpha}\nu\delta\rho\alpha$
V.	$\pi\acute{\alpha}\tau\epsilon\rho$		$\theta\acute{\upsilon}\gamma\alpha\tau\epsilon\rho$	$\ddot{\alpha}\nu\epsilon\rho$

Plural

N. V.	$\pi\alpha\tau\acute{\epsilon}\rho\epsilon s$	$\mu\eta\tau\acute{\epsilon}\rho\epsilon s$	$\theta\upsilon\gamma\alpha\tau\acute{\epsilon}\rho\epsilon s$	$\ddot{\alpha}\nu\delta\rho\epsilon s$
G. Ab.	$\pi\alpha\tau\acute{\epsilon}\rho\omega\nu$	$\mu\eta\tau\acute{\epsilon}\rho\omega\nu$	$\theta\upsilon\gamma\alpha\tau\acute{\epsilon}\rho\omega\nu$	$\dot{\alpha}\nu\delta\rho\hat{\omega}\nu$
D. L. I.	$\pi\alpha\tau\rho\acute{\alpha}\sigma\iota(\nu)$	$\mu\eta\tau\rho\acute{\alpha}\sigma\iota(\nu)$	$\theta\upsilon\gamma\alpha\tau\rho\acute{\alpha}\sigma\iota(\nu)$	$\dot{\alpha}\nu\delta\rho\acute{\alpha}\sigma\iota(\nu)$
A.	$\pi\alpha\tau\acute{\epsilon}\rho\alpha s$	$\mu\eta\tau\acute{\epsilon}\rho\alpha s$	$\theta\upsilon\gamma\alpha\tau\acute{\epsilon}\rho\alpha s$	$\ddot{\alpha}\nu\delta\rho\alpha s$

a. Except in the nom. and voc. sing. the relationship nouns are in every case accented alike.

b. No vocative of μήτηρ occurs in the N. T. But μήτηρ is found as vocative in papyri [Preis. Samm. 439 (i / B. C.), B. G. U. III, 846, 10 (ii / A. D.)]. In the Gospels πατήρ and θυγάτηρ appear as vocatives [Vid. πατήρ, Wilcken Arch. VI, 205 (159 B. C.)]. For accent of the vocatives here see §147.

c. Originally the strong grade (–τηρ, –τωρ, –ηρ) belonged to the nominative singular only; the middle grade (–τερ, –τορ, –ερ) to the locative sing., and the nominative plu., the weak grade (–τρ, –τρ, –ρ) to gen. sing. and plural and acc. plural; and in the locative plural sonant or vocalic ρ (=ρα) was developed because it (ρ) was followed by a consonant (σ) of the case-ending. The original distinction between these vowel grades is better preserved in these relationship nouns than in any other.

d. In the forms of ἀνδρ– the consonant δ is developed between ν and ρ for the sake of euphony in transition from ν to ρ. Cf. our *gander* and *thunder* with O. E. *gan(d)ra* and *thunor*; *cinder* with Lat. *cineris*.

e. γαστήρ (γαστερ–), ἡ, is declined like πατήρ; but in the N. T. the dat. loc. ins. sing. γαστρί and the nom. plural γαστέρες only are found.

186. Liquid Stems showing very little or no vowel gradation.

Singular

A.	σωτήρ (ὁ)	ῥήτωρ (ὁ)	ἀστήρ (ὁ)
Stem	σωτηρ	ῥητορ	ἀστερ
	saviour	*orator*	*star*
N.	σωτήρ	ῥήτωρ	ἀστήρ
G. Ab.	σωτῆρος	ῥήτορος	ἀστέρος
D. L. I.	σωτῆρι	ῥήτορι	[ἀστέρι]
A.	σωτῆρα	ῥήτορα	ἀστέρα

Plural

N.	σωτῆρες	ῥήτορες	ἀστέρες
G. Ab.	[σωτήρων]	ῥητόρων	ἀστέρων
D. L. I.	[σωτῆρσι(ν)]	[ῥήτορσι(ν)]	[See note a.]
A.	σωτῆρας	ῥήτορας	ἀστέρας

a. The dat. loc. inst. plural is not found in the N. T. But the dat. loc. inst. plural forms of words of the types of σωτήρ and ῥήτωρ occur in the papyri and inscriptions. Stephanus (Thes.) quotes τοῖς φράτορσιν from Hesychius. So far there seems to be no dat. loc. inst. plural of ἀστήρ found in the papyri or inscriptions. The Attic form is ἀστράσι(ν) (the weak grade —τρ). It would be unwise to guess the κοινή form; because ἀστράσι(ν) occurs in late writers, ἀστῆρσι(ν) is cited by Stephanus and Sophocles as found in Geminius (i / B. C.?), and Steph. quotes φράτερσιν from Hesychius. Cronert (173) quotes also ἀστέροις from a MS. of Geminius. In Luke 21:25 ἄστροις (from ἄστρον) occurs.

b. ἀήρ (ἀέρος), air, is declined like ἀστήρ. Only these two substantives of the ἀστήρ type occur in the N. T.

c. There are five substantives in the N. T. declined like σωτήρ: νιπτήρ, στατήρ, σωτήρ, φωστήρ, χαρακτήρ (only in nom. sing). There are nine like ῥήτωρ.

d. No vocatives of this type are found.

Singular

B.	χείρ (ἡ)	μάρτυς (ὁ)
Stem	χειρ–, χερ–	μαρτυρ–
	hand	witness
N.	χείρ	μάρτυς
G. Ab.	χειρός	μάρτυρος
D. L. I.	χειρί	[μάρτυρι]
A.	χεῖρα	μάρτυρα

Plural

N.	χεῖρες	μάρτυρες
G. Ab.	χειρῶν	μαρτύρων
D. L. I.	χερσί(ν)	μάρτυσι(ν)
A.	χεῖρας	μάρτυρας

a. What was the original stem of χείρ is not certain. χερ-, χερι-, and χερσ- have been proposed. Whatever the stem, it seems clear that the present (Att., κοινή) nom. was formed from the frequent oblique cases and the form χειρ- was generalized (except dat. loc. inst. plural χερσί). The Ionic has χερός, χερί, χέρα etc. Homer has χερί, and χείρεσσι χείρεσι.

b. The Att. and κοινή nom. μάρτυς (from μαρτυρς) is a new formation after the analogy of the nominatives in -s. The form μάρτυρ does not appear in N. T.

c. πῦρ (πυρ-), τό, *fire*, in sing. only, is N. πῦρ, G. Ab. πυρός, D. L. I. πυρί, A. πῦρ.

187.   Stems Ending in a Nasal (ν) (§§187–189c.).

a. In proethnic Greek there were stems in -μ; but final μ of the nom. sing. regularly became ν. Thus the few -μ- stems became -ν- stems, as χιών (from χιωμ) and ἕν, *one*, (from σεμ). Consequently -ν- stems are the only nasal stems surviving in Greek.

b. Originally stems in μον-, -μεν-, -ον-, -εν- (nom. μων, -μην, -ων, -ην), had vowel gradation in the different cases (as did the Liquids, see §184, a):

Strong	Middle	Weak
-μων	-μον	-μν
-μην	-μεν	-μν
-ων	-ον	-ν
-ην	-εν	-ν

c. In the nom. singular ω and η regularly appear. In some words the oblique cases have levelled out the ο or ε of the middle grade; and in other words the nominative was levelled out into the oblique cases; but in a few words the stem of the weak grade was levelled out in the oblique cases; as ποιμήν (ποιμεν-), ἡγεμών (ἡγεμον-); Ἕλλην (Ἑλλην-), αἰών (αἰων-); ἀρήν, (ἀρν-), κύων (κυν-).

188. Stems showing effects of vowel gradation.

Singular

	ἡγεμών (ὁ)	ποιμήν (ὁ)
Stem	ἡγεμον–	ποιμεν–
	leader	shepherd
N.	ἡγεμών	ποιμήν
G. Ab.	ἡγεμόνος	ποιμένος
D. L. I.	ἡγεμόνι	ποιμένι
A.	ἡγεμόνα	ποιμένα

Plural

N.	ἡγεμόνες	ποιμένες
G. Ab.	ἡγεμόνων	ποιμένων
D. L. I.	ἡγεμόσι(ν)	ποιμέσι(ν)
A.	ἡγεμόνας	ποιμένας

a. The dat., loc., inst. plu. ἡγεμόσι(ν), ποιμέσι(ν) are new formations with the substitution of the vowel (ο and ε) of the generalized stem for α (=vocalic ν) of the weak grade stem (–μν, see § 187), before the case-ending –σι. If the middle grade stem (–μον, –μεν) had been used, such forms as –μουσι(ν) and μεισι(ν) would have occurred. See § 173 b. N.

b. κύων (ὁ), dog, levelled out its weak grade stem: κύων, [κυνός], [κυνί], [κύνα], plu. κύνες, [κυνῶν], κυσί(ν), κύνας.

c. In the acc. plu., ἄρνας (Luke 10:3), is the only occurrence in N. T. of a form of the old nom. ἀρήν which had levelled out the weak grade in the oblique cases; ἀμνός or ἀρνίον is used in the N. T. In the N. T. only these two words (b. and c.) survive of the few which had levelled out the weak grade. The D. L. I. plu. κυσί(ν) is formed after the analogy of κυνός.

189. Stems showing no effects of vowel gradation.

Singular

	αἰών (ὁ)	Ἕλλην (ὁ)
Stem	αἰων–	Ἑλλην–
	age	Greek
N.	αἰών	Ἕλλην
G. Ab.	αἰῶνος	Ἕλληνος
D. L. I.	αἰῶνι	Ἕλληνι
A.	αἰῶνα	[Ἕλληνα]

Plural

N.	αἰῶνες	Ἕλληνες
G. Ab.	αἰώνων	Ἑλλήνων
D. L. I.	αἰῶσι(ν)	Ἕλλησι(ν)
A.	αἰῶνας	Ἕλληνας

a. The acc. singular Ἕλληνα does not occur in the N. T., but μῆνα (acc. sing. of μήν) occurs. The papyri frequently show these accusatives.

b. μήν [gen. μηνός], ὁ, *month*, was originally an –s stem. The Ion. has μείς and the Dor. μής, from μενς for μηνς (§61, e). The Aeolic gen. μῆνος and the Att. Ion. Dor. gen. μηνός are from μηνσος, from which was formed a new (Attic) nom. μήν after analogy of stems in –ν. Then it was declined regularly like Ἕλλην, the forms in the N. T. being sing. nom. μήν, dat. loc. ins. μηνί, acc. μῆνα, plural acc. μῆνας.

c. In ὠδίν, stem ὠδιν–, ἡ, *pang*, appears the formation of the nom. after the analogy of –ν– stems in –μον, –μεν. The old nom. ὠδίς is not found in the N. T. In ὠδίν is a survival of stems which had the vowel gradation –ιων, –ιην, –ιον, –ιεν, –ιν, –ιν. In some stems the weak grade –ιν became generalized. From the generalized stem in –ιν a new nominative in primitive Greek was formed after the analogy of nominatives in –s; thus ὠδίς; the ν of the stem disappeared before s. Then much later a new nominative in –ν, as ὠδίν, was formed. The cases of ὠδίν are: Sing. N. ὠδίν, G. Ab. [ὠδῖνος], D. L. I. ὠδῖνι, A. [ὠδῖνα], plu. N. [ὠδῖνες], G. Ab. ὠδίνων, D. L. I. [ὠδῖσι(ν)], A. ὠδῖνας. Nom. forms like ὀξύρριν, *with a sharp nose*, occur frequently in the papyri.

d. Two nouns ending in –αν with stems in ν are declined on the analogy of Ἕλλην: μεγιστάν, (ὁ), *grandee*, occurring only in the plural forms, nom. μεγιστᾶνες and dat. μεγιστᾶσι(ν); μέλαν, (τὸ), *ink*, occurring only in the singular forms, gen. μέλανος and dat. loc. inst. μέλανι.

190. Stems Ending in –σ– (§§190–196).

Words with stems in –σ– in the parent language were neuter

substantives, to which are related adjectives in $-\epsilon\sigma$ (§212A), and
masculine or feminine substantives in $-o\sigma-$.

191 Neuter Substantives with stems in $-a\sigma-$.

Substantives of this stem were never numerous. The two
substantives (γῆρας, τό, *old age*, and κρέας, τό, *flesh*) which show
traces of this inflection were discussed in §179, a, b under $-\tau$
stems. In the κοινή period other substantives (with nom. in
$-as$) of this type had passed into the class of neuter stems in $-\tau$

192. Neuter Substantives with stems in $(-o\sigma)$, $-\epsilon\sigma$.

These substantives had vowel gradation throughout the
inflection, but from the proethnic period the grade $-\epsilon\sigma$ was
levelled out into all the cases except the nominative and accusative singular which have $-os$. Neut. substantives with nom.
in $-os$ and stem in $-\epsilon s$ all conform to one type.

Singular

	ἔθνος (τό)	ἔλεος (τό)
Stem	ἐθνεσ–	ἐλεεσ–
	nation	*pity*
N.	ἔθνος	ἔλεος
G. Ab.	ἔθνους (fr. ἔθνεσος)	ἐλέους (fr. ἐλέεσος)
D. L. I.	ἔθνει (fr. ἔθνεσι)	ἐλέει (fr. ἐλέεσι)
A.	ἔθνος	ἔλεος

Plural

N.	ἔθνη (fr. ἔθνεσα)
G. Ab.	ἐθνῶν (fr. ἐθνέσων)
D. L. I.	ἔθνεσι(ν) (fr. ἔθνεσσι)
A.	ἔθνη (fr. ἔθνεσα)

a. Intervocalic σ dropped out in proethnic Greek, and there
occurred the contraction of the concurrent vowels in all cases
except nom. and acc. singular. The parentheses show what
would be the original uncontracted form.

b. The uncontracted gen. plural appears in ὀρέων (Rev. 6:15)
and χειλέων (Heb. 13:15). The gen. plural of these two words
is always uncontracted in the LXX.

c. In the dat. loc. inst. plural σσ, resulting from the union
of the stem-ending $-\sigma$ with the case-ending $-\sigma\iota$ is simplied to σ.

193. In ἔλεος is exhibited the normal inflection when the stem -εσ- is preceded by ε.

194. Masculine proper names with nom. in -ης (stem -ες) were in Attic declined like the masculine of adjectives with stems in -ες. But in iii / B. C. the process of assimilation to the forms of the first declension began; and by the end of i/A. D. the process was practically complete.

195. Other nouns with stems in -ες are adjectives. See §212A.

196. Substantives with stems in -οσ.

One substantive of this type with nom. in -ως, viz. αἰδώς, *modesty*, is found in the N. T. It is in W H used once (I Tim. 2:9) and in the gen., αἰδοῦς (fr. αἰδόσος); in Heb. 12: 28 the MSS. Aleph^c D ^{b. c.} K L al. have it as a var. lect. Thus far it is not found in the papyri.

197. Stems in the Semi-vowels ι and υ (§§197-201D).

The obvious irregularities in the inflection of these stems are due to the fact that originally the stem-forms contained various vowel gradations (grades of ablaut). Just what their order and connection is not certain. New formations in the cases from various causes supplanted the old grades.

198. Stems in $\begin{cases} ει \\ ι \end{cases}$

Before vowels of the case-endings ει appears, and before consonants ι. In the dat. loc. inst. plural ε comes from the nominative plural. The strong ending ει lost the consonant ι before vowels, as in dat. loc. inst. sing. πολε(ι)ι contracted to πόλει; nom. plu. πολε(ι)ες contracted to πόλεις. See §31a.

Singular

Stem	πόλις (ἡ)	σίναπι (τό)
	$\begin{cases} πολει- \\ πολι- \end{cases}$	$\begin{cases} σιναπει- \\ σιναπι- \end{cases}$
	city	*mustard*
N.	πόλις	[σίναπι]
G. Ab.	πόλεως	σινάπεως
D. L. I.	πόλει	[σινάπει]
A.	πόλιν	[σίναπι]

Plural

N.	πόλεις	
G. Ab.	πόλεων	No plural
D. L. I.	πόλεσι(ν)	
A.	πόλεις	

a. The gen. abl. sing. πόλεως is from an older πόληος (cf. πόληος Hom.) by transference of quantity (quantitative metathesis) and retains the accent of the older form. The accent of the gen. abl. plural follows that of the gen. abl. sing.

b. The acc. plural is borrowed from the nominative. Attic inscriptions since 307 B. C. show the acc. plu. ending in —εις. The original ending is seen in the Cret. πόλινς.

c. Substantives in —σις (Ind.=G. tej), with πίστις and ὄψις, form the bulk of words in this class.

d. One neuter, σίναπι, occurs. The papyri show neuters frequently, as ἄμι, στίμι, πέπερι, etc.—all foreign words as σίναπι itself.

199. Stems in $\begin{cases} ευ \\ υ \end{cases}$

A. As ι of ει in the $\left. \begin{matrix} ει \\ ι \end{matrix} \right\}$ stems represents the consonant value of ι(= y) so also the υ of ευ represents the consonant value of υ (ϝ =w). Before vowels of the case-endings ευ was used, and before consonants υ. In the dat. loc. inst. plural ε comes from the nom. plural. The strong ending ευ lost the consonant υ before vowels, as in dat. loc. inst. sing. πηχε(υ)ι contracted to πήχει, nom. plu. πηχε(υ)ες contracted to πήχεις. See §31, b for disappearance of υ(ϝ) between vowels.

B.

	Stem	πῆχυς (ὁ) $\begin{cases} πηχευ- \\ πηχυ- \end{cases}$ cubit	
		Singular	Plural
N.		[πῆχυς]	[πήχεις]
G. Ab.		[πήχεως, πήχεος]	πήχεων, πηχῶν
D. L. I.		[πήχει]	[πήχεσι(ν)]
A.		πῆχυν	[πήχεις]

a. Of $\left.\begin{array}{c} \epsilon v \\ v \end{array}\right\}$ stems πῆχυς is the only substantive found in the N. T.

b. The gen. abl. sing. πήχεως was formed after the analogy πόλεως of the $\left.\begin{array}{c} \epsilon\iota \\ \iota \end{array}\right\}$ stems. The form πήχεος is from the older πηχεϝος. The gen. abl. sing. in the LXX is generally πήχεος. The gen. abl. plural πήχεων came from πηχεϝων (a new formation with εϝ from the nominative). The contracted form πηχῶν comes from assimilation to gen. plu. of neuters in –εσ– (nom. –ος). The form πηχῶν is general in the papyri, and occurs in LXX along with πήχεων.

c. The dat. loc. inst. plu. πήχεσι(ν) has ε from the nominative plural with the consonant case-ending –σι.

d. The acc. plural πήχεις is borrowed from the nominative.

200. Stems in –υ.

In this stem υϝ alternated with ῡ in primitive Greek; before vowels υϝ was used, and υ before consonants. The combination υϝ regularly became υ.

Singular

Stem	στάχυς (ὁ)	ἰχθύς (ὁ)	ὀσφύς (ἡ)
	σταχυ–	ἰχθυ–	ὀσφυ–
	ear of corn	fish	loins
N.	στάχυς	ἰχθύς	ὀσφύς
G. Ab.	στάχυος	ἰχθύος	ὀσφύος
D. L. I.	στάχυϊ	ἰχθύϊ	ὀσφύϊ
A.	στάχυν	ἰχθύν	ὀσφύν

Plural

N.	στάχυες	ἰχθύες	ὀσφύες
G. Ab.	σταχύων	ἰχθύων	ὀσφύων
D. L. I.	στάχυσι(ν)	ἰχθύσι(ν)	ὀσφύσι(ν)
A.	στάχυας	ἰχθύας	ὀσφύας

a. An old Ionic and Attic acc. plural form ἰχθῦς (from ἰχθυνς) does not appear in the New Testament.

b. A few grammarians write the circumflex accent in the

nom. and acc. sing. of oxytone words of this class: as ἰχθῦς, ἰχθῦν; ὀσφῦς, ὀσφῦν.

c. An old neuter, δάκρυ *tear*, of this class is found only in the dat. loc. inst. plu., δάκρυσι(ν). The gen. abl. plural form δακρύων may be from δάκρυον (τό).

d. There are nine substantives (including δάκρυ) of this class found in the New Testament.

201. Stems in –ᾱυ, –ευ, –ου, –οι.

Originally vowel gradation was present in the inflection of each of these stems. But in each stem one or other of the grades was generally levelled out into all the cases.

A. Stems in –ᾱυ–.

In this stem –ᾱϝ alternated with ᾱυ; ᾱϝ before vowels of the case-endings, ᾱυ before consonants. ϝ between vowels regularly disappeared.

a. A single substantive of this class appears once in the N. T., ναῦς (ἡ), *ship*, and in the acc. ναῦν (Acts 27:41). This acc. form (Attic also) is a new formation from the nominative.

b. The word occurs infrequently in the non-literary papyri. In the vernacular πλοῖον gradually supplanted ναῦς.

B. Stems in –ευ– (older –ηυ–).

In stem gradation ηυ originally belonged to the nom. sing. The –ηυ–(–ηϝ before vowels) was levelled out into all the cases except the voc. sing. which retained the old grade –ευ.

Singular

βασιλεύς (ὁ)

Stem   βασιλευ–

king

Endings in prim. Greek

N.	βασιλεύς	–ηυς
G. Ab.	βασιλέως	–ηϝος
D. L. I.	βασιλεῖ.	–ηϝι
A.	βασιλέα	–ηϝα
V.	βασιλεῦ	–ευ

Plural

N. V.	βασιλεῖς	–ηϝες
G. Ab.	βασιλέων	–ηϝων
D. L. I.	βασιλεῦσι(ν)	–ηνσι
A.	βασιλεῖς	–ηϝας

a. The nom. sing. –ηυς was shortened to –ευς in primitive Greek; also in the dat. loc. inst. plural –ηυσι to –ευσι. The endings –ηϝος, –ηϝι, –ηϝα, acc. plu. –ηϝας regularly became –εως, –ει, εᾱ, εᾱς in Attic by the disappearance of ϝ and exchange of quantity of vowels (See § 45). In gen. abl. plu. βασιλέων came from βασιλήων by the shortening of a long vowel before a long vowel. The old nom. plu. βασιλῆες (βασιλῆς) was supplanted after the middle of iv / B. C. by the new formation βασιλεῖς formed after the analogy of words like πήχεις, ἡδεῖς.

b. The acc. plural βασιλεῖς (borrowed from nominative) came into use about the end of the iv / B. C. The older nom. βασιλῆς was used as accusative at an earlier period.

c. The Attic of the middle period had the acc. βασιλέᾱς.

d. Of the old noun Ζεύς (from Ζηυς from Διηυς) the gen. abl. Διός (Acts 14:13) and the acc. Δία (Acts 14:12) are found each in the N. T. Διός came regularly from Διϝος; Δία from Διϝα was new formation with Διϝ from the genitive. In its full inflection Ζεύς shows clearly some of the original vowel gradations.

C. Stems in –ου (older –ωυ?).

In the inflection of βοῦς there were originally three grades of vowel gradation; traces of these are apparent in the present declension. Before consonants –ου appears and before vowels οϝ (ϝ disappears between vowels).

βοῦς (ὁ)

Stem   βου–

ox

	Singular	Plural
N.	βοῦς	[βόες]
G. Ab.	βοός	βοῶν
D. L. I.	βοΐ	[βουσι(ν)]
A.	βοῦν	βόας

a. The nom. sing. βοῦς comes from the shortening of βωυς. The acc. sing. is formed after the analogy of the nominative. From the stem βοϝ come the gen., abl., dat., loc., inst., sing. and the nom., gen., abl., and acc. plural. βοῦς, an acc. plu. in Attic, is formed after the analogy of the acc. singular.

b. The three substantives νοῦς (ὁ), *mind*, πλοῦς (ὁ), *voyage*, and χοῦς(ὁ), *dust*, which were originally (also Attic) inflected in the Second Declension are declined in the κοινή and N. T. like βοῦς.

D. Stems in –οι (older –ωι?).

In the inflection of words of this stem there were originally three grades of vowel gradation. The grade –οι became generalized in the oblique cases. Before vowels of the case-endings ι was regularly changed to y (the consonant value of ι) which disappeared, then contraction of the concurrent vowels took place. The nom. may have ended in –ωι beside –ω in the proethnic period. The declension of these stems concerns the N. T. student if the form ἠχους (Luke 21:25) be taken from ἠχώ, *sound*, and accented ἠχοῦς, and if the MSS. F G be followed in writing πειθοῖ instead of πειθοῖς in I Cor. 2:4. The dat. loc. inst. form πειθοῖ (nom. πειθώ) is found in a papyrus of 184 A. D., P. Oxy. III. 487, 37.

Stem ἠχώ (ἡ)
ἠχοι–
sound

N. [ἠχώ or –ῷ]
G. Ab. ἠχοῦς (ἠχογος)
D. L. I. ἠχοῖ (ἠχογι)
A. [ἠχώ (ἠχογα)]

N. The plural forms of this declension are wanting. When the plurals of words of this declension occur they are in the second declension.

202. There is a large number of proper names of mixed declension. The most familiar is:

N. Ἰησοῦς, G.-Ab. Ἰησοῦ, D. L. I. Ἰησοῦ, Acc. Ἰησοῦ, V. Ἰησοῦ.

203. There are many indeclinable foreign (to Greek) proper

names and other words: Μαριάμ, Συμεών, etc., and κορβᾶν, μάννα, πάσχα, ῥακά etc.

Declension of Adjectives

204. The explanations of case-forms have been given in connection with the substantive. The origin of the adjective is given in the Syntax. All that is necessary to give under the declension is the forms that occur in the N. T.

205. Adjectives of the First and Second Declensions. Most adjectives of the vowel (first and second) declension have three endings (–ος, –η or –ᾱ, –ον). The feminine is declined according to the first declension, and the masculine and neuter according to the second declension.

N. When –ος is preceded by ε, ι or ρ, the feminine has –α, otherwise –η.

206. Adjectives of Three Endings (First and Second Declensions):

A.

Singular

	Masc.	Fem.	Neut.
N.	καλός	καλή	καλόν
G. Ab.	καλοῦ	καλῆς	καλοῦ
D. L. I.	καλῷ	καλῇ	καλῷ
A.	καλόν	καλήν	καλόν
V.	καλέ		

Plural

	Masc.	Fem.	Neut.
N. V.	καλοί	καλαί	καλά
G. Ab.	καλῶν	καλῶν	καλῶν
D. L. I.	καλοῖς	καλαῖς	καλοῖς
A.	καλούς	καλάς	καλά

B.

Singular

	Masc.	Fem.	Neut.
N.	ἅγιος	ἁγία	ἅγιον
G. Ab.	ἁγίου	ἁγίας	ἁγίου
D. L. I.	ἁγίῳ	ἁγίᾳ	ἁγίῳ
A.	ἅγιον	ἁγίαν	ἅγιον
V.	ἅγιε		

Plural

N. V.	ἅγιοι	ἅγιαι	ἅγια
G. Ab.	ἁγίων	ἁγίων	ἁγίων
D. L. I.	ἁγίοις	ἁγίαις	ἁγίοις
A.	ἁγίους	ἁγίας	ἅγια

N. The accent of nom. and gen. plu. of the fem. follows that of the masculine.

C. Participles.

All middle and passive participles (except the first and second aorist passive participles) are declined (except for accent) like καλός. The accent follows the general principles of accentuation. The accent of the fem. nom. and gen.-abl. plural follows the masculine. In the perf. middle and passive participle the accent is on the penult.

a. Present Participle (middle and passive).

Singular

	Masc.	Fem.	Neut.
N.	λυόμενος	λυομένη	λυόμενον
G. Ab.	λυομένου	λυομένης	λυομένου
	etc.	etc.	etc.

Plural

N.	λυόμενοι	λυόμεναι	λυόμενα
G. Ab.	λυομένων	λυομένων	λυομένων
	etc.	etc.	etc.

b. Perfect Participle (middle and passive).

Singular

	Masc.	Fem.	Neut.
N.	λελυμένος	λελυμένη	λελυμένον
	etc.	etc.	etc.

Plural

N.	λελυμένοι	λελυμέναι	λελυμένα
G. Ab.	λελυμένων	λελυμένων	λελυμένων

207. Adjectives of Two Endings (Second Declension).

Adjectives of the second declension having the same form for the masculine and feminine are called adjectives of two endings. Most such adjectives are compounds; but there are exceptions when the feminine would be −α (and not −η).

Singular

	Masc. and Fem.	Neut.
N.	ἄπιστος	ἄπιστον
G. Ab.	ἀπίστου	ἀπίστου
D. L. I.	ἀπίστῳ	ἀπίστῳ
A.	ἄπιστον	ἄπιστον

Plural

N. V.	ἄπιστοι	ἄπιστα
G. Ab.	ἀπίστων	ἀπίστων
D. L. I.	ἀπίστοις	ἀπίστοις
A.	ἀπίστους	ἄπιστα

208. Some simple adjectives have two endings, and some compound adjectives have three endings.

a. Adjectives in –ιος, both simple and compound, may have two or three endings.

b. Some simple adjectives showing variation:

αἰώνιος usually has two endings, –ος, –ον; but the feminine form αἰωνίαν occurs twice (Heb. 9:12; 2 Thes. 2:16).

ἔρημος is of two endings; in Attic three.

κόσμιος has two endings; in Attic three.

ὅσιος is probably of two endings.

οὐράνιος is probably of two endings; but some MSS. have a fem. ending in Lk. 2:13.

στεῖρος is usually of two endings. But a fem. form στεῖρα occurs in the N. T., or it seems best so to consider the forms in the N. T. rather than as a fem. substantive στεῖρα, because the dat. is written στείρᾳ in Lk. 1:36.

c. Some compound adjectives showing variation:

ἀργός has three endings; fem. form in 1 Tim. 5:13; Tit. 1:12.

αὐτόματος has three endings (also in classical writers); fem-form in Mk. 4:28.

ἐκλεκτός has a fem. form in 2 Jno. 13.

παραθαλάσσιος has a fem. form in Matt. 4:13.

209.   Contracted Adjectives.

Adjectives in –εος and –οος are generally contracted.

Declension of χρυσοῦς (χρύσεος).

Singular

	Masc.	Fem.	Neut.
N.	χρυσοῦς	χρυσῆ	[χρυσοῦν]
G. Ab.	[χρυσοῦ]	χρυσῆς	χρυσοῦ
D. L. I.	[χρυσῷ]	[χρυσῇ]	[χρυσῷ]
A.	χρυσοῦν	χρυσῆν	χρυσοῦν

Plural

N.	[χρυσοῖ]	[χρυσαῖ]	χρυσᾶ
G. Ab.	[χρυσῶν]	χρυσῶν	[χρυσῶν]
D. L. I.	[χρυσοῖς]	[χρυσαῖς]	[χρυσοῖς]
A.	χρυσοῦς	χρισᾶς	χρυσᾶ

a.   διπλοῦς is declined like χρυσοῦς. The only difference in the resultant forms of contracted adjectives in –εος and –οος is found in the feminine singular of endings in –ρεος: Thus N. [ἀργυρᾶ], G. Ab. [ἀργυρᾶς], D. L. I. ἀργυρᾷ, A. ἀργυρᾶν.

b.   The following words appear in the N. T.:

ἁπλοῦς(–ῆ, –οῦν), *single*; διπλοῦς (–ῆ, –οῦν), *double*; τετραπλοῦς (–ῆ, –οῦν), *four fold*; ἀργυροῦς (–ᾶ, –οῦν), *silvern*; σιδηροῦς (–ᾶ, –οῦν), *iron*; πορφυροῦς, (–ᾶ, –οῦν) *purple*; χαλκοῦς (–ῆ, –οῦν) *brazen*; χρυσοῦς (ῆ, –οῦν) *golden*.

c.   νέος, ὄγδοος, στερεός, and ὑπήκοος do not contract; but ὄγδοος is found in a contracted form in the papyri.

d.   In some MSS. uncontracted forms of χρυσοῦς and χαλκοῦς appear in Rev.

e.   In Rev. 1:13 Westcott and Hort have χρυσᾶν (fem. acc. sing.). In the papyri are found χρυσᾶν ἢ ἀργυρᾶν and χρυσῆν ἢ ἀργυρῆν.

f.   ἁπλῆ, διπλῆ etc. are from ἁπλεα, διπλεα, not ἁπλοα and διπλοα.

210. Adjectives of the Third Declension. When adjectives of the consonant (third) declension have a separate form for the feminine, the feminine is declined like substantives of the first declension in –α.

Participles are treated together, § 214.

211. Adjectives of Three Endings (the Third and First Declensions). The feminine is formed by adding ια (ya) to the stem).

A. Stems in $\begin{cases} ευ \ (ε_F). \\ υ \end{cases}$

The feminine was formed by adding ya to the stem –ε_F, as ὀξε_Fya = ὀξεῖα.

a. Declension of ὀξύς, ὀξεῖα, ὀξύ.

Singular

	Masc.	Fem.	Neut.
N.	ὀξύς	ὀξεῖα	ὀξύ
G. Ab.	ὀξέως	ὀξείας	ὀξέως
D. L. I.	ὀξεῖ	[ὀξείᾳ]	ὀξεῖ
A.	[ὀξύν]	ὀξεῖαν	ὀξύ

Plural

	Masc.	Fem.	Neut.
N.	ὀξεῖς	[ὀξεῖαι]	ὀξέα
G. Ab.	ὀξέων	ὀξειῶν	ὀξέων
D. L. I.	[ὀξέσι(ν)]	ὀξείαις	[ὀξέσι(ν)]
A.	ὀξεῖς	ὀξείας	ὀξέα

So are declined βαθύς, βαρύς, γλυκύς, ταχύς, etc.

(a) The gen. sing. in –εος (Attic) is found in some MSS. The ending, –εως is due to the analogy of the declension of such nouns as πόλις, G. Ab. πόλεως.

(b) The masc. nom. plu. ὀξεῖς is used for the accusative.

b. Declension of πολύς.

The declension of πολύς is made up of the blending of two different stems. The masculine nom. and acc. sing. πολύς, πολύν, and the neuter nom. and acc. sing., πολύ are formed from the stem πολυ. The feminine πολλή is from πολ(F)ya from

which was formed a masculine and neuter stem πολ(ϝ)yo–
=πολλο–, used in all the other forms of the masc. and neut.

Singular

	Masc.	Fem.	Neut.
N.	πολύs	πολλή	πολύ
G. Ab.	πολλοῦ	πολλῆs	πολλοῦ
D. L. I.	πολλῷ	πολλῇ	πολλῷ
A.	πολύν	πολλήν	πολύ

Plural

	Masc.	Fem.	Neut.
N.	πολλοί	πολλαί	πολλά
G. Ab.	πολλῶν	πολλῶν	πολλῶν
D. L. I.	πολλοῖς	πολλαῖς	πολλοῖς
A.	πολλούς	πολλάς	πολλά

B. Stems in –ν.

a. Declension of μέλας, μέλαινα, μέλαν; stem μελαν–. The masc. nom. sing. μέλας was formed from the generalized stem μελαν– by adding s after the analogy of the nominatives in –s. The feminine μέλαινα came from μελανya = μέλαινα.

Singular

	Masc.	Fem.	Neut.
N.	μέλας	[μέλαινα]	[μέλαν]
G. Ab.	[μέλανος]	[μελαίνης]	μέλανος
D. L. I.	[μέλανι]	[μελαίνῃ]	μέλανι
A.	[μέλανα]	μέλαιναν	[μέλαν]

Plural

	Masc.	Fem.	Neut.
N.	[μέλανες]	[μέλαιναι]	[μέλανα]
G. Ab.	[μελάνων]	[μελαινῶν]	[μελάνων]
D. L. I.	[μέλασι(ν)]	[μελαίναις]	[μέλασι(ν)]
A.	[μέλανας]	[μελαίνας]	[μέλανα]

b. Declension of μέγας, μεγάλα, μέγα. It seems that the masc. nom. and acc. sing. μέγας, μέγαν and the neut. nom. and acc. sing. μέγα came from a –ν– stem, μεγν (or μεγντ), the ν becom-

ing sonant ν; then was formed a feminine μεγάλη from which
the stem μεγαλο– was formed for all the other cases of the masc.
and neut.

Singular

	Masc.	Fem.	Neut.
N.	μέγας	μεγάλη	μέγα
G. Ab.	μεγάλου	μεγάλης	μεγάλου
D. L. I.	μεγάλῳ	μεγάλῃ	μεγάλῳ
A.	μέγαν	μεγάλην	μέγα

Plural

	Masc.	Fem.	Neut.
N.	μεγάλοι	μεγάλαι	μεγάλα
G. Ab.	μεγάλων	μεγάλων	μεγάλων
D. L. I.	μεγάλοις	μεγάλαις	μεγάλοις
A.	μεγάλους	μεγάλας	μεγάλα

C. Stems in –ντ–.

The participles are treated separately for convenience.

Adjective stems in –ϝεντ (nom. –εις, –εσσα, –εν) are not found
in the N. T.

a. Stems in –αντ–.

Declension of πᾶς, πᾶσα, πᾶν; stem παντ–.

Singular

	Masc.	Fem.	Neut.
N.	πᾶς	πᾶσα	πᾶν
G. Ab.	παντός	πάσης	παντός
D. L. I.	παντί	πάσῃ	παντί
A.	πάντα	πᾶσαν	πᾶν

Plural

	Masc.	Fem.	Neut.
N.	πάντες	πᾶσαι	πάντα
G. Ab.	πάντων	πασῶν	πάντων
D. L. I.	πᾶσι(ν)	πάσαις	πᾶσι(ν)
A.	πάντας	πάσας	πάντα

N. So are declined (except for accent) ἅπας and all participles whose masc. nom. sing. end in –ας.

(a) The fem. πᾶσα is from παντya = πανσα = πᾶσα.

(b) The neut. πᾶν takes ᾶ from πᾶς.

b. Stems in –οντ–.

The two adjectives ἑκών (stem ἑκοντ–) and ἄκων (stem ἀκοντ–) with stem –οντ– were originally participles. The forms appearing in the N. T. are masc. nom. sing. ἑκών, fem. nom. sing. ἑκοῦσα; and masc. nom. sing. ἄκων.

212. Adjectives of Two Endings. Adjectives wholly in the third (consonant) declension have only two endings.

A. Stems in –εσ.

Adjectives with masc. nom. sing. in –ης are closely related to neuter substantives with stem in –εσ.

Declension of ἀληθής, –ές.

	Singular		Plural	
	M. and F.	N.	M. and F.	N.
N.	ἀληθής	ἀληθές	ἀληθεῖς	ἀληθῆ
			(fr. –εσες)	(fr. –εσα)
G. Ab.		ἀληθοῦς (fr. –εσος)	ἀληθῶν	
D. L. I.		ἀληθεῖ (fr. –εσι)	ἀληθέσι(ν)	
A.	ἀληθῆ,	ἀληθές	ἀληθεῖς	ἀληθῆ
	(fr. –εσα)			

a. The masc. and fem. acc. plu. –εις is from the nominative.

b. A few times in some MSS. ν is found added to the masc. (fem.) acc. sing., as in ἀσεβῆν (Rom. 4:5). This is probably due to the strong influence of the first declension and to the tendency to add an irrational final ν after long vowels.

c. πλήρης in many instances seems to be indeclinable: see John 1:14.

B. Stems in $-\epsilon\nu$ and $-o\nu$.   See declension of substantives with stems in $-\epsilon\nu$, $-o\nu$, or $-\mu\epsilon\nu$, $-\mu o\nu$.

a. The few forms from stems in $-\epsilon\nu$, masc. in $-\eta\nu$ and neut. in $-\epsilon\nu$ are declined like subst. in $-\epsilon\nu$, as ἄρσην (ἄρρην), *male.* See §§187, 188.

b. Declension of ἄφρων, ἄφρον.

	Singular		Plural	
	M. and F.	N.	M. and F.	N.
N.	ἄφρων	[ἄφρον]	ἄφρονες	ἄφρονα
G. Ab.	[ἄφρονος]		ἀφρόνων	
D. L. I.	[ἄφρονι]		[ἄφροσι(ν)]	
A.	ἄφρονα	ἄφρον	ἄφρονας	[ἄφρονα]
V.	ἄφρων			

C. Comparatives with nom. in $-\omega\nu$, $-o\nu$ are made up of two different stems, $-\iota yo\sigma$ and $-\iota\sigma o\nu = -\iota(y)o\sigma$, $-\iota(\sigma)o\nu$.

Declension of μείζων, μεῖζον.

	Singular	
	Masc. and Fem.	Neut.
N.	μείζων	μεῖζον
G. Ab.	μείζονος	
D. L. I.	μείζονι	
A.	⎰μείζονα ⎱μείζω (fr. $-o\sigma a$)	μεῖζον

	Plural	
N.	⎰μείζονες ⎱μείζους (fr. $-o\sigma\epsilon\sigma$)	⎰μείζονα ⎱μείζω (fr. $-o\sigma a$)
G. Ab.	μειζόνων	
D. L. I.	μείζοσι(ν)	
A.	⎰μείζονας ⎱μείζους (from nom.)	⎰μείζονα ⎱μείζω

213. Adjectives of One Ending.

A few adjectives have one ending with the masc. and fem. alike; as ἀμήτωρ and ἀπάτωρ, which are used only in the masc. nom. in the N. T.; ἅρπαξ, [gen. ἅρπαγος], has nom. plu. ἅρπαγες and dat., loc., inst. plu. ἅρπαξιν; νῆστις has nom. plu. νήστεις.

214. Declension of Participles.

Participles of the active voice and the aorist passive participle have stems in –ντ (except the perfect active participle). The masculine and neuter are of the third declension, the feminine is of the first declension.

Most stems in –οντ do not add anything to form the nom. masc. sing. Stems in –αντ, –εντ, –υντ and –οντ of μι– verbs add s to form the nom. masc. singular. The neut. nom. sing. is the stem, τ drops off.

The feminine is formed from the stem by adding –ya, as λυοντya = λύουσα; τιθεντya = τιθεῖσα; λυσαντya =λύσασα.

A. Stems in –αντ. Except for accent they are declined like πᾶς, πᾶσα, πᾶν; as λύσας, λύσασα, λῦσαν.

B. Stems in –εντ.
Declension of τιθείς, –εῖσα, –έν.

<table>
<tr><td></td><td colspan="3" align="center">Singular</td></tr>
<tr><td></td><td>Masc.</td><td>Fem.</td><td>Neut.</td></tr>
<tr><td>N.</td><td>τιθείς</td><td>τιθεῖσα</td><td>τιθέν</td></tr>
<tr><td>G. Ab.</td><td>τιθέντος</td><td>τιθείσης</td><td>τιθέντος</td></tr>
<tr><td>D. L. I.</td><td>τιθέντι</td><td>τιθείσῃ</td><td>τιθέντι</td></tr>
<tr><td>A.</td><td>τιθέντα</td><td>τιθεῖσαν</td><td>τιθέν</td></tr>
<tr><td></td><td colspan="3" align="center">Plural</td></tr>
<tr><td>N.</td><td>τιθέντες</td><td>τιθεῖσαι</td><td>τιθέντα</td></tr>
<tr><td>G. Ab.</td><td>τιθέντων</td><td>τιθεισῶν</td><td>τιθέντων</td></tr>
<tr><td>D. L. I.</td><td>τιθεῖσι(ν)</td><td>τιθείσαις</td><td>τιθεῖσι(ν)</td></tr>
<tr><td>A.</td><td>τιθέντας</td><td>τιθείσας</td><td>τιθέντα</td></tr>
</table>

So are declined all aorist passive partciples in –εντ (nom. masc. –εις).

C.   Stems in –οντ, with masc. nom. sing. in ων.

a.   Declension of λύων, –ουσα, –ον.

Singular

	Masc.	Fem.	Neut.
N.	λύων	λύουσα	λῦον
G. Ab.	λύοντος	λυούσης	λύοντος
D. L. I.	λύοντι	λυούσῃ	λύοντι
A.	λύοντα	λύουσαν	λῦον

Plural

N.	λύοντες	λύουσαι	λύοντα
G. Ab.	λυόντων	λυουσῶν	λυόντων
D. L. I.	λύουσι(ν)	λυούσαις	λύουσι(ν)
A.	λύοντας	λυούσας	λύοντα

N.   Accent of neut. participle with more than two syllables is like βασιλεῦον, or ἀπαγγέλλον.

b.   Declension of ὤν, ὄντος, ὄν.

Singular

	Masc.	Fem.	Neut.
N.	ὤν	οὖσα	ὄν
G. Ab.	ὄντος	οὔσης	ὄντος
D. L. I.	ὄντι	οὔσῃ	ὄντι
A.	ὄντα	οὖσαν	ὄν

Plural

N.	ὄντες	οὖσαι	ὄντα
G. Ab.	ὄντων	οὐσῶν	ὄντων
D. L. I.	οὖσι(ν)	οὔσαις	οὖσι(ν)
A.	ὄντας	οὔσας	ὄντα

N.   Second aorist participles with nom. masc. in –ών are accented like ὤν, etc.

D.   Contract Participles with ending –ουντ (= –εοντ or –οοντ), from contract verbs in –έω and –όω.

Declension of φιλῶν (φιλέων), φιλοῦσα (φιλέουσα), φιλοῦν (φιλέον).

Singular

	Masc.	Fem.	Neut.
N.	φιλῶν	φιλοῦσα	φιλοῦν
G. Ab.	φιλοῦντος	φιλούσης	φιλοῦντος
D. L. I.	φιλοῦντι	φιλούσῃ	φιλοῦντι
A.	φιλοῦντα	φιλοῦσαν	φιλοῦν

Plural

N.	φιλοῦντες	φιλοῦσαι	φιλοῦντα
G. Ab.	φιλούντων	φιλουσῶν	φιλούντων
D. L. I.	φιλοῦσι(ν)	φιλούσαις	φιλοῦσι(ν)
A.	φιλοῦντας	φιλούσας	φιλοῦντα

N. The present participles of the –όω verbs are declined like φιλῶν; as δηλῶν, δηλοῦσα, δηλοῦν, G. Ab. δηλοῦντος, δηλούσης, δηλοῦντος, etc.

E. Contract Participles with ending –ωντ (= –αοντ or –ηοντ), from contract verbs in –άω and –ήω.

Declension of τιμῶν (τιμάων), τιμῶσα (τιμάουσα), τιμῶν (τιμάον).

Singular

	Masc.	Fem.	Neut.
N.	τιμῶν	τιμῶσα	τιμῶν
G. Ab.	τιμῶντος	τιμώσης	τιμῶντος
D. L. I.	τιμῶντι	τιμώσῃ	τιμῶντι
A.	τιμῶντα	τιμῶσαν	τιμῶν

Plural

N.	τιμῶντες	τιμῶσαι	τιμῶντα
G. Ab.	τιμώντων	τιμωσῶν	τιμώντων
D. L. I.	τιμῶσι(ν)	τιμώσαις	τιμῶσι(ν)
A.	τιμῶντας	τιμώσας	τιμῶντα

F. Stems in –οντ, with masc. nom. sing. in –ους (μι– verbs).
Declension of διδούς, διδοῦσα, διδόν.

Singular

	Masc.	Fem.	Neut.
N.	διδούς	διδοῦσα	διδόν
G. Ab.	διδόντος	διδούσης	διδόντος
D. L. I.	διδόντι	διδούσῃ	διδόντι
A.	διδόντα	διδοῦσαν	διδόν

Plural

N.	διδόντες	διδοῦσαι	διδόντα
G. Ab.	διδόντων	διδουσῶν	διδόντων
D. L. I.	διδοῦσι(ν)	διδούσαις	διδοῦσι(ν)
A.	διδόντας	διδούσας	διδόντα

N. So is declined the μι– aorist participle δούς, δοῦσα, δόν.

G. Stems in –υντ.

Only a few forms occur in the N. T. from participles like δεικνύς. The forms are:

	Masc.	Fem.	Neut.
Nom. sing.	δεικνύς	δεικνῦσα	δεικνύν
G. Ab. sing.	δεικνύντος	δεικνύσης	δεικνύντος
	etc.	etc.	etc.
Nom. plu.	δεικνύντες	δεικνῦσαι	δεικνύντα
D. L. I. plu.	δεικνῦσι(ν)	δεικνύσαις	δεικνῦσι(ν)
	etc.	etc.	etc.

215. Perfect Active Participles.

Two different stems [–ϝοσ–(–υσ–) and –ϝοτ] were blended in the declension of the perfect active part. The feminine is a new formation from the stem form of the masculine, gen. υσγας = –υιας which was levelled out in all cases.

Declension of λελυκώς, –κυῖα, –κός.

Singular

	Masc.	Fem.	Neut.
N.	λελυκώς	λελυκυῖα	λελυκός
G. Ab.	λελυκότος	λελυκυίας	λελυκότος
D. L. I.	λελυκότι	λελυκυίᾳ	λελυκότι
A.	λελυκότα	λελυκυῖαν	λελυκός

Plural

N.	λελυκότες	λελυκυῖαι	λελυκότα
G. Ab.	λελυκότων	λελυκυιῶν	λελυκότων
D. L. I.	λελυκόσι(ν)	λελυκυίαις	λελυκόσι(ν)
A.	λελυκότας	λελυκυίας	λελυκότα

a. In the fem. gen., abl. sing. a form like λελυκυίης sometimes occurs.

b. Like λελυκώς is declined εἰδώς, εἰδυῖα, εἰδός, gen. εἰδότος, εἰδυίας, εἰδότος, etc.

c. In ἑστώς (perf. act. part. of ἵστημι) contraction has taken place, and a new feminine was formed from the present part., as:

Sing. N.	ἑστώς,	ἑστῶσα,	ἑστός
G. Ab.	ἑστῶτος,	ἑστώσης,	ἑστῶτος
	etc.	etc.	etc.
Plu. D. L. I.	ἑστῶσι(ν),	ἑστώσαις,	ἑστῶσι(ν)

Comparison of Adjectives

216. The suffixes most frequently used in comparison are: for the comparative, masc. −τερος, fem. −τερα, neut. −τερον; for the superlative, masc. −τατος, fem. −τατη, neut. −τατον. The endings are added to the masc. stem of the positive:

Positive	Comp.	Superl.
μικρός,	μικρότερος,	[μικρότατος]
μακάριος,	μακαριώτερος,	[μακαριώτατος]
ἀσθενής,	ἀσθενέστερος	[ἀσθενέστατος]

a. Comparatives are declined like ἅγιος, and superlatives like καλός (except for accent).

b. Generally adjectives with masc. nom. in −ος lengthen o to ω if preceded by a short syllable; see μακαριώτερος above. There are occasional substitutions of −ώτερος for −ότερος, and vice versa.

c. The only instances of superlative forms in –τατος in the N. T. are ἁγιώτατος, ἀκριβέστατος and τιμιώτατος.

d. The stem from which a comparative is made may be an adverb:

ἄνω,	ἀνώτερος
ἔξω,	ἐξώτερος
κάτω,	κατώτερος

217. Comparison with the suffixes –ιων (or –γων), –ιστος.

Some adjectives add to the root the suffix –ιων (–γων) to form the masc. and fem. comparative, –ιον (–γον) to form the neuter, and –ιστος (–η, –ον) to form the superlative. Forms in –ιων (–γων) are declined like μείζων, and forms in –ιστος like καλός (except for accent).

Positive	Comp.	Superl.
μέγας	μείζων	μέγιστος

a. Some formations of comparison are irregular by reason of change of sounds or because different words are used:

Positive	Comp.	Superl.
ἀγαθός	βελτίων	———
	κρείσσων	———
	κρείττων	κράτιστος
κακός	ἥσσων	———
	χείρων	———
μικρός	μικρότερος	———
	ἐλάσσων	ἐλάχιστος
πολύς	πλείων	πλεῖστος
	πλέων	———

b. Sometimes a double comparison occurs: μειζότερος (3 John 4); ἐλαχιστότερος.

218. Comparison may be expressed by μᾶλλον (*more*) with a positive for the comparative, and μάλιστα (*most*) with a positive for the superlative. This is the regular method of comparing participles.

Declension of Pronouns

219. Pronominal Roots.

a. Substantives are kin to verbs in root and adjectives are variations of the substantive. But pronouns belong to a separate stock and Bopp has rightly divided roots into verbal and pronominal. All other forms as adverbs, prepositions, conjunctions, intensive particles, are really case forms of nouns or pronouns. Hence three sets of stems stand out with special prominence built on two root stocks. These stems are verbs, nouns, pronouns.

b. Once more noun and pronoun are vitally connected with the verb. The noun is so employed in root formation and the pronoun is used to form the personal endings of the verb. Hence the actual verb form is made up from the two roots of the language, the verbal and the pronominal.

c. Monro (*Homeric Grammar*, p. 57) remarks that noun stems name or describe while pronouns only point out, the one is predicative, the other demonstrative. In a sense then all pronouns were originally demonstrative. In the Sanskrit the pronominal roots are demonstrative and differ fundamentally from the roots of nouns.

d. Some of the forms are the most primitive known in the Indogermanic languages. In the Sanskrit personal pronouns of the first and second persons have no distinction of gender and are made up of fragments of various roots.

220. The Personal Pronouns are ἐγώ *I*, σύ *thou*, αὐτός, –ή, –ό *he, she, it*, and declined as follows:

Singular

					Masc.	Fem.	Neut.
N.	ἐγώ	N. V.	σύ	N.	αὐτός	–ή	–ό
G. Ab.	ἐμοῦ, μου		σοῦ, σου		αὐτοῦ	–ῆς	–οῦ
D. L. I.	ἐμοί, μοι		σοί, σοι		αὐτῷ	–ῇ	–ῷ
A.	ἐμέ, με		σέ, σε		αὐτόν	–ήν	–ό

Plural

					Masc.	Fem.	Neut.
N.	ἡμεῖς	N. V.	ὑμεῖς	N.	αὐτοί	–αί	–ά
G. Ab.	ἡμῶν		ὑμῶν		αὐτῶν	–ῶν	–ῶν
D. L. I.	ἡμῖν		ὑμῖν		αὐτοῖς	–αῖς	–οῖς
A.	ἡμᾶς		ὑμᾶς		αὐτούς	–άς	–ά

a. The New Testament does not use the third personal form οὗ, οἷ, ἕ, σφεῖς, etc. Instead the forms of αὐτός occur in all genders and both numbers.

b. The enclitic forms μου, σου, etc. are not used with prepositions, except πρός με. αὐτός is properly a demonstrative pronoun. It is doubtful that the nom. of αὐτός was weakened to simply the third personal pronoun. After the article αὐτός means *same*; when not after article and modifying a word it is intensive, *self*.

c. In Greek ἐγώ was originally ἐγών like the Sanskrit *aham*. This ἐγώ form appears in Latin *ego*, Gothic *ik*, German *ich*, French *je*, Anglo-Saxon *ic*, English *I*. So σύ is in Doric τύ like the Latin *tu*, etc. The Sanskrit is *tuam*. Compare *aham*. The oblique forms in the singular come from another stem which is practically the same in all the above languages, *mam*, (*Sans.*) ἐμέ, *me*, etc. (σέ, is from τέ, original *tue*) for the accusative; ἐμέσιο, ἐμέο, ἐμοῦ (μοῦ) and σεῖο, σέο, σοῦ for the genitive-ablative; ἐμοί, σοί have the locative ending used for locative, dative, instrumental; in the plural ἡμεῖς, ὑμεῖς come from the Lesbian ἀμμές, ὑμμές; ἡμῶν, ὑμῶν are new formations (Giles); ἡμῖν, ὑμῖν are locative forms.

221. The Reflexive Pronouns are formed from personal pronouns and the oblique cases of αὐτός. Of course there is no nominative. Their declensions are:

Singular

	First Pers.		Sec. Pers.		Third Pers.		
	M.	F.	M.	F.	M.	F.	N.
G. Ab.	ἐμαυτοῦ,	–ῆς	σεαυτοῦ,	–ῆς	ἑαυτοῦ,	–ῆς,	–οῦ
D. L. I.	ἐμαυτῷ,	–ῇ	σεαυτῷ,	–ῇ	ἑαυτῷ,	–ῇ,	–ῷ
A.	ἐμαυτόν,	–ήν	σεαυτόν,	–ήν	ἑαυτόν,	–ήν	–ό

Plural
For all persons

	M.	F.	N.
G. Ab.	ἑαυτῶν,	–ῶν,	–ῶν
D. L. I.	ἑαυτοῖς,	–αῖς,	–οῖς
A.	ἑαυτούς,	–άς,	–ά

a. In the third pers. sing. a shortened form is frequently met, as αὐτόν in place of ἑαυτόν, etc.

b. The old reflexive form ὑμῶν αὐτῶν is found in 1 Cor. 7:35.

222. Possessive Pronouns are formed from the personal pronouns and are declined like καλός and ἅγιος.

ἐμός, –ή, –όν, *my*, *mine*; ἡμέτερος, –α, –ον, *our*.

σός, –ή, –όν, *thy*, *thine*; ὑμέτερος, –α, –ον, *your*.

ἡμέτερος and ὑμέτερος are really comparative forms.

a. For *his*, *her*, *its* αὐτοῦ, αὐτῆς, αὐτοῦ are used.

b. For *their*, αὐτῶν is used.

223. The Reciprocal Pronoun, meaning *one another*, *each other*, is gen. abl. ἀλλήλων, dat. loc., inst. ἀλλήλοις, acc. ἀλλήλους. No fem. and neut. forms are found in the N. T. It seems that forms of ἑαυτῶν are sometimes used in a reciprocal sense.

224. The Definite Article was originally a demonstrative.

	Singular			Plural		
	M.	F.	N.	M.	F.	N.
N.	ὁ	ἡ	τό	οἱ	αἱ	τά
G. Ab.	τοῦ	τῆς	τοῦ	τῶν	τῶν	τῶν
D. L. I.	τῷ	τῇ	τῷ	τοῖς	ταῖς	τοῖς
A.	τόν	τήν	τό	τούς	τάς	τά

225. The Chief Demonstrative Pronouns are οὗτος *this*, and ἐκεῖνος, *that*.

a. οὗτος, αὕτη, τοῦτο.

	Singular		
	Masc.	Fem.	Neut.
N.	οὗτος	αὕτη	τοῦτο
G. Ab.	τούτου	ταύτης	τούτου
D. L. I.	τούτῳ	ταύτῃ	τούτῳ
A.	τοῦτον	ταύτην	τοῦτο

Plural

	Masc.	Fem.	Neut.
N.	οὗτοι	αὗται	ταῦτα
G. Ab.	τούτων	τούτων	τούτων
D. L. I.	τούτοις	ταύταις	τούτοις
A.	τούτους	ταύτας	ταῦτα

b. ἐκεῖνος, ἐκείνη, ἐκεῖνο.

Singular

	Masc.	Fem.	Neut.
N.	ἐκεῖνος	ἐκείνη	ἐκεῖνο
G. Ab.	ἐκείνου	ἐκείνης	ἐκείνου
D. L. I.	ἐκείνῳ	ἐκείνῃ	ἐκείνῳ
A.	ἐκεῖνον	ἐκείνην	ἐκεῖνο

Plural

	Masc.	Fem.	Neut.
N.	ἐκεῖνοι	ἐκεῖναι	ἐκεῖνα
G. Ab.	ἐκείνων	ἐκείνων	ἐκείνων
D. L. I.	ἐκείνοις	ἐκείναις	ἐκείνοις
A.	ἐκείνους	ἐκείνας	ἐκεῖνα

c. ὅδε occurs rarely, and is declined as ὁ with the enclitic δε added.

d. Other demonstrative pronouns are τοιοῦτος *such*, τοσοῦτος *so much*, τηλικοῦτος *so great*, τοιόσδε *such*.

226. The indefinite ἄλλος, –η, –ο *other*, is declined like ἐκεῖνος. The demonstrative ἕτερος, –α, –ον (declined like ἅγιος) *other of two, different*, seems sometimes to be used like ἄλλος.

a. δεῖνα, *such a one*, is found once in N. T., τὸν δεῖνα (Matt. 26:18).

227. The Relative Pronoun ὅς, ἥ, ὅ *who, which, that* is declined thus:

	Singular			Plural		
	M.	F.	N.	M.	F.	N.
N.	ὅς	ἥ	ὅ	οἵ	αἵ	ἅ
G. Ab.	οὗ	ἧς	οὗ	ὧν	ὧν	ὧν
D. L. I.	ᾧ	ᾗ	ᾧ	οἷς	αἷς	οἷς
A.	ὅν	ἥν	ὅ	οὕς	ἅς	ἅ

a. The relative ὅs is a development from an old demonstrative, like English *that*. In Homer ὥs is often demonstrative *thus*.

b. Other relatives are:

ὅσγε and ὅσπερ (simply ὅs+an enclitic).

οἷοs *of which kind* (declined like ἅγιοs).

ὁποῖοs *such as* (declined like ἅγιοs).

ὅσοs *as much as, as many as* (declined like καλόs, except accent).

228. The General Relative Pronoun ὅστις is used in the indefinite sense *any one who* or in a particular sense *some one* (in particular).

It is found in the N. T. in the following cases:

	Singular			Plural		
	M.	F.	N.	M.	F.	N.
N.	ὅστις	ἥτις	ὅτι	οἵτινες	αἵτινες	ἅτινα
A.			ὅτι			

a. There is one instance of the gen. abl. ὅτου in the phrase ἕως ὅτου (Matt. 5:25).

b. ὅστις is made up of the relative ὅs and the indefinite τις.

229. The Interrogative Pronoun τίς, τί, *who, which, what* is declined thus:

	Singular		Plural	
	M. and F.	N.	M. and F.	N.
N.	τίς	τί	τίνες	τίνα
G. Ab.	τίνος		τίνων	
D. L. I.	τίνι		τίσι(ν)	
A.	τίνα	τί	τίνας	τίνα

N. The interrogative τίς, τί always is written with the acute accent—never the grave.

a. τίς has the same root as the Latin *quis*, Sans. *kas*, Gothic *hwas*, Ger. *wer*, Anglo-Saxon *hwa* (English *who*). Both Latin and Greek made an indefinite form from this root, as *aliquis*, τις.

230. The Indefinite Pronoun τὶς, τὶ, *any, some* is an enclitic. It is declined like τίς, τί (except for accent).

	Singular		Plural	
	M. and F.	N.	M. and F.	N.
N.	τὶς	τὶ	τινές	τινά
G. Ab.		τινός		τινῶν
D. L. I.		τινί		τισί(ν)
A.	τινά	τὶ	τινάς	τινά

Adverbs

231. Adverbs were originally case-forms that became fixed, made from substantives, adjectives, and pronouns. Some are remnants of obsolete case-forms. The stems of some have gone out of use as nouns or pronouns. The case-forms are illustrated in the following:

Nom.: ἅπαξ, *once*.

Gen.: ποῦ, *where*; ἑξῆς, *next*.

Abl.: All adverbs in –ως are probably ablatives: as ὡς, *as*; οὕτως, *thus*; ἑτέρως, *otherwise*.

Dat.: δημοσίᾳ, *publicly*.

Loc.: ἀεί, *always*; [οἴκοι, *at home*]; ἐκεῖ *there*; πανοικεί(–ί) *with all the house*.

Inst.: λάθρα(or –ᾳ), *secretly*; πάντη(–ῃ), *in every way*; πόρρω, *far*.

Acc.: πολύ, *much*; ταχύ, *quickly*; ἀκμήν, *up to this point*; πολλά, *often*; δωρεάν, *freely*.

232. Other adverbs were formed by suffixes which may be relics of lost case-endings:

–θεν: ἐκεῖθεν, *from that place, thence*; παιδιόθεν, (παιδόθεν), *from childhood*.

–κις: πολλάκις, *oftentimes*; ποσάκις, *how often*.

–δον: ὁμοθυμαδόν, *with one accord*; σχεδόν, *nearly, almost*.

–στι: Ἑλληνιστί, *in Greek (fashion)*; Ἑβραϊστί, *in Hebrew*; Ῥωμαϊστί, *in Latin*.

233. Adverbs in –ως expressing manner are formed from adjectives and pronouns. A mechanical rule is that the adverb may be formed by changing the final –ων (–ῶν) of the masc. gen. abl. plu. into –ως (–ῶς), retaining the accent of the adjective. The adverbs in –ως (–ῶς) were originally old ablatives

from *o* stems, –ωδ =–ως; then –ως was transferred to other
stems.

Gen. Abl. Plu. δικαίων,   adv. δικαίως *justly*.
   "   "   "   ἄλλων,   adv. ἄλλως *otherwise*.
   "   "   "   κακῶν,   adv. κακῶς *ill*.
   "   "   "   ὄντων,   adv. ὄντως *really*.
   "   "   "   φειδομένων, adv. φειδομένως *sparingly*.

234. Comparison of Adverbs. The comparative of adverbs
is the same as the neuter accusative sing. of the comparative
adjective; and the superlative is the same as the neuter accusative plural of the superlative adjective. Thus:

Positive	Comp.	Superl.
ἀκριβῶς	ἀκριβέστερον	————
ἐγγύς	ἐγγύτερον	ἔγγιστα
[μάλα]	μᾶλλον	μάλιστα
πόρρω	πορρώτερον	————
————	ὕστερον	————
ἄνω	ἀνώτερον	————

N. But some comparatives end in –ω and –ως; as κατωτέρω
(κατώτερος), περισσοτέρως (περισσότερον). The superlative form
πρῶτος has πρῶτον and πρώτως; and ἔσχατος has ἐσχάτως.

Numerals

235. The numeral adjectives and adverbs occurring in the
N. T. are as follows:

Sign.	Cardinals	Ordinals	Adverb
1. ā	εἷς, μία, ἕν	πρῶτος	ἅπαξ
2. β̄	δύο	δεύτερος	δίς
3. γ̄	τρεῖς, τρία	τρίτος	τρίς
4. δ̄	τέσσαρες, τέσσαρα	τέταρτος	
5. ε̄	πέντε	πέμπτος	πεντάκις
6. ϛ̄	ἕξ	ἕκτος	
7. ζ̄	ἑπτά	ἕβδομος	ἑπτάκις
8. η̄	ὀκτώ	ὄγδοος	
9. θ̄	ἐννέα	ἔνατος	

Sign.	Cardinals	Ordinals	Adverb
10. ῑ	δέκα	δέκατος	
11. ιᾱ	ἕνδεκα	ἑνδέκατος	
12. ιβ̄	δώδεκα, δεκαδύο	δωδέκατος	
14. ιδ̄	δεκατέσσαρες	τεσσαρεσκαιδέκατος	
15. ιε̄	δεκαπέντε	πεντεκαιδέκατος	
18. ιη̄	δέκα ὀκτώ, δέκα καὶ ὀκτώ		
20. κ̄	εἴκοσι(ν)		
25. κε̄	εἴκοσι πέντε		
30. λ̄	τριάκοντα		
40. μ̄	τεσσαράκοντα, τεσσεράκοντα		
50. ν̄	πεντήκοντα	πεντηκοστός	
60. ξ	ἑξήκοντα		
70. ō	ἑβδομήκοντα		ἑβδομηκοντάκις
80. π̄	ὀγδοήκοντα		
90. ϙ̄	ἐνενήκοντα		
100. ρ̄	ἑκατόν		
200. σ̄	διακόσιοι		
300. τ̄	τριακόσιοι		
400. ῡ	τετρακόσιοι		
500. φ̄	πεντακόσιοι		
600. χ̄	ἑξακόσιοι		
1,000. ͵α	χίλιοι		
2,000. ͵β	δισχίλιοι		
3,000. ͵γ	τρισχίλιοι		
4,000. ͵δ	τετρακισχίλιοι		
5,000. ͵ε	πεντακισχίλιοι		
7,000. ͵ζ	χιλιάδες ἑπτά, ἑπτακισχίλιοι		
10,000. Μ̄^{a}	μύριοι or δέκα χιλιάδες		
20,000. Μ̄^{β}	εἴκοσι χιλιάδες		
50,000. Μ̄^{ε}	μυριάδες πέντε		

N. In addition to the 24 letters of the alphabet three obsolete signs were used: (1) ϛ(= στ) in place of ϝ for 6; (2) ϙ (koppa) for 90; and (3) ϡ or ϡ (sampi or san) for 900, but this sign is not found in N. T. The straight lines over the letters note them as numerals. When the letters are used again as from 1,000 to 9,000 a sloping line is placed under the letters. From 10,000 up M with the proper sign written above was used. In modern books accents take place of the straight line.

236. The Declension of the Cardinals from 1 to 4:

a. εἷς, μία, ἕν one.   b. δύο two.

	M.	F.	N.	
N.	εἷς	μία	ἕν	δύο
G. Ab.	ἑνός	μιᾶς	ἑνός	δύο
D. L. I.	ἑνί	μιᾷ	ἑνί	δυσί(ν)
A.	ἕνα	μίαν	ἕν	δύο

c. τρεῖς, τρία three.   d. τέσσαρες, τέσσαρα four.

	M. and F.	N.	M. and F.	N.
N.	τρεῖς	τρία	τέσσαρες	τέσσαρα
G. Ab.	τριῶν		τεσσάρων	
D. L. I.	τρισί(ν)		τέσσαρσι(ν)	
A.	τρεῖς	τρία	τέσσαρας	τέσσαρα

N. Like εἷς are declined οὐδείς, οὐδεμία, οὐδέν and μηδείς etc.
NN. τέσσαρες as an accusative is found in many MSS.

237. The Cardinals from 5 to 199 are indeclinable; but from 200 up they are declinable. All the ordinals are declinable (like καλός, except for accent).

238 Distributives proper are expressed in Greek by repetition; as δύο δύο two by two, or by ἀνὰ δύο or κατὰ δύο.

239. Multiplicative distributives with ending –πλοῦς, fold, are ἁπλοῦς, διπλοῦς. Proportional distributives with ending –πλασίων are found, as ἑκατονταπλασίων and πολλαπλασίων.

240. The suffix –αῖος forms adjectives answering the question on what day? as δευτεραῖος, τεταρταῖος.

CHAPTER VII

INFLECTION OF THE VERB

241. The forms of the Greek verbal-system are of two kinds: (1) the finite forms and (2) the infinite forms. The finite forms are the indicative, subjunctive, optative, and imperative. The infinite forms are the infinitive, participle, and verbal adjective in —τός and —τέος.

242. The Greek verb shows distinctions in person, number, voice, mode and tense.

243. There are three persons, first, second and third, in each number of the indicative, subjunctive, and optative; of the imperative, the second and third.

244. There were three numbers; singular, dual, and plural. The dual early fell into disuse, so that it does not appear in the vernacular κοινή.

245. There are three voices: active, middle, and passive. Voice pertains to the action of the verb as regards the subject of the action.

a. The middle voice indicates that the subject is acting with reference to himself.

b. The parent Indo-ger. language probably had only two voices—active and middle. The middle forms came to be used to express the passive idea. The second aorist passive in —ην was originally active in form, and the first aorist passive in —θην was a special new formation. The passive has the same forms as the middle in all tenses except the aorist and future.

c. Some verbs were used only in the form of the middle and passive voices seemingly with an active meaning. They have been called (wrongly) middle and passive deponents.

A. There are four modes (or moods): indicative, subunctive, optative, and imperative; which are called finite because they are limited to a subject by the personal endings.

N. There was in the parent language an injunctive mode (unaugmented indicative forms with secondary endings) which became a part of the imperative system.

246. There are seven tenses in the indicative: the present, imperfect, future, aorist, perfect, pluperfect, and future perfect. There are three tenses in the subjunctive and imperative: the present, aorist, and perfect. In the optative, infinitive, and participle there are five tenses: the present, future, aorist, perfect, (and future perfect).

247. The tenses of the indicative are commonly divided into two classes:

a. Primary (or Principal) tenses—the present, future, perfect, and future perfect.

b. Secondary (or Historical) tenses—the imperfect, aorist, and pluperfect.

248. Many verbs have tenses known as the *second* or *strong* aorists (in all voices), the *second* or *strong* perfect and pluperfect (in active voice only), and the *second* or *strong* future (passive). Few verbs have both the *first* and *second* forms in any tense, but when a verb has both forms in a tense, the two forms usually differ in meaning (one transitive, the other intransitive), but not always.

249. There were originally two verb-types, one denoting *durative* or *linear* action, the other *momentary* or *punctiliar* action. Thus in ἐσθίω the verb-stem is *durative* or linear, and in ἔφαγον the verb-stem is *punctiliar*. So in English "blink the eye" is a different kind of action from "live a life"; and "seek" has a different kind of action from "find." In Greek this matter of the "kind of action" in the verb-stem (or root) itself, called *Aktionsart*, existed before there was any idea of the later tense development.

The aorist tense at first was used with verb-stems of punctiliar sense; and the present tense with verb-stems of durative action.

A present (durative action) could not be formed from a verb-stem expressing punctiliar action unless the verb-stem was modified by a formative element; and no verb-stem expressing durative action would occur in the second aorist. Hence arose what are called defective verbs, that is, verbs with presents but no aorists, or with aorists but no presents. Then the aorist (especially the first aorist) tense came gradually to be made on verbs of durative action. And the present tense came to be made on verbs of punctiliar action. Thus the tense came to be used for the expression of the idea that once belonged only to the verb-stem (or root). That is, the aorist tense imposed a punctiliar idea on a durative verb-stem; and the present tense imposed a durative idea on a punctiliar verb-stem.

250. The infinite forms are called verbal nouns because they have properties of both verb and noun. They are of two kinds:

a. Substantive: the infinitive. The infinitives were originally isolated singular case-forms of nouns of action, dative and locative.

b. Adjective: (1) participles (inflected like adjectives) in the active, middle, and passive voice. (2) Verbal adjectives in $-\tau \acute{o}s$ and $-\tau \acute{e}os$.

251. The tenses of the verb in Greek are divided into nine tense-systems. Each tense-system has a distinct stem, called tense-stem.

<table>
<tr><td>Systems.</td><td>Tenses.</td></tr>
</table>

1. Present, including present and imperfect in all voices.
2. Future, including future active and middle.
3. First aorist, including first aorist active and middle.
4. Second aorist, including second aorist active and middle.
5. First perfect, including first perfect and pluperfect active.
6. Second perfect, including second perfect and pluperfect active.
7. Perfect middle, including perfect and pluperfect middle and passive, and future perfect.

8. First passive, including first aorist and first future passive.
9. Second passive, including second aorist and second future passive.

N. Most verbs have only six of these nine systems, since very few verbs have both the first and second forms of the same tense; many verbs have less than six.

252. The principal parts of a Greek verb are the first person singular indicative of every system used in it.

a. In verbs which have no active voice the principal parts are the present, future, perfect, and aorist (both aorists, middle and passive, if they occur) indicative.

253. Stems.

a. Each tense-system has a distinct stem, called *tense-stem*, to which the endings are attached.

b. The various tense-stems are made from a fundamental stem called the verb-stem. The verb-stem may be either a root (as λεγ in λέγω) or a root to which a derivative suffix has been added (as τιμα- is the verb-stem of τιμάω, and τι is the root).

c. Tense-stems are generally made from verb-stems by prefixes and suffixes and modifications of stem. The tense-stem and the verb-stem may be identical; as πιστευ- in πιστεύω is both the present stem and the verb-stem.

d. A verb which forms its tense-stems directly from a root is called a *primitive* verb, as λύω, root λυ. A verb forming its tense-stems from the stem of a substantive or adjective is called a *denominative* verb; as τιμάω from stem τιμα- of the substantive τιμή; φανερόω from stem φανερο- of the adjective φανερός.

N. A verb may form its tense-stem from a stem of another verb or from an adverb; as γνωρίζω from verb-root of γινώσκω; χωρίζω from adv. χωρίς.

e. The verb-stem may show modifications in different verb-systems:

      Vowel gradation: λείπω, λέλοιπα, ἔλιπον.
      Change in quantity: λῡω, perf. λέλῠκα.

254. The *inflection* of a verb consists in the addition, to its different stems, of certain endings which, in the finite modes, indicate person, number, and voice.

a. The final vowel of some tense-stems varies between o and ε (or ω and η) in certain forms, as λέγομεν, λέγετε. This is called the *thematic* (or *variable*) vowel. It is indicated as ᵒ/ε or ω/η, as λεγᵒ/ε, λεγω/η.

255. There are two different ways of inflecting the verb, the *athematic* and the *thematic*. In the athematic the personal endings are added directly to the stem. The thematic has the thematic vowel ᵒ/ε (ω/η) before the personal endings.

a. The primary endings of the first person sing. active were –μι in the athematic and –ω in the thematic. So verbs are called μι– verbs or ω– verbs according to the ending of the first person sing. active.

b. To the athematic inflection belong the athematic presents and imperfects of μι– verbs; all aorists passives (except subj.); strong aorists which do not have the thematic vowel; all perfects and pluperfects middle (and passive); and the strong perfect and pluperfect active of a few verbs.

c. To the thematic inflection belong all futures and the forms of the present, imperfect, and strong aorists, which have the thematic vowel.

d. According to the final letter of the verb-stem, ω– verbs are named:

(1) Vowel (or pure) verbs, when stem ends in a vowel;
  (a) Not contracted, when ending in ι or υ.
  (b) Contracted, when ending in α, ε, η, o.
(2) Consonant verbs, when stem ends in a consonant;
  (a) Liquids, when ending in λ or ρ.
  (b) Nasals, when ending in μ or ν.
  (c) Stop (or mutes) when ending in a stop (mute) (35).

256. To *conjugate* a verb is to give all its forms in voice, tense, mode, number, and person. In the following sections (§§257-270) are given the paradigms of the conjugation of the various tense-stems.

257. The Root or Strong Aorist (also called the Second Aorist).

A. Athematic

Pres. ἵστημι, ἀφίημι, τίθημι, δίδωμι, γινώσκω.
Stem. στη/ἀ, ἡ/ἑ, θη/ε, δω/ο, γνω.

Active Voice

Indicative—

S. 1.	ἔστην	ἀφῆκα	ἔθηκα	ἔδωκα	ἔγνων
2.	[ἔστης]	ἀφῆκας	ἔθηκας	ἔδωκας	ἔγνως
3.	ἔστη	ἀφῆκε	ἔθηκε	ἔδωκε	ἔγνω
P. 1.	ἔστημεν	ἀφήκαμεν	ἐθήκαμεν	ἐδώκαμεν	ἔγνωμεν
2.	ἔστητε	ἀφήκατε	ἐθήκατε	ἐδώκατε	ἔγνωτε
3.	ἔστησαν	ἀφῆκαν	ἔθηκαν	ἔδωκαν	ἔγνωσαν

N. The ind. act. of ἀφίημι, τίθημι, δίδωμι are formed from an alternative root in –κ with the endings of the weak aorist, and the κ forms in the ind. act. of these three verbs wholly displaced the strong (athematic) forms, with the single exception of a strong form of δίδωμι in the 3 plu., παρέδοσαν in Luke 1:2. Like ἔστην are the forms of –ἔβην. Two forms from ἔδυν are found, 3rd sing. ἔδυ and 3rd plu. ἔδυσαν.

Subjunctive—

S. 1.	[στῶ]	ἀφῶ	θῶ	δῶ	γνῶ
2.	[στῇς]	[ἀφῇς]	θῇς	δῷς, δοῖς	γνῷς
3.	στῇ	ἀφῇ	θῇ	δῷ, δοῖ, δώῃ	γνῷ, γνοῖ
P. 1.	[στῶμεν]	ἀφῶμεν	θῶμεν	δῶμεν	[γνῶμεν]
2.	στῆτε	ἀφῆτε	[θῆτε]	δῶτε	γνῶτε
3.	στῶσι(ν)	ἀφῶσι(ν)	θῶσι(ν)	δῶσι(ν)	γνῶσι(ν)

Optative—

S. 1.	[σταίην]	[ἀφείην]	[θείην]	[δοίην]	[γνοίην]
2.	[σταίης]	[ἀφείης]	[θείης]	[δοίης]	[γνοίης]
3.	[σταίη]	[ἀφείη]	[θείη]	[δοίη], δώῃ	[γνοίη]
P. 1.	[σταίημεν]	[ἀφείημεν]	[θείημεν]	[δοῖμεν]	[γνοίημεν]
2.	[σταίητε]	[ἀφείητε]	[θείητε]	[δοῖτε]	[γνοίητε]
3.	[σταίησαν]	[ἀφείησαν]	[θείησαν]	[δοίησαν]	[γνοίησαν]

N.   Of these forms in the optative δῴη alone occurs in the N. T. Except for σταίη, θείη and the forms of δοίην, the forms given above are uncertain for the papyri.

Imperative—

S. 2.	στῆθι	ἄφες	θές	δός	γνῶθι
3.	στήτω	[ἀφέτω]	[θέτω]	δότω	γνώτω
P. 2.	στῆτε	ἄφετε	θέτε	δότε	γνῶτε
3.	[στήτωσαν]	[ἀφέτωσαν]	[θέτωσαν]	[δότωσαν]	[γνώτωσαν]

N.   In compounds –στα as well as –στηθι is found in 2 pers. sing. Of βαίνω only compound forms are found:

    S. 2.   –βηθι, –βα,   3.   –βάτω,   P. 2.   –βατε.

Infinitive—

    στῆναι   ἀφεῖναι   θεῖναι   δοῦναι   γνῶναι

N.   The infinitive from βαίνω is found only in the compound form, –βῆναι.

Participle—

	στάς,	ἀφείς,	θείς,	δούς,	γνούς,
	–ᾶσα	–εῖσα	–εῖσα	–οῦσα	–οῦσα,
	–άν	–έν	–έν	–όν	–όν.

Middle Voice.

Indicative—

S. 1.	(Lacking)	(No forms	ἐθέμην	[ἐδόμην]	(Lacking)
2.		occur in	ἔθου	[ἔδου]	
3.		N. T.)	ἔθετο	ἔδοτο	
P. 1.			[ἐθέμεθα]	[ἐδόμεθα]	
2.			ἔθεσθε	ἔδοσθε	
3.			ἔθεντο	ἔδοντο	

Subjunctive—

S. 1.	[θῶμαι]
2.	[θῇ]
3.	[θῆται]
P. 1.	θώμεθα
2.	[θῆσθε]
3.	[θῶνται]

Optative—

S. 1.   The only form from athematic verbs is ὀναίμην (present ὀνίναμαι).

Imperative—

S. 2.		θοῦ
3.		[θέσθω]
P. 2.		θέσθε
3.		[θέσθωσαν]

Infinitive—

θέσθαι

Participle—

θέμενος

B. Thematic

Stem λαβο/ε

Active Voice

	Sing.	Plural

Indicative—

1.	ἔλαβον	ἐλάβομεν
2.	ἔλαβες	ἐλάβετε
3.	ἔλαβε(ν)	ἔλαβον

Subjunctive—

1.	λάβω	λάβωμεν
2.	λάβῃς	λάβητε
3.	λάβῃ	λάβωσιν

Optative—

1.	[λάβοιμι]	[λάβοιμεν]
2.	[λάβοις]	[λάβοιτε]
3.	λάβοι	λάβοιεν

Imperative—

2.	λάβε	λάβετε
3.	λαβέτω	λαβέτωσαν

Infinitive—

λαβεῖν

Participle—

λαβών, -οῦσα, -όν.

N.   In the Ind. the endings -α, -ας, -ε(ν) in the sing. and -αμεν, -ατε, -αν in the plural are frequently found.   The α in these endings came from the α of the σ- aorist.   Almost all the aorist act. ind. forms of εἶπον and ἤνεγκον are found with these endings, as εἶπα, εἶπας, εἴπαμεν, εἴπατε, εἶπαν.

Middle Voice

	Sing.	Plural
Indicative—		
1.	ἐλαβόμην	ἐλαβόμεθα
2.	ἐλάβου	ἐλάβεσθε
3.	ἐλάβετο	ἐλάβοντο
Subjunctive—		
1.	λάβωμαι	λαβώμεθα
2.	λάβῃ	λάβησθε
3.	λάβηται	λάβωνται
Optative—		
1.	[λαβοίμην]	[λαβοίμεθα]
2.	[λάβοιο]	[λάβοισθε]
3.	λάβοιτο	[λάβοιντο]
Imperative—		
	λαβοῦ	λάβεσθε
	λαβέσθω	λαβέσθωσαν

Infinitive—

λαβέσθαι

Participle—

λαβόμενος, —η, —ον.

Passive Voice

The Root or Strong Aorist in the passive is not thematic. Aorists in —ην were originally active athematic formations which came to be used to express the passive.

	Sing.	Plural
Indicative—		
1.	ἐτράπην	ἐτράπημεν
2.	ἐτράπης	ἐτράπητε
3.	ἐτράπη	ἐτράπησαν
Subjunctive—		
1.	τραπῶ	τραπῶμεν
2.	τραπῇς	τραπῆτε
3.	τραπῇ	τραπῶσι(ν)
Optative—		
1.	[τραπείην]	[τραπείημεν]
2.	[τραπείης]	[τραπείητε]
3.	[τραπείη]	[τραπείησαν]
Imperative—		
2.	τράπηθι	τράπητε
3.	τραπήτω	τραπήτωσαν

Infinitive—

τραπῆναι

Participle—

τραπείς, —εῖσα, —έν.

258.   The σ– Aorist (also called the Weak or First Aorist).

Active Voice

	Sing.	Plural	Sing.	Plural
Indicative—				
1.	ἔλυσα	ἐλύσαμεν	ἔμεινα	ἐμείναμεν
2.	ἔλυσας	ἐλύσατε	ἔμεινας	ἐμείνατε
3.	ἔλυσε(ν)	ἔλυσαν	ἔμεινε(ν)	ἔμειναν
Subjunctive—				
1.	λύσω	λύσωμεν	μείνω	μείνωμεν
2.	λύσῃς	λύσητε	μείνῃς	μείνητε
3.	λύσῃ	λύσωσι(ν)	μείνῃ	μείνωσι(ν)
Optative—				
1.	[λύσαιμι]	[λύσαιμεν]	[μείναιμι]	[μείναιμεν]
2.	[λύσαις]	[λύσαιτε]	[μειναις]	[μείναιτε]
3.	λύσαι	λύσειαν, or −αιεν	μείναι	μείνειαν, or −αιεν
Imperative—				
2.	λῦσον	λύσατε	μεῖνον	μείνατε
3.	λυσάτω	λυσάτωσαν	μεινάτω	μεινάτωσαν
Infinitive—	λῦσαι		μεῖναι	
Participle—	λύσας, −ασα, −αν.		μείνας, −ασα, −αν.	

Middle Voice

Instead of μένω the aor. Midd. of ἀγγέλλω is given.

	Sing.	Plural	Sing.	Plural
Indicative—				
1.	ἐλυσάμην	ἐλυσάμεθα	ἠγγειλάμην	ἠγγειλάμεθα
2.	ἐλύσω	ἐλύσασθε	ἠγγείλω	ἠγγείλασθε
3.	ἐλύσατο	ἐλύσαντο	ἠγγείλατο	ἠγγείλαντο

Subjunctive—

1.	λύσωμαι	λυσώμεθα	ἀγγείλωμαι	ἀγγειλώμεθα
2.	λύσῃ	λύσησθε	ἀγγείλῃ	ἀγγείλησθε
3.	λύσηται	λύσωνται	ἀγγείληται	ἀγγείλωνται

Optative—

1.	λυσαίμην	[λυσαίμεθα]	[ἀγγειλαίμην]	[ἀγγειλαίμεθα]
2.	[λύσαιο]	[λύσαισθε]	[ἀγγείλαιο]	[ἀγγείλαισθε]
3.	[λύσαιτο]	[λύσαιντο]	[ἀγγείλατο]	[ἀγγείλαιντο]

Imperative—

2.	λῦσαι	λύσασθε	ἄγγειλαι	ἀγγείλασθε
3.	λυσάσθω	λυσάσθωσαν	ἀγγειλάσθω	ἀγγειλάσθωσαν

Infinitive—

λύσασθαι   ἀγγείλασθαι

Participle—

λυσάμενος —η, —ον   ἀγγειλάμενος, —η, —ον.

Passive Voice

The aorist passive of ἐγείρω is given instead of μένω or ἀγγέλλω.

	Sing.	Plural	Sing.	Plural
Indicative—				
1.	ἐλύθην	ἐλύθημεν	ἠγέρθην	ἠγέρθημεν
2.	ἐλύθης	ἐλύθητε	ἠγέρθης	ἠγέρθητε
3.	ἐλύθη	ἐλύθησαν	ἠγέρθη	ἠγέρθησαν

Subjunctive—

1.	λυθῶ	λυθῶμεν	ἐγερθῶ	ἐγερθῶμεν
2.	λυθῇς	λυθῆτε	ἐγερθῇς	ἐγερθῆτε
3.	λυθῇ	λυθῶσι(ν)	ἐγερθῇ	ἐγερθῶσι(ν)

Optative—

1.	[λυθείην]	[λυθείημεν]	[ἐγερθείην]	[ἐγερθείημεν]
2	[λυθείης]	[λυθείητε]	[ἐγερθείης]	[ἐγερθείητε]
3.	λυθείη	[λυθείησαν]	ἐγερθείη	[ἐγερθείησαν]

Imperative—

2.	λύθητι	λύθητε	ἐγέρθητι	ἐγέρθητε
3.	λυθήτω	λυθήτωσαν	ἐγερθήτω	ἐγερθήτωσαν

Infinitive—

λυθῆναι   ἐγερθῆναι

Participle—

λυθείς, –εῖσα, –έν   ἐγερθείς, –εῖσα, –έν

259. The Present.

A. Athematic

Present Stem ἱστη/ἄ, τιθη/ε, διδω/ο, δεικνῡ/υ.

Active Voice

Indicative—

S. 1.	ἵστημι	τίθημι	δίδωμι	δείκνυμι
2.	[ἵστης]	[τίθης]	δίδως	[δείκνυς]
3.	ἵστησι(ν)	τίθησι(ν)	δίδωσι(ν)	δείκνυσι(ν)
P. 1.	[ἵσταμεν]	τίθεμεν	[δίδομεν]	[δείκνυμεν]
2.	[ἵστατε]	τίθετε	[δίδοτε]	[δείκνυτε]
3.	[ἱστᾶσι(ν)]	τιθέασι(ν)	διδόασι(ν)	[δεικνύασι(ν)]

Subjunctive—

S. 1.	[ἱστῶ]	τιθῶ	[διδῶ]	[δεικνύω]
2.	[ἱστῇς]	[τιθῇς]	[διδῷς, διδοῖς]	[δεικνύῃς]
3.	[ἱστῇ]	[τιθῇ]	διδῷ, διδοῖ	[δεικνύῃ]
P. 1.	[ἱστῶμεν]	[τιθῶμεν]	[διδῶμεν]	[δεικνύωμεν]
2.	[ἱστῆτε]	[τιθῆτε]	[διδῶτε]	[δεικνύητε]
3.	[ἱστῶσι(ν)]	τιθῶσι(ν)	διδῶσι(ν)	[δεικνύωσι(ν)]

Optative—
No present act. optative of any of these verbs occurs in
the N. T.

Imperative—

S. 2.	[ἴστη]	τίθει	δίδου	[δείκνυ]
3.	[ἱστάτω]	τιθέτω	διδότω	[δεικνύτω]

P. 2.	[ἴστατε]	τίθετε	δίδοτε	δείκνυτε
3.	[ἱστάτωσαν]	[τιθέτωσαν]	[διδότωσαν]	[δεικνύτωσαν]

Infinitive—

ἱστάναι	τιθέναι	διδόναι	δεικνύναι

Participle—
ἱστάς, –ᾶσα, –άν, τιθείς, –εῖσα, –έν, διδούς, –οῦσα, –όν, –δεικνύς,
ῦσα, –ύν.

Imperfect Active

S. 1.	[ἵστην]	[ἐτίθην]	[ἐδίδουν]	[ἐδείκνυν]
2.	[ἵστης]	[ἐτίθεις]	[ἐδίδους]	[ἐδείκνυς]
3.	[ἵστη]	ἐτίθει	ἐδίδου	[ἐδείκνυ]

P. 1.	[ἵσταμεν]	[ἐτίθεμεν]	[ἐδίδομεν]	[ἐδείκνυμεν]
2.	[ἵστατε]	[ἐτίθετε]	[ἐδίδοτε]	[ἐδείκνυτε]
3.	[ἵστασαν]	ἐτίθεσαν	[ἐδίδοσαν]	[ἐδείκνυσαν]

Middle and Passive Voices

Indicative—

S. 1.	ἵσταμαι	τίθεμαι	[δίδομαι]	δείκνυμαι
2.	ἵστασαι	[τίθεσαι]	[δίδοσαι]	[δείκνυσαι]
3.	ἵσταται	τίθεται	δίδοται	δείκνυται

P. 1.	ἱστάμεθα	[τιθέμεθα]	διδόμεθα	δεικνύμεθα
2.	ἵστασθε	τίθεσθε	[δίδοσθε]	[δείκνυσθε]
3.	ἵστανται	τίθενται	[δίδονται]	δείκνυνται

Subjunctive—

S. 1.	[ἱστῶμαι]	[τιθῶμαι]	[διδῶμαι]	[δεικνύωμαι]
2.	[ἱστῇ]	[τιθῇ]	[διδῷ]	[δεικνύῃ]
3.	[ἱστῆται]	[τιθῆται]	[διδῶται]	[δεικνύηται]

P. 1.	[ἱστώμεθα]	[τιθώμεθα]	[διδώμεθα]	[δεικνυώμεθα]
2.	[ἱστῆσθε]	[τιθῆσθε]	[διδῶσθε]	[δεικνύησθε]
3.	[ἱστῶνται]	[τιθῶνται]	[διδῶνται]	[δεικνύωνται]

The forms above are given in full because forms of δύναμαι
occur: δύνηται, δύνωνται.

Optative—

No present middle or passive optative of any of these
verbs occurs in the N. T.   Two forms from δύναμαι are found:
1. sing. δυναίμην, 3. plu. δύναιντο.

Imperative—

S. 2.	ἵστασο	[τίθεσο]	[δίδοσο]	[δείκνυσο]
3.	[ἱστάσθω]	[τιθέσθω]	[διδόσθω]	[δεικνύσθω]

P. 2.	[ἵστασθε]	[τίθεσθε]	[δίδοσθε]	δείκνυσθε
3.	[ἱστάσθωσαν]	τιθέσθωσαν	[διδόσθωσαν]	[δεικνύσθωσαν]

Infinitive—

ἵστασθαι   τίθεσθαι   δίδοσθαι   δείκνυσθαι

Participle—

ἱστάμενος   τιθέμενος   διδόμενος   δεικνύμενος

Imperfect, Middle and Passive

S. 1.	ἱστάμην	[ἐτιθέμην]	[ἐδιδόμην]	[ἐδεικνύμην]
2.	[ἵστασο]	[ἐτίθεσο]	[ἐδίδοσο]	[ἐδείκνυσο]
3.	ἵστατο	ἐτίθετο	ἐδίδοτο	ἐδείκνυτο

P. 1.	[ἱστάμεθα]	[ἐτιθέμεθα]	[ἐδιδόμεθα]	[ἐδεικνύμεθα]
2.	ἵστασθε	[ἐτίθεσθε]	[ἐδίδοσθε]	[ἐδείκνυσθε]
3.	ἵσταντο	ἐτίθεντο	[ἐδίδοντο]	ἐδείκνυντο

260. Conjugation of ἀφίημι and συνίημι. Stems (ἀφ–, συν–) ἱη/ε.

Present
Active Voice

Indicative—

	Sing.	Plural	Sing.	Plural
1.	ἀφίημι	ἀφίεμεν	[συνίημι]	[συνίεμεν]
2.	ἀφεῖς	ἀφίετε	[συνεῖς]	συνίετε
3.	ἀφίησι(ν)	ἀφίουσι(ν)	[συνίησι(ν)]	συνιᾶσι(ν)

N. 2. Sing. ἀφεῖς is from ἀφίω; from the same form occur 1 plu. ἀφίομεν, 3 plu. ἀφίουσι(ν) and συνίουσι(ν).

Subjunctive—

1.	[ἀφιῶ]	[ἀφιῶμεν]	[συνιῶ]	[συνιῶμεν]
2.	[ἀφιῇς]	ἀφιῆτε	[συνιῇς]	[συνιῆτε]
3.	ἀφιῇ	[ἀφιῶσι(ν)]	[συνιῇ]	συνιῶσι(ν)

Optative—
No forms occur in N. T.

Imperative—

2.	[ἀφίει]	ἀφίετε	[συνίει]	[συνίετε]
3.	ἀφιέτω	[ἀφιέτωσαν]	[συνιέτω]	[συνιέτωσαν]

Infinitive—

ἀφιέναι   συνιέναι

Participle—

[ἀφιείς, –εῖσα, –έν]   συνιείς and συνίων

Imperfect Indicative

The only form found in the N. T. is 3 sing. ἤφιεν as if from ἀφίω.

Middle and Passive Voices

Indicative—

	Sing.	Plural	
1.	[ἀφίεμαι]	[ἀφιέμεθα]	No forms from
2.	[ἀφίεσαι]	[ἀφίεσθε]	συνίεμαι occur in the N. T.
3.	ἀφίεται	ἀφίενται	
		and ἀφίονται	

Subjunctive—

No forms occur in N. T.

Optative—

No forms occur in N. T.

Imperative—

No forms occur in N. T.

Infinitive—

Not found in N. T.

Participle—

From καθίημι occurs καθιέμενος.

Imperfect Indicative

No forms occur in the N. T.

261. Conjugation of φημί, εἰμί, and εἶμι. Stems φη/α; ἐσ; and εἰ/ἰ.

Present

Active Voice

Indicative—

	Sing.	Plural	Sing.	Plural	Sing.	Plural
1.	φημί	[φαμέν]	εἰμί	ἐσμέν	[εἶμι]	[ἴμεν]
2.	[φής]	[φατέ]	εἶ	ἐστέ	[εἶ]	[ἴτε]
3.	φησί	φασί	ἐστί(ν)	εἰσί(ν)	[εἶσι]	ἴασι(ν)

Subjunctive—

	Sing.	Plural	Sing.	Plural	Sing.	Plural
1.	[φῶ]	[φῶμεν]	ὦ	ὦμεν	[ἴω]	[ἴωμεν]
2.	[φῇς[	[φῆτε]	ᾖς	ἦτε	[ἴῃς]	[ἴητε]
3.	[φῇ]	[φῶσι]	ᾖ	ὦσι	[ἴῃ]	[ἴωσι]

Optative

	Sing.	Plural
1.	[εἴην]	[εἴημεν]
2.	[εἴης]	[εἴητε]
3.	εἴη	[εἴησαν]

Imperative—

	Sing.	Plural	Sing.	Plural
2.	ἴσθι	[ἔστε]	ἴθι	[ἴτε]
3.	ἔστω, ἤτω	ἔστωσαν	[ἴτω]	[ἴτωσαν]

Infinitive—

[φάναι]   εἶναι   [ἰέναι]

Participle—

ὤν, οὖσα, ὄν

Imperfect

1.	[ἔφην]	[ἔφαμεν]	[ἦν], ἤμην	ἦμεν, ἤμεθα	[ᾖειν]	
2.	[ἔφης]	[ἔφατε]	ἦς, ἦσθα	ἦτε	[ᾖεις]	
3.	ἔφη	[ἔφασαν]	ἦν	ἦσαν	ᾖει	ᾖεσαν

262. Conjugation of κάθημαι and κεῖμαι. Stems ἦσ; and κει.

Present
Middle Voice

Indicative—

	Sing.	Plural	Sing.	Plural
1.	κάθημαι	[καθήμεθα]	κεῖμαι	κείμεθα
2.	κάθῃ	[κάθησθε]	[κεῖσαι]	[κεῖσθε]
3.	κάθηται	κάθηνται	κεῖται	κεῖνται

Subjunctive—

1.	[καθῶμαι]	[καθώμεθα]
2.	[καθῇ]	[καθῆσθε]
3.	[καθῆται]	[καθῶνται]

Optative—
No form found in the N. T.

Imperative—

2.	[κάθησο], κάθου	[κάθησθε]	[κεῖσο]	[κεῖσθε]
3.	καθήσθω	[καθήσθωσαν]	[κείσθω]	[κείσθωσαν]

Infinitive—

        καθῆσθαι   κεῖσθαι

Participle—

        καθήμενος   κείμενος

Imperfect Indicative

1.	[ἐκαθήμην]	[ἐκαθήμεθα]	[ἐκείμην]	[ἐκείμεθα}
2.	[ἐκάθησο]	[ἐκάθησθε]	[ἔκεισο]	[ἔκεισθε]
3.	ἐκάθητο	ἐκάθηντο	ἔκειτο	ἔκειντο

263.   Present (Continued).

B.   Thematic

(a).   Uncontracted Vowel Stems and Consonant Stems. Pres. Stem λυο/ε.

Active Voice

	Sing.	Plural

Indicative—

	Sing.	Plural
1.	λύω	λύομεν
2.	λύεις	λύετε
3.	λύει	λύουσι(ν)

Subjunctive—

	Sing.	Plural
1.	λύω	λύωμεν
2.	λύῃς	λύητε
3.	λύῃ	λύωσι(ν)

Optative—

	Sing.	Plural
1.	[λύοιμι]	[λύοιμεν]
2.	[λύοις]	λύοιτε
3.	λύοι	λύοιεν

Imperative—

	Sing.	Plural
2.	λῦε	λύετε
3.	λυέτω	λυέτωσαν

Infinitive—

λύειν

Participle—

λύων, −ουσα, −ον

Imperfect Active

	Sing.	Plural
1.	ἔλυον	ἐλύομεν
2.	ἔλυες	ἐλύετε
3.	ἔλυε(ν)	ἔλυον

Middle and Passive Voices

	Sing.	Plural

Indicative—

1.	λύομαι	λυόμεθα
2.	λύῃ	λύεσθε
3.	λύεται	λύονται

Subjunctive—

1.	λύωμαι	λυώμεθα
2.	λύῃ	λύησθε
3.	λύηται	λύωνται

Optative—

1.	[λυοίμην]	[λυοίμεθα]
2.	[λύοιο]	[λύοισθε]
3.	λύοιτο	[λύοιντο]

Imperative—

2.	λύου	λύεσθε
3.	λυέσθω	λυέσθωσαν

Infinitive—

λύεσθαι

Participle—

λυόμενος, —η, —ον

Imperfect, Middle and Passive

1.	ἐλυόμην	ἐλυόμεθα
2.	ἐλύου	ἐλύεσθε
3.	ἐλύετο	ἐλύοντο

264.   (b)   Contracted Vowel Stems.

Pres. Stems.   τιμαο/ε, ποιεο/ε, πληροο/ε.

Active Voice
Indicative—

S. 1.	τιμῶ	ποιῶ	πληρῶ
2.	τιμᾷς	ποιεῖς	πληροῖς
3.	τιμᾷ	ποιεῖ	πληροῖ
P. 1.	τιμῶμεν	ποιοῦμεν	πληροῦμεν
2.	τιμᾶτε	ποιεῖτε	πληροῦτε
3.	τιμῶσι(ν)	ποιοῦσι(ν)	πληροῦσι(ν)

Subjunctive—

S. 1.	τιμῶ	ποιῶ	[πληρῶ]
2.	τιμᾷς	ποιῇς	[πληροῖς]
3.	τιμᾷ	ποιῇ	[πληροῖ]
P. 1.	τιμῶμεν	ποιῶμεν	[πληρῶμεν]
2.	τιμᾶτε	ποιῆτε	[πληροῦτε]
3.	τιμῶσι(ν)	ποιῶσι(ν)	[πληροῦσι(ν)]

Optative—

No form of the pres. act. opt. of [any regular contract verb appears in N. T.

Imperative—

S. 2.	τίμα	ποίει	πλήρου
3.	τιμάτω	ποιείτω	πληρούτω
P. 2.	τιμᾶτε	ποιεῖτε	πληροῦτε
3.	τιμάτωσαν	ποιείτωσαν	πληρούτωσαν

Infinitive—

τιμᾶν	ποιεῖν	πληροῦν

Participle—

   τιμῶν, –ῶσα, –ῶν   ποιῶν, –οῦσα, –οῦν πληρῶν, –οῦσα, –οῦν

Imperfect Active

S. 1.	ἐτίμων	ἐποίουν	ἐπλήρουν
2.	ἐτίμας	ἐποίεις	ἐπλήρους
3.	ἐτίμα	ἐποίει	ἐπλήρου
P. 1.	ἐτιμῶμεν	ἐποιοῦμεν	ἐπληροῦμεν
2.	ἐτιμᾶτε	ἐποιεῖτε	ἐπληροῦτε
3.	ἐτίμων	ἐποίουν	ἐπλήρουν

Middle and Passive Voices

Indicative—

S. 1.	τιμῶμαι	ποιοῦμαι	πληροῦμαι
2.	τιμᾶσαι	ποιῇ	πληροῖ
3.	τιμᾶται	ποιεῖται	πληροῦται
P. 1.	τιμώμεθα	ποιούμεθα	πληρούμεθα
2.	τιμᾶσθε	ποιεῖσθε	πληροῦσθε
3.	τιμῶνται	ποιοῦνται	πληροῦνται

Subjunctive—

S. 1.	τιμῶμαι	ποιῶμαι	πληρῶμαι
2.	[τιμᾷ]	[ποιῇ]	[πληροῖ]
3.	τιμᾶται	ποιῆται	πληρῶται
P. 1.	τιμώμεθα	ποιώμεθα	[πληρώμεθα]
2.	τιμᾶσθε	ποιῆσθε	[πληρῶσθε]
3.	τιμῶνται	ποιῶνται	[πληρῶνται]

It is probable that the plural of όω verbs in the pres. midd. and pass. subj. was the same in form as indicative.

Optative—

No optative form of contract verbs appears in N. T.

Imperative—

S. 2.	τιμῶ	ποιοῦ	πληροῦ
3.	τιμάσθω	ποιείσθω	πληρούσθω
P. 2.	τιμᾶσθε	ποιεῖσθε	πληροῦσθε
3.	τιμάσθωσαν	ποιείσθωσαν	πληρούσθωσαν

Infinitive—

| | τιμᾶσθαι | ποιεῖσθαι | πληροῦσθαι |

Participle—

τιμώμενος, —η, —ον. ποιούμενος, —η, —ον. πληρούμενος, —η, —ον.

Imperfect Middle and Passive.

S. 1.	ἐτιμώμην	ἐποιούμην	ἐπληρούμην
2.	ἐτιμῶ	ἐποιοῦ	ἐπληροῦ
3.	ἐτιμᾶτο	ἐποιεῖτο	ἐπληροῦτο
P. 1.	ἐτιμώμεθα	ἐποιούμεθα	ἐπληρούμεθα
2.	ἐτιμᾶσθε	ἐποιεῖσθε	ἐπληροῦσθε
3.	ἐτιμῶντο	ἐποιοῦντο	ἐπληροῦντο

265. (c) Conjugation of ζήω and χρήομαι.

Pres. Stem ζηο/ε; χρηο/ε.

Present

	Active Voice		Middle and Passive Voice	
	Sing.	Plural	Sing.	Plural

Indicative—

1.	ζῶ	ζῶμεν	[χρῶμαι]	χρώμεθα.
2.	ζῇς	ζῆτε	[χρᾶσαι]	[χρᾶσθε]
3.	ζῇ	ζῶσι(ν)	[χρᾶται]	χρῶνται

Subjunctive—

1.	[ζῶ]	ζῶμεν	[χρῶμαι]	[χρώμεθα]
2.	[ζῇς]	[ζῆτε]	[χρῇ]	[χρῆσθε]
3.	[ζῇ]	ζῶσι(ν)	χρῆται	[χρῶνται]

Optative—

No form of pres. opt. of these verbs occurs in N. T.

Imperative—

2.	[ζῇ, ζῆθι]	[ζῆτε]	χρῶ	[χρᾶσθε]
3.	[ζήτω]	[ζήτωσαν]	[χράσθω]	[χράσθωσαν]

Infinitive—

ζῆν (ζῆν)   [χρᾶσθαι, χρῆσθαι]

Participle—

ζῶν, –ῶσα, –ῶν χρώμενος, –η, –ον

Imperfect Indicative

1.	ἔζων, ἔζην	[ἐζῶμεν]	[ἐχρώμην]	[ἐχρώμεθα]
2.	[ἔζης]	ἐζῆτε	[ἐχρῶ]	[ἐχρᾶσθε or ἐχρῆσθε.]
3.	[ἔζη]	[ἔζων]	[ἐχρᾶτο or ἐχρῆτο]	ἐχρῶντο

266.   (d)   Conjugation of πλέω and δέομαι (*to beg*).
Pres. Stem. πλεϝο/ε; δεϝο/ε.

Present

	Active Voice		Middle and Passive Voice	
	Sing.	Plural	Sing.	Plural

Indicative—

1.	[πλέω]	[πλέομεν]	δέομαι	δεόμεθα
2.	[πλεῖς]	[πλεῖτε]	[δέῃ]	[δεῖσθε]
3.	πλεῖ	[πλέουσι(ν)]	δεῖται	[δέονται]

Subjunctive—

1.	[πλέω]	[πλέωμεν]	‖[δέωμαι]‖	[δεώμεθα]
2.	[πλέῃς]	[πλέητε]	‖[δέῃ]‖	‖[δέησθε]‖
3.	πλέῃ	[πλέωσι(ν)]	‖[δέηται]‖	‖[δέωνται]‖

Optative—

No form of the optative of these verbs occurs in N. T.

Imperative—

No form of the imperative occurs in the N. T.

Infinitive—

πλεῖν   [δεῖσθαι]

Participle—

πλέων, —ουσα, —ον   δεόμενος, —η, —ον

Imperfect Indicative

	Active Voice		Middle and Passive Voice	
	Sing.	Plural	Sing.	Plural
1.	[ἔπλεον]	ἐπλέομεν	[ἐδεόμην]	[ἐδεόμεθα]
2.	[ἔπλεις]	[ἐπλεῖτε]	[ἐδέου]	[ἐδεῖσθε]
3.	ἔπλει	ἔπλεον	ἐδεῖτο	[ἐδέοντο]

267. The Future.

A. Active Voice

Indicative—

	Sing.	Plural	Sing.	Plural
1.	λύσω	λύσομεν	κρινῶ	κρινοῦμεν
2.	λύσεις	λύσετε	κρινεῖς	κρινεῖται
3.	λύσει	λύσουσι(ν)	κρινεῖ	κρινοῦσι(ν)

Optative—

Not found in the N. T.

Infinitive—

λύσειν   [κρινεῖν]

Participle—

λύσων, –ουσα –ον   κρινῶν, [–οῦσα], [–οῦν]

B. Middle Voice

Indicative

1.	λύσομαι	λυσόμεθα	[κρινοῦμαι]	[κρινούμεθα]
2.	λύσῃ	λύσεσθε	[κρινῇ]	κρινεῖσθε
3.	λύσεται	λύσονται	κρινεῖται	κρινοῦνται

Optative—

Not found in the N. T.

Infinitive—
λύσεσθαι   [κρινεῖσθαι]

Participle—
λυσόμενος, —η, —ον   [κρινούμενος]

C. Passive Voice

The First or Weak and the Second or Strong Future Passive:
λυθησο/ε, τραπησο/ε (pres. τρέπω).

	Sing.	Plural	Sing.	Plural
Indicative—				
1.	λυθήσομαι	λυθησόμεθα	τραπήσομαι	τραπησόμεθα
2.	λυθήσῃ	λυθήσεσθε	τραπήσῃ	τραπήσεσθε
3.	λυθήσεται	λυθήσονται	τραπήσεται	τραπήσονται

Optative—
Not found in the N. T.

Infinitive—
[λυθήσεσθαι]   [τραπήσεσθαι]

Participle—
λυθησόμενος   τραπησόμενος

D. The Future of εἰμί.

Indicative—

	Sing.	Plural
1.	ἔσομαι	ἐσόμεθα
2.	ἔσῃ	ἔσεσθε
3.	ἔσται	ἔσονται

Optative—
Not found in the N. T.

Infinitive—
ἔσεσθαι

Participle—
ἐσόμενος, —η, —ον

268.   *A.*   The Strong or Second Perfect.

Active Voice

Indicative—

	Sing.	Plural	Sing.	Plural
1.	γέγονα	γεγόναμεν	οἶδα	οἴδαμεν
2.	γέγονας	γεγόνατε	οἶδας	οἴδατε
3.	γέγονε(ν)	γεγόνασι(ν),–αν	οἶδε(ν)	οἴδασι(ν), ἴσασι(ν)

Subjunctive—

1.	γεγονώς	ὦ γεγονότες ὦμεν	εἰδῶ	εἰδῶμεν
2.	etc.	etc.	εἰδῇς	εἰδῆτε
3.			εἰδῇ	[εἰδῶσι(ν)]

Optative—
No forms occur in the N. T.

Imperative—

2.	Not found in N. T.	[ἴσθι]	ἴστε
3.		[ἴστω]	[ἴστωσαν]

Infinitive—

γεγονέναι   εἰδέναι

The old strong perf. infinitive ἑστάναι occurs three times in the N. T. —present ἵστημι.

Participle—

γεγονώς, –υῖα, –ός   εἰδώς, –υῖα, –ός

From ἵστημι is found old strong part. ἑστώς, –ῶσα, –ός (See page 99).

Pluperfect Indicative

1.	[(ἐ)γεγόνειν]	[(ἐ)γεγόνειμεν]	ᾔδειν	[ᾔδειμεν]
2.	[(ἐ)γεγόνεις]	[(ἐ)γεγόνειτε]	ᾔδεις	ᾔδειτε
3.	(ἐ)γεγόνει	(ἐ)γεγόνεισαν	ᾔδει	ᾔδεισαν

B.   The κ– Perfect (also called the First or Weak Perfect).

Active Voice

Indicative—

	Sing.	Plural	Sing.	Plural
1.	λέλυκα	λελύκαμεν	ἔσταλκα	ἐστάλκαμεν
2.	λέλυκας	λελύκατε	ἔσταλκας	ἐστάλκατε
3.	λέλυκε(ν)	λελύκασι(ν)	ἔσταλκε(ν)	ἐστάλκασι(ν)

In the 3 plu. occurs the form λέλυκαν.

Subjunctive—

1.	λελυκώς ὦ	λελυκότες ὦμεν
	etc.	etc.

Subjunctive made with participle and subj. of εἰμί.

Optative—
No forms occur in the N. T.

Imperative—
No forms occur in the N. T.

Infinitive—

    λελυκέναι   ἐσταλκέναι

Participle—

    λελυκώς, –υῖα, –ός   ἐσταλκώς, –υῖα, –ός

Pluperfect Indicative

1.	[(ἐ)λελύκειν]	[(ἐ)λελύκειμεν]	[ἐστάλκειν]	[ἐστάλκειμεν]
2.	[(ἐ)λελύκεις]	(ἐ) λελύκειτε	[ἐστάλκεις]	ἐστάλκειτε
3.	(ἐ)λελύκει	(ἐ)λελύκεισαν	ἐστάλκει	ἐστάλκεισαν

269. The Perfect Middle and Passive Voices.

	(a) Vowel Stems	(b) Labial Stems	(c) Palatal Stems	(d) Dental Stems
	λελυ–	τετριβ–	τεταγ–	πεπειθ–

Indicative—

S. 1	λέλυμαι	[τέτριμμαι]	[τέταγμαι]	πέπεισμαι
2.	λέλυσαι	[τέτριψαι]	[τέταξαι]	[πέπεισαι]
3.	λέλυται	τέτριπται	τέτακται	πέπεισται

P. 1.	λελύμεθα	[τετρίμμεθα]	[τετάγμεθα]	πεπείσμεθα
2.	λέλυσθε	[τέτριφθε]	[τέταχθε]	[πέπεισθε]
3.	λέλυνται	τετριμμένοι	τεταγμένοι	πεπεισμένοι
		εἰσί(ν)	εἰσί(ν)	εἰσί(ν)

Subjunctive—

The subjunctive occurs only in the periphrastic form.

S. 1.	λελυμένος ὦ	τετριμμένος ὦ	τεταγμένος ὦ	πεπεισμένος ὦ
2.	λελυμένος ᾖς	etc.	etc.	etc.
3.	λελυμένος ᾖ			
P. 1.	λελυμένοι ὦμεν	etc.	etc.	etc.
2.	λελυμένοι ἦτε			
3.	λελυμένοι ὦσι(ν)			

Optative—

No forms occurs in the the N. T.

Imperative—

S. 2.	λέλυσο	No form of the imperative of mute (stop)
3.	[λελύσθω]	stems occurs in the N. T.
P. 2.	λέλυσθε	
3.	[λελύσθωσαν]	

Infinitive—

λελύσθαι	[τετρίφθαι]	[τετάχθαι]	[πεπεῖσθαι]

Participle—

λελυμένος, –η, –ον   τετριμμένος, –η, ον   τεταγμένος, –η, –ον
πεπεισμένος, –η, –ον.

Pluperfect Indicative

S. 1.	[(ἐ)λελύμην]	[(ἐ)τετρίμμην]	[(ἐ)τετάγμην]	[(ἐ)πεπείσμην]
2.	[(ἐ)λέλυσο]	[(ἐ)τέτριψο]	[(ἐ)τέταξο]	[(ἐ)πέπεισο]
3.	(ἐ)λέλυτο	(ἐ)τέτριπτο	[(ἐ)τέτακτο]	[(ἐ)πέπειστο]
P. 1.	[(ἐ)λελύμεθα]	[(ἐ)τετρίμμεθα]	[(ἐ)τετάγμεθα]	[(ἐ)πεπείσμεθα]
2.	[(ἐ)λέλυσθε]	[(ἐ)τέτριφθε]	[(ἐ)τέταχθε]	[(ἐ)πέπεισθε]
3.	(ἐ)λέλυντο	[τετριμμένοι ἦσαν]	[τεταγμένοι ἦσαν]	[πεπεισμένοι ἦσαν]

The periphrastic 3 plu. occurs in vowel stems, as ἦσαν βεβαρημένοι (Matt. 26:43).

<table>
<tr><td>(e) Liquid Stems</td><td>(f) Nasal Stems</td></tr>
<tr><td>ἐσταλ– (pres. στέλλω)</td><td>ἐξηραν– (pres ξηραίνω)</td></tr>
</table>

Indicative—

	Sing.	Plural	Sing.	Plural
1.	[ἔσταλμαι]	[ἐστάλμεθα]	[ἐξήραμμαι]	[ἐξηράμμεθα]
2.	[ἔσταλσαι]	[ἔσταλθε]	[ἐξήρανσαι]	[ἐξήρανθε]
3.	ἔσταλται	ἐσταλμένοι εἰσί(ν)	ἐξήρανται	[ἐξηραμμένοι] εἰσί(ν)

Subjunctive—
Periphrastic as in (a).

Optative—
No forms occur in N. T.

Imperative—
No imperative of these stems occurs in the N. T.

Infinitive—
[ἐστάλθαι]   [ἐξηράνθαι]

Participle—
ἐσταλμένος, –η, –ον   ἐξηραμμένος, –η, –ον

Pluperfect Indicative
No form of these stems occurs in the N. T.

270. The Future Perfect.

Active Voice
No future perfect active forms occur in the N. T. except εἰδήσουσιν (Heb. 8:11), the future of οἶδα, and the periphrastic form ἔσομαι πεποιθώς (Heb. 2:13).

Passive Voice
Except for κεκράξονται (Luke 19:40) in some MSS., the future perfect passive occurs in the N. T. only in the periphrastic

form (the perf. pass. participle and the future indicative of εἰμί), as ἔσται δεδεμένον (Matt. 16:19), ἔσονται διαμεμερισμένοι (Luke 12:52).

The normal form for vowel verbs was:

Indicative—

	Sing.	Plural
1.	[λελύσομαι]	[λελυσόμεθα]
2.	[λελύσῃ]	[λελύσεσθε]
3.	[λελύσεται]	|λελύσονται|

271. Perfect stems which end in a Mute (§35), liquid, or nasal suffer certain phonological changes in the perfect and pluperfect middle (passive) before the personal endings.

a. Mute (or Stop) Stems:

(1) A labial mute (πβφ) before μ becomes μ; thus τετριβμαι becomes τέτριμμαι.

(2) A palatal mute (κχ) before γ becomes γ, γ remains γ; thus δεδιωκμαι becomes δεδίωγμαι; γ remains γ as in τέταγμαι (stem τεταγ-).

(3) A lingual mute (τδθ) before μ by analogy becomes σ; thus πεπειθμαι becomes πέπεισμαι.

(4) A mute of the stem before a mute of the personal ending becomes coordinate (§35, b.), thus βτ > πτ, φτ > πτ; γτ > κτ, χτ > κτ, πθ > φθ; βθ > φθ, κθ > χθ; γθ > χθ. Thus τετριβται becomes τέτριπται; τεταγται becomes τέτακται; τετριβφε becomes τέτριφθε; τεταγθε becomes τέταχθε.

(5) A labial mute +σ = ψ; thus τετριβσαι becomes τέτριψαι.

(6) A palatal mute + σ = ξ; thus τεταγσαι becomes τέταξαι.

(7) A lingual mute +σ is assimilated (σσ) and one σ is dropped; thus πεπειθσαι becomes πεπεισσαι, then πέπεισαι.

(8) A lingual mute before another lingual mute becomes σ; thus πεπειθται becomes πέπεισται.

(9) σ between two consonants is dropped; thus ἐσταλ(σ)θε becomes ἔσταλθε.

b. Liquid Stems are conjugated like ἔσταλμαι. See (9) above.

c. Nasal Stems. ν before μ is assimilated (μμ); thus ἐξήρανμαι becomes ἐξήραμμαι.

d. Some stems that originally ended in σ are conjugated like πέπεισμαι after the analogy of endings like –σται; thus τετέλεσμαι from τελέω (stem τελεσγ–).

272. Accent of Verb.

According to the so-called trisyllabic law finite verb forms (simple or compound) throw the accent as far back as the quantity of the final syllable permits: as βασιλεύω, βασιλεύετε, ἐβασιλευόμην, ἄπειμι.

A. There are exceptions to this rule:

a. Infinitives and participles, being substantives or adjectives, do not come under this rule; they are accented as substantives or adjectives.

(1) All infinitives in –ναι accent the penult.

(2) The infinitive of contract verbs and the infinitive of the strong aorist active in –ειν have the circumflex accent on the ultima; as φιλεῖν, λιπεῖν.

b. Imperatives as εἰπέ, εἰπόν, λαβέ, λαβοῦ preserve the original accent of the verb when it began a sentence. But W H have ἴδε and λάβε.

c. In compound verbs the accent cannot go behind the augment or reduplication, as εἰσῆλθον.

d. Contract verbs are only apparent exceptions.

B. In the optative final –αι and –οι are regarded as long, elsewhere as short. Note the accent of the following forms (of first aorist):

βασιλεῦσαι, aor. act. inf.; βασιλεύσαι, aor. act. opt., 3 sing.; βασίλευσαι, aor. mid. imperative, 2 sing.

273. The augment (ἐ) is commonly treated as of two kinds, the syllabic and the temporal. It probably was originally a temporal adverb (locative case) denoting past time, and came to be used with the imperfect, aorist, and pluperfect

indicative to express the past tense, because these verb forms (although with secondary endings) were felt to have no inherent characteristic which indicated definitely past time. It is found in Sanskrit (in the form *a*), Iranian, Armenian, and Greek. In the ethnic period when the time of the action of the verb was clearly indicated by the context the augment was not used. Then after the analogy of the augmented forms the unaugmented forms acquired a meaning of past time that was independent of context.

274. A. When the augment (ἐ) is prefixed to verbs beginning with a consonant it is called the *syllabic* augment. Thus ἔβαλλον, ἔλυσα, ἐλελύκει.

N. 1. There seems to have been a form ἠ besides ἐ, in the primitive parent language; as ᾔδειν (Hom. ἠ–ειδη). By some scholars is so explained the ἠ in ἠβουλόμην and ἤθελον; but this ἠ is probably due to the analogy of η in ἤθελον from ἐθέλω; so also ἠ in ἠδυνήθην.

N. 2. The augment in such forms as ἑώρων (ὁράω), ἀνέῳξα (ἀνοίγω) is not satisfactorily explained. It may have been by quantitative metathesis of the augment ἠ and the initial vowel of the verb, as ἠο>ἐω.

N. 3. Some verbs beginning with a vowel have the syllabic augment because they formerly began with σ, ϝ, or y; as ἀνέῳξα (pres. ἀνοίγω from ἀν-ϝοιγνυμι); εἴασα (pres. ἐάω from σεϝαω); εἶχον (pres. ἔχω from σεχω). When ε + ε resulted, contraction (ει) regularly followed.

N. 4. The ρρ sometimes found after the augment is due to the assimilation of ϝ to ρ (ϝρ>ρρ), as ἔρρηξεν.

B. When the initial vowel of a verb beginning with a vowel is lengthened it is called *temporal* augment. Thus ἦγον (ἄγω). This is probably due to analogy of verbs that

began with ε (or ο) and then extended to all verbs beginning
with a vowel.

α becomes η		αι becomes ῃ	
ε	" η	αυ	" ηυ
ι	" ῑ	ει	" ῃ
ο	" ω	ευ	" ηυ
υ.	" ῡ	οι	" ῳ
ᾳ	" ῃ		

N. But diphthongs are frequently unaugmented.

275. In the pluperfect the augment is usually dropped, as
τεθεμελίωτο (Matt. 7:25). The syllabic augment is absent in
προορώμην (Acts 2:25). The temporal augment is sometimes
absent, as in ἀφέθησαν (Rom. 4:7).

276. In verbs compounded with a preposition the augment
stands between the compound parts, as ἀπέβαλλον (ἀποβάλλω). In
a few verbs the compound form came to be considered as a simple
verb and was augmented before the preposition, as ἐκάθευδον.

277. Verbs derived from compound nouns receive the augment as simple verbs, as ἐθηριομάχησα (I Cor. 15:32).

278. Sometimes double augment is found, as ἀπεκατεστάθη
(Mk. 3:5); and triple aug. in ἠνεῴχθησαν (Matt. 9:30).

279. *Reduplication* is the repetition of the initial sound of
a word. It was originally used to express iterative or intensive action. Then later it came to be used as a tense-forming
element (perfect). There were originally three types of
reduplication: (1) with ι in the reduplicated syllable; (2) with
ε in the reduplicated syllable; (3) the whole syllable reduplicated. The tense-systems that show reduplication are the
present, aorist, and perfect.

280. a. A few verbs have in the present system reduplication of type (1) in §279, made by prefixing the initial consonant + ι. Thus γίνομαι (γίγνομαι); γινώσκω (γιγνώσκω); δίδωμι;
τίθημι (θιθημι); ἵστημι (σιστημι); πίπτω, etc.

N. Probably the reduplication in διδάσκω belongs to the verb-stem.

b. Of type (3) there are γογγύζω, ἀραρίσκω, etc.

281. A few verbs have reduplication in the aorist (second) system, some of type (2) and some of type (3) in §279.

a. Type (2): reduplication made by prefixing the initial consonant +ε; as πέπιθον (pres. πείθω). This form occurs in Homer but not in the N. T.

b. Type (3): the whole syllable reduplicated when the word began with a vowel; as ἤγαγον (pres. ἄγω); ἤνεγκα and ἤνεγκον (stem ἐνεκ–).

282. Reduplication in the Perfect. The most common reduplication in Greek is that in the perfect tense, where it is not like augment, mode-sign or personal endings. It is an integral part of the tense in all modes, voices, and persons, until its disappearance in the later Greek. But originally there were some perfects without reduplication, a remnant of which is seen in οἶδα. Reduplication in the perfect system is the effort to express the idea of completion in the verb form.

283. Originally there were two types of reduplication in the perfect, types (2) and (3) in §279.

A. The oldest mode of reduplication [type (3)] consisted of the reduplication of the whole syllable; as ἐγρήγορα, ὄλωλα, etc.

a. In a few verbs which begin with α, ε, or ο reduplication of the whole syllable is made and α, ε, or ο of the verb-stem is lengthened, α and ε to η, and ο to ω. This is generally called "Attic" reduplication (yet Homer used it much more than did the Attic writers). Thus ἀκήκοα (pres. ἀκούω); ἐλήλυθα (stem ἐλυθ–); ὄλωλα (pres. ὄλλυμι).

B. The perfect generally had reduplication with ε in the reduplicated syllable.

a. When the verb-stem began with a single consonant, the reduplication consisted of the consonant + ε; as λέλοιπα (λείπω); βέβηκα (βαίνω). There is dissimilation of aspirates when the verb-stem began with a rough mute; as τέθεικα (stem θε); πέφευγα (pres. φεύγω).

b. When the verb-stem began with a mute and liquid or nasal, the reduplication consisted of the mute + ε; as γέγραφα (γράφω); τέθλιμμαι (with dissimilation of the aspirate), pres. θλίβω.

c. But when the verb-stem began with such combinations as γν–, βλ–, κτ–, πτ–, ζ–, ξ–, ψ–, and with other combinations than b (above), generally simple ε was prefixed for the reduplicated syllable; as ἔγνωκα (stem γνο); ἔσπαρμαι (σπείρω); ἔζωσμαι (ζώννυμι).

N. In these perfects it is probable that the form of reduplication is due to analogy of perfects like ἔσχηκα (ἔχω, from σεχω, see d below).

d. Verb-stems originally beginning with σ, ϝ, or ϝ + a consonant reduplicated regularly as in a above; but when the reduplicated consonant disappeared, only ε was left and it often contracted with the following vowel (initial vowel of the resultant stem); as ἔσχηκα; ἔοικα from ϝεϝοικα; ἔστηκα from σεστηκα; εἴρηκα from ϝεϝρηκα; εἴληφα from σεσληφα.

N. εἴληχα (λαγχάνω) and εἴλοχα (λέγω, collect) are due to analogy of εἴληφα in d above.

e. When the verb stem begins with ῥ, sometimes the ρ is (or is not) doubled and ε is prefixed to form the reduplicated syllable, as in d above; sometimes the reduplication is regularly made according to a above; as ἔρρωμαι (pres. ῥώννυμαι); ῥεράντισμαι (pres. ῥαντίζω); ἔριμμαι (ῥίπτω).

C. In verb-stems originally beginning with a vowel the ε would regularly contract with the vowel in the parent language. And through the analogy of some verbs in ἀ– and ὀ–, contracting to ἠ– and ὠ–, the vowel was lengthened, like the augment, as reduplication. Thus ἦγμαι (ἄγω); ἤγγελκα (ἀγγέλλω).

284. Double reduplication sometimes occurs, as ἀνεῳγμένη (in Rev.). Sometimes reduplication is absent εὐαρεστηκέναι (Heb. 11:5).

285.   As a rule with compound verbs (preposition + verb) in the N. T. reduplication comes between the preposition and the verb, as generally in the case of augment (which see).

286.   When the pluperfect has the augment, the augment is prefixed to the reduplicated syllable, as ἐλελύκει.

287.   The tense-suffixes, which are added to the verb-stem to form the various tense-stems, consist of the thematic vowel and one or more letters affixed directly to the verb-stem. But there are no tense-suffixes: (1) in the second aor. active and middle and second perfect and pluperfect of μι– verbs; and (2) in the perfect and pluperfect middle (and passive) of all verbs.

The tense-suffixes are:

a.   Present system, $-^o/_\epsilon$, $-y\,^o/_\epsilon$, $-\nu\,^o/_\epsilon$, $-a\nu\,^o/_\epsilon$, $-\nu a,$ $-\nu\nu,$ $-\tau\,^o/_\epsilon$, $-\sigma\kappa\,^o/_\epsilon$, $-\theta\,^o/_\epsilon$; or none, as in φαμέν.

b.   Future system, $-\sigma\,^o/_\epsilon$; (subj. of second aor. stem also used).

c.   First aorist system, $-\sigma a$ (a from vocalic μ).

d.   Second aorist system, $-^o/_\epsilon$ ($^o/_\epsilon$ was originally an integral part of stem); or none, as in ἔβην.

e.   First perfect system, $-\kappa a$ (pluperf. $-\kappa\eta$ from $-\kappa\epsilon a$; $-\kappa\epsilon\iota$ from $\kappa\epsilon\epsilon$; $-\kappa\epsilon$).

f.   Second perfect system, $-a$ (pluperf. $-\eta$; $-\epsilon\iota$; $-\epsilon$); or none, as in old second perf. [ἕσταμεν].

g.   Perfect middle system, none; future perf. $-\sigma\,^o/_\epsilon$.

h.   First passive system, $-\theta\eta$, $-\theta\epsilon$; fut. pass. $-\theta\eta\sigma\,^o/_\epsilon$.

i.   Second passive system, $-\eta$, $-\epsilon$; fut. pass. $-\eta\sigma\,^o/_\epsilon$.

N.   The $-a$ in the first and second perf. systems (e and f above) arose in the σ– aorist (c above) from vocalic μ = a of the personal ending, and then became extended by analogy to the perfect.

288.   The thematic (or variable) vowel $^o/_\epsilon$, originally an integral part of a verb-stem, is found at the end of the verb-

stems in the present, imperfect, second aorist act. and middle of ω– verbs, and in all futures and future perfects. In the indicative the thematic vowel appears as *o* before μ and ν (and in the optative of the tenses named), elsewhere as ε.

a. The lengthened thematic vowel ($^\omega/_\eta$) is found in the subjunctive of all verbs.

b. The mode-suffixes of the optative are –ι– or –ιη– (see §307).

289. The Personal Endings. To the tense-stems in the finite modes are attached certain endings called personal endings. Of the origin of these endings nothing is known with any degree of certainty. But it is generally assumed that they were partly or entirely of pronominal origin. These personal endings have two cross divisions: (1) the active and middle have a separate list, the passive having no endings of its own; (2) there is another cleavage on the line of primary and secondary tenses in the indicative, i. e. the unaugmented and the augmented tenses. The subjunctive mode falls in with the primary endings, and the optative uses the secondary endings (except 1 sing. in –μι). In many forms distinctive endings are preserved only in the μι– verbs.

290. Table of Personal Endings.

A. Active

		Indicative (Primary) and Subjunctive	Indicative (Secondary) and Optative
Sing.	1.	–ω or –μι	–ν, (–α from vocalic μ)
	2.	–s (for –σι), –θα (–σθα)	–s, –σθα
	3.	–σι (for –τι)	—— (–τ disappeared)
Plu.	1.	–μεν, (–μες)	–μεν
	2.	–τε,	–τε
	3.	–νσι (for –ντι)	–ν, –σαν

B. Middle

		Indicative (Primary) and Subjunctive	Indicative (Secondary) and Optative
Sing.	1.	$-\mu\alpha\iota$	$-\mu\eta\nu$
	2.	$-\sigma\alpha\iota$	$-\sigma o$
	3.	$-\tau\alpha\iota$	$-\tau o$
Plu.	1.	$-\mu\epsilon\theta\alpha$	$-\mu\epsilon\theta\alpha$
	2.	$-\sigma\theta\epsilon$	$-\sigma\theta\epsilon$
	3.	$-\nu\tau\alpha\iota$	$-\nu\tau o$

C. The imperative has no regular set of endings of its own. The imperative system was made up of (1) injunctive forms, (2) forms with the bare stem, and (3) compound forms:

Imperative

		Active	Middle
Sing.	2.	$—, -s, -\theta\iota$	$-\sigma o$
	3.	$-\tau\omega$	$-\sigma\theta\omega$
Plu.	2.	$-\tau\epsilon$	$-\sigma\theta\epsilon$
	3.	$-\nu\tau\omega\nu, -\tau\omega\sigma\alpha\nu$	$-\sigma\theta\omega\nu, -\sigma\theta\omega\sigma\alpha\nu$

291. Remarks on the Primary Endings of the Active (indicative and subjunctive):

a. 1 sing.— $-\omega$ is the primary termination of thematic stems. $-\mu\iota$ occurs in the pres. indicative of $\mu\iota-$ verbs. $-\alpha$ of the perfect indic. came from the $-\alpha$ of the $\sigma-$ aorist.

b. 2 sing.— $-\sigma\iota$ is only preserved in Homer. The form with $-s$, is really a secondary ending after analogy of forms like ἔφερες. $-\theta\alpha$ is an old perfect ending which spread to other tenses.

N. Sometimes $-\epsilon s$ instead of $-\alpha s$ is found in the perfect.

c. 3 sing.— $-\tau\iota$ occurs in $-\mu\iota$ verbs; $-\tau\iota$ became $-\sigma\iota$ in Attic, Ionic, and Doric. The form λύει was formed on the analogy of the 2 sing. λύ-εις (see b above).

d. 3 plu.— $\nu\tau$ was the original ending for thematic verbs (Doric φέροντι); in Attic it became $-\nu\sigma\iota$ as φέρουσι from φερονσι.

In some μι- verbs is found the analogical ending αντι– (from ατι from ντι). The ending –ατι from ντι (vocalic ν) was preserved in some Homeric perfects in the form of –ᾰσι which was later replaced by –ᾱσι from –αντι (from –ντι). For αν - in perfect see §292 N.

292. Secondary Endings of the Active (indicative and optative):

a. 1 sing.— –ν is for μ which was vocalic after a consonant and became α (so ἔλυσα from ἔλυσμ). [In the pluperf. –η is from εα (see §287e).]

In the opt. –ν is found when the mode-suffix is –ιη; elsewhere the opt. has the primary ending –μι.

b. 3 sing.—The secondary ending –τ regularly disappeared in primitive Greek.

c. 3 plu.— –ν is from –ντ (with τ dropped). –σαν came from such forms as aorist ἔλυσαν and ἦσαν; –ντ after consonants became –α (τ), then after analogy of such forms as ἔφερον was formed –αν which was attached to the σ– aorist and verbs in –σ–, then –σαν was taken as an ending. Analogically a later ending –οσαν was extracted and frequently used.

N. –αν is sometimes found in the 3 plu. of the perfect.

293. Primary and Secondary Endings of the Middle.

a. 1 sing.—The primary ending –μαι and the secondary ending –μην are not found in any of the other Indo-ger. languages.

b. 2 sing.—The original primary ending was –σαι, the σ of which regularly disappeared in early Greek when it was intervocalic; but σ was retained in perfects whose stem ended in a consonant (as γέγραψαι), and after the analogy of the perfects ending in consonants σ was early in Attic and Ionic restored in the present ind. of μι– verbs and to all other perfects. The form η– is the result of contraction from εαι after σ had dropped out; and η is written ει on Attic inscriptions from the fourth century B. C. onwards.

N.   Both δύνῃ and δύνασαι (δύναμαι) are found in the N. T.
On the other side occur φάγεσαι and πίεσαι in Luke 17:8; and
in some contract verbs –σαι appears as ὀδυνᾶσαι (Luke 16:25).

c.   2 sing.— –σο was the original secondary ending in
thematic verbs, and –θης in athematic verbs and was probably
preserved in the aor. passive, as in ἐδόθης.   But –σο was generalized.   In the imperfect of μι– verbs σ occurs and in all
pluperfects.   For the disappearance of σ elsewhere see b
above and §64b.

d.   2 plu.— –σθε was used for the primary and secondary
endings.   Its origin is unknown.   On the loss of σ in such
forms as ἔσταλθε see §63.

e.   3 plu.—The original primary endings were –νται after
vowels and –αται (vocalic ν =a) after consonants.   But after
about the beginning of the fourth century B. C. the perfects
in –αται and –ατο (see below) disappeared and their place was
taken by the periphrastic forms.

f.   3 plu.— –ντο after vowels and –ατο after consonants
were the secondary endings.   For the disappearance of –ατο
(a = vocalic ν) see e above.

294.   Remarks on the Endings of the Imperative.   An old
injunctive mode (in appearance consisting of unaugmented
indicative forms with secondary endings) is responsible for
more of the imperative forms than any other single source
(see §290 c).

A. Active

a.   2 sing.—An early imperative was just the athematic
present stem.   In forms like λέγε, λῦε, λάβε, it is the root plus
the thematic vowel (as an integral part of the stem).   –θι
(probably an old adverb) is used with athematic stems.   Forms
like σχές, δός, θές are probably old injunctive forms.   The
aorist form λῦσον may be injunctive or verbal substantive.

b.   3 sing.— –τω is probably the ablative of a demonstrative pronoun.

c. 3 plu.—The ending $-\nu\tau\omega\nu$ probably came from an old injunctive form $\phi\epsilon\rho o\nu$ $+\tau\omega$ $+\nu$ (plural ending) $= \phi\epsilon\rho o\nu\tau\omega\nu$. The ending $-\tau\omega\sigma\alpha\nu$ probably arose from a pluralizing of the singular by the addition of the plural ending $-\sigma\alpha\nu$.

B. Middle

a. 2 sing.— $-\sigma o$ probably came from an old injunctive. σ has been restored in the present of $\mu\iota-$ verbs. The aorist form $\lambda\hat{v}\sigma\alpha\iota$ is probably the $\sigma-$ aorist act. infinitive used as imperative.

b. 3 plu.—The endings $-\sigma\theta\omega\nu$ and $-\sigma\theta\omega\sigma\alpha\nu$ were probably due to a development like that of the active (third plu.).

295. The Endings of the Pluperfect Active. The usual mode of forming the pluperfect active began originally with stems ending in $-\epsilon$. To the stem in ϵ were added the singular endings of the perfect $-a$, $-as$, $-\epsilon$, which in Attic contracted with ϵ of the stem into $-\eta$, $-\eta s$, $-\epsilon\iota$; and in the plural the personal endings were added directly to the stem in ϵ, as $-\epsilon\mu\epsilon\nu$, $-\epsilon\tau\epsilon$, $-\epsilon\sigma\alpha\nu$. The ϵ (originally of the stem) became extended to other verbs. Later the endings $-\epsilon\iota\nu$ and $-\epsilon\iota s$ were formed with $\epsilon\iota$ from the third person singular, then $\epsilon\iota$ was extended to the plural.

296. Endings of the Infinitive.

a. Dative case-forms:

(1) $-\nu\alpha\iota$, in present act. and the second perfect active, of $\mu\iota-$ verbs, and in the first and second aorist active.

(2) $-\epsilon\nu\alpha\iota$, in the perfect active, and in $\delta o\hat{v}\nu\alpha\iota$.

(3) $-\alpha\iota$ (probably from an old noun of action in $-\sigma$), in the $\sigma-$ aorist active.

(4) $-\sigma\theta\alpha\iota$ (origin uncertain), in other tenses of middle (passive) not mentioned above and below in *b*.

b. Locative case-forms:

(1) $-\epsilon\nu$, in the present and second aorist active of $\omega-$ verbs, and all active futures.

(2) $[-\mu\epsilon\nu]$, obsolete in the $\kappa o\iota\nu\dot{\eta}$.

297.   Endings of the Participle.

a.   –ντ– is the formative element of all active participles (except the perfect) and of the passive participles of the first and second aorist. The second aor. pass. is really active in form, and the first pass. part. was formed on analogy of the second aor. part.

b.   For the stem of the perfect active participle see §215.

c.   –μενο– is the formative element in all middle and passive (except the aorist) participles.

298.   In the tense-stems many verbs still show vowel-gradation (see §§44-47), generally two strong grades and a weak grade.   The most important grades are:

	Strong	Strong	Weak
a.	ε	ο	α
	τρέπω	[τέτροφα]	ἐτράπην
b.	ει	οι	ι
	λείπω	λέλοιπα	ἔλιπον
	πείθω	πέποιθα	
c.	ευ	ου	υ
	φεύγω		ἐφυγον
	[ἐλευθ–]	[ἐλήλουθα]	[ἤλυθον]

299.   Verb-stems ending in a short vowel (α, ε, ο) generally lengthen the vowel before the tense-suffix (except in the present system).   Here α (except after ε, ι, and ρ) becomes ·η.   Thus:

τιμάω, τιμήσω, ἐτίμησα, etc.

ἐάω, ἐάσω, εἴασα, etc.

φιλέω, φιλήσω, ἐφίλησα, etc.

δηλόω, δηλώσω, ἐδήλωσα, etc.

N.   Many verbs have a short vowel as τελέω, τελέσω, ἐτέλεσα, because the stem originally ended in σ.

300.   a.   What may appear to be *metathesis* in some verbs is probably due to vowel-gradation, as θνῆσκω, ἔθανον,

b.   Also what is sometimes called *syncope* in some verbs is a form of vowel-gradation, as πίπτω (for πιπετω).

The Tenses [1]

301. *The Aorist*. The New Testament preserves the original second aorist of the μι form (non-thematic) which is really the original verb-form, as ἔστην, ἔγνων. The second aorist form (thematic) with the variable vowel ⁰/ε appears also as ἔλιπον. The reduplicated aorist also survives as ἤγαγον (Luke 22:54). There is even a reduplicated first aorist, ἐκέκραξα (Acts 24:21). The first aorist forms with ᵃ/ε (with or without σ) are frequent as ἔλεξα, ἔκρινα. To obtain the root, ᵃ/ε, ⁰/ε, or σ ᵃ/ε must be dropped. One of the peculiarities of the New Testament usage is the increased use of ᵃ/ε even with second aorist stems. This usage existed already in the case of εἶπα, ἤνεγκα, ἔπεσα along with εἶπον, ἤνεγκον, ἔπεσον. In the New Testament, as in the papyri, it is extended greatly to such forms as ἦλθαν, εἶδαν, ἀνεῦραν, ἀνεῖλαν. In fact, the modern Greek uses only some dozen of the old second aorists. Everywhere else the later first aorist has the field. The ending οσαν, common in Septuagint, existing in papyri, and frequent in modern Greek vernacular, is strongly attested for παρελάβοσαν (Mg. of W. H) in 2 Thess. 3:6. Ἡμάρτησα (Rom. 5:14) as well as ἥμαρτον (1 Cor. 7:28) is found. The growth is towards aorists with σα. We have ἐδώκαμεν in 1 Thess. 4:2. Again forms like ἀφῆκες (Rev. 2:4) occur as in the papyri and the modern Greek. Ἐγενήθην is found also (Acts 4:4). In Acts 28:26 εἰπόν, not εἰπέ, is the imperative form. In Mark 12:1 ἐξέδετο, not ἐξέδοτο, has lost the root vowel and the thematic vowel ε has taken its place. The New Testament preserves the three aorists in κα (ἔδωκα, ἔθηκα, ἧκα).

302. *The Present Tense System*. (For the classification of the present stems and the formation of the present stem from the verb-stem see §317). In no part of the Greek verb (and Sanskrit) do we have such a complicated system as in the present system. There are (Brugmann) thirty-two classes of

---

1. §§ 301-311 are taken *verbatim* from the Eighth Edition of Robertson's *Short Grammar*.

Indo-Germanic verbs in the tense system, thirty of which the Greek possesses. However, they can all be grouped under seven simple divisions which are practically the same as the Sanskrit systems. If the present is built on the aorist (or identical with it as is often true like $\phi\eta-\mu\iota$), the obvious and easy way to make the present would be to add the primary personal endings to the aorist or present stems, and this is seen in such forms as $\phi\eta-\mu\iota$. Here $\check{\epsilon}-\phi\eta-\nu$ is either aorist or imperfect, for there would be no distinction in forms. The imperfect is merely a variation of the present stem with secondary endings. Some of these presents are reduplicated like $\delta\iota-\delta\omega-\mu\iota$, for reduplication is not confined to the perfect. Rather it seems to begin with some aorists, continue with some presents, and then be taken up by the perfect tense. What is called the variable (thematic) vowel class is but a step removed from the root class, for $\check{\epsilon}-\lambda\epsilon\gamma-o-\nu$ is exactly like $\check{\epsilon}-\lambda\iota\pi-o-\nu$ (Giles) in form. Hence we may argue that $\lambda\acute{\epsilon}\gamma-o-\mu\iota$ ($\lambda\acute{\epsilon}\gamma\omega$) is made from the same stem by the addition of the thematic vowel. If so, $\check{\epsilon}\lambda\epsilon\gamma o\nu$ was originally aorist as well as later imperfect like $\check{\epsilon}-\phi\eta-\nu$. This fact throws some light on the frequent use of $\check{\epsilon}\lambda\epsilon\gamma o\nu$ in the New Testament, for instance. The ν class (nasal class) comprises both of the previous classes, those that merely add one of the ν combinations of the root (non-thematic) as $\sigma\beta\acute{\epsilon}-\nu\nu\nu-\mu\iota$, and those that use the variable vowel also (thematic) as $\dot{\alpha}\mu\alpha\rho\tau-\acute{\alpha}\nu-\omega$, $\lambda\alpha\mu\beta\acute{\alpha}\nu\omega$. The aorist and the imperfect, of course, differ as $\check{\epsilon}-\lambda\alpha\beta-o\nu$, $\dot{\epsilon}-\lambda\acute{\alpha}\mu\beta\alpha\nu-o\nu$. The strong vowel class is just like the variable vowel class save that the root vowel has been strengthened. Here a distinction, as in the ν class, exists between the aorist and the imperfect, as $\check{\epsilon}-\phi\upsilon\gamma-o\nu$, $\check{\epsilon}-\phi\epsilon\upsilon\gamma-o\nu$. The τ class differs from the variable vowel class only in the insertion of τ before the variable vowel and the consequent euphonic changes $\dot{\epsilon}-\beta\acute{\alpha}\phi-\eta\nu$, $\beta\acute{\alpha}\pi-\tau\omega$. The ι class likewise inserts ι before the variable vowel with various euphonic results such as $\sigma\tau\acute{\epsilon}\lambda-\lambda\omega$, $\kappa\eta\rho\acute{\upsilon}\sigma-\sigma\omega$. Not all the verbs in the $\sigma\kappa^{o}/_{\epsilon}$ or $\iota\sigma\kappa^{o}/_{\epsilon}$ class are inceptive, and some have reduplication as $\gamma\iota-\gamma\nu\acute{\omega}-\sigma\kappa\omega$. The New Testament writes γινώσκω, γίνομαι. The uncontracted form δύνασαι (Matt. 5:36) and the contracted form δύνῃ (Mark 9:22) both exist. So η, and not ει, is the usual form of contracts in εω for second person middle singular indicative. New presents like στήκω (Phil. 1:27) are built from the perfect stem. Ἥφιεν (Mark 1:34) is treated like an uncompounded ω verb. In Rev. 2:20 note ἀφεῖς from ἀφίω. In ἠρώτουν (Matt. 15:23) we have Ionic contraction of αω verbs like εω. Note reading of A νικοῦντι (Rev. 2:7). The imperfect, like the aorist, has forms in α. So εἶχαν (Mark 8:7). In εἴχοσαν (John 15:22, 24) and ἐδολιοῦσαν (Rom. 3:13, from the Septuagint) the imperfect follows the aorist in the use of οσαν like the papyri and the modern Greek. Winer is in error, however, in citing ἐδίδοσαν (John 19:3) as an example, for δο is here the root and σαν the usual secondary ending with μι verbs in the third person plural. This example does not appear in Winer-Schmiedel, sec. 13, 14. Ἐτίθουν (Acts 3:2) and ἐδίδουν (Acts 4:33) sometimes displace the μι forms, as do ἀφίουσιν (Rev. 11:9), συνίουσιν (Matt. 13:13).

303. *The Future System.* The future tense is a later development and the tense has had a varied history. The Sanskrit had a periphrastic future made by a future active participle usually with an auxiliary. This method of making the future by an auxiliary and participle or infinitive has persisted till now. In the Germanic tongues the auxiliary and the infinitive is the only way of forming this tense. English has no future by the use of suffix. In the modern Greek the commonest way of forming the future is by means of θέλω and the infinitive (like English). Jebb thinks that Herodotus shows that the vernacular early began this usage. Here the origin of the idiom is seen in the purpose expressed by the auxiliary verb. But in the New Testament we must insist on the full force of θέλω as in John 7:17. Perhaps the original method was to have neither special form nor auxiliary, but to leave it to the imagination to tell when to project a verb into the future. Thus we still say: "I go home next week." So Jesus

said ἔρχομαι καὶ παραλήμψομαι (John 14:3). Some verbs never formed a future tense at all as εἰμι, though ἐλεύσομαι is made from ἔρχομαι. Εἰμι as future is not in the New Testament. Another device used to express time is μέλλω with the infinitive (aorist or present and thrice the future in the New Testament, as in earlier Greek) as in Matt. 11:14; Acts 3:3; 11:28. However, the Sanskrit, Greek, Latin and other languages, have developed a distinct future tense form. The Sanskrit did it by the use of *sya* or *isya*, but this suffix, which means "go" as the Coptic suffix NA does, was rarely· used (Whitney) partly because the subjunctive mode was practically a future in sense. In the Greek the future form in σ is much more common, though in Homer little distinction exists between the aorist subjunctive and the future indicative. The two forms may have a common origin (Giles), though this is not certain, for the future may be a variation from the present. This latter is the opinion of Delbrueck. The modern Greek has no future form at all and, when not using θέλω and infinitive, has θά and the subjunctive (cf. Homer). Forms like πίομαι (Luke 17:8), φάγομαι (*ibid.*) give color to the aoristic origin of the future form. It may be that some verbs make the future from the aorist and some from the present. In the New Testament we have ἐκχεῶ, however, as in Acts 2:17. Ἐλπιοῦσιν (Matt. 12:21) and similar verbs drop the σ, like the Attic future, but βαπτίσω retains it (Matt. 3:11). Καλέσω, τελέσω retain the σ, while both ἀπολέσω (Matt. 21:41) and ἀπολῶ (1 Cor. 1:19) occur. The form (Doric) πεσοῦμαι (made from σ ε ο/ε) is in the New Testament, but φεύξομαι. In Rev. 22:19 we have ἀφελῶ (so Septuagint) from ἀφαιρέω. The usual future of liquid verbs (ε ο/ε) like κρινῶ is common. So also ἀποθανοῦμαι. The Doric future seems like a combination of σ and ε (liquid verbs), or is it that σε ο/ε is an original ending? This latter is entirely possible and the fact that the old Doric and Homer both have σε ο/ε (cf. Sanskrit *syo*) lends color to the idea that the Indo-Germanic had such a suffix. Cf. Kuehner-Blass, *Laut-und Formenlehre*, II, S. 105 f. Hirt (*Handbuch*, etc., S. 403 f.), however, considers $\sigma\epsilon^{0}/_{\epsilon}$ to be a union of σ and the liquid ϵ. The future appears in the New Testament only in the indicative mode and in the verbal nouns (infinitives and participles).

304. *The Perfect System.* This tense presents some special difficulties both as to formation and signification. We are concerned only with the formation, though it may be remarked that in the Sanskrit, as the aorist disappears, the perfect increases in use with apparent loss of precise distinctions. Both Greek and Sanskrit preserve reduplication, probably originating from the iterative and reduplicated present like γιγνώσκω. The perfect then is in form a variation from the present. However, we are utterly at sea as to the origin of κα which is usually added to the perfect active stem before the personal ending. The κ may be due to some reduplicated κ stems in the present, which set the style. Some color is lent to this idea by the presence of some older perfect forms without the κ as οἶδα, γέγονα, λέλοιπα, and the aspirated forms like γέγραφα. In fact a form without κ or α appears in some verbs like ἑ–στά–ναι (Acts 12:14). Besides ἥκω, though present in form, has the meaning of the perfect. Note ἐξῆλθον καὶ ἥκω (Jo. 8:42). All this seems to show that the common κα for the active was a gradual development. This κα was used with a few aorists (ἔδωκα, ἔθηκα, ἧκα). Compare modern Greek ἐλύθηκα for ἐλύθην. In the Latin a similar phenomenon occurs in the ending *vi* as in *ama-vi*, which has not been explained. The Latin has some reduplicated perfects like *dedi* and aorist forms in *s* like *scripsi*. This form with double origin does double service in the Latin (both aorist and perfect). The modern Greek has wholly dropped the perfect form save in the passive participle. Instead ἔχω with the aorist infinitive (ει, not αι) is used as ἔχω λύσει much like the English. In the Attic we have sometimes ἔχω and the aorist participle. The past perfect in modern Greek is expressed by εἶχον λύσει. The Sanskrit has merely a trace of the past perfect. It was never common in the Greek, though it was always at hand when needed. In the

modern Greek, as in the old, the common tenses are the aorist, the present, and the imperfect. The perfect middle adds the personal endings directly to the reduplicated stem like ἑστα– μεν in the active. In the New Testament οἶδα is conjugated regularly in singular and plural of the indicative. Future perfect is εἰδήσω. In Acts 26:4 we have ἴσασι. Outside of the indicative the form is εἰδῶ, ἴστε, εἰδέναι, εἰδώς. The opt. εἰδείην is not in the N. T. It is not only in Rev. (19:3) that forms like εἴρηκαν appear; they are in the rest of the New Testament (John 17:6, τετήρηκαν) and in the papyri. Ανσι, originally αντι, by analogy of aorist, is αν. Κεκοπίακες Rev. 2:3 is like the aorist ἀφῆκες (Rev. 2:4) and such forms occur in the papyri among the ignorant scribes (Moulton). 'Αφέωνται (Luke 5:20) is a Doric form for ἀφεῖνται, though similar forms occur in Ionic and Arcadian. The past perfect like the imperfect, is confined to the indicative, and like it also usually has an augment besides the secondary personal endings. However, we have only κειν forms in the active. The Sanskrit had no future perfect nor has the modern Greek. In the ancient Greek are only two such active forms, ἑστήξω and τεθνήξω. The rest are in the middle voice. In the New Testament we have only εἰδήσω and that is from the Septuagint (Heb. 8:11). In Luke 19:40 some manuscripts read κεκράξονται. In Heb. 2:13 we have the periphrastic form ἔσομαι πεποιθώς. Such forms occur for the present perfect and the past perfect also. This analytic use of the verb forms is more common in all the tenses in the New Testament idiom (like κοινή and Hebrew too), especially in Luke's writings, and finally in the modern Greek wholly destroys the perfect verb forms.

The Modes

305. *The Indicative.* There is no mode suffix for the indicative. It is, of course, the normal mode for all the Indo-germanic languages, and is always used by them unless there is special reason for using one of the other modes. It is the only mode which uses all the tenses in Sanskrit and Greek. In

the Sanskrit the future occurs only in the indicative, and the perfect appears only in the indicative and the participle save a few examples in the early Sanskrit (the Veda) of the other modes. The imperfect and the past perfect, of course, belong to the indicative only. Hence in Sanskrit it is only the aorist and the present that use modes other than the indicative. This is interesting as showing the gradual growth of the modes. In modern English we have nearly come round again to the position of the Sanskrit in our almost exclusive use of the indicative. The subjunctive, optative, and imperative are variations from the indicative and the old injunctive mode.

306. *The Subjunctive.* In the early Sanskrit the subjunctive is very common with the aorist and the present and has a special mode sign *a*. But the later Sanskrit nearly loses this mode as we have in English nearly ceased to use it. The first person survives as a practical imperative. In Greek the earliest form of the subjunctive with non-thematic stems is not different from the indicative with thematic stems and uses $^o/_\epsilon$ not $^\omega/_\eta$, just like the indicative thematic stems. So ἴομεν is subjunctive in Homer, while ἴμεν is indicative. In the early Ionic the non-thematic stems do in some cases use $^\omega/_\eta$, but not always. It would seem therefore that the subjunctive mode sign was first the variable vowel $^o/_\epsilon$ already in use. This sign was gradually lengthened into $^\omega/_\eta$. Even in the fifth century B. C. the Ionic has aorist subjunctives like ποιήσει. Hence, "the distinction between indicative and subjunctive cannot always be easily drawn" (Giles). It is also probable that the Attic future ἔδομαι, πίομαι, and the New Testament φάγομαι (Jas. 5:3) were originally aorist subjunctives. The mode suffix was first added to the stem as in the μι forms (δό–η = δῶ) and in the aorist passive forms (λυ–θέ–ω = λυθῶ). In Mark 8:37 δοῖ is subjunctive (as in papyri), δῷ = οἶ as often. But with thematic stems the variable vowel $^o/_\epsilon$ was merely changed to $^\omega/_\eta$ and the σ aorist makes the subjunctive σω/ση. In δύνωμαι, δύνηται we either have irregular

accent and contraction (so ἰστῆται, αη = η instead of α) or the
mode sign ω/η displaces α of the stem. So the optative δύναιτο
has irregular accent (compare ἰσταῖτο). Homer frequently
uses μι with the subjunctive of verbs, ἐθέλωμι, ἴδωμι. The subjunctive used only primary personal endings in both Sanskrit
and Greek. In Greek the subjunctive has increased in the
frequency with which it is used, and in the modern Greek has
displaced both the optative and the infinitive (save with
auxiliary verbs). The Greek used a perfect subjunctive also,
though it was never very common in the nature of the case.
In the New Testament besides εἰδῶ (1 Cor. 2:12) we only have
examples of the *periphrastic perfect subjunctive* like ᾖ πεποιηκώς
(Jas. 5:15), ᾖ κεκλημένος (Luke 14:8). The later Byzantine
Greek, like the Latin, developed a future subjunctive which is
not, however, preserved in the modern Greek where the ancient
future forms are lost. Occasionally manuscripts of the New
Testament give such forms in some verbs as κερδηθήσωνται (1
Pet. 3:1), and in Luke 13:28 Westcott and Hort print ὄψησθε in
the text and ὄψεσθε in the margin. This may, however, be a
late first aorist form. Cf. mg. ἄρξησθε (Lu. 13:26) with text
ἄρξεσθε.

307. *The Optative.* The Greek is the only language that
preserved both subjunctive and optative in its flourishing
period. In the Sanskrit the optative displaced the subjunctive save in a few special uses, while in the Latin the subjunctive was extended in its scope to partial future time as
well as present, like the indicative, and the optative was not
used. As a matter of fact both subj. and imperative are future
in idea. The Gothic has only one such mode whether subjunctive or optative is not clear. In Homer the subjunctive
and optative struggle together, the optative gains a firm place,
especially in the literary style, and then loses it gradually
till in the modern Greek it does not exist. In the New Testament it occurs only sixty-seven times, Luke using it twenty-
eight and Paul thirty-one, John, Matthew and James do not

have it at all, and Mark, and Hebrews one each, Jude twice, Peter using it four times. It seems never to have been common in the vernacular and is correspondingly scarce in the papyri. The Sanskrit had two mode signs for the optative either *ya* or *i*. So the Greek has two mode signs for the optative either ι or ιη. The latter is used with non-thematic tense stems like δο–ιη–ν, the former with thematic stems like λιπ–ο–ι–μι, λύ–σα–ι–μι. The subjunctive and the optative mode suffixes are an addition to the tense stem and hence seem to show that these modes grew after the origin of tenses. The personal endings of the optative are chiefly secondary, though μι is primary. The mode doubtless was meant to be secondary and the subjunctive primary, but in actual usage this is not always true. In the Sanskrit the optative is used in all sorts of ways as the subjunctive is in Latin save that it has no future, but its use to express a wish is really future and μι in the Greek suggests connection with primary ideas as well as secondary. The subjunctive in Latin, and often also in Greek, is used after secondary tenses. The Greek, moreover, developed a future optative which was used only in indirect discourse after secondary tenses. This tense does not appear in the New Testament. The aorist and present optative are the tenses always used. The ancient Greek had a perfect optative, but in the New Testament we have no perfect. Indeed in all late Greek the perfect subj., opt., and imperatives are very rare. Cf. J. E. Harry in *The Classical Review* for 1905-1906. The Attic εια (ειε) instead of αι in the first aorist is found in the Textus Receptus as ποιήσειαν (Luke 6:11), but in W H and Nestle ποιήσαιεν. But in Acts 17:27 the critical text has ψηλαφήσειαν.

308. *The Imperative.* The imperative is in a way a makeshift and seems a development from the indicative and injunctive. Some of the forms are just like the indicative as λέγετε and this only the context can decide. Cf. Jo. 5:39 and 14:1. The imperative. like the indicative, has no mode suffix. In

fact the future indicative in Greek, as in Hebrew and English, is often used where the imperative could have been employed as οὐ φονεύσεις (Matt. 5:21). And for the first person both in Sanskrit and Greek the subjunctive is used for the hortatory idea. There is no first person imperative form, though in English we say "Charge we the foe." Moreover, in Latin the third person can be used for exhortations also, but in Sanskrit and Greek the aorist subjunctive was early used with ma, μή, in prohibitions, probably before there was an aorist imperative. In Sanskrit the imperative is little used outside of the present tense. With this late mode the present comes before the aorist in time and the aorist imperative is nearly confined to positive commands. However in the New Testament we have for the third person μή καταβάτω (Mk. 13:15) and similar aorist negative imperatives. Other imperative forms use merely the stem like the original vocative (Giles) as ἵστη. Other imperatives again use the variable vowel like λέγε, λαβέ, λίπε, probably interjectional forms if ε is part of the root (Moulton, Prolegomena, p. 171). Brugmann considers that the accent of λαβέ, εἰπέ, ἐλθέ, εὑρέ , ἰδέ, is that of all imperatives originally when at the beginning of a sentence. But in the N. T. we have ἴδε, λάβε. Some imperative forms are possible substantives as βάπτισον, βάπτισαι (Acts 22:16). See use of στοιχεῖν (Phil. 3:16) and the common χαίρειν (James 1:1) like papyri. Again other imperative forms use personal endings like στῆ–θι, with which compare the Sanskrit dhi, or like τω (Sanskrit tu, originally tod the ablative of the demonstrative pronoun). The plural in ντων is like the Sanskrit ntu with ν added. But the Doric makes the plural ντω. But this Attic form is displaced in the later κοινή (New Testament and papyri) by τω–σαν (compare σαν in plural of secondary tense). Thus also σθων became σθωσαν. It remains to speak of θές, ἔς, δός, σχές which seem kin to the unaugmented aorist indicative (injunctive like λύθητε). In the modern Greek the first and third persons are expressed by ἄς (ἄφες) and the subjunctive much like the English "let" and the infinitive. In the New

Testament we already see ἄφες ἐκβάλω (Luke 6:42). In the use of φάγοι (Mark 11:14) the optative clearly approaches the imperative. There is, of course, no future imperative, for all imperatives are future in idea. The perfect is sometimes used in Greek as πεφίμωσο (Mark 4:39) as in the earlier Sanskrit. But it is not used in the modern Greek. In Lu. 12:35 we find ἔστωσαν περιεζωσμέναι. Forms like ἀνάβα (Rev. 4:1) merely use the stem. Ἥτω (ἔστω) appears in the New Testament and the papyri (possibly Doric) as in 1 Cor. 16:22. Sometimes the imperative form is used with either number and is practically interjectional as ἄγε (Jas. 4:13) as in the older Greek. Compare ἀγέτω in Greek and *agito* in Latin. The periphrastic imperative occurs also as in ἴσθι εὐνοῶν (Matt. 5:25). Cf. γίνεσθε ἑτεροζυγοῦντες (2 Cor. 6:14). Note two persons in Mk. 14:42.

The Voices

309. *The Active.* It is probable, though by no means certain, that the active is the original voice. The personal endings of the active are evidently kin to the pronouns. Compare μι and μεν (μες) with the oblique forms of ἐγώ, σι and τε with σύ, τι and ντι (νσι) with the demonstrative τός (ὅς). In a wonderful way these pronominal suffixes express person, number, and voice. The secondary endings differ from the primary in being shorter and in having a few special forms like σαν and in the fact that ν replaces μ (μι). There is in Greek a certain tendency towards abbreviation of these suffixes. So μι continually drops off, σι in full form appears only in ἐσ-σί and τι only in ἐσ-τί. We have the same situation in the English verbal suffixes, retaining them only in the second and third person singular.

310. *The Middle.* The middle is the only other voice that appears in the Sanskrit where every active ending has a corresponding middle. However, not all verbs have both voices, some having only the active, some only the middle, and some enses using only one voice. In Homer the middle is more common (Monro, *Homeric Grammar*, p. 7) than in any other period of the Greek language. In the modern Greek it is well-nigh displaced by the passive, and the distinctively passive forms (aorist) are used, though the vernacular uses aorist middle imperative λῦσον rather than λύθητι. In the New Testament the middle is disappearing before the passive. In Latin the passive has wholly supplanted the middle though some verbs retain a middle sense. It is supposed by some (Donaldson, *New Cratylus,*) that the middle endings are formed by doubling the suffix for the active. So then μαι is from μαμι, the second μ having dropped out. This is in entire accord with the idea of the middle voice, though it is wholly conjectural. Still it is just as possible (Moulton, *Prolegomena,* p. 152) that the active τίθημι may be a weakening of μαι to μι in τίθεμαι with a corresponding lengthening of ε to η (cf. τίθεμεν in plural). Some middle forms occur, however, in the later Greek that are not common in the older Greek like ἤμην (Matt. 25:35). In the modern Greek εἰμί is always middle save in the form εἶνε (εἶναι), etc., which takes the place of ἐστί (ἐντί). The contraction in the second person singular of the indicative of εσαι into ει is rare in the later Greek. It is usually η. So even with ὄψη (Matt. 27:4), though uncontracted forms like ὀδυνᾶσαι (Luke 16:25) occur. So also φάγεσαι, πίεσαι (Luke 17:8). But βούλει is found in Luke 22:42.

311. *The Passive.* In the Sanskrit, as in the Coptic, there is no passive voice. However the Sanskrit shows the beginning of a passive formation. In the present tense verbs of the *ya* class form a virtual passive by accenting it as *ya*. Such verbs use the middle endings and are conjugated in the same way except the accent. But in the Greek more progress has been made. Two tenses in the Greek have distinctive passive conjugation, the aorist and the future. But here again the aorist passive uses the active endings and the future passive the middle endings. The Greek passive then has no endings of its own. In most tenses it merely borrows the entire middle

inflection, while in the two tenses above it draws on the active and middle both. The so-called second aorist passive like ἐ–στάλ–η–ν is really the second aorist active (root aorist) like ἔ–βη–ν, ἔ–φη–ν. And the special suffix θε (θη) which the passive uses for the first aorist stem is sometimes used as an active form (Giles, *Comparative Philology*, p. 411). The future passive is merely the addition of σο/ε to θη. But even here some future middle forms like ἀδικήσομαι are used in a passive sense just as in the other middle forms. Clearly then the passive is later in origin than both active and middle and is built out of both of them though it never did have a complete set of distinctive endings. In the Latin the passive early displaced the middle, but in the Greek the process was much more slow. In the New Testament the passive has greatly increased in use. New passive forms appear like ἐγενήθην (Matt. 6:10) not common in the earlier Greek. So ἐφύην in Luke 8:6, ἠγγέλην (Luke 8:20), διετάγην (Gal. 3:19). The future passive is also common as κοιμηθησόμεθα (1 Cor. 15:51), and the second future passive as ἀλλαγησόμεθα (*ibid*). For all three voices of γινώσκω see 1 Cor. 13:12.

PART III

THE BUILDING OF WORDS

CHAPTER VIII

WORD FORMATION

312. *Words in the* κοινή.

There are few distinctly New Testament Greek words, not over 50 out of the 5,000 used in it, and many of these may disappear as more papyri are read. But the κοινή shows a large number of words not in the older Greek. The new Liddell and Scott's *Lexicon* is revealing that. Dr. W. Hersey Davis has himself found 3,000 words in the papyri that are not in the older lexicons. Fortunately Preisigke's *Wörterbuch der griechischen Papyrusurkunden* makes it possible to see the evidence. The new words in the New Testament, as in the κοινή, are formed acording to well established principles of the language. Ἡρῳδιανός (Matt. 22:16) and χριστιανός (Acts 11:26) are Latin formations like *Romanus, Africanus.* The proper names in the New Testament are like those in current vernacular use at the time, many of them Greek, many Roman, many Aramaic, some of them abbreviated like Ἀπολλώς from Ἀπολλώνιος. There is a decided increase in the number of compound words in the κοινή There is also a continual change of –μι verbs to –ω verbs. All that can be done in this chapter is to show how New Testament words illustrate the principles of the language.

313. *Simple and Compound Words.*

This is the first thing to note about the formation of words. A word formed from a single stem is called *simple* like λόγ-ο-ς *word* from λέγ-ω. A word formed by combining two or more stems is called *compound* like οἰκο-νόμος *manager of the house.*

314. *Roots.*

Roots represent the original stock from which words are made. They probably never existed in the form of separate roots. Apparently only some 400 roots of Greek words are known for some 90,000 words in Liddell and Scott's *Lexicon* and less than half of these words appear in the so-called classic Greek. The two ultimate kinds of words were verbs and pronouns combined in a verb like φη–μί *says I*. Verbal and nominal roots are so old that it is difficult to distinguish between them. Verbs, substantives, and pronouns are the oldest parts of speech. Adjectives are merely variations from substantives or pronouns. There are a few root words in the New Testament where the case ending is added directly to the root like ἅλ–ς (ἅλ–α Mk. 9:50) *salt*, εἷς = ἕν–ς one, and verbs without thematic vowel º/ε and sometimes without tense suffix like φη–μί. Words formed directly from a verb stem are called verbals like ἀρχ–ή *beginning*, those from noun stems are termed denominatives like ἀρχα–ῖος *of the beginning*.

315. *Suffixes for Substantives.*

Suffixes are the formative endings. These may be added to the root or to the stem. There are formative suffixes, case suffixes for nouns (substantives and adjectives), personal suffixes for the verb. We are here concerned with formative suffixes for substantives, adjectives, and verbs. First then we take up the formative suffixes for substantives. These formative suffixes may be added directly to the root (primary or primitive words) or to a derived stem (derivative words). Only a few specimens of the main kinds can be given here with no extended discussion of the meaning of the suffixes.

(a) *Abstracts (verbals).*

Mainly primitives.

For –α and –η take χαρ–ά (χαίρ–ω) *joy*, ἀρχ–ή (ἄρχ–ω) *beginning*.

For –ο, nom. –ο–ς take λόγ–ο–ς (λέγ–ω) *speech*, τρόπ–ο–ς (τρέπ–ω) *turn*.

(b) *Agent.*

–εύ–ς.

In verbals the one who does an action like γον–εύ–s *parent* (γέ–γον–α).

In denominatives it is one who has to do with something like γραμματ–εύ–s *scribe* (γράμματ–).

Other suffixes for the agent are –τηρ, –τωρ, –της. Masculine –τηρ like σω–τήρ *Saviour* (σώζ–ω), feminine like μαθή–τρια the only New Testament example (Acts 9:36); masc. –τορ, nom. τωρ like πράκτωρ *exactor* (πράσσ–ω), masc. –τα, nom. –τη–s like μαθη–τής *learner* (μανθάν–ω), βαπτισ–τή–s *baptizer* (βαπτίζ–ω). The great majority of the words for the agent are formed in –τη–s. They are formed from many kinds of verbs as those in –άω like ἀκροα–τής *hearer* from ἀκροά–ομαι, those in –έω like ποιη–τής *doer* from ποι–έω, those in –όω like ζηλω–τής *zealot* from ζηλ–όω, those in –εύω like βουλευ–τής *councillor* from βουλ–εύω, those in –άζω like δικασ–τής *judge* from δικ–άζω, those in –ίζω like εὐαγγελισ–τής *evangelist* from εὐαγγελ–ίζω, those in –ύζω like γογγυσ–τής *murmurer* from γογγ–ύζω.

(c) *Action.*

The old form –τι–s survives in only a few words like πίσ–τι–s *faith* from πείθ–ω (πιθ–). Usually τ has changed to σ as –σι–s in the verbals like γνῶ–σι–s *knowledge* (γι–γνώ–σκω), κρί–σι–s *judging* (κρίν–ω), λύτρω–σι–s *redemption* (λυτρ–όω).

For –σια note θυ–σία *sacrifice* (θύ–ω), δοκιμα–σία *proving* (denominative verbal stem δοκιμ–άζω), ἐκκλη–σία *assembly* (ἐκ–καλ–έω).

For –μο–s note verbals like ψαλ–μό–s *twanging a chord* or *psalm* (ψάλλ–ω), from derivative verbs as βαπτισ–μόs *baptism* for –ίζω verbs (βαπτ–ίζω), ἁγιασ–μός *sanctification* for –άζω verbs (ἁγι–άζω), γογγυσ–μός *murmuring* for –ύζω verbs (γογγ–ύζω).

For –εια from verbs in –εύω note βασιλ–εία *kingdom* βασιλ–εύω.

(d) *Result.*

The dental suffix –ματ, nom. –μα, is added to primary verbal stems like γράμ–μα (γράφ–ω) *letter*, πνεῦ–μα (πνέ–ω) *spirit*, or to denominative verbal stems like κήρυγ–μα (κήρυξ, κηρύσσ–ω) *preaching*, πλήρω–μα (πληρ–όω) *fulness*.

With dental stems like –άζω, –ίζω the form is –σμα like βάπτισ–μα (βαπτ–ίζω) *baptism* or with verbs with perfect passive in –σμαι like χρίσ–μα (χρί–ω) *anointing*.

From primary verbals the suffix –ες, nom. –ος, short words like γέν–ος (γι–γέν–ομαι, γίν–ομαι) *offspring*, ἔθος (root ἔθ–ω) *custom*.

(e) *Instrument or Means.*

The chief one is –τρο, nom. –τρον (Latin-*trum*), like ἄρο–τρον (ἀρό–ω) *plough*, λύ–τρον (λύ–ω) *ransom*.

The suffix –τηριο, nom. –τήριον, is used for instrument also like αἰσθη–τήριον (αἰσθάν–ομαι) *organ of perception*, ἱλασ–τήριον (ἱλά–σκομαι) *means of propitiation*.

(f) *Place.*

Here –τηρι, nom. –τήριον, only in verbals like ἀκροα– τήριον (ἀκροά–ομαι) *auditorium*, κρι–τήριον (κρίνω) *judgment seat*.

Less common is –ειο, nom. –εῖον in denominative like ἀγγ–εῖον (ἄγγ–ος) *vessel*, πανδοχ–εῖον (παν–δοχ–εύς) *inn*.

In denominatives also appears the suffix –ων, nom. –ών like ἀμπελ–ών (ἄμπελ–ος) *vineyard*, ἐλαι–ών (ἐλαί–α) *olive orchard*.

(g) *Quality.*

From adjective stems.

Those in –τητ, nom. –της, are mainly from adjective stems in –ο like ἁγιό–της (ἅγι–ος) *holiness*, νεό–της (νέ–ος) *youth*, but εὐθύ–της (εὐθ–ύς) *rectitude*.

For –συνα, nom. –σύνη take δικαιο–σύνη (δίκαιος) *righteousness*, σωφρο–σύνη (σώφρων) *soundness of mind*.

For –ια, nom. –ια, take ἀλήθε–ια (ἀληθής) *truth*, σοφ–ία (σοφός) *wisdom*.

So also –ες, nom. –ος (see under Result), βάθ–ος (βαθ–ύς) *depth*, βάρ–ος (βαρ–ύς) *weight*.

(h) *Diminutives.*

From substantive stems and some of them "hypocoristic" for tender affection.

For –ιο, nom. –ιον, note θυγάτρ–ιον (θυγάτηρ) *little daughter* κοράσ–ιον (κόρη) *little girl*, παιδ–ίον (παῖς) *little child*, all hypocoristic.

Note also αριο nom. –άριον, like γυνυκ–άριον (γυνή) *little woman* (in contempt sometimes), παιδ–άριον (παῖς) *little child*.

Then there is –διο, nom. –ίδιον, like κλιν–ίδιον (κλίν–η) *small bed*, and –αριο, nom. –άριον, like κλιν–άριον *couch*.

In βιβλ–αρ–ίδιον (Rev. 10:9,10) we find a double diminutive (βίβλος, βιβλ–άριον) *a little book*.

For –ισκο, nom. –ίσκος (masc.), –ίσκη (fem.) take νεαν–ίσκος (νεαν–ίας) *young man*, παιδ–ίσκη (παῖς) *young girl*.

(i) *Patronymics.*

These substantives express descent and the suffixes are added to proper names. So –δα, masc. nom. –δης, fem. nom. –s, like Ἡρῳδιάς(–δs = s) *daughter of Herod*. Place names like Ἑλλάs Greece. (Δορκάς) means a gazelle.

(j) *Gentiles (Ethnica)*

These suffixes designate a person as belonging to some people or country.

For –ευ, nom. –εύς, note Ἀλεξανδρ–εύς (Ἀλεξανδρ–ία) *an Alexandrian*, Ταρσ–εύς (Ταρσός) *a Tarsian*.

For –ικός take Γαλατ–ικός (Γαλατία) *Galatian*.

So with –δ, nom. –s, with ι as connecting vowel like Ἑλλην–ί–s (Ἑλλην) *a Greek woman*.

So –ιο–s to city or country like Ἀθηνα–ῖος (Ἀθῆναι) *Athenian*.

316. *Suffixes for Adjectives.*

Only the principal ones can be noted.

(a) *That which pertains to a substantive.*

The suffix –ιο, nom. –ιο–s, is very common like οὐράν–ιος (οὐρανός) *heavenly*, τίμ–ιο–s (τιμή) *precious*. From verbals like ἄγ–ιο–s (ἄζομαι). Added to some τ stems we get –σιος like θαυμάσιος (θαῦματ) *wonderful*. Denominatives in –κο, nom. –κος (generally with connecting vowel ι) like βασιλ–ι–κός (βασιλεύς) *kingly*, φυσ–ι–κός (φύσις) *natural*.

So also –ιακό–s like κυρ–ιακός (κύριος) *relating to the Lord* οἰκ–ιακός (οἰκία) *belonging to the house*.

(b)   *Ability or Fitness.*

The suffix –ικό–s may have spread from forms like φυσ–ι–κός which has an ι connecting vowel. It spread from the notion of pertaining or belonging to as seen in βασιλ–ι–κός to that of likeness, fitness, ability and is the most common adjectival suffix after –ιο–s. Note λογ–ικός (λόγος) *rational,* μουσ–ικός (μοῦσα) *capable of music* (musical). In particular note πνευματ–ικός (πνεῦμα) *spiritual,* σαρκ–ικός (σάρξ) *fleshly,* σωματ–ικός (σῶμα) *bodily,* ψυχ–ικος (ψυχή) *sensual,* where a sharp distinction exists between the forms in –ικός *like* and those in –ινος *made of* as σάρκ–ινος in 1 Cor. 3:1 in contrast with σαρκ–ικός in verse 3.

So also –τικό–s to verbals like αἱρε–τικός (αἱρέ–ομαι) *capable of choosing* (factious. heretic), διδακ–τικός (διδάσκω) *apt at teaching.*

(c)   *Material.*

A large group of adjectives in –ινος meaning *made of a thing* like λίθ–ινος (λίθος) *made of stone,* ὀστράκ–ινος (ὄστρακον) *made of clay,* σάρκ–ινος (σάρξ) *made of flesh.*

Another suffix for material is –εος (–οῦς) like ἀργυρ–οῦς, χρυσ–οῦς.

(d)   *Temporal Adjectives.*

In –ινο–s due to locatives or adverbs in ι like πρω–ϊνός (πρωΐ) *pertaining to morning,* ὀρθρ–ινός (ὄρθρος) *early.*

(e)   *Less Definite Meanings.*

Numerous adjectival suffixes convey no very definite idea. So –ο–s, for simple words like καλ–ός, ὀλίγ–ος, φίλ–ος, for compound words like ἄπειρ–ος, ἀργ–ός.

For –λο–s (m.), –λη (f.), take δοῦ–λος (δέω) *bound to,* τυφ–λός (τύφω) *blind.* So from –ιλος we get ποικ–ίλος *many-colored* and from –ωλος ἁμαρτ–ωλός (ἁμαρτάνω) *devoted to sin.*

For –νος, –νη, –νον note λυμ–νός *naked,* σεμ–νός *to be revered.*

For –ανος take ἱκ–ανός *fit,* ὀρφ–ανός *bereft.*

For –μος (mainly compounds) take ἄ–μω–μος *spotless*, πρό–θυμος **ready**. For –ιμος note ἀδόκ–ιμος *rejected*, ὠφέλ–ιμος *helpful* and for –(σ)ιμος take βρώ–σιμος *edible*, χρή–σιμος *useful*.

For –ρος note αἰσχ–ρός *shameful*, μικ–ρός *little*, νεκ–ρός *dead*. Then come –αρος like χλι–αρός *lukewarm*, –ερος like φαν–ερός *manifest*, –ᾱρος like φλυ–αρός (φλύ–ω) *babbling*, –ηρος like πον–ηρός (πονέω) *evil*, –υρος like ἰσχ–υρός (ἰσχύς) *strong*.

For –ες, nom. –ης., chiefly in compounds take ἀληθ–ής (ἀ privative, λήθω) *true*.

(f) *Comparative Relationship.*

Originally –τερος was relationship rather than comparison, correlatives or opposites like ἀρίσ–τερος *left* as opposed to right (δεξί–τερος), ἡμέ–τερος *ours* as opposed to ὑμέ–τερος *yours*. Duality appears in ἀμφό–τεροι *both*, ἕ–τερος *another*, δεύ–τερος *second*.

(g) *Verbal Adjectives.*

In particular those in –τος which are very numerous from all the classes of verbs like ἄ–πισ–τος, διδακ–τός, κλη –τός, χρησ–τός.

Only one verbal in –τέος occurs in the New Testament, βλη–τέον (Lu. 5:38).

(h) *Some Special Adjectives.*

Some adjectives refuse to come under any rule like βραχ–ύς, –εῖα, –ύ (slow) with ε instead of υ in most cases of masc. and neuter and –εῖα in feminine. Irregular also are μέγας and πολύς. Compound adjectives usually have feminine like the masculine like ἄ–τοπος *out of place*, but not δι–πλοῦς *two-fold*. So αἰώνιος usually. Adjectives like ἀληθής have only two endings. Some adjectives have only one ending like ἄρπαξ *rapacious*, πένης *poor*.

317. *Suffixes for Verbs.*

The structure of the Greek verb has been adequately treated in Chapter VII, Inflection of the Verb. All that can be done here is to give some illustrations of the various suffixes

employed for the first personal singular present indicative of
the several classes of verbs according to the outline in Robertson's *Grammar of the Greek New Testament in the Light of His-
torial Research*, pp. 350-353.

(a)   *The Root Class Without Thematic Vowel.*
This is probably the oldest and simplest form of the verb
with –μι like φη–μί *I say*, εἰ–μί *I am*, κεῖ–μαι *I lie*.   It is disappearing in the κοινή.

(b)   *The Non-Thematic Reduplicated Present.*
Here come some of the most common verbs like δί–δω–μι *I
give*, ἵ–η–μι *I send*, ἵ–στη–μι *I place*, τί–θη–μι *I put.*
(c)   *The Non-Thematic Present with –να– and –νυ–.*
A number of important verbs belong here, but they all
have –ω forms also in the New Testament, like δείκ–νυ–μι *I
show*, ζεύγ– νυ–μι *I join*, μίγ–νυ–μι *I mix*, σβέ–ννυ–μι *I quench.*

(d)   *The Simple Thematic Present.*
This class constantly encroached on the –μι verbs.   It is a
very large class with several branches.

(1)   *Root-verbs.*
Here the thematic vowel is added to the root like ἄγ–ω
I lead, γράφ–ω *I write*, θέλ–ω *I will.*

(2)   *Strengthened Vowel Verbs.*
Here belong verbs like λείπ–ω (λιπ) *I leave*, πείθ–ω (πιθ)
I persuade, φεύγ–ω (φυγ) *I pursue.*

(e)   *The Reduplicated Thematic Present.*
Here come the common verbs γίν–ομαι (γι–γέν–ο–μαι) *I
become*, πίπτ–ω (πι–πέτ–ω) *I fall*, τίκτ–ω(τι–τέκ–ω) *I bear.*

(f)   *The Thematic Present With a Suffix.*
Here there are five divisions, each with a large group of verbs.

(1)   *The ι (Consonant) Class.*
This is a very large class with various subdivisions.   Originally the suffix was –y– (or y°/ι).

Denominative verbs come here. Some of these are causative in –όω like δουλ–όω to enslave. Some are intensive or iterative like –ιζω in βαπτ–ίζω (βάπ–τω) I *baptize*, ῥαντ–ίζω (ῥαίν–ω) I *sprinkle*. Some are desiderative like –ιάω in κοπ–ιάω (κόπ–os) I *grow weary*. But the edge wears off all these special senses and there is a great increase in the number of denominative verbs. The y between the two vowels disappears in these vowel verbs.

For –άω note ἀγαπ–άω (–άγω) I *love*, διψ–άω I *thirst*, νικ–άω I *conquer*, σιγ–άω I *am silent*, τιμ–άω I *honor*.

For –έω note αἱρ–έω (–εγω) I *take*, αἰτ–έω I *ask*, καλ–έω I *call*, λαλ–έω I *speak*.

For –όω note δικαι–όω (–oγω) I *count righteous*, λυτρ–όω I *ransom*, σταυρ–όω I *crucify*.

For –εύω (by analogy) note βασιλ–εύω I *reign*, κελ–εύω I *order*, παιδ–εύω I *train a child*.

The ζ forms belong to the ι class of which there are three: –άζω like ἀρπ–άζω (ἀρπαγ–yω) I *seize*, λιθάζω (λιθαδ–yω) I *stone*; –ίζω like ἐλπ–ίζω (ἐλπιδ–yω) I *hope*, σαλπ–ίζω (σαλπιγ–yω) I *sound a trumpet*, while βαπτ–ίζω is from the verbal βαπ–τός (βάπ–τω); –ύζω in onomatopoetic words like γογγύζω I *murmur*.

–σσω *stems* are usually guttural like κηρύ–σσω (κηρυκ–yω) I *preach*, πρά–σσω (πραγ–yω) I *practice*, φυλά–σσω (φυλακ–yω) I *guard*.

–άλλω and –έλλω are primary like βάλ–λω (βαλ–yω) I *throw*, ἀγγέλ–λω (ἀγγελ–yω) I *announce*.

–αίνω forms (–ανy–ω) can be illustrated by ποιμ–αίνω (ποιμαν–yω) I *shepherd*, σημ–αίνω (σημαν–yω) I *signify*.

–ύνω forms appear in αἰσχ–ύνω (–υνy–ω) I *make ashamed*: παροξ–ύνω I *sharpen*.

–ίνω form appears in κρ–ίνω (κριν–yω) I *judge*.

–αίρω form appears (metathesis) in αἴρω (αρ–yω) I *lift up*, καθαίρω (καθαρ–yω) I *cleanse*.

–είρω form is seen in ἐγείρω (ἐγερ–yω) I *raise*, σπείρω (σπερ–yω) I *sow*.

Two verbs in –αίω have roots in –αϝγ as καίω (καϝγω) *I burn*, κλαίω (κλαϝγω) *I weep*.

(2)   *The* (ν) *Class.*

Take κάμ–νω *I am sick*, πί–νω *I drink*; with –ανο– note ἁμαρτ–άνω *I sin*, αἰσθ–άνο–μαι *I perceive*; with ν inserted in root λα–μ–β–άνω (λαβ) *I take*, μα–ν–θ–άνω (μαθ) *I learn*.

(3)   *The* –σκ– *Class.*

This class is often called inceptive or iterative and some are also reduplicated. Note γι(γ)νώ–σκω *I know*, διδά–σκω (διδάχ–σκω) *I teach*, πά–σχω (πάθ–σκω) *I suffer*, ἀρέ–σκω *I please*.

(4)   *The* τ *Class.*

Only about 18 such verbs like ἅπ–τω *I fasten*, βάπ–τω *I dip*, καλύπ–τω *I cover*.

(5)   *The* θ *Class.*

A small class like ἀλή–θω *I grind*, κνή–θω *I tickle*.

318.   *Compound Words.*

This is a most complicated subject and there is much difficulty in avoiding recrossing one's path several times. The Greek makes combinations of words much better than Latin, though not so extensively as Sanskrit. Most of our modern scientific terms are made by combining Greek words like lexicography, telephone. The κοινή is very fond of compound words. The most important new ones from Aristotle on are given in Robertson's *Grammar*, pp. 160 to 173. Only the outline of the subject can be presented here.

(a)   *Inseparable Prefixes.*

These prefixes do not occur apart from the verbs, substantives, adjectives, or adverbs with which they are used. A few examples of the new κοινή formations in the New Testament (from Aristotle on) may be given here.

For ἀ– (ἀν–) privative note ἀ–γνοέω *I am ignorant*, ἀ–κατάκριτος *uncondemned*, ἄ–σπιλος *unspotted*.

For ἀρχι- *chief-* (*arch-*) take ἀρχ-ιερεύς *chief priest,* ἀρχι-ποιμήν *chief shepherd.*

For δυσ- note δυσ-εντέριον *dysentery,* δυσ-ερμήνευτος *hard to explain.*

For ἡμι- (Latin *semi*) note ἡμι-θανής *half dead,* ἡμί-ωρον *half an hour.*

For νη- note νη-πιάζω (νή, ἔπος, Latin *nequam*) *I speak as a babe* (infant). So νή-πιος *infant.*

(b) Prepositions.

A whole chapter (XIV) is devoted to these important words, both "proper" and "improper" prepositions. The name implies that the primary use was in composition, but this is now known to be untrue. These are merely fixed case-forms (adverbs) that came to be used to help out cases. A start towards this was made in Sanskrit. Now Modern French has dropped the case-forms entirely save in personal pronouns. Only a limited number (eighteen) of these adverbs used with cases were used in composition with verbs. More than twice that number developed in the κοινή that were not used in composition with verbs. The use of prepositions in composition with Greek verbs was slow at first, but became very common in the κοινή. This use of prepositions represents the simplest form of composition by juxta-position (παράθεσις), copulative or paratactic, by placing two words together like ὑπερ-άνω, παρά-κλησις, δώ-δεκα (common in numerals), what the Sanskrit grammarians called *Dvandva* (coordinative compounds). The use of prepositions in compound verbs gives a vivid touch to the picture in the word like the double compound in ἀντι-παρ-ῆλθεν in Lu. 10:31f and συν-αντι-λάβηται in Lu. 10:40. There are literally "sermons in Greek Prepositions" (cf. my *The Minister and His Greek New Testament*). For further discussion see Chapter XIV on Prepositions in this grammar.

(c) *Objective Compounds or Dependent Determinatives.*

With these compounds the first part is related to the other

as a sort of grammatical object or case relationship. It is possible often to see the case that is represented in the compound.

Accusative θεο–μάχος *fighting God,* σπερμο–λόγος *picking up seeds.*

Genitive νομο–διδάσκαλος, *teacher of law,* οἰκο–νόμος, *manager of a house.*

Ablative θεο–δίδακτος, *taught of God* like διδακτοὶ θεοῦ (Is. 6:45), διο–πετής *fallen from Zeus.*

Locative ἀκρο–γωνιαῖος *at the extreme corner,* εὐ–πάρ– εδρος *sitting beside,* χείμα–ερος *flowing in winter.*

Instrumental αἰχμ–άλωτος *captured by a spear,* θεό–πνευστος *inspired by God,* χειρο–ποίητος *made by hand.*

Dative εἰδωλο – λατρεία *idolatry or giving worship to idols,* ἀνθρωπ–άρεσκος *pleasing men.*

(d) *Descriptive Determinative Compounds.*

Here the first element describes the second. The first element may be substantive, adjective, or adverb. Here are some illustrations: ἀγρι–έλαιος *wild olive,* αὐτ–όπτης *self seer or eye-witness,* μονο–γενής *only begotten,* μεγαλο–πρεπής *grand-befitting,* συν–πρεσβύτερος *fellow elder.*

(e) *Possessive Compounds.*

Here the first part qualifies the second part like an adjective or adverb and the whole has the notion of belonging to something or having something. As examples note ὀλιγό–πιστος *having little faith,* ὁμό–τεχνος *of the same trade,* σκληρο– τράχηλος *stiff-necked,* χρυσο–δακτύλιος *having gold ring on finger.*

(f) *Denominative Compound Verbs.*

I have given a list of the most striking new compound verbs seen in the New Testament in my large *Grammar,* pp. 163 to 165, many of which are denominative like ἀλλ–ηγορέω, ἀντ–οφθαλμέω, δι–ερμηνεύω, εἰρηνο–ποιέω, ἐπι–χορηγέω, λιθο–βολέω, λογο–μαχέω, ὀρθο–τομέω, προσωπο–λημπτέω.

319. *Synonyms.*

The history of words is as interesting as the history of people and sometimes as perplexing.   But a single word may have as plain a record of the change of ideas in man's mind as the rocks preserve the story of previous ages.   We begin with etymology, but we must go on and note the changes wrought by suffixes and usage.   Take the root κριν–, for instance, and run it through all the New Testament words.   Start with the verbs κρίν–ω, ἀνα–κρίνω, ἀπο–κρίν–ομαι, ἀντ–απο–κρίν–ομαι, δια–κρίνω–, ἐγ–κρίν–ω, ἐπι–κρίν–ω, κατα–κρίν–ω, συγ–κρίν–ω, ὑπο–κρίν–ω, συν–υπο–κρίν–ω.   Then take the substantives κρί–σις, κρί–μα, κρι–τής, κρι–τήριον, ἀνά–κρι–σις, ἀπό–κρι–σις, διά–κρι–σις, κατά–κρι–σις, ὑπό–κρι–σις, ἀπό–κρι–μα, κατα–κρι–μα, πρό–κρι–μα, ὑπο–κρι–τής, εἰλι–κρίν–εια.   Then come the adjectives, κρι–τικός, ἀ–διά–κρι–τος, ἀ–κατά–κρι–τος, ἀν–υπό–κρι–τος, αὐτο–κατά–κρι–τος, εἰλι–κριν–ής.   There are contrasts in words as important as kinships.   What is the difference, for instance, between ἀγαθός, ἅγιος, δίκαιος, καθαρός, καλός, ὅσιος?   Or between ἀμαρτωλός, κακός, πανοῦργος, πονηρός?   Or between, ἔργον, δύναμις, σημεῖον, τέρας?   Words have histories, kinships, contrasts.   The preacher is a linguistic expert by profession as an interpreter and user of words.   Wise is the preacher who knows his parts of speech and in particular the rich language of the Greek New Testament.

CHAPTER IX

PRINCIPAL PARTS OF SOME IMPORTANT VERBS

320. The perfectly regular verbs like λύω, φιλέω, φωτίζω, etc., call for no comment. All that is here attempted is a summary of the most important verbs in the New Testament that have anything specially noteworthy about any of the tenses. It will be a handy list for the student. Only the forms that occur in the N. T. are given including the compounds. Few things are more essential in Greek than a ready knowledge of the verb.

Ἀγαλλιάω (–άομαι), ἠγαλλίασα (–ασάμην), ἠγαλλιάθην (–άσθην B L in Jo. 5:35).

Ἀγγέλλω (comp. ἀν–, ἀπ–, δι–, ἐξ–, ἐπ–, προ–επ–, κατ–, προ–κατ–, παρ–), ἤγγελλον, ἀγγελῶ, ἤγγειλα, –ήγγελμαι, –ηγγέλην.

Ἄγω (comp. ἀν–, ἐπ–αν–, ἀπ–, συν–απ–, δι–, εἰσ–, παρ–εισ–, ἐξ–, ἐπ–, κατ–, μετ–, παρ–, περι–, προ–, προσ–, συν–, ἐπι–συν–, ὑπ–), ἦγον, ἄξω, ἤγαγον and ἦξα, ἤχθην, ἀχθήσομαι.

Αἰνέω (comp. ἐπ–, παρ -), –ῄνουν, –αινέσω, –ῄνεσα.

Αἱρέω (comp. ἀν–, ἀφ–, δι–, ἐξ–, καθ–, περι–, προ–), –ῃρούμην, –ελῶ and αἱρήσομαι, –εῖλον and –εῖλα, εἱλάμην, –ῄρημαι, ᾑρέθην, αἱρεθήσομαι.

Αἴρω (comp. ἀπ–, ἐξ–, ἐπ–, μετ–, συν–, ὑπερ–), ἀρῶ, ἦρα, ἦρκα, ἦρμαι, ἤρθην, ἀρθήσομαι. Imper. ἆρον and inf. ἆραι.

Αἰσθάνομαι, ᾐσθόμην.

Ἀκούω (comp. δι–, εἰσ–, ἐπ–, παρ–, προ–, ὑπ–), ἤκουον, ἀκούσω and ἀκούσομαι, ἤκουσα, ἀκήκοα, ἠκούσθην, ἀκουσθήσομαι.

Ἀλλάσσω (comp. ἀπ–, δι–, κατ–, ἀπο–κατ–, μετ–, συν–), ἤλλασσον ἀλλάξω, ἤλλαξα, –ήλλαγμαι, –ηλλάγην, ἀλλαγήσομαι.

Ἁμαρτάνω (προ–), ἁμαρτήσω, ἥμαρτον and ἡμάρτησα, ἡμάρτηκα.

Ἀμφι–έννυμι, ἠμφίεσμαι, but ἀμφιάζει (late word) in Lu. 12:28.

'Ανα–βαίνω (only in comp., ἀνα–, προσ–ανα–, συν–ανα–, ἀπο–, δια–, ἐκ–, ἐμ–, ἐπι–, κατα–, μετα–, παρα–, προ–, συμ–, ὑπερ), –ἐβαινον, –βήσομαι, –ἐβην, –βέβηκα. Short forms ἀνάβα, ἀνάβατε in imperative.

'Ανα–θάλλω, only ἀν–έθαλον (Phil. 4:10).

'Αν–αλίσκω (only in comp., ἀν–, προσ–αν–, κατ–αν–). Other forms from ἀναλόω, ἀναλώσω, ἠνάλωσα and ἀνάλωσα, ἀνηλώθην.

'Ανα–τέλλω see under ἐν–τέλλομαι.

'Ανα–τρέπω (only comp., ἀνα–, ἀπω–, ἐκ–, ἐν–, ἐπι–, μετα–, περι–, προ–), –τρέπομαι, –ετρεπόμην, –ἐτρεψα, –ετρεψάμην, –ετράπην, –τραπήσομαι.

'Αν–ίημι, ἀφ–ίημι see under ἵημι.

'Αν–οίγω (only in comp., ἀν–, δι–αν–), ἤνοιγον, ἀνοίξω, ἀνέῳξα, ἤνοιξα, and ἠνέῳξα, ἠνέῳγα, ἀνεῳγμένος and ἠνεῳγμένος, ἠνοίγην, ἀνοιγήσομαι, ἀνεῴχθην, ἠνοίχθην, and ἠνεῴχθην, ἀνοιχθήσομαι.

'Απαντάω (only in comp., ἀπ–, κατ–, συν–, ὑπ–), –αντήσω, –ήντησα, –ήντηκα.

'Αποκτείνω (only in comp.), ἀποκτενῶ, ἀπέκτεινα, ἀπεκτάνθην. Pres. inf. also ἀποκτέννεσθαι.

'Απο–κυέω (only in comp.), ἀπ–εκύησα, Nestle ἀποκύει (Jas. 1:15).

'Απόλλυμι and ἀπολλύω (only in comp., ἀπ–, συν–απ–), ἀπολέσω and ἀπολῶ, ἀπώλεσα, ἀπολωλώς; midd. ἀπόλλυμαι, ἀπωλλύμην, ἀπολοῦμαι, ἀπωλόμην.

Ἅπτω (ἀν–, καθ–, περι–), ἡπτόμην, ἧψα, ἡψάμην, ἥφθην.

'Απ–ωθέω (only comp., ἀπ–, ἐξ–), –ῶσα, –ωσάμην.

'Αρέσκω, ἤρεσκον, ἀρέσω, ἤρεσα.

'Αρκέω (ἐπ–), ἤρκεσα, ἀρκεσθήσομαι.

'Αρνέομαι (ἀπ–), ἠρνούμην, ἀρνήσομαι, –ηρνησάμην, ἤρνημαι, –αρνηθήσομαι.

Ἁρπάζω (δι–, συν–), ἁρπάσω, ἥρπασα, –ηρπάκειν, ἡρπάγην, ἡρπάσθην, ἁρπαγήσομαι.

Ἄρχω (ἐν–, προ–εν–, ὑπ–, προ–ὑπ–), ἦρχον, ἄρξομαι, ἠρξάμην.

Αὐξάνω (συν–, ὑπερ–), ηὔξανον, αὐξήσω, ηὔξησα, ηὐξήθην.

'Αφ–ικνέομαι (only comp., ἀφ–, δι–, ἐφ–), ἀφικόμην.

Βαίνω, see ἀναβαίνω. Causal—βιβάζω (ἀνα–, ἐμ–, ἐπι–, κατα–, προ–, συν–).

Βάλλω (ἀμφι–, ἀνα–, ἀντι–, ἀπο–, δια–, ἐκ–, ἐμ–, παρ–εμ–, ἐπι–, κατα–, μετα–, παρα–, περι–, προ–, συμ–, ὑπερ–, ὑπο–), ἔβαλλον, βαλῶ, βαλοῦμαι, ἔβαλον and once ἔβαλα, –εβαλόμην, βέβληκα, –βεβλήκειν, βέβλημαι, ἐβεβλήμην, ἐβλήθην, βληθήσομαι.
Βαπτίζω, ἐβάπτιζον, ἐβαπτιζόμην, βαπτίσω, ἐβάπτισα, (–σάμην), βεβάπτισμαι, ἐβαπτίσθην, βαπτισθήσομαι.
Βιόω, ἐβίωσα.
Βλάπτω, βλάψω, ἔβλαψα.
Βλαστάνω, ἐβλάστησα, βλαστᾷ (Mk. 4:27) from βλαστάω.
Βλέπω (ἀνα–, ἀπο–, δια–, ἐμ–, ἐπι–, περι–, προ–), ἔβλεπον, ἐβλεπόμην, βλέψω, ἔβλεψα, βλεψάμενος.
Βούλομαι, ἐβουλόμην, ἐβουλήθην. Note βούλει (Lu. 22:42)

Γαμέω, ἐγάμουν, ἔγημα and ἐγάμησα, γεγάμηκα, ἐγαμήθην. Γαμίσκω only in present.
Γελάω (κατα–), –εγέλων, γελάσω.
Γίνομαι (ἀπο–, δια–, ἐπι–, παρα–, συμ–παρα–, προ–), ἐγινόμην, γενήσομαι, ἐγενόμην, and ἐγενήθην, γέγονα, ἐγεγόνειν, γεγόνειν, γεγένημαι. Never γίγνομαι as in Attic.
Γινώσκω (ἀνα–, δια–, ἐπι–, κατα–, προ–), ἐγίνωσκον, γνώσομαι, ἔγνων, ἔγνωκα, ἐγνώκειν, ἔγνωσμαι, ἐγνώσθην, γνωσθήσομαι. subj. γνῷ and γνοῖ, imper. γνῶθι, inf. γνῶναι, part. γνούς. Never γιγνώσκω.
Γράφω (ἀπο–, ἐγ–, ἐπι–, κατα–, προ–), ἔγραφον, γράψω, ἔγραψα, –εγραψάμην, γέγραφα, γέγραμμαι, –εγεγράμμην, ἐγράφην.

Δείκνυμι and δεικνύω (ἀνα–, ἀπο–, ἐν–, ἐπι–, ὑπο–), δείξω, ἔδειξα, –εδειξάμην, ἐδείχθην, –δεδειγμένος.
Δέομαι (προσ–), ἐδεόμην, ἐδεήθην. In Lu. 8:38 W H read ἐδεῖτο. Impersonal δεῖ and ἔδει.
Δέρω, ἔδειρα, δαρήσομαι.
Δέχομαι (ἀνα–, ἀπο–, δια–, εἰσ–, ἐκ–, ἀπ–εκ–, ἐν–, ἐπι–, προσ–, παρα–, ὑπο–), ἐδεχόμην, δέξομαι, ἐδεξάμην, δέδεγμαι, –εδέχθην.
Δέω (κατα–, περι–, συν–, ὑπο–), δήσω, ἔδησα, –εδησάμην, δέδεκα, δέδεμαι, –εδεδέμην, ἐδέθην.
Διακονέω (only thus), διηκόνουν, διακονήσω, διηκόνησα, διηκονήθην.

Δια–τρίβω (only comp., συν–), –έτριβον, τρίψω, –έτριψα, –τέτριμμαι, –τριβήσομαι.

Διδάσκω, ἐδίδασκον, διδάξω, ἐδίδαξα, ἐδιδάχθην.

Δίδωμι and occasionally διδόω (ἀνα–, ἀπο–, ἀντ–απο–, δια–, ἐκ–, ἐπι–, μετα–, παρα–, προ–), ἐδίδουν, δώσω, δώσομαι, ἔδωκα and sometimes ἔδωσα, δέδωκα, δεδώκειν and ἐδεδώκειν, δέδομαι, ἐδόθην, δοθήσομαι. 2 aorist ind. plural ἐδώκαμεν, subj. δῷ, δοῖ, and δώῃ, opt. δῴη in Eph. 1:17 (W H text) instead of δοίη. Imperf. ind. midd. occasionally ἐδίδετο and 2 aor. ind. midd. sometimes ἔδετο.

Δι–ορύσσω (only comp., ἐξ–), –ώρυξα, –ωρύγην, –ωρύχθην.

Διψάω, διψήσω, ἐδίψησα.   In Jo. 7:37 διψᾷ.

Διώκω (ἐκ–, κατα–), ἐδίωκον, διώξω, ἐδίωξα, δεδίωγμαι, διωχθήσομαι.

Δοκέω (εὐ–, συν–ευ–), ἐδόκουν, ηὐδόκουν, ἔδοξα, εὐδόκησα, ηὐδόκησα.

Δύναμαι, ἐδυνάμην and ἠδυνάμην, δυνήσομαι, ἠδυνήθην and ἠδυνάμην, ἠδυνάσθην.   Both δύνασαι and δύνῃ.

Δύω and δύνω (ἐκ–, ἀπ–εκ–, in midd. ἐν–, ἐπι–, ἐπ–εν–, παρ–εισ–), ἔδυν and ἔδυσα (–εδυσάμην), –εδύην.

Ἐάω (προσ–), εἴων, ἐάσω, εἴασα.

Ἐγγίζω (προσ–), ἤγγιζον, ἐγγίσω, ἤγγισα, ἤγγικα.

Ἐγείρω (δι–, ἐξ–, ἐπ–, συν–), ἐγείρομαι, –εγειρόμην (Jo. 6:18), ἐγερῶ, ἤγειρα, ἐγήγερμαι, ἠγέρθην, ἐγερθήσομαι.

Εἶδον, see ὁράω.

Εἴδω is obsolete in present, but perfect is common. Οἶδα (in both numbers, ἴσασιν once in Acts 26:4 and ἴστε), subj. εἰδῶ, opt. absent, imper. ἴστε (Jas. 1:19), inf. εἰδέναι, part, εἰδώς, past perfect ᾔδειν, future perf. εἰδήσω (Heb. 8:11).

Ἔθω is obsolete, but εἴωθα and εἰώθειν occur.

Εἴκω (ὑπο–), εἶξα.

Ἔοικα is from obsolete present εἴκω.

Εἰμί (ἀπ–, ἐν–, ἐξ–, πάρ, συμ–πάρ–, σύν–), ἦν and ἤμην, ἔσομαι (ἔσται). Ἔστω and ἤτω. Cf. ἴσθι and ἦσθα.

Εἶμι (only comp., ἀπ–, εἴσ–, ἐξ–, ἐπ–, σύν–), –ῄειν. Present always in future sense.

Εἶπον from ἔπω obsolete present, (ἀντ–, ἀπ–, προ–) and εἶπα, –ειπάμην, ἐρῶ, εἴρηκα, εἰρήκειν, εἴρημαι, ἐρρέθην and ἐρρήθην (Attic). Both εἰρήκασιν and εἴρηκαν, εἰπόν and εἰπέ, εἰπών and εἴπας, εἶπες, and εἶπας, but only εἰπάτω, εἴπατε, εἰπάτωσαν.

Ἐκ–τείνω (only comp., ἐκ–, ἐπ–εκ–, παρα–, προ–, ὑπερ–εκ–) –τείνομαι, –ἔτεινον, –τενῶ, –ἔτεινα.

Ἐκ–χέω and ἐκ–χύν(ν)ω (only comp., ἐκ–, ἐπι–, κατα–, συγ–, ὑπερ–εκ–), –χέομαι, –ἔχεον, χύννομαι, –εχυννόμην, –ἔχυννον, –χεῶ, –ἔχεα, –κέχυμαι, –εχύθην, –χυθήσομαι. Uncontracted forms ἐκχέετε and ἐξέχεεν.·

Ελαύνω (ἀπ–), ἐλαύνομαι, ἠλαυνόμην, –ἤλασα, ἐλήλακα.

Ἐλέγχω (δια–κατ–), ἐλέγχομαι, –ηλεγχόμην, ἐλέγξω, ἤλεγξα (–άμην), ἠλέγχθην.

Ἕλκω, εἷλκον, ἑλκύσω, εἵλκυσα.

Ἐλπίζω (ἀπ–, προ–), ἤλπιζον, ἐλπιῶ, ἤλπισα, ἤλπικα.

Ἐν–τέλλομαι (only comp. and midd.), –τελοῦμαι, –ετειλάμην, –τέταλμαι, but also ἀνα–, ἐξ–ανα–(–ἔτειλα,– τέ–ταλκα).

Ἐργάζομαι (κατ–, περι–,προσ–), εἰργαζόμην (some MSS) and ἠργαζόμην (so W H), ἠργασάμην, εἴργασμαι (passive), –εἰργάσθην.

Ἔρχομαι (ἀν–, ἐπ–αν–, ἀπ–, δι–, εἰσ–, ἐπ–εισ–, παρ–εισ–, συν–εισ–, ἐξ–, δι–εξ–, ἐπ–, κατ–, παρ–, ἀντι–παρ–, περι–, προ–, προσ–, συν–), ἠρχόμην, ἐλεύσομαι, ἦλθον, and ἦλθα, ἐλήλυθα, ἐληλύθειν.

Ἐρωτάω (δι–, ἐπ–), ἠρώτων and ἠρώτουν, ἐρωτήσω, ἠρώτησα, ἠρωτήθην.

Ἐσθίω and ἔσθω (κατ–, συν–), ἤσθιον, φάγομαι, ἔφαγον.

Εὐαγγελίζω (προ–), εὐαγγελίζομαι, εὐηγγελιζόμην, εὐηγγέλισα (–σάμην), εὐηγγέλισμαι, εὐηγγελίσθην.

Εὐδοκέω. See δοκέω.

Εὐκαιρέω, εὐκαίρουν (also ηὐκ–), εὐκαίρησα.

Εὐλογέω goes regularly with εὐ (not ηὐ) in most MSS.

Εὑρίσκω (ἀν–), εὑρίσκομαι, εὕρισκον, and ηὑρ–, ηὑρισκόμην, εὑρήσω, εὗρον, (εὕραμεν, etc.), εὑρόμην and εὕρησα (some MSS.) εὕρηκα, εὑρέθην, εὑρεθήσομαι.

Εὐφραίνω, εὐφραίνομαι, εὐφραινόμην, ηὐφράνθην, εὐφρανθήσομαι.

Εὔχομαι (προσ–), ηὐχόμην, –εὔξομαι, εὐξάμην.

Ἔχω (ἀν–, ἀντ–, ἀπ–, ἐν–, ἐπ–, κατ–, μετ–, παρ–, περι–, προ–, προσ–, συν–, ὑπερ–, ὑπο–), ἔχομαι, εἶχον, (εἴχαμεν, etc.), εἰχόμην, ἕξω, ἕξομαι, ἔσχον, (ἔσχα), ἐσχόμην, ἔσχηκα. Εἴχοσαν as well as εἶχαν and εἶχον.

Ζάω (ζήω) (ἀνα–, συ–), ἔζων, ζήσω (–ζήσομαι), ἔζησα. Ind. ζῆς, inf. ζῆν.
Ζώννυμι and ζωννύω (ἀνα–, δια–, περι–, ὑπο–), ἐζώννυον, ζώσω, –ζώ-σομαι, –έζωσα, ἐζωσάμην, –έζωσμαι.

Ἥκω (ἀν–, καθ–), ἦκον, ἥξω, ἦξα, ἦκα (some MSS. in Mk. 8:3). Some MSS. ἥκασιν instead of ἥκουσιν.

Ἡττάομαι, ἥττημαι, ἡσσώθην (2 Cor. 12:13) from ἡσσόω (Text. Rec. ἡττήθην).

Θάπτω (συν–), ἔθαψα, ἐτάφην.

Θαυμάζω (ἐκ–), ἐθαύμαζον, θαυμάσω, ἐθαύμασα, ἐθαυμάσθην, θαυμασ-θήσομαι.

Θέλω (not ἐθέλω), ἤθελον, θελήσω, ἠθέλησα.

Θιγγάνω, ἔθιγον.

Θλίβω (ἀπο–, συν–), ἔθλιβον, τέθλιμμαι.

Θνῄσκω (ἀπο–, συν–απο–), –έθνησκον, –θανοῦμαι, –έθανον, τέθνηκα, ἐτεθνήκειν. Both τεθνάναι and τεθνηκέναι, but only τεθνηκώς. Simplex perfect only,

Θύω, θύομαι, ἔθυον, ἔθυσα, τέθυμαι, ἐτύθην.

Ἵημι (comp. only, ἀν–, ἀφ–, καθ–, παρ–, συν–).

1 Ἀν–ίημι (–ιέντες, –ῶ, –έντες, –έθην).

2 Ἀφ–ίημι (also ἀφ–ίω, –ιουσιν Rev. 11:9, –ιομεν Lu. 11: 4, –ιονται W H mg. Jo. 20:23, ἤφιε Mk. 1:34 and 11:16. Tisch. reads, ἀφ–ιουσιν Rev. 11:9 as if from ἀφ–ιέω W H read ἀφεῖς Rev. 2:20 contr. for ἀφίεις), –ίεμαι, –ήσω, –ῆκα (–ῆκες Rev. 2:4, but ἄφ–ες, ἄφ–ετε, ἀφ–ῶ, ἀφ–εῖναι, ἀφ–είς), ἀφ–έωνται in Lu. 6:20 (Doric perfect for ἀφ–εῖνται), –έθην, –εθήσομαι.

3 Καθ–ίημι, –ιέμενος (Acts 10:11), –ῆκα.

4 Παρ–ίημι, –ειμένος (Heb. 12:12), –εῖναι Lu. 11:42.

5 Συν–ίημι (MSS. –ιοῦσιν Matt. 13:13 and 2 Cor. 10:12 from συν–ιέω, but W H read συν–ιᾶσιν. In Mk. 4:12 and Lu. 8:10 W H have –ίωσιν from –ίω. So –ίων in Rom. 3:11, but –ιείς in Matt. 13:23), –ήσω, –ῆκα (–ῶ, σύν–ετε Mk. 7:14).

Ἱλάσκομαι, ἱλάσθητι (Lu. 18:13).

Ἵστημι, ἱστάνω, ἱστάω, (ἀν–, ἐπ–αν–, ἐξ–αν–, ἀνθ–, ἐξ–ανθ–, ἀφ–, δι–, ἐν–, ἐξ–, ἐπ–(ἐπίσταμαι), ἐφ–, κατ–εφ–, συν–εφ–, καθ–, ἀντι–καθ–, ἀπο–καθ–, μεθ–, παρ–, περι–, προ–, συν–), –ιστά-μην, στήσω (–ήσομαι), ἔστην, ἔστησα, ἔστηκα (intr.) and εἰ(ι)στήκειν, ἐστάθην, σταθήσομαι. Both ἑστώς and ἑστηκώς, but always ἑστάναι.

Καθαίρω (δια–, ἐκ–) –εκάθαρα, κεκάθαρμαι.

Καθαρίζω (δια–), καθαριῶ, ἐκαθάρισα, κεκαθάρισμαι, ἐκαθαρίσθην, ἐκαθε-ρίσθη (Matt. 8:3).

Κάθημαι (συγ–), καθέζομαι (παρα–), καθίζω (ἀνα–, ἐπι–, παρα–, περι–, συγ–); ἐκαθήμην, καθήσομαι. Κάθου (κάθησο); ἐκαθεζόμην, καθίσω (–ίσομαι), ἐκάθισα, ἐκαθισάμην, κεκάθικα.

Καίω (ἐκ–, κατα–), καίομαι, –έκαιον, καύσω, –έκαυσα, κέκαυμαι, –εκάην, –εκαύθην, –καήσομαι, καυθήσομαι. In 1 Cor. 13:3 some MSS. have καυθήσωμαι.

Κάμνω, ἔκαμον.

Καλέω (ἀντι–, ἐν–, εἰσ–, ἐπι–, μετα–, παρα–, συν–παρα–, προ–, προσ–, συν–), καλέομαι, ἐκάλουν, καλέσω, καλέσομαι, ἐκάλεσα, ἐκαλεσάμην, κέκληκα, κέκλημαι, (ἐ)κεκλήμην, ἐκλήθην, κληθήσομαι.

Κατ–άγνυμι (only compound), –εάξει (sic with augment in future Matt. 12:20 where LXX has κατάξει), –έαξαν in Jo. 19:32f and subj. κατεαγῶσιν in Jo. 19:31 (augment again) from κατεάγην.

Κεράννυμι (συγ–) and κεραννύω, ἐκέρασα, κεκέρασμαι, κέκραμαι.

Κερδαίνω, κερδήσω, κερδανῶ, ἐκέρδησα (κερδάνω some MSS, in 1 Cor. 9:21), κερδηθήσομαι.

Κλαίω, ἔκλαιον, κλαύσω, κλαύσομαι, ἔκλαυσα.

Κλάω (ἐκ–, κατα–) –κλάομαι, ἔκλασα, ἐκλάσθην.

Κλείω (ἀπο–, ἐκ–, κατα–, συγ–), κλείσω, ἔκλεισα, κέκλεισμαι, ἐκλείσθην.

Κλίνω (ἀνα–, ἐκ–, κατα–, προσ–), κλινῶ, ἔκλινα, κέκλικα, ἐκλίθην, κλιθήσομαι.

Κομίζω (ἐκ–, συγ–), –εκομιζόμην, κομίσομαι and κομιοῦμαι, ἐκόμισα, ἐκομισάμην.

Κόπτω (ἀνα–, ἐκ–, ἐν–, κατα–, προ–, προσ–), κόπτομαι, ἐκοπόμην ἔκοπτον, κόψω, κόψομαι, –ἔκοψα, ἐκοψάμην, –εκόπην, κοπήσομαι.

Κορέννυμι, κεκόρεσμαι, ἐκορέσθην.

Κράζω (ἀνα–), ἔκραζον, κράξω, ἔκραξα and ἐκέκραξα, –ἔκραγον, κέκραγα. Some MSS. κεκράξομαι.

Κρέμαμαι (ἐκ–), κρεμαννύω, κρεμάζω, and κρεμάω, ἐξ–εκρέμετο (Lu. 19:48), ἐκρέμασα, ἐκρεμάσθην.

Κρίνω (ἀνα–, ἀπο–, ἀντ–απο–, δια–, ἐν–, ἐπι–, κατα–, συν–, ὑπο–, συν–υπο–), κρίνομαι, ἔκρινον, ἐκρινόμην, κρινῶ, ἔκρινα, –εκρινάμην, κέκρικα, κεκρίκειν, κέκριμαι, ἐκρίθην, κριθήσομαι.

Κρύπτω (ἀπο–, ἐν–, περι–), ἔκρυψα, κέκρυμμαι, ἐκρύβην, –ἔκρυβον.

Κυλίω (ἀνα–, ἀπο–, προσ–), –εκυλιόμην, κυλίσω, –εκύλισα, –κεκύλισμαι.

Λαγχάνω, ἔλαχον.

Λαμβάνω (ἀνα–, ἀντι–, συν–αντι–, ἀπο–, ἐπι–, κατα–, μετα–, παρα–, συν–παρα–, προ–, προσ–, συλ–, συν–περι–, ὑπο–), λαμβάνομαι, ἐλάμβανον, λήμψομαι, ἔλαβον, (ἐλάβατε, 1 Jo. 2:27), ἐλαβόμην, εἴληφα, –εἴλημμαι, –ελήμφθην, λημφθήσομαι. Λάβε, not λαβέ. Εἴληφες in Rev. 11:17.

Λανθάνω (ἐκ–, ἐπι–), ἔλαθον, –ελαθόμην, –λέλησμαι.

Λέγω (ἀντι–, δια–, ἐπι–, προ–) to say, λέγομαι, ἔλεγον, ἐλεγόμην, –ελεξάμην, –ελέχθην. Some MSS. ἔλεγαν in Jo. 11:56. Cf. εἶπον.

Λέγω to collect (only comp. ἐκ–, ἐπι–, κατα–, παρα–, συλ–), –λέγομαι, –ελεγόμην, –λέξω, –ἔλεξα (–άμην), –λέλεγμαι.

Λείπω (ἀπό–, δια–, ἐκ–, ἐπι–, κατα–, ἐν–κατα–, περι–, ὑπο–), ἔλειπον, –λείψω, –ἔλιπον, ἔλειψα, –λέλειμμαι, –ελείφθην.

Λούω (ἀπο–), λούομαι, ἔλουσα, ἐλουσάμην, λέλουμαι (λέλουσμαι MSS. Heb. 10:22).

Μανθάνω (κατα–), ἔμαθον, μεμάθηκα.

Μέλω, only μέλει impersonal, ἔμελε and μελέτω (1 Cor. 7:21). Ἐπι–μέλομαι and ἐπι–μελέομαι, –μελήσομαι, –εμελήθην. Μετα–μέλομαι, –εμελόμην, –εμελήθην, –μελεθήσομαι.

Μέλλω, ἔμελλον and ἤμελλον, μελλήσω.

Μένω (ἀνα–, δια–, ἐν–, ἐπι–, κατα–, παρα–, συν–παρα– in Receptus only Phil. 1:25, περι–, προσ–, ὑπο–), ἔμενον, μενῶ, ἔμεινα, –μεμένηκα, μεμενήκειν.

Μίγνυμι and μίσγω (συν–ανα–), μίγνυμαι, ἔμιξα, μέμιγμαι.

Μιμνήσκω (ἀνα–, ἐπ–ανα–, ὑπο–), μιμνήσκομαι, –μνήσω, –ἐμνησα, μέμνημαι, ἐμνήσθην, μνησθήσομαι.

Νύσσω (κατα–), ἔνυξα, –ενύγην.

Ξηραίνω, present active does not occur, ξηραίνομαι, ἐξήρανα, ἐξήραμμαι, ἐξηράνθην.

Ξυρέω and late form ξυράω, and ξύρω (possibly ξύρασθαι in 1 Cor. 11:6), ξυρήσομαι, ἐξυράμην, ἐξύρημαι.

Οἰκοδομέω (ἀν–, ἐπ–, συν–), οἰκοδομοῦμαι, ᾠκοδόμουν, οἰκοδομήσω, ᾠκοδόμησα (also οἰκοδ–), ᾠκοδόμημαι, οἰκοδομῆσθαι (Lu. 6:48), ᾠκοδομήμην, ᾠκοδομήθην, οἰκοδομήθην (Jo. 2:20), οἰκοδομηθήσομαι.

Ὄμνυμι (Mk. 14:71), ὀμνύω (Matt. 26:74), ὤμοσα Matt. 23:18) from root ὀμο–.

Ὀνίνημι, only opt. ὀναίμην (Philemon 20) second aorist middle ὠνάμην.

Ὁράω (ἀφ–, καθ–, προ–), ὁρῶμαι, ἑώρων (some MSS. in Jo. 6:2), –ωράμην (–ορώμην), ὄψομαι, ὠψάμην (Lu. 13:28), ἑώρακα and ἑόρακα, ἑωράκειν, ὤφθην, ὀφθήσομαι. Εἶδον (εἶδα, εἴδαμεν) is from obsolete stem ιδ (Latin *video*). Subj. ἴδω, Imper. ἴδε, (not ἰδέ), inf., ἰδεῖν, part. ἰδών.

Παίζω (ἐν–), –ἔπαιζον, παίξω, –ἔπαιξα, –ἐπαίχθην, –παιχθήσομαι.

Πάσχω (προ–, συμ–), ἔπαθον, πέπονθα.

Παύω (ἀνα–, ἐπ–ανα–, συν–ανα–, κατα–) is regular save ἀναπαήσομαι.

Πείθω (ἀνα–), πείθομαι, ἔπειθον, (–όμην), πείσω, ἔπεισα, πέποιθα, ἐπεποίθειν, πέπεισμαι, ἐπείσθην, πεισθήσομαι.

Πεινάω, πεινάσω, ἐπείνασα. Inf. πεινᾶν.

Περι–τέμνω (only comp., συν–), –έτεμον, –τέτμημαι, –ετμήθην.

Πήγνυμι (προσ–), ἔπηξα.

Πιάζω and πιέζω (ὑπο–), ἐπίασα, πεπίεσμαι, ἐπιάσθην.

Πίμπλημι (ἐμ–) and ἐμ–πιμπλάω, ἔπλησα, ἐπλήσθην, πλησθήσομαι, πεπλησμένος in Luke 6:25.

Πίμπρημι and πιμπράω (ἐμ–), –έπρησα.

Πίνω (κατα–, συμ–), ἔπινον, πίομαι, ἔπιον, πέπωκα, –επόθην. Both πεῖν (MSS. even πῖν) and πιεῖν, but only πίε. Cf. πίεσαι.

Πιπράσκω, ἐπίπρασκον, πέπρακα, πέπραμαι, ἐπράθην.

Πίπτω (ἀνα–, ἀντι–, ἀπο–, ἐκ–, ἐν–, ἐπι–, κατα–, παρα–, περι–, προσ–, συμ–), ἔπιπτον, πεσοῦμαι, ἔπεσον and ἔπεσα, πέπτωκα. Cf. πέπτωκες (Rev. 2:25) and πέπτωκαν (Rev. 18:3).

Πλάσσω, ἔπλασα, ἐπλάσθην.

Πλέκω (ἐμ–), –πλέκομαι, ἔπλεξα, –επλάκην.

Πλέω (ἀπο–, δια–, ἐκ–, κατα–, παρα–, ὑπο–), –έπλεον, –έπλευσα.

Πλήσσω (ἐκ–, ἐπι–), –πλήσσομαι, –επλησσόμην, –έπληξα, ἐπλήγην (–επλάγην).

Πνέω (ἐκ–, ἐν–, ὑπο–), ἔπνευσα.

Πνίγω (ἀπο–, συμ–), –πνίγομαι, ἔπνιγον, ἐπνιγόμην, ἔπνιξα, –επνίγην.

Πράσσω, πράξω, ἔπραξα, πέπραχα, πέπραγμαι.

Πυνθάνομαι, ἐπυνθανόμην, ἐπυθόμην.

Ῥαντίζω, ἐράντισα (some MSS. ἐρράντ–), ἐραντισάμην, ῥεράντισμαι (some MSS. ἐρρ).

Ῥέω (παρα–), ῥεύσω, –ερρύην.

Ῥήγνυμι and ῥήσσω, (δια–, περι–, προσ–), ῥήγνυμαι, –ερησσόμην, ῥήξω, ἔρ(ρ)ηξα.

Ῥίπτω (ἀπο–, ἐπι–) and ῥιπτέω, ἔριψα (and ἔρρ–), ἔρριμμαι (and ἔρ–).

Σβέννυμι and σβεννύω, σβέννυμαι, σβέσω, ἔσβεσα, σβεσθήσομαι.

Σημαίνω, ἐσήμαινον, ἐσήμανα.

Σπάω (ἀνα–, ἀπο–, δια–, ἐπι–, περι–), –εσπώμην, σπάσω, –έσπασα, ἐσπασάμην, ἔσπασμαι, –εσπάσθην.

Σπείρω (δια–, ἐπι–), σπείρομαι, ἔσπειρον, ἔσπειρα, ἔσπαρμαι, ἐσπάρην.

Στέλλω (ἀπο–, ἐξ–απο–, συν–απο–, δια–, ἐπι–, κατα–, συν– or συ–, ὑπο–), στέλλομαι, –έστελλον, –εστελλόμην, –στελῶ, –έστειλα (–άμην), –έσταλκα, –έσταλμαι, –εστάλην. Cf. ἀπέσταλκαν in Acts 16:36.

Στήκω (cf. mod. Gk. στέκω) pres. from ἕστηκα (cf. γρηγορέω from ἐγρήγορα), imperf. ἕστηκον in Jo. 8:44 and Rev. 12:4 acc. to W H.

Στηρίζω (ἐπι–), στηρίξω and στηρίσω in some MSS. (cf. στηριῶ in LXX), ἐστήριξα and ἐστήρισα, ἐστήριγμαι, ἐστηρίχθην.

Στρέφω (ἀνα–, ἀπο–, δια–, ἐκ–, ἐπι–, κατα–, μετα–, συν–, or συ–, ὑπο–), στρέφομαι, –έστρεφον, –στρέψω, ἔστρεψα, –έστραμμαι, ἐστράφην, στραφήσομαι.

Στρωννύω and στρώννυμι (κατα–, ὑπο–), ἐστρώννυον, ἔστρωσα, ἔστρωμαι, ἐστρώθην.

Συ–ζεύγνυμι (only comp.), συνέζευξα.

Συν–τέμνω (only comp.), συντετμημένος in some MSS (Rom. 9:28).

Σφάζω (κατα–), σφάξω, ἔσφαξα, ἔσφαγμαι, ἐσφάγην.

Σώζω (δια–, ἐκ–), σώζομαι, ἐσωζόμην, σώσω, ἔσωσα, σέσωκα, σέσωσμαι, ἐσώθην, σωθήσομαι.

Τάσσω (ἀνα–, ἀντι–, ἀπο–, δια–, ἐπι–δια–, ἐπι–, προ–, προσ–, συν–, ὑπο–), τάσσομαι, –τάξομαι, ἔταξα (–άμην), τέταχα, τέταγμαι, –ετάγην, –ετάχθην, –ταγήσομαι.

Τελέω (ἀπο–, διά–, ἐκ–, ἐπι–, συν–), τελοῦμαι, τελέσω, ἐτέλεσα, τετέλεκα, τετέλεσμαι, ἐτελέσθην, τελεσθήσομαι.

Τίθημι (ἀνα–, προσ–ανα–, ἀπο–, δια–, ἀντι–δια–, ἐκ–, ἐπι–, κατα–, συν–επι–, συν–κατα–, μετα–, παρα–, περι–, προ–, προσ–, συν–, ὑπο–) and τιθέω (ἐτίθει 2 Cor. 3:13; ἐτίθουν some MSS. Mk. 6:56, but W H ἐτίθεσαν as in Acts. 3:2; 4:35. But ἐπι–τίθει in 1 Tim. 5:22 and τιθέασιν in Mt. 5:15), τίθεμαι, –ετιθέμην, θήσω (–θήσομαι), ἔθηκα (θῶ, –θες Mt. 9:18 and Lk. 17:5, θέτε Lk. 21:14, θεῖναι, θείς), ἐθέμην (–τέθεικα, τέθειμαι, –ετεθείμην, ἐτέθην, –τεθήσομαι.

Τίκτω, τέξομαι, ἔτεκον, ἐτέχθην.

Τρέφω (ἀνα–, ἐκ–, ἐν–) ἔθρεψα, –εθρεψάμην, τέθραμμαι –ετράφην.

Τρέχω (εἰσ–, κατα–, περι–, προ–, προσ–, συν–, ἐπι–συν–, ὑπο–), ἔτρεχον, ἔδραμον.

Τυγχάνω (ἐν–, ὑπερ–εν–, ἐπι–, παρα–, συν–), ἔτυχον, τέτυχα and τέτευχα (or even τετύχηκα in MSS. in Heb. 8:6).

Τύπτω has only present stem in N. T., τύπτομαι, ἔτυπτον. See πατάσσω and πλήγνυμι.

Φαίνω (ἀνα–, ἐπι–), φαίνομαι, φανοῦμαι, –ἔφανα, ἐφάνην, φανήσομαι.

Φέρω (ἀνα–, ἀπο–, δια–, εἰσ–, παρ–εισ–, ἐκ–, ἐπι–, κατα–, παρα–, περι–, προ–, προσ–, συν–, ὑπο–), φέρομαι, ἔφερον (–όμην), οἴσω, –ἤνεγκον and ἤνεγκα, –ενήνοχα, ἠνέχθην.

Φεύγω (ἀπο–, δια–, ἐκ–, κατα–), φεύξομαι, –πέφευγα, ἔφυγον.

Φθάνω (προ–), ἔφθασα, ἔφθακα.

Φθείρω (δια–, κατα–), φθείρεσαι, ἔφθειρον, φθερῶ, ἔφθειρα, –ἐφθάρμαι, ἐφθάρην, φθαρήσομαι.

Φοβέομαι (ἐκ–), ἐφοβούμην, ἐφοβήθην, φοβηθήσομαι. But active ἐκφοβεῖν in 2 Cor. 10:9.

Φορέω, φορέσω, ἐφόρεσα.

Φράσσω, ἔφραξα, ἐφράγην, φραγήσομαι.

Φύω (ἐκ–, συμ–), ἐφύην.

Χαίρω (συν–), ἔχαιρον, ἐχάρην, χαρήσομαι (Textus Receptus χαρῶ in Rev. 11:10).

Χαλάω, χαλάσω, ἐχάλασα, ἐχαλάσθην.

Χαρίζομαι, χαρίσομαι, ἐχαρισάμην, κεχάρισμαι, ἐχαρίσθην, χαρισθήσομαι.

Χράομαι (χρήομαι) (κατα–), ἐχρώμην, ἐχρησάμην, κέχρημαι. Χρή (impersonal) only once, Jas. 3:10.

Ψύχω (ἀνα–, ἀπο–, ἐκ–, κατα–), ψυγήσομαι.

Ὠνέομαι, ὠνησάμην, not ἐπριάμην.

PART IV

SYNTAX

CHAPTER X

THE SENTENCE

321. *The Meaning of Syntax.*

Accidence gives the changes in the inflections of words in their relations with each other. Syntax (σύνταξις) explains the meaning of these word changes, the orderly arrangement of words. Syntax deals not merely with the form, but with the function, and not merely with the relation of words with words, but of clauses with clauses, of sentences with sentences, of paragraphs with paragraphs. Naturally we begin with words. In order to understand the meaning of a sentence in Greek one needs to know the original meaning of each word, the development of these words in history, the meaning of each form, the particular stage reached at the time of writing, the context in the given instance. Do not translate a Greek sentence until you understand its meaning. Never try to explain the Greek idiom by a conjectural translation into English. Syntax is the interpretation of the facts, not a set of rules.

322. *The Meaning of Sentence.*

The Latin *sententia* is the expression of an opinion. This expression of an idea is complex. One makes a statement about something. Here then we have subject and predicate which are the two foci of the sentence considered as an ellipse. The normal sentence involves both subject and predicate as in *Jesus spoke* ('Ιησοῦς ἐλάλησεν, Matt. 23:1). But one word in Greek may involve both subject and predicate as in ἀπέχει (Mk. 14:41, *It is enough*). The personal endings of the verb can indicate the subject as here. As a matter of fact, an idea can be implied, not formally expressed, without either subject or predicate as in the sharp refusal of Elisabeth to allow the boy to be named Zacharias when she said Οὐχί (Lu. 1:60ʻ

Not so).   Martha's "Yea, Lord" Ναί, Κύριε (Jo. 11:27) likewise carries a full idea.

323. *The Subject and Its Modifiers.*

Around the subject may be grouped any number of words (substantives, adjectives, pronouns, article, adverbs, prepositions, participles, relative sentences, etc.) connected by the article, apposition, or merely by position. This center may have various ramifications all made plain by agreement in gender, number, case, and sometimes person. The article may be repeated to make plain that the phrase added is attributive as in Rom. 7:10 ἡ ἐντολὴ ἡ εἰς ζωήν, the commandment the one (meant) for life. Another good example is in Rev. 1:9 ἐγὼ Ἰωάνης, ὁ ἀδελφὸς ὑμῶν καὶ συνκοινωνὸς ἐν τῇ θλίψει καὶ βασιλείᾳ καὶ ὑπομονῇ ἐν Ἰησοῦ *I John* (apposition), *the brother* (apposition) *of you* (genitive) *and co-partner* (following adjuncts without ὁ repeated like ἡ in Rom. 7:10, one article with all three) *in tribulation and kingdom and patience* (no article before adjunct just as after συνκοινωνὸς) *in Jesus*. See in particular Rom. 1:1-6 where all the clauses cling around Παῦλος.

324. *The Predicate and Its Modifiers.*

The predicate makes the statement and is a verb or a copula (like εἰμί, καλοῦμαι, etc.) with a substantive, adjective, etc. Sometimes the copula is not expressed, but only implied as in Rom. 1:7 where neither ἐστίν nor εἴη appears and in Rom. 7:12 ὁ νόμος ἅγιος, *the law is holy*, where ἐστίν is not used. A normal example of the use of the copula is seen in John 10:11 ἐγώ εἰμι ὁ ποιμὴν ὁ καλός, *I am the shepherd the good one*. The predicate may have any number of amplifications by means of object, apposition, adjective, adverb, pronoun, article, participle, relative, conjunctions, etc. A good example appears in Rom. 16:17 παρακαλῶ δὲ ὑμᾶς, ἀδελφοί, σκοπεῖν τοὺς τὰς διχο—στασίας καὶ τὰ σκάνδαλα παρὰ τὴν διδαχὴν ἣν ὑμεῖς ἐμάθετε ποιοῦντας *Now I exhort you, brethren, to keep an eye on those who are making divisions and putting stumbling-blocks contrary to the teaching which you received*. The verb (predicate) has two accusatives (ὑμᾶς, σκοπεῖν). This infinitive σκοπεῖν has an object, the articular participle τοὺς ποιοῦντας. This participle ποιοῦντας has two substantives as object and one prepositional adjunct παρὰ τὴν διδαχήν. The substantive διδαχήν is further described by the relative clause ἣν ὑμεῖς ἐμάθετε. It is all beautifully linked together in a perfectly transparent way radiating from the predicate verb παρακαλῶ (the infinitive to the predicate, the participle to the infinitive, the substantive to the participle, the adjunct to the substantives, the relative clause to the adjunct). The long sentence in Luke 1:1-4 illustrates well how by means of the two foci in the sentence (subject and predicate) in both principal and subordinate clauses, a well-rounded period with literary finish is produced. In Rom. 8:3 it makes a deal of difference in meaning whether ἐν τῇ σαρκί be taken with κατέκρινε, as it should, or with τὴν ἁμαρτίαν as it should not.

325. Apposition both with Subject and Predicate.

This was the earliest method of expanding both subject and predicate as for the subject in ἀνὴρ προφήτης (Lu. 24:19) a man a prophet where the main idea is in the word in apposition, and for the predicate in Rom. 3:25 ὃν προέθετο ὁ θεὸς ἱλαστήριον. Whom God set forth as a propitiation where ἱλαστήριον expands ὃν the object of προέθετο. The word in apposition normally agrees in case with the other word, but this was not always true in the ancient Greek. The papyri give numerous examples of failure to observe this point, particularly with the articular participle. So in Rev. 3:12 ἡ καταβαίνουσα (the one coming down) does not agree in case with the preceding genitive with which it is in apposition τῆς καινῆς Ἰερουσαλήμ (the new Jerusalem).

326. Agreement between Subject and Predicate.

As a rule the predicate agrees with the subject in number, person, and gender (where called for as with adjectives and participles in predicate). So in 1 Cor. 15:9 ὃς οὐκ εἰμὶ ἱκανὸς καλεῖσθαι ἀπόστολος. Who am not fit to be called an apostle.

Εἰμί is used, not ἐστίν, for ὅς is in agreement in person as well as number with ἐγώ. When several persons occur the first prevails over the second and third as in Jo. 10:30 ἐγὼ καὶ ὁ πατὴρ ἔν ἐσμεν. *I and the Father are one*, where in English we usually reverse the order and say *The Father and I are one*. But in this order the first person prevails (Lu. 2:48 ζητοῦμεν). But the agreement is not by mechanical rule, but according to sense very often. This applies to number as in Matt. 21:8 ὁ ὄχλος ἔστρωσαν where the plural verb occurs with a collective substantive. Neuter plural substantives occur with singular or plural verbs indifferently as in Lu. 4:41 where some manuscripts give ἐξήρχετο and some ἐξήρχοντο with δαιμόνια. So in Lu. 8:30 with δαιμόνια again we have εἰσῆλθεν (singular) and the next verse παρεκάλουν (plural). The verb may agree with first subject expressed and be understood with the rest. So in Acts 11:14 ἐν οἷς σωθήσῃ σὺ καὶ πᾶς ὁ οἶκός σου *by which thou wilt be saved and all thy house*, where we have the second person singular (σωθήσῃ) future indicative and merely understood with οἶκος. A striking example occurs in Lu. 2:33 ἦν ὁ πατὴρ αὐτοῦ καὶ ἡ μήτηρ θαυμάζοντες *his father and his mother were wondering* we have to say in English though ἦν is singular with πατὴρ (coming first) and θαυμάζοντες (participle in periphrastic imperfect) is masculine plural agreeing with both πατὴρ and μήτηρ (coming after both). The literary plural is common with Paul as in 1 Thess. 2:18 ἠθελήσαμεν—ἐγὼ Παῦλος *I Paul wished*.

327. *Agreement between Substantive and Adjective (and Participle).*

This agreement in number and gender as in John 10:11 ὁ ποιμὴν ὁ καλός *the shepherd the good one* is often according to sense as ὁ ὄχλος ἐπάρατοι (Jo. 7:49) where the plural verbal ἐπάρατοι (accursed) occurs with the singular ὄχλος (multitude), collective substantive. So as to gender in ἔθνη ἐσκοτισμένοι (Eph. 4:17f). The Greek has grammatical gender as well as natural gender and either may be followed. Some adjectives have no distinctive feminine form or the masculine may be used as feminine as in ζωὴν αἰώνιον (Jo. 6:47) *life eternal* and αἰωνίαν λύτρωσιν (Heb. 9:12) *eternal redemption* (the regular form).

328. *The Use of Anacoluthon.*

Speakers and writers are not slaves of grammatical rules or even of principles. If a sentence becomes involved, a new start can be made by cutting the Gordian Knot without formal agreement. This failure to follow (ἀνακόλουθον) is common in all stages of the Greek language. It appears in the New Testament also in Mk. 7:19 where καθαρίζων agrees with nothing nearer than λέγει at the beginning of verse 18. Westcott and Hort put a dash before it. Colloquial Greek shows it often as in the papyri and it appears in long sentences as in Acts 15:22f where πρεσβυτέροις, ἐκλεξαμένους, γράψαντες do not agree in case. The Book of Revelation in particular has numerous examples, but Paul has it also in his impassioned passages as in 2 Cor. 8:18-20 οὗ—χειροτονηθεὶς (genitive and nominative). In an example like ἀπὸ ὁ ὤν (Rev. 1:4) the nominative is retained on purpose rather than the ablative with ἀπὸ in the same verse to accent the unchangeableness of God.

329. *Simple and Compound Sentences.*

Sentences are either simple (single) or compound. The simple sentence is the earliest, just a single statement. The compound sentence may be either co-ordinate (paratactic) or subordinate (hypotactic). That is, independent statements may be made parallel with each other or dependent on one another. The paratactic sentences may have connective conjunctions (copulative like τε, καί, δέ, ἀλλά; adversative like δέ, ἀλλά, πλήν; disjunctive like ἤ, εἴτε, οὔτε, μήτε; inferential like ἄρα, γάρ, οὖν). There may be asyndeton with no conjunction as in 1 Cor. 13:4-7. The hypotactic sentence likewise will either have conjunctions (relative like ὡς; temporal like ὅτε; comparative like ὥσπερ, causal like ὅτι; final like ἵνα; conditional like εἰ, ἐάν; declarative like ὅτι, etc.) or asyndeton may occur here also as in Lu. 9:54 θέλεις εἴπωμεν; *Dost thou wish that we speak?* where ἵνα is not used.

CHAPTER XI

NOUNS (SUBSTANTIVE AND ADJECTIVE)

330. *The Elements of Speech.*

These are probably verb, noun, and pronoun. It is not certain which is the earliest, verb or noun, possibly now one, now the other. There is little real distinction between a verb root and the noun. Compare the modern English use of the word "work" either as verb or noun. The pronoun is itself of independent origin and has been remarkably persistent in the Indo-Germanic family of languages as can be illustrated by the presence of "me" in them. This shows the personal and social side of speech. Book language is an afterthought. The Greek verb is a combination of the verb-stem and the personal pronoun like δίδω–μι (*give I*). It is not hard to see how the various parts of speech are all linked together. Adverbs, for instance, are formed from verbs, participles, substantives, adjectives, pronouns. χάριν is originally substantive (grace) as in Jo. 1:16, then an adverbial preposition with the genitive as in Eph. 3:14 τούτου χάριν *for this cause*. In 1 Tim. 3:16 ὁμολογουμένως (*confessedly, without controversy*) is made from the participle ὁμολογούμενος.

331. *Noun Includes both Substantive and Adjective.*

The word "noun" is from the Latin *nomen* name and is an appellation applied to a person, thing, or quality. In common usage it is often confined to substantives, but grammatically considered in syntax it includes both substantive and adjective, for both are names (ὀνόματα) applied to persons or things or qualities.

332.   The Adjective a Variation from the Substantive.

In Whitney's *Sanskrit Grammar* there is no separate treatment for adjective. The English word adjective is from the
Latin verb *adjicio* and means something placed beside the
substantive, an added (ἐπίθετον) description. Originally substantives served to express this added idea and that usage
never died out, as γυναῖκα χήραν (Lu. 4:26) *a widow woman*,
ἐν τῷ Ἰορδάνῃ ποταμῷ (Matt. 3:6) *the Jordan River*. Compare
our use of professor, doctor, captain, president, with the proper
name (President Hoover, for instance.)   In Hebrew the genitive case with *ben* (son) often took the place of an adjective
and that is seen in the Greek New Testament as in υἱὸν γεέννης
(Matt. 23:15) *son of hell*. Most of the Sanskrit adjectives
have only one or two endings, though some have all three
genders.   So in Greek ἅρπαξ *rapacious* or *ravening* (Matt. 7:15)
has only one form. Many adjectives in Greek have only
two forms, one for masculine and feminine, one for the neuter.
This is specially true of compound words like ἐπιθυμίαι ἀνόητοι
(1 Tim. 6:9) *foolish lusts*. Some adjectives like αἰώνιος are used
with two or three endings as in 2 Thess. 2:16 παράκλησιν αἰωνίαν
(separate feminine) and Matt. 25:46 ζωὴν αἰώνιον (same as
masculine). The articular neuter adjective is often used in
the same sense as an abstract like τὸ πονηρόν (Rom. 12:9) *the
evil* (*thing*).

333.   Adjectives and Substantives.

Sometimes the substantive is so well known as not to call
for expression as in τῇ ἐπιούσῃ (ἡμέρᾳ) in Acts 16:11 *on the next
day* where the participle in the feminine locative singular
plainly implies ἡμέρᾳ (day). The neuter plural often occurs
with the adjective where only the context can decide the
precise idea as in πνευματικοῖς πνευματικὰ συνκρίνοντες (1 Cor. 2:13)
combining spiritual ideas with spiritual words. Sometimes
only the context can decide whether the articular adjective
in an oblique case is masculine or neuter as in ἀπὸ τοῦ πονηροῦ

(Matt. 6:13) *from the evil one* (Satan or man) or *from what is evil* (the evil thing).

334. Attributive or Predicate Adjectives.

A good example of the attributive adjective without the article is ζωὴν αἰώνιον in Matt. 25:46 *life eternal* and with the article take ὁ ποιμὴν ὁ καλός in Jo. 10:11 *the good shepherd*. Without the article the adjective may be either attributive or predicate. For the predicate adjective see Heb. 7:24 ἀπαρ–άβατον ἔχει τὴν ἱερωσύνην *he holds the priesthood indissoluble* (untransferable) and the repeated use of μακάριοι *happy* in the Beatitudes (Matt. 5:3-11).

335. Comparison of Adjectives.

The positive form may be absolute as with ἀγαθός (*good*) of God in Mk. 10:18. The comparative originally expressed duality or contrast as in πρότερος but it gradually was extended till it began to displace the superlative as in Matt. 18:4 ὁ μείζων *the greatest*. On the other hand the superlative, as with us, occurs where only two are contrasted as in πρῶτός μου *before me* (ablative of comparison) in John 1:15. This idiom is common in modern Greek. The superlative is usually elative like our "very" as in 2 Pet. 1:4 μέγιστα *very great*. A few true superlatives survive like τὴν ἀκριβεστάτην αἵρεσιν (Acts 26:5) *the strictest sect*.

336. The Adjective Frequently an Adverb.

This use of the neuter accusative singular πολύ *much* as an adverb (2 Cor. 8:22) is common as is the plural πολλά (Mk. 9:26). So with the article τὸ πρῶτον (John 12:16) *at the first* and τὸ λοιπόν (Phil. 3:1) *as for the rest*. This accusative of general reference may be the earliest form of the adverb. But the Greek adjective also occurs in a peculiar idiom difficult to render into English as in δευτεραῖοι ἤλθομεν (Acts 28:13) *We ⁀ame second day men* (on the second day). A sharp distinction is observed between πρῶτος in Jo. 20:4, 8 *first* (before Peter) and πρῶτον as in Lu. 10:5 πρῶτον λέγετε *say first* (before doing anything else).

337. *Adjectives Followed by Various Cases.*

So with the genitive as πλήρης χάριτος (Jo. 1:14) *full of grace*, with the ablative as μείζων τοῦ πατρός (Jo. 8:53) *greater than the Father*, with the dative as ἔνοχος τῇ κρίσει (Matt. 5:21) *liable to the judgment*, with the associative instrumental as ὅμοιος ἀνθρώπῳ (Matt. 20:1) *like a man*, and even with the accusative as ὅμοιον υἱὸν ἀνθρώπου (Rev. 14:14) *like a son of man*. The infinitive after the adjective like ἱκανὸς βαστάσαι, (Matt. 3:11) *fit to bear* is also in a case, here the accusative of general reference.

CHAPTER XII

THE CASES

338. *Cases in the Indo-Germanic Tongues.*

(a) *Eight Cases in the Sanskrit.*

The Sanskrit, the oldest known member of the group, has eight well defined cases (nominative, vocative, accusative, genitive, ablative, locative, instrumental, dative). Each of these cases has a separate set of endings except the vocative which is not really a case in the sense that the others are. The Sanskrit case-endings (omitting the dual because it is not used in the κοινή) are:

	Singular	Plural
	m. f. n.	m. f. n.
N.	s or —	as or i
V.	——	——
Acc.	am or —	as or i
G.	as	ām
Abl.	as	bhyas
D.	ē (āi)	bhyas
I.	ā or bhi	bhis (ois or āis)
L.	i	su

It is possible that the old Sanskrit had another case, the associative, which early blended with the instrumental, though Giles (*Comparative Philology*, p. 269) suggests that there may never have been a separate associative case, but only the use of the instrumental with persons or other animate objects (*companions*) in contrast with inanimate objects (*instruments*).

(b) *Varied History of these Eight Case-Forms.*

The Russian language still has the eight case-forms. In modern French, outside of the pronouns, there are no case-forms at all. The others come in between these extremes. Latin had six separate case-forms (the ablative, locative and instrumental appearing under one ending, *i* or *e* for the singular, *is* or *ibus* for the plural like the Sanskrit plural). The Gothic had only four case-forms, the ablative, locative, instrumental, and dative being alike and the vocative now like the nominative and now like the accusative. The German still has five case-forms (nominative, vocative, genitive, accusative, dative). The Anglo-Saxon had six case-forms and in some words all eight. A few Anglo-Saxon words preserve the locative and the ablative endings, though in general these have been blended with the dative and the instrumental (March, *Grammar of the Anglo-Saxon Language*, p. 148). In modern English, outside of the personal pronouns, the eight case-forms have all disappeared save the genitive *s* and it is sometimes represented by the apostrophe or is displaced by the preposition *of*. The κοινή Greek had five case-forms, like the ancient Greek, the genitive and the ablative having the same form like the Sanskrit singular, while the locative, instrumental, and dative have the same endings like the Sanskrit plural. In the modern Greek vernacular the locative, instrumental, and dative cases disappear, εἰς and the accusative being used instead like the English use of *in, with, to*. So modern Greek vernacular has only three case-forms (nominative, accusative, genitive-ablative). But neuter substantives in the old Greek had already blended several case-forms, nominative, vocative, and accusative being alike, genitive and ablative being alike, locative, instrumental, and dative being alike (three case-forms for neuter words). As a matter of fact, the blending had already begun in the Sanskrit, for the ending *as* served for both genitive and ablative singular, while *bhyas* answered for ablative and dative plural and the instrumental *bhis* did not differ greatly. The Greek, unlike the Sanskrit and the Latin, makes the accusative plural in masculine and feminine nouns different (as rather than ες, for instance). But some of the dialects (Northwest Greek, for example) had accusative in ες and papyri examples occur in the κοινή like τοὺς πράκτορες *the tax-gatherers* (B. G. U. 530. i/A. D.). There are remnants of distinctive ablative, locative, and instrumental endings preserved in some Greek words.

339.   *The Origin and Use of the Cases.*

(a)   *Origin of the Endings Unknown.*

They do not exist in separate form. Apparently they are pronominal as the nominative and accusative or local as the ablative and locative. It is all speculation to talk about the purely local cases. The accusative is apparently the oldest of the cases. The ablative was the first case to lose its distinctive ending while the genitive has been the most tenacious (the only separate case-form in English outside of pronouns).

(b)   *The Object of the Cases.*

The purpose of the cases was to show the relation of words to each other. In the isolating languages like the Chinese this is done by the position of the words and by the tone of voice. Hence each case had a distinct idea and these eight cases had to bear the whole burden of expressing the relations of words with each other. The more developed a people became the more difficult it was for the eight cases to make complicated ideas plain.

(c)   *Prepositions to the Rescue.*

The old Sanskrit had no prepositions at all. Some adverbs began to be used with cases to help out the case idea in the later Sanskrit just as we have ἀξίως *worthily* used with τοῦ εὐαγγελίου in Phil. 1:27. In the Greek and Latin this tendency to define more sharply the case idea grew rapidly. "These adverbs, which we now call prepositions. in time became the constant concomitants of some cases; and when this had happened, there is an ever-increasing tendency to find the important part of the meaning in the preposition and not in the case-ending" (Giles, *Comparative Philology*, p. 272). In the Coptic there are no case-endings, but only particles and prepositions as we have seen to be true of French outside of pronouns. The rise of prepositions, therefore, to help the cases bear the burden of word relations marks the beginning of the decline of the case system. But the prepositions have helped preserve the separate ideas confused by the blending of case-endings.

(d) *Recognizing the Case in Spite of the Blending.*

Each of the eight cases had a separate ending and a separate meaning. The only scientific way to interpret the cases is to recognize the case and to give the true meaning to it. It is confusion worse confounded to try to explain the Greek genitive as the "whence-case" as even Winer did. The "whence" idea is ablative, not genitive at all. So also students have been needlessly befuddled by grammars that speak of the dative of place (locative) and the dative of instrument (instrumental). Some grammars now hesitatingly speak of "the true dative", "the locative dative," "the instrumental dative." The "true" dative is the *only* dative, the other examples being locative and instrumental cases. Comparative grammar is the only scientific and historical grammar and it has liberated the minds of all students of the Greek New Testament who are not mere traditionalists. As a rule, the context in the New Testament makes it plain what case idea is present where the endings have blended. Occasionally either case will make sense, though not the same sense. Thus in Rom. 8:24 τῇ ἐλπίδι ἐσώθημεν if ἐλπίδι is in the locative it means *"we are saved* (timeless aorist) *in hope"* while, if it is in the instrumental, the idea is "by hope," and the dative would be "for hope." If there is doubt about the case because of the same ending for two or more cases, try

the meaning of each case in the actual context and see what
the result is.   As a rule that is sufficient.   Thus in Matt. 1:11
ἐπὶ τῆς μετοικεσίας βαβυλῶνος the form βαβυλῶνος can be either
genitive or ablative, but a little knowledge of the Old Testament makes it plain that it is genitive, not ablative, for Jechoniah was not led away *from* Babylon.   It was a Babylon
removal, as a matter of fact *to* Babylon, though the genitive
does not mean *to*, but only a Babylon kind of removal which
we happen to know was to Babylon.   No case is ever used
"for" another (*enallage casuum*).   Each writer or speaker
uses the case in each instance that best expresses the idea
that he has in mind.   He must be allowed full liberty in the
matter.

340.   *The Nominative.*

(a)   *Not the oldest Case.*

That honor belongs to the accusative.   The Hindu grammarians treated it first (*prathama*).   The singular ending *s*
is thought to be demonstrative like the Sanskrit *sas*.

(b)   *The Naming Case.*

So the word nominative means (πτῶσις ὀνομαστική).   Hence
it has come to be the case of the subject where the nominative form is retained unchanged in contrast with the various
oblique cases.   Sometimes the nominative is the mere stem
without *s* as in κεφαλή, sometimes the changed stem as in πατήρ
or ὄνομα.   The real subject in Greek is expressed by the personal ending as in φη–μί *Say I*.   When ἐγώ is also expressed
it is in apposition with μι.   The addition of the pronoun or
noun in apposition with the personal ending is a later development due to the desire for accuracy and clearness.   It is
unscientific, then, to speak of the "omission" of the subject
even in an impersonal verb like ὕει *it rains* or καλῶς ἔχει *it is
well*, for the real subject is expressed in the ending.   Even
in the predicate the nominative is appositional as in Σὺ εἶ Πέτρος

(Matt. 16:18) *Thou art Peter.* Instead of this predicate nominative the New Testament often has εἰs and the accusative as ἔσονται οἱ δύο εἰς σάρκα μίαν (Matt. 19:5) *the two shall be one flesh* as in Gen. 2:24. This idiom occurs occasionally in the κοινή, but is especially common in the Septuagint under the influence of the Hebrew. The French has *c'est moi,* the Latin *dedecori est,* and the English can say *It is me.* The appositional force of the nominative is strikingly illustrated in Αὐτὸs ἐγὼ Παῦλοs παρακαλῶ (2 Cor. 10:1) *I Paul myself exhort.*

(c) *Even in Apposition with Other Cases.*

There was occasional laxity on this point in all writers, particularly in participial phrases. It is common in the papyri. See τῆs καινῆs ᾿Ιερουσαλήμ, ἡ καταβαίνουσα (Rev. 3:12). Sometimes the retention of the nominative form serves in lieu of quotation marks which the ancients did not have as in ὑμεῖs φωνεῖτέ με ὁ διδάσκαλοs καὶ ὁ κύριοs (John 13:13) *Ye call me "The Teacher" and "The Lord."* In a case like ἀπὸ ὁ ὢν καὶ ὁ ἦν καὶ ὁ ἐρχόμενοs the unchangeable nature of God is accented by the retention of the nominative instead of the ablative with ἀπό.

(d) *The Nominative Absolute.*

Moulton naively says that the nominative "has a certain tendency to be residuary legatee of case-relations not obviously appropriated by the other cases." So in the title of books one finds the nominative as in ᾿Αποκάλυψιs ᾿Ιωάνου, in salutations without a verb as in Παῦλοs κλητὸs ἀπόστολοs (1 Cor. 1:1) and even with the infinitive, favorite idiom in letters in the papyri, as in Jas. 1:1 ᾿Ιάκωβοs χαίρειν. Sometimes the construction is changed and the nominative (*nominativus pendens*) is left suspended as in ὁ νικῶν δώσω αὐτῷ (Rev. 3:21). This parenthetic nominative is common in the papyri, and appears often in the New Testament as in ἡμέραι τρεῖs (Matt. 15:32) *three days,* πρασιαὶ πρασιαί (Mk. 6:40) *garden beds garden beds,* ὄνομα αὐτῷ ᾿Ιωάνης (Jo. 1:6) *name to him John,* ὁ γὰρ Μωυσῆς οὗτος (Acts 7:40) *for this Moses.* We have it also in exclamations as in ταλαίπωρος ἐγὼ ἄνθρωπος (Rom. 7:24) *wretched man I.* The nominative form is often used as a vocative and is really a vocative then.

341. *The Vocative.*

(a) *The Case of Address* (πτῶσις κλητική).

Strictly it is not a case since the word in the vocative has no precise relation to the other words in the sentence and it has no special endings. In neuter nouns it is just like the nominative. In all nouns in the plural it has the same form as the nominative. It is only in the singular of masculine or feminine nouns that it has a distinct form at all which may be merely the stem as in πάτερ or a change in the stem vowel ο to ε as in ἄνθρωπε. But sometimes the nominative form occurs as vocative as in θυγάτηρ (Mk. 5:34) instead of θύγατερ and in πατήρ (Jo. 17:24) instead of πάτερ. So also ὦ πλήρης (Acts 13:10) instead of ὦ πλῆρες. We even have πατὴρ δίκαιε (Jo. 17:25) *Righteous Father.* In the Sanskrit "the vocative is not considered and named by the native grammarians as a case like the rest" (Whitney, *Sanskrit Grammar,* p. 89). But for practical syntactical purposes it has to be treated as a case and so the name is justified.

(b) *With or without* ὦ.

It may be used with ὦ like our "O" as in ὦ ἄνθρωπε (Rom. 2:1) *O man* or without ὦ as in πάτερ (Jo. 17:1). So in the plural ὦ ᾿Ιουδαῖοι (Acts 18:14) *O Jews* or ῎Ανδρες ᾿Αθηναῖοι (Acts 17:22) **Athenians** (*men of Athens*).

(c) *The Articular Nominative as Vocative.*

This idiom is not unknown to the old Greek, but it is very common in the New Testament. In the Hebrew and Aramaic it is the rule as seen in ταλειθά translated τὸ κοράσιον (Mk. 5:41)

you little maid (we have to say).   See also ἀββά ὁ πατήρ in
Mk. 14:36 and in Rom. 8:15 and Gal. 4:6 where probably
Jesus and Paul employed both Aramaic and Greek from the
bilingual habit of childhood.   In Lu. 12:32 we have τὸ μικρὸν
ποιμνίον *you little flock* without the Aramaic equivalent.   In
Matt. 11:26 ὁ πατήρ is the equivalent of πάτερ in the preceding
verse.   In the old Greek θεός is usual for the vocative as in
the New Testament save in one quotation from the Septuagint we have θεέ (Matt. 27:46).   So in Rev. 15:3 we have
Κύριε ὁ θεός.   In John 20:28 we have the vocative of address,
ὁ κύριός μου καὶ ὁ θεός μου, not the nominative of exclamation.
Jesus accepts Thomas' words as direct address (vocative).
The form is nominative, but the case is vocative.

342.   *The Accusative.*

(a)   *A Poor Name* (πτῶσις αἰτιατική).

It is more probably derived from αἰτία in the sense of cause
rather than of accusation.   Priscian calls it *casus causativus.*
But even the causative case is vague enough.   In old English
"accuse" meant "betray" or "show", but even so the showing
case would not distinguish it much from the other cases.
Since it is the oldest case, it is possible that the name did not
have the other cases in mind.   They are in reality variations
from the accusative, the normal oblique case for a noun unless
there is some reason for using some other case.   The presump-
tion is thus in favor of using the accusative.   The oldest form
of ἐγώ is ἐγών like *aham* in the Sanskrit.

(b)   *Extension the Root Idea.*

In a general way the accusative case answers the question
"how far" (Giles, *Comparative Philology*, p. 303).   This is
true of verbs, substantives, adjectives, even general reference
or adverbially.   It will thus be seen that the relation of the
noun in the accusative to the verb or other words in the sentence is very indefinite.   The precise relation is determined

by the meaning of the noun and of the verb. It is not known
what the ending μ (ν) in the singular comes from or means.
Some consider it allied to the Sanskrit *ma*, Greek με; others
think it merely a local termination. In general it is not hard
to see the root idea of extension in the accusative.

(c) *The Normal Case in the Vernacular*.

In the vernacular the accusative retained its frequency as
the normal case even with verbs that in the written or literary style use other cases (rather than locative, instrumental,
dative, and even genitive and ablative). This is clearly shown
by Mullach in his *Grammatik der Griechischen Vulgarsprache*,
pp. 323-333. The same thing is observable in the old poets.
Pindar, for example, has "a multiplicity of accusatives"
(Giles). In the modern Greek the accusative has regained
its old ascendancy with the corresponding disuse of the other
cases. "When a fine sense of language is failing, it is natural
to use the direct accusative to express *any* object which verbal
action affects, and so to efface the difference between 'transitive' and 'intransitive' verbs" (Jebb, in Vincent and Dickson's
Handbook to Modern Greek, p. 307). Hence many verbs that
were intransitive in the written style are transitive in the
vernacular as seen in the papyri, New Testament, and modern
Greek. The use of other oblique cases served to make fine
distinctions with more nicety and precision. When these
distinctions were not sharply perceived, the use of the other
cases faded. The accusative then has made a circle. In the
beginning it was the only case. Now in the modern Greek
it is once more the normal oblique case. In the beginning
the accusative continued to be used more or less loosely even
after the other cases arose, when one did not wish to differ-
entiate sharply, so that even a point of time could be expressed
by the accusative in the Sanskrit and even in the New Testament as ὥραν ἐνάτην in Acts 10:3 though Aleph A B C have
περί here before the accusative (*about the ninth hour*), though
ὥραν ἑβδόμην is undoubtedly genuine in Jo. 4:52 *at the seventh*

hour and ποίαν ὥραν in Rev. 3:3 *at what hour*. So again we find οἱ χρώμενοι τὸν κόσμον in 1 Cor. 7:31 *those who use the world* instead of τῷ κόσμῳ, the instrumental case (cf. *utor* in Latin). The accusative with χράομαι appears in Cretan inscriptions and in late Greek. On the contrary in Rev. 2:14 we have ἐδίδασκεν τῷ βαλάκ as in some later writers instead of the accusative, perhaps partly influenced also by the Hebrew.

(d) *With Verbs of Motion.*

This was probably the first use of the accusative. In Sanskrit "it stands especially as the goal of motion, with verbs of going, bringing, sending, and the like" (Whitney, *Sanskrit Grammar*, p. 92). In Homer this use is common with verbs which imply reaching a point and in the poets the idiom continued to be frequent both as to place and persons. In English we say "go home" where home is accusative. This original use of the accusative is not preserved in the New Testament unless it is seen in ὁδὸν θαλάσσης (Matt. 4:15) *the way of the sea.*

(e) *Extension of Space.*

This use of the accusative is a perfectly normal one in answer to the question "how far" as in Lu. 2:44 ἦλθον ἡμέρας ὁδόν *they went a day's journey*, John 6:19 ἐληλακότες οὖν ὡς σταδίους εἴκοσι πέντε ἢ τριάκοντα *having rowed therefore about twenty-five or thirty stadia.* This idiom was in the Sanskrit and Latin also and survives in English.

(f) *Extent of Time.*

The Indo-Germanic languages are fond of this construction with the accusative for duration of time. So we have τοσαῦτα ἔτη δουλεύω σοι (Luke 15:29) *I have been serving thee so many years*, τί ὧδε ἑστήκατε ὅλην τὴν ἡμέραν ἀργοί; (Matt. 20:6) *why stand ye idle all the day?* However, as already noted under (c) the accusative is occasionally used loosely for a point of time (Jo. 4:52).

(g)　*Accusative of the Inner Object or Cognate Accusative.*

Here the action of the verb expresses itself in a word of
the same root as in φυλάσσοντες φυλακάς(Lu. 2:8) *guarding guards,*
ἐφοβήθησαν φόβον μέγαν (Mark 4:41) *they feared a great fear.* In a
way this seems the most obvious of all accusatives with verbs
unless the objective result is even simpler like ἁμαρτάνοντα ἁμαρτίαν
(1 Jo. 5:16) *sinning a sin.* Sometimes the substantive is not
identical in root, but only similar in idea, the analogous cognate accusative, as in μὴ φοβούμεναι μηδεμίαν πτόησιν(1 Pet. 3:6).
Sometimes the relative pronoun represents this cognate accusative as in ὅρκον ὅν ὤμοσεν (Lu. 1:73) *the oath which he swore.*

(h)　*With Transitive Verbs.*

Here the action of the verb extends to the external object,
passes over (transitive, from *transire*). This is a problem
purely for Greek verbs and the corresponding verb in another
language (Sanskrit, Latin, German, English) may be intransitive. So in Jas. 5:12 μὴ ὀμνύετε μήτε τὸν οὐρανὸν μήτε τὴν γῆν
swear not either by heaven or by earth the English verb has to
add "by" to the verb, whereas ὀμνύω needs no preposition.
So in John 8:27 τὸν πατέρα αὐτοῖς ἔλεγεν *he was speaking to them
of the Father* the English must needs use "of". Again the
same Greek verb may be now transitive, as with ἔμενον ἡμᾶς
(Acts 20:5) *they were waiting for us,* now intransitive as ἐμείναμεν
παρ' αὐτῷ (Acts 21:8) *we abode with him.* Moreover, if a Greek
verb is transitive, it does not use the accusative, if some other
oblique case suits the precise idea better. So ἐπιλανθάνομαι
occurs with the accusative τὰ μὲν ὀπίσω (*the things behind*) in
Phil. 3:13 and the genitive τῆς φιλοξενίας (*hospitality*) in Heb.
13:2. Sometimes the difference in case may indicate difference in meaning as in ἀκούοντες μὲν τῆς φωνῆς (Acts 9:7) *hearing the sound* and τὴν δὲ φωνὴν οὐκ ἤκουσαν (Acts 22:9) *but they
did not understand the voice.* Sometimes an intransitive verb
like ἔρχομαι may be rendered transitive by a preposition in
composition like διελθὼν τὴν Μακεδονίαν (Acts 19:21) *passing
through Macedonia.* Then again the object may be implied,

though not expressed as with ἐπέχων πῶς (Lu. 14:7) *observing how* where τὸν νοῦν (*the mind*) must be supplied. But ordinarily the accusative with a transitive verb is simple enough as in ἐκάλεσεν αὐτούς (Matt. 4:21) *he called them.*

(i) *Two Accusatives with One Verb.*

The Sanskrit was fond of the double accusative. The second accusative may be merely in apposition with the first, the predicate accusative as in οὐκέτι λέγω ὑμᾶς δούλους (Jo. 15:15) *I speak of you no longer as slaves.* Occasionally εἰs (like our "as" for "for") occurs with this predicate accusative as in εἰs προφήτην αὐτὸν εἶχον (Matt. 21: 46) *they held him as a prophet.* One accusative may be of the person and the other of the thing as with ἐκεῖνος ὑμᾶς διδάξει πάντα (Jo. 14:26). The Latin *doceo* and the English *teach* agree with the Greek διδάσκω in this use of two accusatives. Plainly one has not succeeded as a teacher who merely teaches a subject. He must also teach the pupil else it is all for naught. But the accusative of the person and of the thing does not always appear. So αἰτέω may use both as in ὃν αἰτήσει ὁ υἱὸς αὐτοῦ ἄρτον (Matt. 7:9) *of whom his son shall ask a loaf* or only the accusative of the person (Mt. 6:8) αἰτῆσαι αὐτόν or only the accusative of the thing (Lu. 1:63) and the person may be in the ablative with ἀπό (1 Jo. 5:15) or with παρά (Acts 3:2). So also with ἐνδιδύσκω *to clothe* we find two accusatives as in ἐνδιδύσκουσιν αὐτὸν πορφύραν (Mk. 15:17) and ἱμάτιον πορφυροῦν περιέβαλον αὐτόν (Jo. 19:2) *they threw a purple robe around him.* But note ἐν ἱματίοις λευκοῖς with this verb in Rev. 3:5. There is much freedom about two accusatives with verbs of clothing and depriving and the second accusative can be otherwise expressed and often is so in the New Testament. Some causative verbs may have two accusatives as in ὁρκίζω σε τὸν θεόν (Mk. 5:7) *I adjure thee by God* and ὃς ἂν ποτίσῃ ὑμᾶς ποτήριον ὕδατος (Mk. 9:41) *whoever shall give you a cup of water.* Some verbs of doing good or ill have two accusatives like μηδὲν βλάψαν αὐτόν (Lu. 4:35) *injuring him not at all.*

(j) *With Passive Verbs.*

It is a mistake to associate the accusative in one's mind simply with the active voice or even including the middle voice. Many verbs are intransitive in the active voice while the middle is just as likely to be transitive as the active, and even the passive may also be transitive, though in the nature of the case this is not so frequent as in the other voices. Whether a verb is transitive or not, is not a matter of the voice, but of the verb force. Essentially voice has nothing to do with the transitiveness of the action in the verb. The passive itself is a later development and simply used the middle forms unchanged save in the aorist where a special termination was employed with the active endings and the future where σ was added to this termination and the middle endings used. It was a makeshift and the verb sometimes retained some of the transitive force in the older voices. The passive made constant inroads on the middle and finally in the modern Greek usurped the functions of that voice. The so-called passive deponents no longer have the passive idea if they ever had it. In the New Testament, for instance, ἀπεκρίθη (Jo. 6:7) is devoid of any passive idea and merely means "he answered", not "he was answered". It is far more frequent than the aorist middle ἀπεκρίνατο (Lu. 3:16). So this use of the passive may be transitive as in μὴ οὖν φοβηθῆτε αὐτούς (Matt. 10:26) *Do not fear them,* without any passive idea, though in verse 28 we have μὴ φοβηθῆτε ἀπὸ τῶν κτλ which is intransitive like our "Do not be afraid of". So the present middle φοβεῖσθε is transitive in verse 28, but intransitive in verse 31. Other examples of transitive passive forms are ἐντραπήσονται τὸν υἱόν μου (Matt. 21:37) *they will reverence my son* (second future passive of ἐντρέπω), ὃς ἐὰν ἐπαισχυνθῇ με—ὁ υἱὸς τοῦ ἀνθρώπου ἐπαισχυνθήσεται αὐτόν. (Mk. 8:38) *whosoever shall be ashamed of me—the Son of man shall be ashamed of him* (first aorist passive subjunctive and future passive indicative of ἐπαισχύνομαι). Here in English we have to translate as if intransitive "be ashamed of," but the Greek is not responsible for the defects of the English. The Sanskrit had no proper passive voice. Some verbs in Greek, Latin, and English that use two accusatives retain the accusative of the thing in the passive. This is natural for the other alternative would be the predicate nominative as happens with verbs of calling like υἱοὶ θεοῦ κληθήσονται (Matt. 5:9) *shall be called sons of God* or to put it in some other oblique case instead of the accusative. With the passive of διδάσκω the accusative of the thing is the only recourse, as with the Latin *doceo* and the English *teach*. So ἃς ἐδιδάχθητε (2 Thess. 2:15) *which we were taught* (first aorist passive). But with περιβάλλω either the accusative is retained, as is usual, as in περιβεβλημένους στολὰς λευκάς (Rev. 7:9) *clad in white robes* or the locative (without or with ἐν) as in περιβεβλημένους ἱματίοις λευκοῖς (Rev. 4:4) *clad in white garments* (some Mss. have ἐν). In John 11:44 δεδεμένος τοὺς πόδας καὶ τὰς χεῖρας κειρίαις *bound as to the feet and the hands with grave bands* the accusative is retained as well as the instrumental case (κειρίαις) where only one accusative was used in the active voice. So the single accusative of the active (that of the thing) is retained in ὃ ἐγὼ βαπτίζομαι (Mk. 10:38) *with which I am baptized*, δαρήσεται ὀλίγας the second future passive of δέρω (Lu. 12:47) *shall be beaten with few stripes* (πληγάς), οἰκονομίαν πεπίστευμαι (1 Cor. 9:17) *I have been instructed with a stewardship*, διεφθαρμένων τὸν νοῦν (1 Tim. 6:5) *corrupted in mind*. The Greek has more liberty here than the Latin and is not hindered from turning a dative of the person with the active into the subject of the passive voice. By analogy the Greek can greatly extend this construction as in τὴν αὐτὴν εἰκόνα μεταμορφούμεθα (2 Cor. 3:18) *we are being changed into the same image*, πεπληρωμένοι καρπὸν δικαιοσύνης (Phil. 1:11) *filled with the fruit of righteousness*, and even τὴν ἅλυσιν περίκειμαι (Acts 28:20) where περίκειμαι, according to ancient usage, is used as the passive of περιτίθημι though literally meaning *I lie around the chain* (by metonymy for the chain lying around Paul). There is only one example of the accusative with the verbal in -τέον after the ancient idiom (Luke 5:38) οἶνον νέον—βλητέον *new wine must be put*.

(k) The Accusative of General Reference.

Here the notion of extension exists irrespective of a transitive verb.   In the Sanskrit "the neuter accusative of innumerable adjectives, simple or compound, is used adverbially" (Whitney, *Sanskrit Grammar*, p. 93).   The adverb is merely a word in a fixed case, often in the accusative.   So ὀλίγον (Mk. 6:31) *for a little time*, πολύ (2 Cor. 8:22) *much*, πολλά (Jas. 3:2) *in many things.*   The masculine and feminine genders also may be used in this accusative of general reference as ὃν τρόπον (Matt. 23:37) *in which manner*, τὸν ἀριθμόν (Jo. 6:10) *in number*, τὰ πρὸς θεόν (Heb. 2:17) *in the things pertaining to God*, δωρεάν (Matt. 10:8) *freely* or *as a gift*, τὴν ἀρχήν (Jo. 8:25) *at the beginning.*   This use of the accusative is easy to understand.

(l) With the Infinitive.

What is here considered is not the object of the infinitive, but what is often loosely called the "subject" of the infinitive. As a matter of fact, the infinitive cannot have a subject anymore than the participle.   Neither has any personal endings by which the subject is expressed, and voice in the infinitive is only by analogy and does not relate the action to the subject.   The infinitive was substantival in origin and is in a fixed case.   But the infinitive can allow the person who has to do with the action to be predicate nominative as in φάσκοντες εἶναι σοφοί (Rom. 1:22) *alleging being wise (about themselves).* Otherwise the accusative of general reference as in νομίζοντες αὐτὸν τεθνηκέναι *thinking being dead as to him.*   The trouble about understanding this Greek idiom is that we read back into the Greek our English translation where we use conjunctions and say "alleging that they were wise," "thinking that he was dead."   Now the Greek often used ὅτι (*that*) and the indicative in indirect declarative clauses, but the infinitive is not the ὅτι construction.   It must be explained according to its own genius.   Take πάλιν χρείαν ἔχετε τοῦ διδάσκειν ὑμᾶς τινὰ τὰ στοιχεῖα (Heb. 5:12) *You again have need of the* (note article τοῦ) *teaching you the elements* (two accusatives of person and thing) *as to some one.* This third accusative (τινὰ) can only be explained as the accusative of general reference by which alone this infinitive can express the agent of the action (having no personal endings). It must be recalled that the Greeks did not concern themselves with the awkwardness of such an idiom rendered literally into English. After we see precisely what the Greek idiom means we are at liberty to put it into idiomatic English, but we have no right to try to explain the Greek idiom by the English. This use of the accusative is common in Latin and occurs in Anglo-Saxon. The action expressed by the infinitive holds good so far as the person mentioned by the accusative is concerned. Take once more ἐν τῷ εἰσαγαγεῖν τοὺς γονεῖς τὸ παιδίον 'Ιησοῦν (Lu. 2:27) *in the bringing the child Jesus as to the parents.* This again is very awkward English, but clear Greek. Note ἐν with the article τῷ with the infinitive. We have no right to try to explain this idiom as if we had here ὅτε εἰσήγαγον instead of ἐν τῷ εἰσαγαγεῖν. Clearly τὸ παιδίον is the object of εἰσαγαγεῖν. The other accusative τοὺς γονεῖς is due to the idea of general reference. In English we have to say *when the parents brought the child Jesus,* but that is not a strict translation of Luke's favorite idiom which makes literally impossible English.

(m) *The Accusative Absolute.*

The grammars usually mean by this expression a participle and substantive in the accusative in place of the common genitive absolute. Such an accusative would simply be the accusative of general reference with the participle agreeing with it. An example is found in γνώστην ὄντα σε (Acts 26:3) *thou being an expert,* unless an anacoluthon is allowed. In 1 Cor. 16:6 τυχόν is the neuter accusative absolute of the participle τυχών from τυγχάνω and is used as an adverb (*it happening, by chance, perhaps*). In Rom. 8:3 τὸ ἀδύνατον τοῦ νόμου *the impossibility of the law* can be explained either as the nominative absolute or the accusative absolute without a

participle.   Certainly τὸ ἐξ ὑμῶν (Rom. 12:18) *so far depends
on you* (the thing from you) is accusative of general reference.

(n)   *The Accusative of Inverse Attraction.*

Here the antecedent (substantive) is attracted into the case
of the relative as in τὸν ἄρτον ὃν κλῶμεν (1 Cor. 10:16) *the bread
which we break.*

(o)   *The Accusative with Prepositions.*

It is not the preposition that "governs" the accusative,
but simply that the prepositions define more precisely the
notion of extension already in the accusative, being themselves
properly adverbs in various cases.   The thing to do is to see
exactly what each preposition by reason of its own meaning
adds to the case idea of the accusative.   Translation into
English should only come after this process has been carried
through.   The translation is a result of the process.   Try
that method on ἀνὰ μέσον (Mk. 7:31), διὰ τὸν φόβον (Jo. 7:13),
εἰς τὴν πόλιν (Matt. 26:18), ἐπὶ τὴν γῆν (Matt. 15:35), κατὰ
τὸν νόμον (Lu. 2:22), μετὰ ἡμέρας τρεῖς (Lu. 2:46), παρὰ τὴν ὁδόν
(Matt. 20:30), περὶ αὐτόν (Matt. 8:18), πρὸς αὐτόν (Matt. 3:25),
ὑπὲρ δοῦλον (Philemon 16), ὑπὸ τὸν μόδιον (Matt. 5:15).

343.   *The Genitive.*

(a)   *Two Cases with One Form.*

It is no longer open to dispute that in Greek we have two
cases (genitive and ablative) with the same ending.   Already
in the Sanskrit that was true in the singular (*as*) though not
in the plural.   It is simply grotesque to try to explain all the
uses of the one form in Greek as either genitive or ablative.
Moulton properly calls Winer's definition of the genitive as
"unquestionably   the   *whence-case*"   "an   utterly   obsolete
procedure."   Even Kühner and Crosby found the explanation of the genitive in the ablative and Madvig tried to
derive the ablative ideas from the genitive.   Comparative

grammar has settled this matter. The two cases happen in Greek to have the same form, but they differ in idea. Examples occur which can be explained as either case.

(b)   *The Case of Genus or Kind.*

The genitive has the wrong name. It is not *casus genitivus* (πτῶσις γεννητική), but rather *casus generalis* from *genus* (kind or species) as Priscian calls it, that is πτῶσις γενική from γένος, in a word the specifying case. It is thus a descriptive case like the adjective in function, though not adjectival in origin, like ἡμέρα παρασκευῆς (Lu. 23:54), *day of preparation* (*preparation day*). It is not known what the origin of the ending—os is, though it may be pronominal. This ending has survived best of any of the case-endings in the Indo-Germanic tongues and in English is the only one that has survived outside of pronouns. The genitive case means "this and not that" or "this and no other" while the accusative answers the question "how far". Both ideas are general and admit a wide range of application. In a word the genitive is the *general* or genus case and the precise specifying lies in the word, not the case. βάπτισμα μετανοίας (Mk. 1:4) is therefore *repentance baptism*, though the precise relation is not defined. It is baptism marked by repentance, whether based on and preceded by repentance or to induce repentance the case does not say. So in τὴν γέενναν τοῦ πυρός (Matt. 5:22) Gehenna is described as characterized by fire. The genitive may come before the limiting word as in Ἑλλήνων πολὺ πλῆθος (Acts 14:1) or between the article and substantive as in ἡ τοῦ πνεύματος βλασφημία (Matt. 12:31). Two or even three genitives can be used together as in τὸν φωτισμὸν τοῦ εὐαγγελίου τῆς δόξης τοῦ χριστοῦ (2 Cor. 4:4) *the illumination of the gospel of the glory of Christ.*

(c)   *The Resultant Idea Due to a Variety of Causes.*

The idea of the genitive is single and simple, but may be applied to different words and different contexts. One of the

follies of some students is to explain the genitive by the resultant translation of these different contexts as different
kinds of genitives, thus mistaking the resultant translation
for the philosophical and historical explanation of the case
itself. The root of the case remains the same. Take μετοικεσίαν
βαβυλῶνος (Matt. 1:12). All that the case says is that it is a
Babylon-removal, but whether *to* Babylon or *of* Babylon or,
if ablative, *from* Babylon, we do not know from the form of
the case. The mention of Jechoniah in the verse makes it
plain from the Old Testament history that it was the removal
of the people of Judah to Babylon and not *from* Babylon
(hence genitive, not ablative). The genitive does not mean
to, but that is the resultant idea. It is difficult to make a
satisfactory grouping of the uses of a case with so many possible combinations in detail and the simplest analysis is best.

(d) *The Local Use of the Genitive.*

This is probably the earliest and is certainly the most objective. It thus means "here and not there." It is probable
that the common adverbs of place αὐτοῦ (*here*), οὗ and ὅπου
(*where*), ποῦ; (*where?*), πανταχοῦ (*everywhere*), ὁμοῦ (*together*) are
all in the genitive, though they could be shortened locatives.
In Homer the genitive was freely used for place as οὐκ Ἄργεος
ἦεν (*not at Argos*). This usage survived in the vernacular
and with the poets. The poets are often the best source for
the actual usage of the people. Compare ποῦ γῆς; (*where
on earth?*). Luke uses ἐκείνης (19:4) *by that way* and ποίας;
(5:19) *by what way?* Homer can say λούεσθαι ποταμοῖο (Homeric
form for –ου) *to bathe in a river* and Luke (16:24) can say ἵνα
βάψῃ τὸ ἄκρον τοῦ δακτύλου αὐτοῦ ὕδατος *that he may dip the tip of
his finger in water* (not *oil*, but *water*). So in Acts 19:26 we have
οὐ μόνον Ἐφέσου, ἀλλὰ σχεδὸν πάσης τῆς Ἀσίας *not only at Ephesus,
but in almost all Asia*, clear instance of the local use of the
genitive. Once more note ὁδὸς ἐθνῶν (Matt. 10:5) *way to the
Gentiles* and ἡ διασπορὰ τῶν Ἑλλήνων (Jo. 7:35) *the dispersion*

among the Greeks. So in Matt. 1:11, 12, 17 μετοικεσίας (-αν) βαβυλῶνος means removal to Babylon as already shown by the context. Various prepositions may be used to make clearer the local use of the genitive as ἀντί, ἐναντίον, ἕνεκα, ἐντός, ἐπί, μετά, περί, πλησίον.

(e) *Expressions of Time.*

The genitive with words of time means this time rather than some other time. So in Lu. 18:7 ἡμέρας καὶ νυκτός the genitive calls attention to the fact that the elect cry to God *by day and by night.* In Lu. 2:37 νύκτα καὶ ἡμέραν the accusative means that Anna served in the temple *all night and all day.* See the same distinction between τοῦ λοιποῦ *in respect of the rest of the time* (Gal. 6:17) and τὸ λοιπόν (Heb. 10:13) *for the rest of the time.* In Matt. 24:20 note the distinction between the genitive χειμῶνος *by winter* in contrast with summer and the locative σαββάτῳ *on a sabbath* as a point of time. Note the adverbs with the genitive of time δὶς τοῦ σαββάτου (Lu. 18:12) *twice on the Sabbath,* ἅπαξ τοῦ ἐνιαυτοῦ (Heb. 9:7) *once for all within the year.* In Matt. 25:6 μέσης νυκτός means *in the middle of the night.* Prepositions in the New Testament are often used to make plainer the expression of time like εἰς πολλὰ ἔτη (Lu. 12:19) *for many years,* δι' ἡμερῶν (Mk. 2:1) *after some days* (days coming in between, διά), ἐν τῷ πάσχα ἐν τῇ ἑορτῇ (Jo. 2:23) *at the passover at the feast.*

(f) *Subjective or Objective Genitive.*

Here again it is not the case that determines this point, but the relation of the words to each other. Thus in ἡ ἀγάπη τοῦ χριστοῦ συνέχει ἡμᾶς (2 Cor. 5:14) it is clearly the subjective genitive and Paul means *the love of Christ holds us (me) together,* that is, *the love that Christ has for me,* not my love for Christ. But in ἔχετε πίστιν θεοῦ (Mk. 11:22) *have faith in God* θεοῦ is plainly the objective genitive, not the subjective. It is not the faith that God has, but the faith of which God is the object. In itself the case means only the God-kind of faith. So in ἐπὶ εὐεργεσίᾳ ἀνθρώπου ἀσθενοῦς (Acts 4:9) *for a good deed to an impotent man*, it is not a good deed done by an impotent man, but one done to him. The genitive does not mean "to" any more than it means "in" in Mk. 11:22. In ἡ τοῦ πνεύματος βλασφημία (Matt. 12:31) it is the blasphemy "against" the Holy Spirit and so clearly objective genitive. The examples of both kinds are almost endless. Each example is decided by its own context. In itself the genitive is neither subjective nor objective.

(g) Possession the Most Common Use.

Take τὸν δοῦλον τοῦ ἀρχιερέως (Matt. 26:51) *the slave of the high-priest*, not of another, and αὐτοῦ τὸ ὠτίον *his ear*, that of the slave, not of another. Sometimes the relationship is not clearly defined, but is simply assumed as plain. So Μαρία Ἰακώβου (Lu. 24:10) *James' Mary*, but whether mother, wife, daughter, or even sister is not stated. We learn elsewhere that it is his mother. Often the article alone occurs and the context has to determine the meaning as in οἱ τοῦ χριστοῦ Ἰησοῦ (Gal. 5:24) *those (followers, disciples) of Christ Jesus*. So in particular the neuter article as τὰ Καίσαρος (Mk. 12:17) *the (things) of Caesar*. The genitive in the predicate does not differ from the possessive use as in πάντα ὑμῶν ἐστιν (1 Cor. 3:21).

(h) The Qualitative Use of the Genitive.

This is a natural idiom like τὸ σῶμα τῆς ἁμαρτίας (Rom. 6:6) *the body of sin* (marked by, characterized by sin). There may be practical identity (apposition) at times as in ἡ οἰκία τοῦ σκήνους (2 Cor. 5:1) *the house of the tent* (consisting in the tent), πόλεις Σοδόμων καὶ Γομόρρας (2 Pet. 2:6). Even expressions like υἱοὶ φωτός (1 Thess. 5:5) *sons of light* are shown by the papyri to be not mere Hebraisms though more common in Hebrew. The genitive must not be considered as the precise equivalent of the adjective, though it is older than the adjective as the Sanskrit shows. Hence ἐν καινότητι ζωῆς (Rom. 6:4) *in newness of life* does not mean simply *in new life*. The quality is sharpened by the two substantives. The genitive is the natural case for the expression of price as δηναρίου (Rev. 6:6) *for a denary*.

(i) The So-called Partitive Genitive.

This use approaches closely to the ablative idea as in τὸ δεκατὸν τῆς πόλεως (Rev. 11:13) *the tenth of the city*. Sometimes the partitive genitive alone occurs as subject probably with τινὲς (*some*) understood as in συνῆλθον καὶ τῶν μαθητῶν (Acts 21:16) *some of the disciples went together*. The ablative case is plain because of ἐκ in John 16:17 εἶπαν ἐκ τῶν μαθητῶν αὐτοῦ *some of his disciples said*.

(j) With Adjectives.

This use is naturally parallel to that with substantives. So with ἄξιον τῆς μετανοίας (Matt. 3:8) *worthy of repentance*, πλήρης χάριτος (Jo. 1:14) *full of grace*, συμμόρφους τῆς εἰκόνος (Rom. 8:29) *conformed to the image*, ἔνοχος αἰωνίου ἁμαρτήματος (Mk. 3:29) *liable to (guilty of) an eternal sin*, ἔννομος χριστοῦ (1 Cor. 9:21) *under law to Christ*. Our translation of the genitive with adjectives varies precisely as with substantives. Occasionally the participle is used with the genitive as if a neuter adjective as in τὸ εἰθισμένον τοῦ νόμου (Lu. 2:27) *the custom (accustomed thing) of the law*.

(k) With Adverbs and Prepositions.

As examples take ἀξίως τῶν ἁγίων (Rom. 16:2) *worthily of the saints*, ἀντὶ πολλῶν (Matt. 20:28) *instead of many*, ἄντικρυς Χίου (Acts 20:15) *opposite Chios*, ἄχρι Πάφου (Acts 13:6) *as far as Paphos*, διὰ τοῦ προφήτου (Matt. 1:22) *by the prophet*, ἐγγὺς τῆς Λύδδας (Acts 9:38) *near to Lydda*, ἔναντι τοῦ θεοῦ (Lu. 1:8) *before God*, ἐναντίον τοῦ λαοῦ (Lu. 20:26) *before the people*, ἕνεκεν ἐμοῦ (Matt. 10:18) *for my sake*, ἐντὸς ὑμῶν (Lu. 17:21) *within you*, ἐνώπιον κυρίου (Lu. 1:15) *before the Lord*, ἐπάνω ὄρους (Matt. 5:14) *upon a mountain*, ἐπὶ τῆς γῆς (Col. 1:16) *upon the earth*, ἔσω τῆς αὐλῆς (Mk. 15:16) *within the court*, ἕως τοῦ χριστοῦ (Matt. 1:17) *until Christ*, κατ' ἐμοῦ (Lu. 11:23) *against me*, κατέναντι ὑμῶν (Mk. 11:2) *over against you*, κατενώπιον τῆς δόξης (Jude 24) *before the glory*, κύκλῳ τοῦ θρόνου (Rev. 4:6) *around the throne*, μέσον γενεᾶς σκολιᾶς (Phil. 2:15) *in the midst of a crooked generation*, μετὰ τῶν θηρίων (Mk. 1:13) *with the wild beasts*, μεταξὺ δύο στρατιωτῶν (Acts 12:6) *between two soldiers*, μέχρι μεσονυκτίου (Acts 20:7) *until midnight*, παραπλήσιον θανάτου (Phil. 2:27) *near to death*, πλησίον τοῦ χωρίου (Jo. 4:5) *near the place*, περὶ τοῦ Ἰησοῦ (Acts 28:23) *concerning Jesus*, τούτου χάριν (Eph. 3:1) *for this reason*. These various adverbs and prepositions were called upon to make plainer the precise aspect of the genitive case involved.

(1) *With Verbs.*

"With verbs the genitive means this and no other, while the accusative with verbs means this and no more" (Broadus). Hence it is very common with verbs when such a distinction is made. Some verbs naturally use the genitive, some the accusative (see previous discussion of the accusative), some now one and now the other. Thus verbs of sensation may have the genitive (cf. vernacular English "remember of") as in μνημονεύετε τῆς γυναικὸς Λώτ (Lu. 17:32) *remember Lot's wife* or the accusative as in μνημονεύετε τοὺς πέντε ἄρτους (Matt. 16:9) *remember the five loaves.* So also note ἐπιλαθέσθαι τοῦ ἔργου ὑμῶν (Heb. 6:10) *to forget your work*, but τὰ μὲν ὀπίσω ἐπιλανθανόμενος (Phil. 3:13) *forgetting the things behind*; γεύσεταί μου τοῦ δείπνου (Lu. 14:24) *shall taste my dinner*, but ἐγεύσατο τὸ ὕδωρ (John 2:9) *tasted the water*; αὐτοῦ ἀκούετε (Mk. 9:7) *hear him*, but ἤκουσεν τὸν ἀσπασμόν (Lu. 1:41) *heard the salutation*; καλοῦ ἔργου ἐπιθυμεῖ (1 Tim. 3:1) *desires a good work*, but ἐπιθυμῆσαι αὐτήν (Matt. 5:28) *to lust after her*; γέμουσιν ὀστέων (Matt. 23:27) *full of bones*, but γέμοντα ὀνόματα βλασφημίας (Rev. 17:3) *full of names of blasphemy.* The distinction in the two cases (genitive and accusative) is real here, but it is not to be pressed too far, since the accusative made constant inroads on the genitive. See further the genitive with ἐγώ σου ὀναίμην (Philemon 20) *may I have joy of thee,* ἐμπνέων ἀπειλῆς (Acts 9:1) *breathing in* (and *out*) *threatening,* κἂν θηρίον θίγῃ τοῦ ὄρους (Heb. 12:20) *if a wild beast touch the mountain,* ἐπισκοπῆς ὀρέγεται (1 Tim. 3:1) *longs for the office of bishop.* These are merely samples of the large number of verbs of emotion and sensation that use the genitive like ἐπέτυχον ἐπαγγελιῶν (Heb. 11:33) *obtained promises,* ἐπεμελήθη αὐτοῦ (Lu. 10:34) *cared for him,* τοῦ ἰδίου υἱοῦ οὐκ ἐφείσατο (Rom. 8:32) *spared not his own Son.* Other verbs of a somewhat more objective nature also use the genitive like γεμίσατε ὕδατος (Jo. 2:7) *fill with water,* ἐγκαλεῖσθαι στάσεως (Acts 19:40) *to be accused of riot,* πραθῆναι πολλοῦ (Matt. 26:9) *to be sold for much,* βασιλεύει τῆς Ἰουδαίας (Matt. 2:22) *is king of Judea,* μετέχων γάλακτος (Heb. 5:13) *partaking of milk,* ἐπελάβετο αὐτοῦ (Matt. 14:31) *took hold of him,* ἐκράτησε τῆς χειρὸς αὐτῆς (Matt. 9:25) *took hold of her hand,* τοῦ ἑνὸς ἀνθέξεται (Lu. 16:13) *shall cleave to the one.* Some verbs use the genitive as the result of κατά in composition as in αἰσχύνης καταφρονήσας (Heb. 12:2) *despising shame,* κατεγέλων αὐτοῦ (Matt. 9:24) *were laughing at him.*

(m) *The Genitive Absolute.*

It is not possible to decide certainly whether the use of the participle with a substantive or pronoun in the absolute idiom so common in Greek is genitive or ablative. In Latin the ablative case is the one so used (ablative absolute), unless it is the instrumental which in Latin has the same form. In Sanskrit the instrumental (associative) is sometimes so used and the locative often. In the Anglo-Saxon the dative is often so used and is common in Wycliff. Mullach (*Grammatik,* p. 357) says that the Greek genitive absolute belongs to the literary style and is not common in the vernacular Attic. Jebb notes that in the modern Greek vernacular the idiom has practically disappeared and conjunctions and finite verbs are employed. But in the papyri this construction is used with great frequency and freedom. In the New Testament it appears chiefly in the historical books, particularly in Acts as in Γαλλίωνος ἀνθυπάτου ὄντος (Acts 18:12) *Gallio being proconsul.* Sometimes the participle occurs alone with the pronoun or substantive understood as in ἐλθόντων (Matt. 17:14) *they having come.* Sometimes the construction occurs when another case could have been used as in ταῦτα αὐτοῦ ἐνθυμηθέντος ἐφάνη αὐτῷ (Matt. 1:20) *he having thought on these things there appeared unto him,* where ἐνθυμηθέντι could have been used to agree with αὐτῷ The idiom may even occur when the nominative is present as in μνηστευθείσης τῆς μητρὸς αὐτοῦ Μαρίας εὑρέθη (Matt. 1:18) *his mother Mary being betrothed she was found.* If the case is really genitive, as is possible, it is merely the usual specifying case and the participle agrees with the substantive or pronoun.

The use of the genitive articular infinitive for purpose is an old and common one as in τοῦ σπείρειν (Matt. 13:3) *to sow.* The attraction of the relative pronoun to the genitive case of the antecedent is thoroughly idiomatic as in περὶ πάντων ὧν ἐποίησεν (Lu. 3:19) *concerning all things which he did.* It was by no means always done.

344. *The Ablative.*

(a) *Old Ablative Ending in Singular.*

Already in the Sanskrit the ending for the ablative singular is the same as the genitive. But the separate ablative ending *t* or *d* survives in Latin inscriptions like *domod,* the Greek ὡς(τ), πῶς(τ), οὐρανόθεν (doubted by some philologists), Umbrian *tu* (out of), Anglo-Saxon *ut* (out of), and it is held by some to be demonstrative like Sanskrit *ta.* But, whatever may be true as to the origin of the case-ending, the idea of the case is clear. It is the case of origin or separation, *casus ablativus* as Julius Caesar called it, πτῶσις ἀφαιρετική, Winer's "whence" case. The Greek ablative used the same ending as the genitive in both singular and plural.

(b) *Rare with Substantives.*

Homer could say ἀνάπαυσις πολέμοιο *rest from war*. But it became rare in Greek after substantives as in Latin. Still we find in the New Testament διαστολὴ 'Ιουδαίου τε καὶ ῞Ελληνος (Rom. 10:12) *distinction between Jew and Greek*, διάκρισις καλοῦ καὶ κακοῦ (Heb. 5:14) *discernment between good and evil*. In 2 Pet. 1:20 ἐπιλύσεως is clearly ablative in the predicate after the copula γίνεται *no prophecy comes of private disclosure*. As already noted, it is possible to consider the partitive genitive as ablative. Compare ἐν τούτων (Matt. 6:29) with ἐν ἐξ αὐτῶν (Matt. 10:29). So also τίνα ἀπὸ τῶν δύο (Matt. 27:21) *which from the two*, clearly ablative.

(c) *With Adjectives.*

It is common enough in the earlier Greek as in Plato ἐπιστή-μης κενός *bereft of understanding*, ἐλεύθερος αἰδοῦς *free from shame*. In the New Testament we find ἀπείραστος κακῶν (James 1:13) *untempted of evil things*, ξένοι τῶν διαθηκῶν (Eph. 2:12) *aliens from the covenants*. So also verbal adjectives like διδακτοὶ θεοῦ (Jo. 6:45) *taught of God*, ἀγαπητοὶ θεοῦ (Rom. 1:7) *beloved of God*. The use of the ablative with adjectives with a priva-tive is common in the papyri. Several such examples occur in the New Testament besides Jas. 1:13 above as with ἀκατάπαστος (2 Pet. 2:14), ἀνάξιος (1 Cor. 6:2), ἄνομος (1 Cor. 9:21), ἄπειρος (Heb. 5:13). Moreover, the ablative may be used after the comparative form of the adjective as μείζων τοῦ κυρίου αὐτοῦ (John 13:16) *greater than his lord*, μικρότερος πάντων (Mk. 4:31) *smaller than all*. It occurs also after the superlative as πρῶτός μου (Jo. 1:15) *first from me* (before me).

(d) *With Prepositions.*

This use is very common in the New Testament and the preposition made plain the distinction in meaning from the genitive. Thus ἄνευ λόγου (1 Pet. 3:1) *without talk*, ἀπέναντι τοῦ τάφου (Matt. 27:61) *before the tomb*, ἀπὸ σοῦ (Matt. 5:29) *from thee*, ἄτερ ὄχλου (Lu. 22:6) *apart from a crowd*, ἐκ τοῦ ὕδατος (Mk. 1:10) *out of the water*, ἐκτὸς τοῦ σώματος (1 Cor. 6:18) *without the body*, ἔμπροσθεν πάντων (Matt. 26:70) *in the presence of all*, ἐπέκεινα βαβυλῶνος (Acts. 7:43) *beyond Babylon*, ἔξω τῆς οἰκίας (Mt. 10:14) *outside the house*, ἔξωθεν τῆς πόλεως (Rev. 14:20) *outside the city*, ὄπισθεν τοῦ 'Ιησοῦ (Lu. 23:26) *behind Jesus*, ὀπίσω μου (Matt. 3:11) *after (behind) me*, παρὰ τοῦ πατρός (Jo. 15:26) *from beside the Father*, παρεκτὸς λόγου (Matt. 5:32) *except the matter*, πέραν τοῦ 'Ιορδάνου (Matt. 4:25) *beyond the Jordan*, πλὴν τοῦ πλοίου (Acts 27:22) *except the boat*, πρὸ καιροῦ (Matt. 8:29) *before time*, πρὸς τῆς ὑμετέρας σωτηρίας (Acts 27:34) *from the side of your safety*, ὑπὲρ τοῦ λαοῦ (Jo. 11:50) *over, in behalf of, in the place of the people*, ὑπεράνω αὐτῆς (Heb. 9:5) *up over it*, ὑπερέκεινα ὑμῶν (2 Cor. 10:16) *beyond you*, ὑπερεκπερισσοῦ ὧν (Eph. 3:20) *above which*, ὑπὸ πάντων (Acts 22:12) *by all*, ὑποκάτω τῶν ποδῶν(Mk. 6:11) *under the feet*, χωρὶς παραβολῆς (Matt. 13:34) *without a parable*.   With πρό, πρός, ὑπέρ the comparative idea calls for the ablative.

(e) *With Verbs.*

It is not so frequent as with the accusative, genitive, and dative, and yet there are undoubted examples in plenty where the idea of origin or separation is dominant.   The ablative ἐπιλύσεως in the predicate with γίνεται (2 Pet. 1:20) has already been noted.   So also we seem to have the ablative in ἐγένετο γνώμης (Acts 20:3), though it is difficult to render it into English (*he became of the purpose*), and in Heb. 12:11 οὐ δοκεῖ εἶναι χαρᾶς ἀλλὰ λύπης *does not seem to be from joy, but from grief*.   But plainly ablative ὧν τινες ἀστοχήσαντες (1 Tim. 1:6) *which some having missed* (aimed at and missed, a privative), ἐκώλυσεν αὐτοὺς τοῦ βουλήματος (Acts 27:43) *hindered them from the purpose*, ἣν ἠκούσατέ μου (Acts 1:4) *which ye heard from me*, ἐκρατοῦντο τοῦ μὴ ἐπιγνῶναι (Lu. 24:16) *were kept from recognizing* (redundant μή), ὑστεροῦνται τῆς δόξης τοῦ θεοῦ (Rom. 3:23) *fall short of the glory of God*, λείπεται σοφίας (James 1:5) *lacks wisdom*, ἐδεήθη αὐτοῦ (Lu. 5:12) *begged of him*, and probably δώσω αὐτῷ τοῦ μάννα (Rev. 2:17) *I will give him part of the manna* where the part is contrasted with the whole as in ἐκ τοῦ ἄρτου ἐσθιέτω (1 Cor. 11:28) and ἐσθίει ἀπὸ τῶν ψιχίων (Matt. 15:27) *eat of the crumbs.* The ablative occurs with a number of compound verbs like οὐκ ἀφίστατο τοῦ ἱεροῦ (Lu. 2:37) *departed not from the temple,* ὑπερβάλλουσαν τῆς γνώσεως (Eph. 3:19) *surpassing knowledge,* ἀπηλλοτριωμένοι τῆς ζωῆς (Eph. 4:18) *alienated from the life,* ἀποστήσονταί τινες τῆς πίστεως (1 Tim. 4:1) *some will depart from the faith,* ἀπεστερημένων τῆς ἀληθείας (1 Tim. 6:5) *deprived of the truth,* διαφέρετε αὐτῶν (Matt. 6:26) *ye differ from them,* τῆς χάριτος ἐξεπέσατε (Gal. 5:4) *ye fell out of grace.*

345. *The Locative.*

(a) *The In Case.*

It is the simplest of the cases in its etymological idea, merely a point within the limits of the context. Delbrück prefers "local" (τοπική) to "locative". The case is very common in the Sanskrit with its distinctive endings *i* in the singular, *su* in the plural. We have thus in Greek three cases (locative, instrumental, dative) with the same endings which are in the main locative endings though remnants of the instrumental and dative endings survive. The English adverbs *here, there, where,* preserve the old locative endings. In Latin the ablative has the same endings with the other three save that sometimes in the singular the dative has a different ending. In English we represent the locative by the use of *in, on, at, among, by, upon, beside.*

(b) *Place.*

In Homer it is very common to have the locative with names of towns, countries, crowds, etc., without prepositions. We have it preserved in later Greek in some adverbs of place like οἴκοι *at home* (cf. οἴκῳ dative), αὐτόθι *here,* ποῖ *whither,* though they do not appear in the New Testament. κύκλῳ (Mk. 3:34) *in a circle* occurs several times. In the New Testament as in the later Greek generally we find ἐν with the locative as ἐν Ἀθήναις (1 Thess. 3:1) *in Athens*, but not always as στοιχοῦσιν τοῖς ἴχνεσιν (Rom. 4:12) *walk in the steps*, λῃσταῖς περιέπεσεν (Lu. 10:30) *he fell among robbers*, πορεύεσθαι ταῖς ὁδοῖς αὐτῶν (Acts 14:16) *to go in their ways*, τῷ πλοιαρίῳ (Jo. 21:8) *came in the boat* whereas in Matt. 14:13 we read ἐν πλοίῳ *in a boat*, ὕδατι βαπτίζω (Lu. 3:16) *I baptize in water* (whereas in Matt. 3:11 we have βαπτίζω ἐν ὕδατι), ἐπέθηκεν αὐτοῦ τῇ κεφαλῇ (Jo. 19:2) *they placed upon his head*, ἀδύνατος τοῖς ποσίν (Acts 14:8) *impotent in his feet*, τῷ θυσιαστηρίῳ παρεδρεύοντες (1 Cor. 9:13) *sitting beside the altar*.

(c) *Time*.

Just the locative case without a preposition is common for a point of time in Greek as in Sanskrit, Latin, Anglo-Saxon. Observe the difference between τὸ σάββατον the accusative for duration, *all through the sabbath*, and the locative τῇ μιᾷ σαββάτων *on the first day of the week*, both in Lu. 24:1. See also again the distinction in case (genitive and locative) in χειμῶνος μηδὲ σαββάτῳ (Matt. 24:20) already explained under genitive. In English we have to use various prepositions for a point of time like *in, on, at*. So with τῇ τρίτῃ ἡμέρᾳ (Matt. 20:19) *on the third day*, ταύτῃ τῇ νυκτί (Lu. 12:20) *on this night*, αὐτῇ τῇ ὥρᾳ (Lu. 2:38) *at the hour itself*, τετάρτῃ φυλακῇ (Matt. 14:25) *at the fourth watch*, τῇ ἑορτῇ (Lu. 2:41) *at the feast*, τοῖς γενεσίοις αὐτοῦ (Mk. 6:21) *at his birthday celebration*. With most of these and similar phrases ἐν is also used. The ἐν adds little, if anything, to what is already plain, except to show that the case is locative, not instrumental or dative. The use of ἐν constantly increased. Some temporal adverbs are themselves in the locative case like ἀεί (2 Cor. 6:10) and πέρυσι (2 Cor. 8:10). Brugmann (*Gr. Gr.*, p. 252) considers πάλαι a dative as he also does χαμαί.

(d) With Figurative Expressions.

This usage occurs with verbs, substantives, or adjectives. Some of these idioms are close to the literal notion of place like τοῖς ἔθεσιν περιπατεῖν (Acts 21:21) to walk in the customs, πορευομένη τῷ φόβῳ (Acts 9:31) walking in the fear, βαπτίσει ὑμᾶς πνεύματι ἁγίῳ (Mk. 1:8) shall baptize you in the Holy Spirit, ὅταν πειρασμοῖς περιπέσητε ποικίλοις (Jas. 1:2) whenever ye fall around in many colored trials. But other examples are just as clearly locative such as οἱ πτωχοὶ τῷ πνεύματι (Matt. 5:3) the poor in spirit, σχήματι εὑρεθείς (Phil. 2:8) found in fashion, τῇ κακίᾳ νηπιάζετε (1 Cor. 14:20) in evil be ye babes, οἱ καθαροὶ τῇ καρδίᾳ (Matt. 5:8) the pure in heart, τὸ χειρόγραφον τοῖς δόγμασιν (Col. 2:14) the hand-writing (bond) in decrees. Here again ἐν can be used if one so desires.

(e) Prepositions.

Originally nearly all the prepositions used the locative as the inscriptions for the dialects show and Homer preserves the locative with many prepositions that drop it in later Greek. In the New Testament the locative no longer appears with ἀμφί, ἀνά, μετά, περί, ὑπό though the locative, as in Homer (Monro, Homeric Grammar, p. 101), often occurs with verbs which have these prepositions in composition like τῇ θλίψει ὑπομένοντες (Rom. 12:12) being patient in tribulation. Here as always the prepositions do not govern the locative, but "stand to it in the relation of adverbial elements strengthening and directing its meaning" (Whitney, Sanskrit Grammar, p. 103). The only prepositions in the New Testament that are employed with the locative are the four following: ἐν as ἐν τῷ Ἰορδάνῃ (Matt. 3:6) in the Jordan, ἐπί as ἐπὶ θύραις (Matt. 24:33) at the doors, παρά as παρὰ τῷ σταυρῷ τοῦ Ἰησοῦ (Jo. 19:25) beside the Cross of Jesus, and πρός as πρὸς τῷ μνημείῳ (Jo. 20:11) at the tomb. Several of the prepositions are themselves in the locative case like ἀμφί, ἐν (ἐνί), ἐπί, περί, πρός (προτί).

(f) *The So-called Pregnant Use of the Locative or the Accusative.*

In the older Greek this idiom occurs without prepositions, but in the New Testament only with ἐν, εἰς and παρά. The accusative suggests extension and the locative location, and a difference of emphasis is presented. Only it must be recalled that originally ἐν was used either with the locative or the accusative like the Latin *in*, that εἰς is merely a longer form of ἐν, and that εἰς with the accusative constantly encroached on ἐν with the locative and finally in the modern Greek displaced it. So that a rigid difference in idea cannot be insisted on. There is no practical difference between ὁ εἰς τὸν ἀγρόν in Mk. 13:16 and ὁ ἐν τῷ ἀγρῷ in Matt. 24:18 (*the one in the field* in both cases), between εἰς τὸ τρυβλίον in Mk. 14:20 and ἐν τῷ τρυβλίῳ in Matt. 26:23 (*in the dish* in both cases), between ἐν οἴκῳ ἐστίν in Mk. 2:1 and the margin of Westcott and Hort εἰς οἶκόν ἐστιν ("*he is at home*" in either case). In ἦν παρὰ τὴν θάλασσαν *he was beside the sea* it is customary to say that the accusative implies previous motion, but in the light of the constant increase in the use of the accusative that point can not be pressed too far. In the English vernacular people constantly say "go in the house," "jump in the river," etc.

346. *The Instrumental.*

(a) *Originally Associative in Idea.*

There are those who hold that originally the Sanskrit had nine cases, the associative and the instrumental blending into one, the instrumental absorbing the associative, an old associative ending *a* as in ἅμα, τάχα and the true instrumental *bhi* for the singular and *bhis* for the plural. It is true that Homer φι does occur in the singular in θεόφι and φιν for the plural θεόφιν. But this φι is used in Homer not only for the instrumental, but also for the locative, the ablative, and possibly the dative (Brugmann, *Gr. Gr.* p. 239). The Sanskrit singular ending is *a* or *bhi* and the plural *bhis*. It remains possible that there never was but the one case, the instru-

mental, which originally was associative in idea. The two
conceptions are closely kin and it is not hard for association
to develop into agent or instrument. Our English *with* is a
pertinent illustration of how association (*with*) runs into instrument (*with*). The same thing is true of *by*. It is proper
therefore to treat it as one case with the original idea of mere
association that developed into that of instrumental association. The notion of association or accompaniment is fairly
common in the New Testament. So ὡμίλει αὐτῷ (Acts 24:26)
he conversed with him, ἠκολούθησαν αὐτῷ (Mk. 1:18) *they followed
him*, ἐκολλήθη ἑνί (Lu. 15:15) *he clave to one*, συνείπετο αὐτῷ (Acts
20:4) *he followed with him*, κοινωνεῖτε τοῖς τοῦ χριστοῦ παθήμασιν
(1 Pet. 4:13) *ye share in the sufferings of Christ*, μεμιγμένην
πυρί (Rev. 15:2) *mixed with fire*, ἑτεροζυγοῦντες ἀπίστοις (2 Cor.
6:14) *yoked with unbelievers*, εἰς ὑπάντησιν αὐτῷ (Jo. 12:13) *for
meeting with him*, μετοχὴ δικαιοσύνῃ καὶ ἀνομίᾳ (2 Cor. 6:14)
sharing with righteousness and lawlessness.

(b) *Expression of time.*

It was once used with expressions of place, but that idiom
no longer appears in the New Testament unless one be found in
ἑτέρᾳ ὁδῷ (Jas. 2:25) *by another way* which may be locative.
We have πανταχῇ in Acts 21:28, but not ὅπῃ or πῇ in the New
Testament. But there are undoubted examples of the associative-instrumental with expressions of time as in χρόνῳ ἱκανῷ
(Lu. 8:27) *with considerable time* (for a long time as in Acts
8:11), probably also πολλοῖς χρόνοις (Lu. 8:29) *for a long time*
as above (but locative *on many occasions* makes sense also),
χρόνοις αἰωνίοις (Rom. 16:25) *through times eternal*, τεσσεράκοντα
καὶ ἓξ ἔτεσιν (Jo. 2:20) *along with forty and six years it was built.*
In this latter case as in Acts 13:20 the accusative for duration
of time could have been used. But the associative-instrumental in such examples is an old Indo-Germanic idiom that
has survived.

(c) *Likeness.*

The correspondence is figurative, but the case is associative-instrumental. So ὅμοιος αὐτῷ (John 9:9) *like him,* ὁμοιωθέντες ἀνθρώποις (Acts 14:11) *likened to men,* ἴσους ἡμῖν (Matt. 20:12) *equal with us,* ἔοικεν κλύδωνι (Jas. 1:6) *he is like a wave,* τὸ αὐτὸ τῇ ἐξυρημένῃ (1 Cor. 11:5) *the same thing with the woman who has been shaved.*

(d) *Manner.*

This idiom is very common as παντὶ τρόπῳ εἴτε προφάσει εἴτε ἀληθείᾳ (Phil. 1:18) *in every way whether in pretence or in truth,* φύσει (Eph. 2:3) *by nature,* τῷ γένει (Acts 4:36) *by race,* ἀκατακαλύπτῳ τῇ κεφαλῇ (1 Cor. 11:5) *with the head unveiled,* προσευχῇ προσηύξατο (Jas. 5:17) *prayed with prayer.* A number of adverbs in the instrumental case illustrate this notion of manner like δημοσίᾳ (Acts 16:37), ἰδίᾳ (1 Cor. 12:11), κρυφῇ (Eph. 5:12), πανοικεί (Acts 16:34), πανπληθεί (Lu. 23:18), πάντῃ (Acts 24:3), τάχα (Rom. 5:7). So also the adverb and preposition ἅμα and the preposition μετά and the conjunction ἵνα have the old instrumental ending α–.

(e) *Cause.*

Here again the idea wavers between association and means. Thus we have τοιαύταις θυσίαις εὐαρεστεῖται (Heb. 13:16) *for with such sacrifices he is well pleased,* τῇ ἀπιστίᾳ ἐξεκλάσθησαν (Rom. 11:20) *they were broken off because of unbelief,* ἵνα μὴ τῷ σταυρῷ τοῦ χριστοῦ διώκωνται (Gal. 6:12) *that they may not be persecuted because of the Cross of Christ.*

(f) *Means or Instrument.*

Means or instrument can be naturally expressed by this case. Donaldson (*New Cratylus,* p. 439) calls it the implementive case. The verb χράομαι obviously, like *utor* in Latin, has the instrumental case as πολλῇ παρρησίᾳ χρώμεθα (2 Cor. 3:12) *we use boldness,* though the accusative also occurs (1 Cor.

7:31) as already shown. Other illustrations are συναπήχθη τῇ
ὑποκρίσει αὐτῶν (Gal. 2:13) *he was carried away by their hypoc-
risy*, ἤλειφεν τῷ μύρῳ (Luke 7:38) *she anointed them with the
ointment*, ἀνεῖλεν δὲ 'Ιάκωβον μαχαίρῃ (Acts 12:2) *he slew James
by the sword*, δεδάμασται τῇ φύσει τῇ ἀνθρωπίνῃ (James 3:7) *has been
tamed by human nature*, ἁλύσεσι δεδέσθαι (Mark 5:4) *bound by
chains*, οὐ φθαρτοῖς, ἀργυρίῳ ἢ χρυσίῳ, ἐλυτρώθητε, ἀλλὰ τιμίῳ αἵματι
(1 Pet. 1:18f.) *ye were redeemed not with corruptible things
(silver or gold), but by the precious blood*, πεπληρωμένους πάσῃ ἀδικίᾳ
(Rom. 1:29) *filled with all unrighteousness*, χάριτί ἐστε σεσωσμένοι
(Eph. 2:8) *ye are saved by grace*, ᾧ τις ἥττηται (2 Peter 2:19) *by
which one has been overcome*; and probably also τῇ γὰρ ἐλπίδι
ἐσώθημεν (Rom. 8:24) *for we were saved by hope*, and κατακαύσει
πυρὶ ἀσβέστῳ (Matt. 3:12) *will burn with unquenchable fire*,
though these could also be locative. The agent with passive
verbs may also be expressed in the instrumental case as οὐδὲν
ἄξιον θανάτου ἐστὶν πεπραγμένον αὐτῷ (Luke 23:15) *nothing worthy
of death has been done by him*, and probably κἀγὼ εὑρεθῶ ὑμῖν (2 Cor.
12:20) *and I may be found by you*, though this may possibly
be a true dative (Brugmann, *Griechische Grammatik*, p. 400).

(g) *Measure.*

The instrumental case is used to express measure in comparative phrases. In English *the* is in the instrumental case
in phrases like *the more*, *the less*, as is shown by the Anglo-
Saxon *thy (the)*. The accusative gradually displaces the instrumental in Greek for this idea, yet it appears several times in
Hebrews as in 10:25, τοσούτῳ μᾶλλον ὅσῳ βλέπετε *(by) so much the
more as (by as much as) ye see*. See also πολλῷ μᾶλλον (Mark
10:48) *by much more (the more a great deal)*.

(h) *With Prepositions.*

Only two prepositions use the instrumental in Greek, ἅμα
at the same time with and σύν *together with*. In Latin *cum* is
used with the instrumental and in Sanskrit *sam* (σύν). See

ἄμα αὐταῖς (Matt. 13:29) *at the same time with* and σὺν τῷ ἀγγέλῳ
(Luke 2:13) *together with the angel*. Verbs compounded with
σύν take the instrumental very often as συνηγέρθητε τῷ χριστῷ
(Col. 3:1), *ye were raised together with Christ*, ἵνα μοι συναντιλάβηται
(Luke 10:40) *that she take hold for her part* (ἀντι–) *together
with me*, συνχαίρετέ μοι (Phil. 2:18) *keep on rejoicing together
with me*. There are other ways of expressing many of the
above ideas in Greek than by the instrumental case as prepositions grew into common use. For instance, cause or ground
can be clearly conveyed by διά and the accusative, manner
by ἐν and the locative, and even means or instrument by ἐν
and the locative as ἀποκτεῖναι ἐν ῥομφαίᾳ (Rev. 6:8) *to kill with
(in, killing located in) the sword*. This last construction is
like the Hebrew idiom, it is true, but is also occasionally
present in the older Greek and survives in the papyri. Greek,
like other languages, and more than some, had flexibility and
variety in the expression of the same idea.

347. The Dative.

(a) *The Last of the Three Cases to Coalesce and Lose Its
Ending.*

This Greek case, according to Brugmann, *Griechische Grammatik*, p. 226f., coalesced in form with the locative and instrumental after they had lost distinction in endings. So
then in Greek the union was first between the locative and
instrumental. The case-endings of the three cases which
thus united are partly locative (ι, ισι), partly dative (αι)
and partly instrumental (α in adverbs and dialects, φι in
Homer, and possibly οις). Clearer traces of the difference
in endings survive in Greek than in the ablative. In a few
words both locative and dative forms occur in Greek (οἴκοι,
οἴκῳ). In Latin the dative singular is often separate from
locative, instrumental, and ablative. But in both Greek and
Latin the function of these cases remains distinct after the
forms are blended. In the modern Greek vernacular this
form for all three vanishes. For the dative it was εἰς and the

accusative or even the genitive form by itself. So in English the dative form has gone save with some pronouns like *him*, *me*, though the case is used either without any sign or usually with *to*, as *I gave John a book* or *I gave a book to John.* See in Wycliff's Bible, "Believe ye to the gospel" (Mark 1:15). Sometimes it is not possible to decide whether we have locative, instrumental or dative as each case makes sense in the context, though a different meaning. Thus in Acts 2:33 τῇ δεξιᾷ τοῦ θεοῦ ὑψωθείς can mean *exalted at* (*locative*) *the right hand of God, exalted by* (instrumental), or *exalted to* (dative).

(b) *The Case of Personal Interest.*

The idea of the dative (πτῶσις δοτική, *casus dativus*, the giving case) is very simple. It is the case of personal interest and accents one's personal advantage or disadvantage. It is chiefly used with persons or things personified. It is thus a purely grammatical case like the nominative and vocative (*rein grammatisch*). Whenever the dative is used, the root idea is that of advantage or disadvantage. What is called the dative of possession illustrates this idea clearly as in ἐὰν γένηταί τινι ἀνθρώπῳ ἑκατὸν πρόβατα (Matt. 18:12) *if a hundred sheep belong to a man*, οὐκ ἦν αὐτοῖς τόπος (Lu. 2:7) *there was no room for them*, ὑμῖν ἐστιν ἡ ἐπαγγελία (Acts 2:39) *to you is the promise.*

(c) *The Ethical Dative.*

This idiom is merely a strong emphasis on the personal idea as in ἐμοὶ γὰρ τὸ ζῆν χριστός (Phil. 1:21) *for me* (*as I look at it*) *living is Christ*, ἀστεῖος τῷ θεῷ (Acts 7:20) *beautiful to God* (*as God looks at it*), τί ἡμῖν καὶ σοί; (Mk. 1:24) *What is it to us and to thee?* Compare the English "hear me this," "look you." See also 1 Cor. 4:3.

(d) *With Place.*

Naturally not often, though a few examples occur like ἐγγίζειν τῇ Δαμασκῷ (Acts 9:3) *draw nigh to Damascus*, προσεληλύθατε

Σιὼν ὄρει (Heb. 12:22, and so verse 18) *ye have come to Mount Sion.* In Rev. 2:16 ἔρχομαί σοι ταχύ *I am coming quickly to thee* the verb of motion is used with a person, not place.

(e) *With Substantives and Adjectives.*

Wherever the idea of personal interest appears the dative is naturally used. Thus τῷ θεῷ χάρις (2 Cor. 2:14) *thanks to God,* μονογενὴς τῇ μητρί (Lu. 7:12) *only begotten to his mother,* καλόν σοί ἐστιν (Matt. 18:8) *it is good for thee,* πιστὴν τῷ κυρίῳ (Acts 16:15) *faithful to the Lord,* ἀπειθὴς τῇ οὐρανίῳ ὀπτασίᾳ (Acts 26:19) *disobedient to the heavenly vision,* ἐναντίος αὐτοῖς (Mk. 6:48) *contrary to them,* ἀρκετὸν τῷ μαθητῇ (Matt. 10:25) *sufficient to the disciple.* There are many more like ἀρεστός, δυνατός, ἔνοχος, ἱκανός, νεκρός, σωτήριος, ὑπήκοος, φανερός, ὠφέλιμος but these will illustrate the point.

(f) *With Adverbs and Prepositions.*

Some of these adverbs are themselves in the dative like οὐαί. Brugmann (*Gr. Gr.,* pp. 226, 228) considers dative forms also καταί, πάλαι, παραί, χαμαί. But clearly the dative case occurs with οὐαί as in οὐαὶ τῷ κόσμῳ (Matt. 18:7) *woe to the world,* though the accusative appears also in Rev. 8:13; 12:12. Cf. also 1 Thess. 2:10 where ὑμῖν is used with ὁσίως καὶ δικαίως καὶ ἀμέμπτως. With prepositions the dative used to be common (Delbrück, *Grund.* p. 130) with ἀντίον, ἐναντίον, πλησίον in the older Greek. In the New Testament we have twice the dative with ἐγγύς as in Acts 9:38 and 27:8 though the genitive is the usual case employed. It is also possible that the dative is occasionally preserved with ἐπί as μακροθύμησον ἐπ' ἐμοί (Matt. 18:26) *be patient with me* where ἐπί merely supplements the idea of the dative. So also 1 Th. 3:7; Rom. 16:19; 2 Cor. 9:14.

(g) *With Verbs.*

The dative is probably commonest as the indirect object of verbs as in προσέφερον αὐτῷ παιδία (Mk. 10:13) *they were bringing little children to him,* ὁ δὲ ἔφη αὐτοῖς (Mk. 9:12) *but he said to them,* ἄφες ἡμῖν τὰ ὀφειλήματα ἡμῶν (Matt. 6:12) *forgive us our debts.* But here prepositions often occur in place of the dative as ἤνεγκον αὐτὸν πρὸς αὐτόν (Mk. 9:20) *they brought him to him.* But the dative may also be the direct object of verbs with a strong idea of personal relation like θεῷ ἀρέσαι (Rom. 8:8) *to please God,* δουλεύω σοι (Lu. 15:29) *I have been serving thee,* βοήθει μοι (Matt. 15:25) *help me,* ἐπείθοντο αὐτῷ (Acts 5:36) *they obeyed him,* ἠπίστουν αὐτοῖς (Lu. 24:11) *they disbelieved them.* There are many more such verbs like ἀπειθέω, διακονέω, λατρεύω, προσκυνέω, ὑπακούω that naturally use the dative case.

Sometimes the dative case sustains a rather loose relation to the verb like ἀπεθάνομεν τῇ ἁμαρτίᾳ (Rom. 6:2) *we died to sin,* ζῇ τῷ θεῷ (Rom. 6:10) *he lives to God,* μὴ μεριμνᾶτε τῇ ψυχῇ (Matt. 6:25) *stop being anxious for the life,* ἐνεῖχεν αὐτῷ (Mk. 6:19) *she held it against him* ("she had it in for him"), μαρτυρεῖτε ἑαυτοῖς (Matt. 23:31) *ye testify against yourselves.* There are many more where it is the dative of advantage as the context makes plain. Some of these are in the predicate, but the explanation is the same.

It can not be clearly determined whether we have dative of personal agent or the instrumental case in Lu. 23:15 οὐδὲν ἄξιον θανάτου ἐστὶν πεπραγμένον αὐτῷ *nothing worthy of death has been done by him* (or "for him" if the dative). So again either the dative or the instrumental is possible in πρὸς τὸ θεαθῆναι αὐτοῖς (Matt. 6:1) *to be seen for them* (or *by them*). Cf. also 2 Pet. 3:14.

The infinitives that end in –αι are in the dative case though they are no longer treated as datives. The Sanskrit and Homer preserve the dative idea. In the New Testament we see the dative idea when the infinitive is used for purpose as in ἤλθομεν προσκυνῆσαι αὐτῷ (Matt. 2:2) *we came to worship him.* Compare the old English, "What went ye out for to see?"

CHAPTER XIII

ADVERBS

348. Origin and Nature of Adverbs.

The adverb is neglected often as an inconsequential part of speech, and yet adverbs include a large portion of the parts of speech like particles, conjunctions, prepositions beside the generally acknowledged adverbs. As a matter of fact it is not possible to draw a sharp line of distinction between adverbs, particle, preposition, and conjunction. The particles, prepositions, and conjunctions are in reality adverbs in that they have fixed case-forms. They have specialized uses and so differ thus from other adverbs and from each other. Our English "but" can be substantive, adjective, pronoun, adverb, preposition, conjunction (Giles *Phil.*, p. 237). This difference has continued from the Sanskrit to modern English. The mere adverb is a fixed case-form of a substantive, adjective, or participle, numeral, pronoun, or phrase used to modify verbs, adjectives, other adverbs or even substantives. Any oblique case may be so used and even the nominative in a set phrase like τὸ καθ' εἷς (Rom. 12:5) where καθ' is not regarded as a preposition. As examples of the accusative case as an adverb note δωρεάν (Matt. 10:8) *freely*, ταχύ (Matt. 5:25) *quickly*; of the genitive note ὅπου (Matt. 6:19) *where*; of the ablative note οὕτως (Matt. 6:30) *thus* or *so*, ὄντως (Lu. 24:34) *really*; of the locative observe κύκλῳ (Mk. 3:34) *in a circle*; of the instrumental take τάχα (Rom. 5:7) *perhaps*; of the dative note χαμαί (Jo. 9:6) *on the ground*.

349. The Use of Adverbs.

The adverb may express manner like σπουδαίως (Lu. 7:4) *earnestly*, place like ἐκεῖ (Matt. 2:13) *there*, or time like ἔπειτα

(Gal. 1:21) *thereupon*. The most common use of the ordinary adverb (not particle, preposition, or conjunction) is with verbs. Note Heb. 1:1 where three adverbs (πολυμερῶς καὶ πολυτρόπως πάλαι) occur with λαλήσας *God having spoken of old times in many portions and in many ways*. Some of these uses with verbs differ from the English idiom greatly. Thus τοὺς κακῶς ἔχοντας (Matt. 14:35) means *those who have it bad*, ἐσχάτως ἔχει (Mk. 5:23) *she has it in the last stages*, a common Greek idiom like βαρέως ἔχω in the papyri. Adverbs can be used with each other, even two comparatives like μᾶλλον περισσότερον ἐκήρυσσον (Mk. 7:36) *more abundantly they proclaimed it*. Adverbs can, of course, be employed with adjectives like ὁμολογουμένως μέγα (1 Tim. 3:16) *confessedly great*. Adverbs can be used with substantives as in τὸν νῦν αἰῶνα (2 Tim. 4:10) *the now age*. Adverbs may even be used as substantives like τίς ἐστίν μου πλησίον (Lu. 10:29) *Who is my neighbor?*

350. *Distinguished from the Adjective.*

So in Lu. 24:18 σὺ μόνος παροικεῖς; means *Hast thou been dwelling alone?* But μόνον πίστευσον (Lu. 8:50) means *only believe*, not *do thou alone believe*. So in Jo. 20:4 ἦλθεν πρῶτος *he came first* (before Peter), but ζητεῖτε πρῶτον (Matt. 6:33) is *seek ye first* (before ye do anything else). The Greek may use an adjective where the English prefers an adverb or adverbial phrase like δευτεραῖοι ἤλθομεν *we came second-day men* (*on the second day*) in Acts 28:13.

351. *Compound Adverbs and Adjuncts.*

Adverbs may be compounded like καθόλου (Acts 4:18) and παραχρῆμα (Acts 3:7). Numerous phrases are used practically as adverbs which are not technically so like κατ' ἰδίαν (Matt. 14:13), καθ' ἡμέραν (Mk. 14:49), τὴν ἀρχήν (Jo. 8:25), τὸ πρότερον (Jo. 6:62).

CHAPTER XIV

PREPOSITIONS

352. The Origin of Prepositions.

(a) Not Originally with Verbs.

The name preposition implies that these adverbs were originally used in composition with verbs. Hence some grammars regard Homer's free use of the eighteen so-called "proper" prepositions as abnormal and call it "tmesis" (cutting or separation) when he so often separates the preposition from the verb. Even in the New Testament the preposition may be a mere adverb as in ὑπὲρ ἐγώ (2 Cor. 11:23) *I more.*

(b) Adverbs Used to Help out the Case Idea.

At first, as in Sanskrit, the case alone expressed word relations. The Sanskrit had no proper class of prepositions, but only some set case-forms of adverbs occasionally employed to make clearer the case-idea, chiefly with the genitive and the accusative, a few with the locative, the instrumental, or the ablative. They were originally local in meaning (Delbrück, *Grundl.* IV. p. 134), and the same root idea is always carried from this local usage to other applications such as time and metaphors. The prepositions sometimes preserve the set case-form as the locative in ἀντί, ἐπί or the accusative in χάριν (still used as a substantive).

(c) Growth in the Use of Prepositions.

The history is a graphic one. Originally in the old Sanskrit it was all case and no preposition, the case-form doing it all. Now in modern French outside of personal pronouns it is all preposition and no case-form, word relations expressed entirely by preposition and position. In English outside of pronouns there is only one case-form (genitive or possessive, *s*) and prepositions and position have to do it all. A similar development in the use of prepositions is shown in the Greek from Homer to the modern Greek. As language developed the various word relations were considered too complicated for the mere case to carry clearly. Prepositions do not govern cases, but merely interpret them.

(d) *Interpreting the Use of the Preposition.*

The historical method is the only true way to understand a given Greek preposition. This method means that one must have a proper idea of the meaning of the case with which the preposition is used. Then see the meaning of the preposition and the case in which it is, if still possible. Then recall the history of both case and preposition and note the precise context and meaning of the words so connected. The resultant idea will come from all these considerations. This does not mean that a given preposition means a half-dozen or more different things as the average lexicon may say. Put each example through this process and you will come out where you do and be ready for the right translation. One should never forget that the Greeks had no translation to help them and yet they understood the various turns with the preposition perfectly.

353. *The So-called Improper Prepositions.*

These are the adverbs used as prepositions with nouns and pronouns, but never employed in composition with verbs. After the wrong definition of prepositions as words placed before verbs in composition (from the Latin *praepono*), the grammarians hesitated to call those never so employed prepositions. And yet they are just as really prepositions as the so-called eighteen "proper" prepositions. The Greek never had any "inseparable" prepositions that were used only in composition. Those used in composition merely went further in the development than the others. That is all. There was a constantly increasing number of adverbs used as prepositions. The already large number in the old Greek grew rapidly in the κοινή till in the New Testament there are 42 such adverbs used as prepositions. Of this list given below χάριν occurs in the New Testament often also as substantive (χάρις); πλησίον as substantive and adjective; μέσον as adjective; ἄχρι, ἕως, μέχρι, πλήν as conjunctions; ἄνευ, ἀντίπερα, ἀπέναντι, ἄτερ, ἔναντι, ἕνεκα(-εν), ἐνώπιον, ἐπέκεινα, κατενώπιον, παραπλήσιον, ὑπερέκεινα, ὑπεράνω, ὑποκάτω only as prepositions. The rest are also adverbs in the New Testament.

Here is the list in the New Testament:

ἅμα *together with* (Matt. 13:29) with the associative instrumental;

ἄνευ *without* (Matt. 10:29) with the ablative;

ἄντικρυς *over against* (Acts 20:15) with genitive;

ἀντίπερα *opposite* (Lu. 8:26) with ablative;

ἀπέναντι *before* (Matt. 27:61) with ablative;

ἄτερ *without* (Lu. 22:6) with ablative;

ἄχρι *until* (Lu. 4:13) with genitive;

ἐγγύς *near* (Jo. 3:23) with genitive or dative (Acts 9:38);

ἐκτός *outside of* (2 Cor. 12:2) with ablative;

ἔμπροσθεν *in front of* (Matt. 5:16) with ablative;

ἔναντι *before* (Lu. 1:8) with genitive;

ἐναντίον *in the presence of* (Lu. 1:6) with genitive;

ἕνεκα (-εν, εἵνεκεν) *on account of* (Lu. 6:22; Matt. 5:10; Lu. 4:18) with genitive;

ἐντός *within* (Lu. 17:21) with genitive;

ἐνώπιον *in the sight of* (Lu. 1:15) with genitive;

ἔξω *outside of* (Matt. 10:14) with ablative;

ἔξωθεν *from without* (Rev. 14:20) with ablative;

ἐπάνω *above* (Matt. 5:14) with genitive;

ἐπέκεινα *beyond* (Acts 7:43) with ablative;

ἔσω *within* (Mk. 15:16) with genitive:

ἕως *as far as* (Lu. 10:15) with genitive;

κατέναντι *over against* (Matt. 21:2) with genitive;

κατενώπιον *before the face of* (Eph. 1:4) with genitive;

κυκλόθεν *from all sides* (Rev. 4:3) with genitive;

κύκλῳ *in a circle* (Rev. 4:6) with genitive;

μέσον *in the midst of* (Phil. 2:15) with genitive;

μεταξύ *between* (Lu. 16:26) with ablative;

μέχρι *as far as* (Matt. 11:23) with genitive;

ὄπισθεν *from behind* (Matt. 15:23) with ablative;

ὀπίσω *behind* (Matt. 4:19) with ablative;

ὀψέ *after* (Matt. 28:1) with ablative;

παρεκτός *except* (Matt. 5:32) with ablative;

παραπλήσιον *near to* (Phil. 2:27) with genitive;

πέραν *on the other side* (Mk. 3:8) with ablative;

πλήν *besides* (Acts 8:1) with ablative;

πλησίον *near* (Jo. 4:5) with genitive;

ὑπεράνω *above* (Eph. 4:10) with ablative;

ὑπερέκεινα *beyond* (2 Cor. 10:16) with ablative;

ὑπερεκπερισσοῦ *far more than* (Eph. 3:20) with ablative;

ὑποκάτω *underneath* (Mk. 6:11) with ablative;

χάριν *for the sake of* (Eph. 3:1) with genitive;

χωρίς *without* (Matt. 13:34) with ablative.

Some of these are compound words, as can be seen, and two are triple compounds, ὑπερ–εκ–περισσοῦ and ἀπ-έν-αντι. There are, besides, a number of circumlocutions that are virtual prepositions like those with μέσος, ὄνομα, πρόσωπον, στόμα, χείρ.

354. *Prepositions in Composition.*

It is often true that the etymological idea of the preposition is retained longest in a compound word. The κοινή shows a growing tendency to use compound words, Polybius far more than the vernacular seen in the New Testament. Διακόσιοι (*two hundred*) is a case in point where the original meaning of διά = δύο survives as it does in διεσπάσθαι (*tear in two*) in Mk. 5:4. The preposition may be repeated after being used in the verb as in διέρχεσθαι δι' ἀνύδρων (Matt. 12:43) *he goes through waterless places.* One (ἀμφί) of the eighteen prepositions in the New Testament occurs only in composition and that leaves only seventeen to be discussed. It is found in ἀμφιβάλλοντας (Mk. 1:16) casting on both sides of the boat, now on one side and now on the other. 'Αμφί is the locative case of ἄμφω, Latin *ambo*, old German *umpi*, English *about*. So ἀμφιέννυμι (Matt. 6:30) means *to put clothing around* one. A careful study of Greek prepositions will enrich one's mind. There are pictures in prepositions.

355. *No Division by Cases.*

There is no scientific division of prepositions according to the cases with which they are used. The cases used are decreasing in the κοινή. Eight use only one case in the New Testament, though a different case (ἀνά, ἀντί, ἀπό, εἰς, ἐκ, ἐν, πρό, σύν). Five (διά, μετά, περί, ὑπέρ, ὑπό) are used with two cases. Three retain three cases (κατά, παρά, πρός), while only one (ἐπί) occurs with four if the pure dative is allowed as in Matt. 18:26.

356. 'Ανά.

Probably in the instrumental case and means up, upwards like ἄνω. Kin to Sanskrit *ana*, Zend *ana*, Gothic *ana*, German *an*, English *on*. Thirteen times in the New Testament, only with the accusative, and chiefly in the distributive use, *up and down, back and forth* as in ἀνὰ δύο (Lu. 10:1) *by twos*, ἀνὰ μέρος (1 Cor. 14:27) *in part*. It is exceedingly common in composition. Moulton and Geden's *Concordance* gives ten pages of such examples like ἀνα–γινώσκω *to know again* or *read* (Acts 8:30), ἀνα–ζω–πυρεῖν *to rekindle, to keep burning* (2 Tim. 1:6), ἀνα–κλίνω *to lie back* or *recline* (Matt. 14:19).

357. 'Αντί.

Locative case of ἄντα like the Sanskrit *anti* (end) and so means *at the end* or facing one from one end of an imaginary line. Compare Latin *ante*, Gothic *and*, German *ant-(ent-)*,

Anglo-Saxon *andlang* (*along*), *andswerian* (*answer*), English *ante-room*, *antagonist*. Two men face each other when each is at one end of the log. It occurs in the New Testament only 22 times except in compounds and there it is not so common as ἀνά. Every usage must be explained from the etymological idea of facing. In Lu. 10:31f. ἀντιπαρῆλθεν we see the original idea plainly preserved. Both priest and Levite crossed over to the opposite side facing (ἀντι–) the poor victim of the bandit and then along (παρ–) till he had passed on the other side. So also in Lu. 24:17 in ἀντι–βάλλετε we see the two disciples casting words back and forth (ἀντι–) as they talk about Jesus. Jesus endured the Cross because he saw the joy at the other end (ἀντι–) of the race. Hence he was willing to give his life a ransom (λύτρον, word used of price for a slave's freedom) for (ἀντί) many, answering over to many, in exchange for many. Another beautiful compound is συν–αντι–λαμβάνομαι used by Martha in her appeal to Jesus (Lu. 10:40) for Mary's help in her turn (ἀντι–) and of the help of the Holy Spirit in Rom. 8:26.

358. 'Από.

It is from adverb ἄψ (*back, backwards*), Sanskrit *apa* (instrumental case), Latin *ab*, Gothic *af*, German *ab*, English *of*, *off*. Old dialects had ἀπύ, ἀπαί. The case of ἀπό is not clear, but it is used in the New Testament only with the ablative and it is very common and also in composition. The meaning is the English *off* and is seen in ἀποκόπτω *to cut off* as in Jo. 18:26 and in ἀποκαλύπτω *to take the veil off* or *unveil* as in Matt. 10:26. So it easily means *from* as in βάλε ἀπὸ σοῦ (Matt. 5:29) *cast it from thee*. So it can have the idea of "*back*" as in ἀποδίδωμι (Matt. 16:27) *to give back*. It may even have a causal use (Lu. 24:41) ἀπὸ τῆς χαρᾶς *as a result of joy*, or agency as in Jas. 1:13.

359. Διά.

Sometimes διαί (Aeschylus), but διά looks like the instrumental case. It is the same word as δύο as seen in διακόσιοι (two hundred). So Sanskrit *dva*, *dvi*, Latin *duo*, *bis*, German *zwei*, English *two*, *twice*, *be-tween* (by twos). The original idea of two or the interval between two is always present. The resultant idea will vary with the case, the meaning of the words, and context. The two cases with which it is used in the New Testament are the genitive and the accusative. There are hundreds of examples and it is common in composition. We see it clearly in ἡμερῶν διαγενομένων τινῶν (Acts 25:13) *some days coming between* (δια–). So διαθήκη (Gal. 3:17) is an arrangement between two or covenant. In Acts 15:9 the δια– in διέκρινεν is explained by μεταξύ (between). So δια–ρήγνυμι (Lu. 8:29) *to rend asunder*, διασπάω (Mk. 5:4) *to draw in two*, διασπορά (Jo. 7:35) *dispersion*. In Mk. 2:1 δι'ἡμερῶν means *"days between"* and so *"after some days"*, but διά does not mean *"after."* It is common for the intermediate agent in contrast with ὑπό the immediate agent as in ὑπὸ κυρίου διὰ τοῦ προφήτου *by the Lord through the prophet*. With the accusative διά gives the ground or reason viewed as coming in between the person and the act as in διὰ φθόνον (Matt. 27:18) *because of envy*. In Heb. 2:10 God is presented as both cause (δι' ὅν) and agent in creation (δι' οὗ). Διά does not mean "through" though that is often the resultant idea as in Jo. 4:4 (go between the sides of and so through).

360. Ἐν.

There is an older form ἐνί (locative case) and in Homer εἰνί or εἰν for metrical reasons. The Arcadian and Cretan dialects wrote ἰν like Latin *in*. Cf. also Latin *en-do* and *in-ter*, Umbrian *en*, German *in* (*ein*), English *in* (*en-*). It simply means a position within boundaries and does not differ from the meaning of the locative case. But originally, as with the Latin *in*, ἐν was used with the accusative or the locative in the Arcadian, Boeotian, Cypriote, Northwest Greek, Thessalian. The Boeotian dialect did not use εἰς at all, but ἐν τὸν πόλεμον (Buck, *Greek Dialects*, p. 197).

In English vernacular we still say "jump in the river," "come in the house." 'Εν is the most common of all prepositions in the New Testament and the so-called *constructio praegnans* is nothing more than the retention of one of the original uses of ἐν except that after εἰς was introduced ἐν is no longer used with the accusative, but only with the locative. Hence it is immaterial whether we have ἐμβαπτόμενος εἰς τὸ τρυβλίον as in Mk. 14:20 *dipping into the dish* or ἐμβάψας ἐν τῷ τρυβλίῳ as in Matt. 26:23 *dipping in the dish*. So also Matt. 3:6 has ἐν where Mark 1:9 has εἰς with βαπτίζω. The various resultant uses of ἐν all come easily and naturally from the simple idea of *in* or *on* or *at*. The context of the word with which ἐν is used needs special attention as it gives color to the resultant idea. Note the three examples of ἐν in John 2:23, one of place ἐν τοῖς Ἱεροσολύμοις, two of time ἐν τῷ πάσχα ἐν τῇ ἑορτῇ *at the passover at the feast*. See also two of place in Jo. 8:20 and two of place in Jo. 4:20. 'Εν adds very little to the locative case and is by no means uniformly employed. So we have it in Matt. 3:11 (=Lu. 3:16), but not in Mk. 1:8, while in Acts 1:5 we have it with πνεύματι, but not with ὕδατι. The so-called instrumental use of ἐν like ἐν μαχαίρῃ (Lu. 22:49) conceives the act (smiting, here) as located in (ἐν) the instrument (sword, here). It is more common in the LXX (due to the Hebrew) than in the current κοινή. Sometimes the use of ἐν, as ἐν ἐμοί (1 Cor. 14:11) *in my case*, borders close on the dative.

361. Εἰς.

It is merely ἐν plus s =ἐνς like ἐνς 'Αθαναίαν preserved in the inscriptions of Argos and Crete. The s seems to have been added by analogy to ἐκ, ἐξ and to have been Aeolic in origin. With the disappearance of the ν before s the resultant form remained ἐς in Thucydides, the Ionic and Doric writers, though εἰς was the common form employed. So the original meaning is precisely the same as ἐν, the only difference being the locative case with ἐν, the accusative with εἰς. The Latin retained both cases with *in* as the English does, though *into* in literary style corresponds to εἰς and the accusative, if a verb of motion calls for it. In itself εἰς means only *in* like ἐν and made constant inroads on ἐν until finally in modern Greek εἰς has displaced ἐν. Hence in the New Testament no hard and fast distinction can be drawn between εἰς and ἐν. It is not so common in composition as ἐν. Hence we find no sharp difference between ὁ εἰς τὸν ἀγρόν (Mk. 13:16) and ὁ ἐν τῷ ἀγρῷ (Matt. 24:18), between εἰς οἶκόν ἐστιν and ἐν οἴκῳ ἐστίν (variations in Mk. 2:1.) With a verb of motion εἰς is more common like εἰς τὸ ὄρος (Matt. 5:1) *into the mountain*, but we have either ἐν τῷ ὀνόματι Ἰησοῦ χριστοῦ βαπτισθῆναι (Acts 10:48) *to be baptized in the name of Jesus Christ* or βεβαπτισμένοι εἰς τὸ ὄνομα τοῦ κυρίου Ἰησοῦ (Acts 8:16) *baptized in the name of the Lord Jesus*, in precisely the same sense. See also Matt. 10:41 εἰς ὄνομα προφήτου *in the name of a prophet*, and Matt. 12:41 εἰς τὸ κήρυγμα Ἰωνᾶ *at the preaching of Jonah*, where it is absurd to insist on "into" as the resultant meaning of εἰς. There is the use of εἰς for purpose like Rom. 11:36 ἐξ αὐτοῦ καὶ δι' αὐτοῦ καὶ εἰς αὐτόν (*out of Him, and by means of Him and unto Him*). Hence a case like Acts 2:38 εἰς ἄφεσιν τῶν ἁμαρτιῶν can mean either *on the basis of forgiveness of sins* (cf. Mk. 1:4f. "confessing their sins") or *with a view to forgiveness of sins*. There is nothing in εἰς to compel either result. One will interpret it according to his theology. The predicate use of εἰς like *as* is in the κοινή though more frequent in the LXX (cf. Matt. 19:5 from Gen. 2:24).

362. Ἐκ (ἐξ before vowels).

There is no Sanskrit equivalent for this word though the same root appears in Latin *ex* (*e*), Gallic *ex*, Cymric *eh*, Old Irish *ess* (so Arcadian, Boeotian, Thessalian ἐς, ἐσς). The original form was ἐξ, then ἐκ. The original meaning is *out of* and it never varies, the limit being marked by the word. It thus differs from ἀπό in implying a previous position within this boundary. So in Mark. 1:10 ἀναβαίνων ἐκ τοῦ ὕδατος *going up out of the water*, (in which he had been, like Acts

8:39), whereas Matt. 3:16 has merely ἀνέβη ἀπὸ τοῦ ὕδατος *he went up from the water*. So ἐκ τοῦ ὀφθαλμοῦ (Lu. 6:42) *out of thy eye*. It is always used with the ablative case and is common in partitive expressions like οὐδεὶς ἐξ αὐτῶν (Jo. 17:12) *no one of them*.

363. Ἐπί.

The Sanskrit *api* (locative), Zend *aipi*, Latin *ob*, Lithuanian *pi*, German *auf*, English *up*. It means *upon* and means resting upon rather than over or above like ὑπέρ. It is common in the New Testament both separately and in composition. It is used with four cases (genitive, locative, accusative, dative) with a great variety of resultant meanings all easily traced from the root idea. The original idea is plain in ἐπιγραφή (Lu. 23:38) *writing upon* and in ἐπιπίπτω (Acts 20:10) *to fall upon*. Sometimes it has the notion of *in addition to* as in ἐπίγνωσις (Col. 1:10) *full knowledge*. See ἐν οὐρανῷ καὶ ἐπὶ γῆς (Matt. 6:10) *in heaven and upon earth*. With the accusative it may be merely *upon* as in Matt. 7:24 ἐπὶ τὴν πέτραν *upon the rock*, or in certain contexts *against* may be the resultant idea as in Matt. 26:55 ἐπὶ λῃστὴν *against a robber*. The locative is common like ἐπὶ τῇ θύρᾳ (Acts 5:9) *at the door*. In Rev. 14:9 both genitive and accusative occur with ἐπί. In Rev. 4:2 we have ἐπὶ τὸν θρόνον while in verse 9 MSS. vary between ἐπὶ τοῦ θρόνου and ἐπὶ τῷ θρόνῳ. There are some examples of the true dative as in 2 Cor. 9:14 τὴν χάριν τοῦ θεοῦ ἐφ' ὑμῖν *the grace of God for you* (cf. Matt. 18:26; Lu. 1:47).

364. Κατά.

καταί (dative) occurs a few times and likewise Arcadian Greek has κατύ. The etymology is uncertain, but the root meaning seems to be *down* like κάτω and opposed to ἀνά(ἄνω) *upward*. It is used with three cases, genitive (*down upon, against*), ablative (*down from*), accusative (*down along*). It is common in composition in the literal sense like κατέβη (Matt. 7:25) *he went down* and in particular in the perfective sense like κατακαίω (Matt. 3:12) *to burn up* (or *down*), κατεσθίω (Matt. 13:4) *to eat up* (we say). The use with the ablative is clear, though infrequent as in κατ' αὐτῆς (Acts 27:14) *down from it* (the island), κατὰ τοῦ κρημνοῦ (Matt. 8:32 = Lu. 8:33) *down from the cliff*. The use with the genitive is very much like our English "down on" or "down upon" one and so "against" as in κατὰ τοῦ 'Ιησοῦ (Mk. 14:55) *against Jesus*. The most of the examples are with the accusative and often with the distributive sense as in κατὰ τὴν χώραν (Lu. 15:14) *up and down (throughout) the country*. Sometimes it has the notion of standard as in κατὰ σάρκα (2 Cor. 5:16) *according to the flesh (as the flesh looks at Christ)*.

365. Μετά.

Instrumental case apparently and seems to be the same root as μέσος *midst* like Sanskrit *mithas*, Latin *medius*, Gothic *mith*, German *mit*, English *mid*. The locative was also used with it in Homer, but in the New Testament only the genitive and the accusative survive. A short form μέ is used in modern Greek. It is quite common and in composition it has the notion "with" as in μετέχω (1 Cor. 10:30) *to have with* or *share* and in μετανοέω (Matt. 3:2) *to change one's mind*. So also μεταμορφόω (2 Cor. 3:18) *to transform*. With the accusative "after" is the resultant notion as in μετὰ δύο ἡμέρας (Matt. 26:2) *after two days*. Probably this idea is reached by the notion of extension in the accusative, "into the midst of" and so after. That led to the notion of "change" as in μετανοέω like our "after thought." So μεταμέλομαι (Matt. 21:30) *to be sorry afterwards*. The usual notion of "midst" or "with" is well illustrated by μετὰ τῶν θηρίων (Mk. 1:13) *with the wild beasts* and μετὰ μαχαιρῶν (Lu. 22:52) *with (accompanied by) swords*.

366. Παρά.

Apparently instrumental case though the Epic has παραί (dative). The etymology is uncertain. It may be kin to

Latin *per*, German *vor*, Anglo-Saxon *fore*, English *for* in for-
swear. The meaning is *alongside, beside*. It appears in our
parallel, parable, paradox. It is very common in composition like παραπλέω (Acts 20:16) *to sail by*, παραρρέω (Heb. 2:1)
to flow by, παρακαλέω (Acts 28:20) *to call to one's side*. It is
used with three cases (locative, ablative, accusative). With
the locative take παρὰ τῷ σταυρῷ (Jo. 19:25) *beside the cross*,
a graphic picture of the desolate mother of Jesus (*stabat Mater*).
With persons it sometimes means at one's house like the
Latin *apud* as παρὰ Σίμωνι (Acts 10:6). With the ablative note
παρὰ τοῦ πατρός (Jo. 16:27) *from the side of the Father*. The
accusative occurs with verbs of motion as ἦλθεν παρὰ τὴν
θάλασσαν (Matt. 15:29) *he came along the sea*, but also with verbs
of rest like ἐκάθητο παρὰ τὴν θάλασσαν (Matt. 13:1) *he was sitting
beside the sea*. It also has the notion of *beyond* after comparative forms as in Heb. 1:4. The notion of opposition comes
naturally after this as in παρὰ δύναμιν (2 Cor. 8:3) *beyond one's
power* and παρὰ νόμον (Acts 18:13) *beyond law* (*contrary to law*).
So παράπτωμα (Matt. 6:14) is *transgression*.

367. Περί.

It is in the locative case like the Sanskrit *pari* and is apparently from the same ultimate root as παρά whatever that is. It
is the same root seen in πέριξ (*round about*), and περισσός (*more
than necessary*) comes from it also. Homer used it as an
adverb πέρι while the Aeolic used πέρ and the intensive enclitic
particle περ is the same word. In Homer it was used with the
locative, genitive, ablative, and accusative. In the New
Testament we have it clearly with the genitive, the most frequent (nearly 300 examples), and the accusative (38). In
Acts 18:25 we have the genitive τὰ περὶ τοῦ Ἰησοῦ *the things
concerning Jesus*, in Acts 13:13 the accusative οἱ περὶ Παῦλον
those around Paul or *Paul and his company*. In 1 Jo. 2:2
περί occurs three times with the genitive. In Mk. 9:42 note
περὶ τὸν τράχηλον αὐτοῦ *around his neck*. It is not certain whether
περί occurs with the ablative in the New Testament, though

that may be true of περὶ ἁμαρτίας in Rom. 8:3 where "concerning sin" may mean to remove sin. In composition περί may mean "from around" as in 2 Cor. 3:16 περιαιρεῖται τὸ κάλυμμα *the veil is taken from around.* In Lu. 10:40 περισπάω means *to draw around.* The MSS. often vary between περί and ὑπέρ. Ἀμφί disappeared before περί and finally περί vanished before ὑπέρ.

368. Πρό.

The case of πρό is not clear, but it is the same root as the Sanskrit *pra,* Zend *fra,* Gothic *fra,* Lithuanian *pra,* Latin *pro,* German *für, vor,* English *fro, for* (forward), *fore* (forefront). In the later Greek it occurs only with the ablative with the notion of comparison. The comparative πρότερος and the superlative πρῶτος are made on πρό. It is more frequent in the New Testament than ἀνά and ἀντί, but less so than most of the others. It is common in composition like προκύλιον (Mk. 14:68) *fore-court,* πρόκριμα (1 Tim. 5:21) *pre-judgment,* προβαίνω (Matt. 4:21) *to go before.* So we have it with place πρὸ τῆς θύρας (Acts 12:6) *before the door,* with time πρὸ χειμῶνος (2 Tim. 4:21) *before winter,* with the notion of superiority πρὸ πάντων (Jas. 5:12) *before all.* In the compound verb προγράφω (Gal. 3:1) *to picture before like an artist* the meaning of προ– means before their eyes.

369. Πρός.

Perhaps a variation of προτί (Sanskrit *prati*) found in Homer, but whether related to πρό, as was once believed, is not certain. The root meaning is to be *near,* though Homer uses πρὸς δέ with the notion of besides or in addition to. In Mk. 4:38 προσκεφάλαιον (*pillow*) means "near the head." It occurs in πρόσωπον (πρός, ὤψ) *face* (near the eye). In 1 Cor. 13:12 we have πρόσωπον πρὸς πρόσωπον *face to face* (*face facing face,* three uses of πρός together). So ὁ λόγος ἦν πρὸς τὸν θεόν (Jo. 1:1) *the Logos was face to face with God.* Originally there were five cases used with πρός, but in the New Testament there are 678 examples with the accusative, 7 with the locative, and only one with the ablative (or genitive, not certain). So it is nearly a one case preposition. The one ablative example is Acts 27:34 πρὸς τῆς ὑμετέρας σωτηρίας (*from the point of view of your safety.* An example of the locative is πρὸς τῷ μνημείῳ (Jo. 20:11) *near the tomb.* The examples with the accusative are many as already stated like πρὸς τὸ φῶς (Mk. 14:54) *near or by the light,* πρὸς ἀλλήλους (Lu. 24:14) *with one another,* πρὸς τοὺς πόδας (Mk. 5:22) *at the feet,* πρὸς τοὺς Ἑβραίους (Acts 6:1) *against the Hebrews.*

370. Σύν.

The old Attic form was ξύν like the Ionic ξυνός (κοινός). One may compare the Latin *cum, con* (accusative). It is never used with any case but the associative instrumental. The Attic prose writers prefer μετά to σύν and Xenophon gave it a place in Attic prose, and the poets preferred σύν to μετά. It is scarce in the New Testament (chiefly in Luke's writings) except in composition where it is extremely frequent. The idea is accompaniment, association, instrument. Thus συνεσθίω (Lu. 15:2) is *to eat together with,* συναντιλαμβάνομαι (Lu. 10:40) *to lay hold together with.* Interesting examples of the preposition are σὺν τῷ χριστῷ (Col. 3:3) *together with Christ,* οἱ σὺν αὐτῷ (Lu. 9:32) *those with him.*

371. Ὑπέρ.

In Homer by anastrophe we have ὑπερ as an adverb as in 2 Cor. 11:23. Ὑπέρα means *upper rope.* It is a comparative form of the positive ὑπό, Sanskrit *upa.* Other comparatives like it are Sanskrit *upari* (locative case), Zend *upairi,* Latin *super,* Gothic *ufar,* German *über,* Anglo-Saxon *ofer,* English *over.* The meaning is thus plain. Chaucer uses over in the sense of upper. The original local sense of ὑπέρ is preserved in composition as in ὑπεράνω (Heb. 9:5) *up over,* ὑπερῷον (Acts

1:13) *upper room*.   The preposition goes down in modern
Greek before ὑπεράνω and διά.   It is used in the New Testament
only with the ablative of comparison, but the notion is ety-
mologically *over* whether the resultant idea is concerning, in
behalf of, instead of.   So ὑπὲρ Τίτου (2 Cor. 8:23) *about Titus*
(over Titus), ὑπὲρ τοῦ ἑνός (1 Cor. 4:6) *in behalf of the one*,
ὑπὲρ τοῦ λαοῦ (Jo. 11:50) *in behalf of the people* which here is
really "instead of the people" as the rest of the clause shows.
In itself ὑπέρ never means "instead of" any more than ἀντί
does or πρό, and yet in the New Testament as in the papyri
and in Euripides (Alcestis) ὑπέρ is the usual preposition used
for the notion of substitution.   Paul makes his meaning clear
on this point in Gal. 3:13 by the contrast with ὑπό, ἐκ.   Hence
one should find no trouble with ὑπέρ in 2 Cor. 5:15; Rom. 5:6;
Heb. 2:9; Tit. 2:14.   The use of ὑπέρ with the accusative
follows naturally with the notion of extension.   So in ὑπὲρ
δύναμιν (2 Cor. 1:8) *beyond ability*, ὑπὲρ τοὺς υἱοὺς τοῦ φωτός
(Lu. 16:8) *beyond the sons of light*.   Here after a comparative
the notion with the accusative is that of going beyond.

372. Ὑπό.

See Sanskrit *upa*, Latin *sub*, Gothic *uf*, English *up*, above.
Homer has ὑπαί (dative).   Unlike κατά, ὑπό never means
downwards.   It is upwards from under.   Hence English *up*
is the top side of line from ὑπό, *sub*.   So ὕψι means aloft and
ὕπτιος facing upwards.   The ideas *on* or *under* depend on standpoint.   The superlative carries on the same idea, Sanskrit
upamas, Greek ὕπατος, ὕψιστος, Latin *summus*, English *oft*,
uppermost.   The single notion of under is common as in ὑπὸ
τὸν μόδιον (Matt. 5:15) *under the bushel*.   It is freely used in
composition in the original sense like ὑποπόδιον (Matt. 5:35)
under foot (sandal), ὑποζώννυμι (Acts 27:17) *to undergird*.   The
locative no longer occurs with ὑπό in the New Testament, but
only the ablative (165 examples) and the accusative (50).
It is common with the ablative for the direct agent as in Matt.

4:1 πειρασθῆναι ὑπὸ τοῦ διαβόλου *to be tempted by the devil.* See Matt. 1:22 where ὑπό is used with κυρίου (immediate agent) and διά with προφήτου (intermediate agent). Other prepositions used to express agency are ἀπό, ἐκ, παρά, πρός. The accusative with ὑπό occurs with verbs of rest as in Matt. 5:15 as well as with verbs of motion (Matt. 8:8). The Johannine writings have ὑπό only five times.

CHAPTER XV

PRONOUNS

373. *The Reason for Pronouns.*

The pronoun is in place of a noun (*pro nomine, πρὸ ὀνόματος*), a device to prevent the repetition of substantive or adjective. In English we very much dislike the repetition of the same word too often. Macaulay is criticised for repeating the substantive. In Jo. 11:22 Martha says to Jesus: ὅσα ἂν αἰτήσῃ τὸν θεὸν δώσει σοι ὁ θεός *Whatsoever thou dost ask of God, God will give thee.* But the noun should be repeated if ambiquity is thus avoided.

The Indo-Germanic pronominal roots are very old, some of them as old as the oldest verbal roots. The pronouns have been the most persistent parts of speech as to retention of case-forms. But a complete set of pronouns was not developed at first. In the vernacular new pronouns arose from time to time.

374. *The Personal Pronouns.*

The pronoun is not so common as in modern European languages. The Greek verb itself contains the personal subject (verb stem plus pronominal root) and even the oblique case of the pronoun was not always expressed. It is not proper to say that the Greek "omits" the pronoun. A Greek writer only employed the personal pronoun when he felt it was necessary to express clearly his ideas. So there is no object expressed for ἰδών (Mk. 10:14). When the nominative pronoun is expressed, there is a certain amount of emphasis for the subject is in the verb already. So with ἐγώ (Matt. 5:22), σύ (Jo. 1:42) ὑμεῖς (Matt. 27:24). In the New Testament the nominative of pronouns, as in the κοινή and the Hebrew, is more frequent than in the earlier Greek. In the case of the redundant pronoun (oblique case) like οἶς αὐτοῖς (Rev. 7:2) there is, of course, no emphasis. The use of αὐτός is usually emphatic "he" in the nominative often to be expressed in English by the tone of voice (Mark 1:8; Matt. 1:21, 8:24; Acts 20:35). The use of καὶ αὐτός in Luke sometimes seems almost to lose emphasis (Lu. 1:22; 15:14; 24:25, 31).

Sometimes the personal pronoun occupies a very prominent position (*prolepsis*) as in σὺ τίς εἶ; (Rom. 14:4) *Thou who art thou?* Sharp contrast may be expressed by bringing two pronouns right together as ἐγώ σε (Jo. 17:4), με σύ (Jo. 17:5). Sometimes the unusual position is for euphony, not for emphasis, as with αὐτοῦ (Jo. 9:6). So with μου and σου in Jo. 9:10, 11, 17 and μου in Matt. 12:50 and note here the emphasis on αὐτός.

The literary plural is common enough in the New Testament where the writer uses "we" when he means only himself. A good example is γράφομεν in 1 Jo. 1:4 with which compare γράφω in 1 Jo. 2:12.

The New Testament never uses the old third personal pronoun (oblique cases), but only oblique cases of αὐτός, like αὐτῷ (dative in Lu. 15:16). The use of ὁ αὐτός for "the same" is still common like τὸ αὐτὸ πνεῦμα (2 Cor. 4:13) *the same spirit.* But this is a very different idiom from the intensive use of αὐτός which see later, like αὐτὸ τὸ πνεῦμα (Rom. 8:26) *the Spirit himself.*

375. *The Possessive Pronouns.*

Possession is expressed in various ways in Greek, each distinctive. Often the article alone is used, though the article does not mean possession. So in Matt. 8:3 ἐκτείνας τὴν χεῖρα *stretching the hand,* that is, *his hand,* though τὴν does not mean *his.* The context makes it perfectly clear that it is the hand of Jesus. See also Mk. 14:47 τὴν μάχαιραν *his sword,* 2 Cor. 12:18 τὸν ἀδελφόν *his brother.*

Often the genitive of the personal pronoun will be added to the article as in ὁ πατήρ μου (Jo. 5:17) *My Father*, τὸν κράβαττόν σου (Jo. 5:8) *thy bed*, τὸν κράβαττον αὐτοῦ (Jo. 5:9) *his bed*. The genitive of the personal pronoun may occur without the article as in φίλοι μου (Jo. 15:14) *friends of mine*, θεὸς ὑμῶν (Jo. 8:54) *God of yours.*

But there is the regular possessive pronoun for the first and second persons singular and plural though not common in the New Testament. For the third person only the devices already mentioned survived. These forms are ἐμός, σός for the singular, ἡμέτερος, ὑμέτερος (comparative -τερος). They occur usually with the article, but not always. So ὁ ἐμὸς καιρός (Jo. 7:8) *my time*, ἐμὸν βρῶμα (Jo. 4:34) *my food*, ἐν τῷ σῷ ὀφθαλμῷ (Matt. 7:3) *in thy eye*, σά (Lu. 15:31 predicate) *thine*, ἐν ταῖς ἡμετέραις γλώσσαις (Acts 2:11) *in our tongues* (no example without article), ἐν τῷ νόμῳ τῷ ὑμετέρῳ (Jo. 8:17) *in your law*, ὑμετέρα (Lu. 6:20 predicate) *yours*. One may find the genitive and the possessive side by side as τὸ ἐμὸν πνεῦμα καὶ τὸ ὑμῶν (1 Cor. 16:18) *my spirit and yours*. The genitive may be in apposition with the idea in the possessive in another case as τῇ ἐμῇ χειρὶ Παύλου (1 Cor. 16:21) *by the hand of me Paul.*

376. *The Intensive Pronoun.*

The intensive αὐτός appears in all persons, genders, and numbers. So αὐτὸς ἐγώ (Rom. 7:25) *I myself*, αὐτοὶ ἀκηκόαμεν (Jo. 4:42) *we ourselves have heard*, δύνασαι αὐτός (Lu. 6:42) *thou thyself art able*, αὐτὸς ὁ 'Ιωάνης (Matt. 3:4) *John himself*, αὐτὰ τὰ ἔργα (Jo. 5:36) *the works themselves*, ἡ φύσις αὐτή (1 Cor. 11:14) *nature itself*. But there are varying degrees of emphasis. It is almost demonstrative in αὐτῇ τῇ ὥρᾳ (Lu. 2:38) *at the hour itself* (at that very hour), an idiom common in Luke and Acts.

377. *Reflexive Pronouns.*

The personal pronouns were originally reflexive and they continued to be so used in the oblique cases especially in the vernacular. So ὡς ἂν ἀφίδω τὰ περὶ ἐμέ (Phil. 2:23) *so soon*

as *I see the affairs concerning me* (*myself*), θησαυρίζετε ὑμῖν
(Matt. 6:20) *treasure for you* (*yourselves*). There is, of course,
no reflexive in the nominative. The distinctive forms for
the reflexive are combinations of the personal pronoun with
the intensive αὐτός. So ἐμφανίσω ἐμαυτόν (Jo. 14:21) *I shall
manifest myself*, βάλε σεαυτόν (Matt. 4:6) *hurl thyself*, εἶπεν
ἐν ἑαυτῷ (Lu. 18:4) *he said in himself*. Note αὐτόν in Jo. 2:24
rather than ἑαυτόν. In the plural ἑαυτῶν has driven out the
first person ἡμῶν αὐτῶν, as in ἀνεθεματίσαμεν ἑαυτούς (Acts 23:14)
we put ourselves under a curse. The second personal plural
reflexive survives as in ὑμῶν αὐτῶν (1 Cor. 7:35) and ὑμῖν αὐτοῖς
(1 Cor. 11:13). But even so the ἑαυτῶν forms are the more
common as in προσέχετε ἑαυτοῖς (Lu. 17:3). For the third person plural see τῷ κυρίῳ ἑαυτῶν (Matt. 18:31) *to their own Lord*.
The genitive of the reflexive may be used with or without
the article and either after the article or before it or after the
substantive (Matt. 8:22; 21:8; 18:31). The use of ἴδιος (*own*)
is also common in the New Testament as in the κοινή. So
εἰς τὸν τόπον τὸν ἴδιον (Acts 1:25) *to his own place*.

378. *The Reciprocal and Distributive Pronouns.*

The reciprocal pronoun, ἀλλήλων (doubling of ἄλλος), occurs
only in oblique cases in the plural. So ἀσπάσασθε ἀλλήλους (1 Cor.
16:20) *salute one another*, ἀγαπῶμεν ἀλλήλους (1 Jo. 4:7) *let us
love one another*, μισήσουσιν ἀλλήλους (Matt. 24:10) *will hate
one another*. There are about a hundred examples in the New
Testament. So also ἑαυτῶν (1 Cor. 6:7). There are also
examples of the old Attic idiom of ἄλλος repeated as ἄλλοι
ἄλλο τι ἔκραζον (Acts 19:32) *some were crying one thing, some
another*. It is also like the Latin use of *alius aliud*. The
distinction between ἄλλος *another* of the same kind and ἕτερος
another of a *different* kind is sometimes observed, as in Gal.
1:6f. where εἰς ἕτερον εὐαγγέλιον is explained as ὃ οὐκ ἔστιν ἄλλο.
But ἕτερος originally meant a second of a pair as in Matt.
11:3, then of three or more as in Lu. 10:1. Contrast is also
expressed by εἷς—εἷς (Mk. 10:37), ὁ εἷς—ὁ ἕτερος (Lu.

7:41), and by the use of τινὲς μέν—τινὲς δέ (Phil. 1:15). The use of ἀμφότεροι for more than two seems to be established now by the papyri as in Acts 19:16 and 23:8. We still find ἕκαστος, but not ἑκάτερος. It is never used with the article (Jo. 6:7), but is common with εἶς (Matt. 26:22). In Rev. 21:21 ἀνὰ εἶς ἕκαστος we have the adverbial use of ἀνά and the nominative case. Ἀλλότριος is like the Latin *alienus* and means *belonging to another* (Rom. 15:20).

379. *The Demonstrative Pronouns.*

The demonstrative pronouns have given the grammarians a deal of trouble. There are a number of them. The simplest of all is ὁ, ἡ, τό which later was weakened into the article like ὁ ὤν (Rev. 1:4) or heightened into the relative as in ὁ ἦν (Rev. 1:4) like the Ionic plural τ forms. Usually the demonstrative ὁ in the New Testament is resumptive as in Matt. 2:5 where οἱ δέ refers to παρ' αὐτῶν. It occurs also for contrast as in οἱ μέν, οἱ δέ (Acts 14:4) though no longer common.

But ὅς is also still demonstrative, though chiefly relative in the New Testament. So ὅς δὲ ἀπεκρίθη (John 5:11) *but this one replied*. But the chief use of this demonstrative is in contrast as ὅς μέν, ὅς δέ (Matt. 22:5).

There are only ten New Testament examples of ὅδε as in Jas. 4:13 εἰς τήνδε τὴν πόλιν *into this city*, though chiefly τάδε as in Rev. 2:1. The peculiar ὁ δεῖνα *such a one* occurs only once (Matt. 26:18).

The most common of all is οὗτος which is employed according to the principles of the language. It is purely deictic in Matt. 21:10 τίς ἐστιν οὗτος; *Who is this?* There is a contemptuous sneer at Peter in the use of οὗτος in Matt. 26:71. The resumptive use is common as in Acts 2:23 where οὗτος refers to Ἰησοῦν in verse 22. So οὗτος may be expanded by a ὅτι clause (Mk. 4:41) or a ἵνα clause (Lu. 1:43).

The article is normally employed with οὗτος as in οὗτος ὁ τελώνης (Lu. 18:11) or ὁ ἄνθρωπος οὗτος (Lu. 23:47). The article is not present if the substantive is in the predicate as in αὕτη

ἀπογραφὴ πρώτη ἐγένετο (Lu. 2:2) *this occurred as a first enrol-
ment.* Some of these predicate examples are awkward in
English like τοῦτο ἀληθὲς εἴρηκας (Jo. 4:18) *this a true thing
thou hast said.* The most difficult example is found in Acts
24:21 περὶ μιᾶς ταύτης φωνῆς *concerning this one voice* where the
article would be called for by the usual rule.

The use of ἐκεῖνος (from ἐκεῖ *there*) is not so common as
οὗτος but follows the same general idiom. It may be purely
deictic as in Jo. 13:26, or contemptuous as in Jo. 9:28, anaphoric
or resumptive as in Jo. 1:8. It is often used in contrast as in
Jo. 3:30 ἐκεῖνον—ἐμέ. It may be quite emphatic as in Jo. 19:35
where ἐκεῖνος points to ὁ ἑωρακώς (John himself). In Mk.
13:11 ἐν ἐκείνῃ τῇ ὥρᾳ is parallel to ἐν αὐτῇ τῇ ὥρᾳ in Lu. 12:12.

Only four correlative demonstratives occur in the New
Testament, one of them τοιόσδε only once and without the
article (2 Pet. 1:17). Τηλικοῦτος occurs once as predicate
(Jas. 3:4), elsewhere attributive though without the article
as in 2 Cor. 1:10. Τοιοῦτος is the usual demonstrative of
quality and it occurs either without the article (Lu. 9:9) or
more usually with it (Matt. 19:14). It is used as the antecedent of οἷος (Mk. 13:19), ὁποῖος (Acts 26:29), ὅς (Heb. 8:1),
or ὅστις (1 Cor. 5:1). The correlative of size or quantity is
τοσοῦτος as in Matt. 8:10; 15:33. Note τοσούτῳ—ὅσῳ (Heb.
1:4), καθ' ὅσον—κατὰ τοσοῦτο (Heb. 7:20-22).

380. *The Relative Pronouns.*

The relative pronoun is so called because it expresses the
relation between clauses. All pronouns express relation
between words, but the special use of uniting clauses justifies
the term. Most conjunctions are relative in origin. The
relative usually agrees with the antecedent in gender and
number and sometimes in case by attraction to the case of the
antecedent as ἧς (Acts 3:25) where ἥν is attracted to the genitive case of the antecedent διαθήκης. Attraction is not always
practiced as is seen in τῷ λόγῳ ὃν εἶπεν (Jo. 2:22). The use of
ὁ as a relative occurs in the phrase ὁ ἦν in Rev. 1:4, 8; 11:17.

The most common relative is, of course, ὅς which far out-numbers all the other relatives. Sometimes the relative agrees with the gender of the predicate as in τῆς αὐλῆς ὅ ἐστιν πραιτώριον (Mk. 15:16) *the court which is the palace.* The agreement may be according to sense rather than grammatical gender as in παιδάριον ὅς ἔχει (Jo. 6:9) *a lad who has* or number and gender as in γενεᾶς ἐν οἷς (Phil. 2:15) *generation among whom.* In 1 Cor. 15:10 Paul purposely says εἰμὶ ὅ εἰμι *I am what I am,* not *who.* In 1 Tim. 3:16 μυστήριον ὅς is a case in point, the correct text, not ὅ or θεὸς. An example of inverse attraction is seen in τὸν ἄρτον ὃν κλῶμεν (1 Cor. 10:16) *the bread which we break.* Sometimes the antecedent is incorporated into the relative clause and is put in the same case as ἐν ᾧ κρίματι κρίνετε (Matt. 7:2) *with what judgment ye judge.* In this example also the one preposition ἐν is used that would be used with both antecedent and relative if put separately. The antecedent is not always expressed. The relative clause is primarily adjectival and describes the antecedent, but, when the antecedent is not expressed, it may be used as a substantive as in Mk. 4:9 ὃς ἔχει ὦτα ἀκούειν ἀκουέτω *who has ears to hear let him hear* where the relative clause is the subject of ἀκουέτω. The articular participle is often parallel to this use of the relative. So in Matt. 7:24 note πᾶς ὅστις ἀκούει and in verse 26 πᾶς ὁ ἀκούων. See also ὅς so used in Matt. 10:42 beside ὁ δεχόμενος in verse 41. In the New Testament ὅστις is not always *whoever,* but sometimes *which very one.* So it may be indefinite as in Matt. 5:39, or more definite than ὅς as in Matt. 27:55 where it is explanatory or even causal as in Acts 10:47. In the New Testament ὅστις is nearly confined to the nominative. The accusative ὅτι appears in Lu. 10:35 and Acts 9:6. In Acts 9:6 we have the only example of ὅστις in the New Testament in an indirect question. The qualitative relative οἷος is rare in the New Testament (1 Thess. 1:5) as is ὁποῖος (Gal. 2:6). A good example of ὁποῖος in an indirect question in Jas. 1:24 ἐπελάθετο ὁποῖος ἦν *he forgot what sort of a man he was.* But ὅσος the quantitative relative is frequent and is, like οἶος and ὁποῖος, either the mere relative (Matt. 7:12) or in an indirect question (Mk. 3:8). There is also ἡλίκος for age (Jo. 9:21) or for stature (Matt. 6:27), only four times in all. The repetition of the relative ὅσα is interesting in Phil. 4:8 and of ὅς in 1 Cor. 15:1f. The use of the relative at the beginning of sentences (like the Latin) occurs in Luke as in Lu. 12:1 ἐν οἷς and 12:3 ἀνθ' ὧν ὅσα (double relative). Recall the demonstrative origin of the relative.

381. The Interrogative Pronouns.

Τίς is the usual interrogative pronoun as in τίς ὑπέδειξεν ὑμῖν; (Matt. 3:7) who suggested to you? It occurs in alternative questions in place of πότερος (πότερον only once in the New Testament Jo. 7:17) as in τίνα θέλετε ἀπολύω ὑμῖν, βαραββᾶν ἢ Ἰησοῦν; (Matt. 27:17) Whom wish ye that I release unto you, Barabbas or Jesus? So τίς—ἤ (Matt. 23:17). Sometimes the copula has dropped out with τί ὅτι (Lu. 2:49) for we have it in τί γέγονεν ὅτι (Jo. 14:22). So as to ἵνα τί in Matt. 9:4. τί alone is almost adverbial (accusative) like "why" (Matt. 7:3) or "how" (Acts 5:9). That is also possible in Lu. 12:49. Note τί rather than τίνα in Acts 13:25. There is nothing peculiar in Paul's use of τί οὖν (Rom. 6:15) or τί ἄρα or τί γάρ. Τί has no effect on the structure of the sentence. The optative with ἄν in Acts 17:18 is merely the apodosis of a fourth class condition. τίς, contrary to earlier usage, is common in indirect questions as in Matt. 20:22. The relative and this indirect interrogative may occur side by side as in ἃ λέγουσιν —περὶ τίνων (1 Tim. 1:7). The subjunctive in τί λαλήσητε (Matt. 10:19) is due to the direct deliberative subjunctive, not to the indirect question. In a case like οἶδά σε τίς εἶ (Mk. 1:24) there is prolepsis of σε and the indirect question as in apposition with σε (I know thee who thou art). There is the double interrogative in Mk. 15:24 τίς τί ἄρῃ who should take what.

The other interrogatives call for little comment. πηλίκος occurs only twice (Heb. 7:4 and possibly Gal. 6:11, but West-

cott and Hort put ἡλίκοις in the margin of Gal. 6:11).   ποταπός
occurs once in a direct question (Matt. 8:27) and four times in
an indirect question (Mk. 13:1; Lu. 1:29; 7:39; 1 Jo. 3:1).
In Lu. 7:39 it is contrasted with τίς.   ποῖος (qualitative)
occurs 16 times in direct questions as in Matt. 21:23 and 16
times in indirect questions (Matt. 21:34). πόσος (quantitative)
is chiefly in the Synoptic Gospels both in direct questions
(Matt. 15:34) and in indirect questions (Matt. 27:13).

382.   *The Indefinite Pronouns.*

The usual one is the enclitic τίς.   It can be used either as
substantive "any body" or "any one" (Matt. 11:27) or "some-
body" in particular as in Acts 5:36.   In Gal. 6:3 both senses
occur.   It may be used with numbers as δύο τινάς (Lu. 7:19)
some two.   It may occur with a substantive almost like an
indefinite article [like ἱερεύς τις (Lu. 1:5) *a priest* just as εἷς
may be the equivalent of τίς as in Mk. 10:17 or they may
occur together as in Mk. 14:47.   It is always enclitic and may
occur at the beginning of a clause like τινὲς δέ (Acts 17:18).

Sometimes πᾶς may be almost equal to τίς as in Matt.
5:22; 13:19.

383.   *Negative Pronouns.*

The most common is οὐδείς.   It is used either absolutely
(Matt. 6:24), with substantives (Lu. 4:24), with other pronouns like ἄλλος (Acts 4:12) or ἕτερος (Acts 17:21).   Sometimes οὐδὲ εἷς appears (Acts 4:32), the uncontracted form,
and more emphatic.   Occasionally εἷς—οὐ is found (Matt.
10:29).   The form οὐθείς (contraction of οὔτε εἷς) occurs in
some passages (Lu. 22:35).   It had quite a run in the κοινή,
but died away by the fifth century A. D.   Μηδείς occurs wherever
the negative μή is allowable (Gal. 6:17) and is naturally not so
frequent as οὐδείς.   Westcott and Hort do not print οὔ τις
and μή τις as single words, except μήτι as an interrogative
particle expecting the answer "No" (Matt. 26:22).

We have both οὐ πᾶς (Matt. 7:21) and πᾶς—οὐ (Matt. 24:22), this latter a Hebrew idiom in the Septuagint with some parallel in the papyri. The result is the same as if οὐδείς had been used with an affirmative verb. In Matt. 24:22 the idea is that "no flesh would have been saved," not that "some flesh would have been lost." Rarely do we find μή—πᾶς (1 Cor. 1:29). Μὴ πᾶς (Jo. 3:16) is according to rule.

CHAPTER XVI

THE ARTICLE

384. *No Indefinite Article in Greek.*

The Sanskrit and the Latin had no article of any kind (definite or indefinite) as the Greek has no indefinite article. Not even has the modern Greek taken up the indefinite article like that developed in the Romance and Teutonic languages. The best that the Greek can do is to use εἷς or τὶς in a weakened sense like εἷς γραμματεύς in Matt. 8:19 *a scribe* or νομικός τις (Lu. 10:25) *a lawyer* where "certain" is too emphatic. The fact is that the English *one*, Scotch *ane*, German *ein*, French *un* are all simply the cardinal *one* adapted to this usage. Children often say: "That was one funny man."

385. *The Definite Article in Greek Originally a Demonstrative Pronoun.*

The Greek was slow in developing the definite article and Homer only shows the beginning of the use of ὁ, ἡ, τό with the force of "the" instead of the demonstrative idea or even the relative. This form was first a demonstrative that was weakened to the article or heightened to the relative. In the Ionic this threefold usage appears for Herodotus uses the τ forms as demonstrative, article, or relative. It is never true to say that the article was used as a demonstrative. The demonstrative use is the oldest and held on in the Attic and is common in the New Testament in ὁ δὲ εἶπεν (Matt. 14:18) and similar phrases οἱ μέν, οἱ δέ (Acts 14:4). And even the relative survives in Rev. 1:4, 8; 11:17.

The Sanskrit demonstrative *sa, sa, tad* is like the Greek ὁ, ἡ, τό, where a rough breathing has taken [the place of *s*.

We see it in the Latin *is-te*, *is-ta*, *is-tud*, the Gothic *sa*, *so* *thata*, the German *der*, *die*, *das*, the Anglo-Saxon *se*, *seo*, *thaet*, the English *this* *(the)*, *that*. In German and in English we see the same form used as demonstrative, article, relative. English "the" is just a weakened form of "this." In the New Testament as in the earlier Attic ὁ, ἡ, τό is usually just the article, while the demonstrative and relative ideas are expressed by other words. The modern Romance languages obtain their definite articles from the Latin *ille*, *iste*.

386. *The Purpose of the Article.*

The Greek grammarians call it ὁριστική and that is close to the idea. It defines, limits, points out from ὁρίζω (cf. our *horizon*). The Greek article is a pointer. It is natural, if not good manners, for children to point at objects. The Greek article does not tell why an object is pointed at nor does it point it out as near or far like the demonstrative. Broadus used to insist that the Greek article points out in one of three ways.

(a) *Individual from Other Individuals.*

This is its most common use. So ἰδὼν τοὺς ὄχλους ἀνέβη εἰς τὸ ὄρος (Matt. 5:1) *Seeing the multitudes he went up into the mountain* (the multitudes gathered there, the mountains rising, just before him). The English renderings often fail to handle properly the Greek article as with τῷ ἁμαρτωλῷ (Lu. 18:13) *the sinner*, not "a sinner." The translators of the Authorized Version were evidently under the influence of the Latin Vulgate which has no article. So in Lu. 4:20 τὸ βιβλίον is the roll that Jesus had just read and τῷ ὑπηρέτῃ is the attendant who had brought it to him. The Greek article is not used when it has no meaning.

(b) *Classes from Other Classes.*

A good illustration occurs in each of the Beatitudes as in οἱ πτωχοὶ τῷ πνεύματι (Matt. 5:3) *the poor in spirit*. About τῷ πνεύματι, see number (c). So the article is used with each class addressed in Col. 3:18 to 4:1 (αἱ γυναῖκες, οἱ ἄνδρες, τὰ τέκνα, οἱ πατέρες, οἱ δοῦλοι, οἱ κύριοι). See also 1 Cor. 1:27; Rom. 2:13. Two classes may be viewed as separate with two articles as οἱ φαρισαῖοι καὶ οἱ γραμματεῖς (Mk. 7:5) or the one article may treat them as one as οἱ Φαρισαῖοι καὶ Σαδδουκαῖοι, (Matt. 16:1). The two articles in Jo. 4:36 accent the distinctness of the two persons as ὁ σπείρων καὶ ὁ θερίζων. The article may be used with the singular to represent the whole class as with ὁ ἐργάτης (Lu. 10:7) *the workman*, ὁ ἄνθρωπος (Matt. 4:4) *mankind*. Classes do not always have the article in Greek as πονηροὺς καὶ ἀγαθούς (Matt. 5:45) *wicked and good*.

(c) *Qualities from Other Qualities.*

The article is not necessary with abstract qualities (cf. 1 Cor. 12:9-11), but in the list of the attributes of God in the songs in Rev. 4:11; 5:13; 7:12 the separate article occurs with each quality as if to single out each one and to sharpen it. In Rev. 5:12 one article (τὴν) is used for the whole list. In 1 Cor. 13 it is interesting to note the variety in the use or absence of the article with the graces mentioned. French and German are like the Greek in the ease with which they employ the article with abstract substantives when it is awkward in the English idiom. In Rom. 16:17 notice how neatly τούς, τάς, τά, τήν all come in. See also Rom. 13:7 and 1 Jo. 4:18 for delicate and precise use of the article. The Greek often has the article with a quality where we cannot handle it in English as with τῷ πνεύματι (in spirit) above.

387. *The Varied Use of the Article.*

(a) *With Word or Clause.*

As a pointer it can point at or out anything not already definite enough without it. As a rule the article has the gender of the thing at which it points, but in ὁ ἀμήν (Rev. 3:14) we have the natural, not the grammatical gender, while τὸ Ἄγαρ (Gal. 4:25) follows the grammatical, not the natural gender. So we have ἀπὸ τοῦ νῦν (Lu. 5:10) where the article points at the adverb νῦν, and τὰ νῦν (Acts 27:22) where the article agrees with things "understood". In τὸ ἀνέβη (Eph. 4:9) the article points at the verb ἀνέβη as in τὸ Εἰ δύνῃ (Mk. 9:23) it points at the clause Εἰ δύνῃ (cf. also Matt. 19:18; Rom. 13:9) where a quotation is so defined. In Lu. 22:4 τὸ πῶς the article points at the indirect question as also with τὸ τίς in verses 23 and 24. The article, of course, is common with the infinitive (Mk. 10:40) and the participle as with other adjectives with a substantive (Acts 21:26) or without a substantive (Lu. 22:27). Often only the article appears where the context is clear as τὰ καίσαρος (Mk. 12:17), *the things of Caesar*, τὸ τῆς συκῆς (Matt. 21:21), *the matter of the fig tree*, οἱ ἐκ νόμου (Rom. 4:14) *those dependent on law.*

(b) *With Attributives.*

There are three kinds of attributive expressions with which the article has to do.

(1) *Adjectives.*

An adjective may be attributive (instead of predicate) without the article as in μικρὰ ζύμη (1 Cor. 5:6) *a little leaven.* But if the article is used before the adjective it is certainly attributive like ὁ ἀγαθὸς ἄνθρωπος (Matt. 12:35) *the good man.* The article may be repeated as in ὁ ποιμὴν ὁ καλός (Jo. 10:11) *the shepherd the good one.* The article may be repeated with each attributive as in τὴν ῥομφαίαν τὴν δίστομον τὴν ὀξεῖαν (Rev. 2:12) *the sword the two mouthed the sharp one.*

(2) *With Genitives.*

From the nature of the case the genitive is generally attributive unless in the predicate with εἰμί,, γίνομαι, etc. So οἰκοδομὴ θεοῦ (1 Cor. 3:9) *God's building* is as really attributive

as τῇ χάριτι τοῦ θεοῦ (1 Cor. 1:4) *the grace of God* or τὸ κήρυγμά μου
(1 Cor. 2:4) *my preaching*. This is true whatever the position
of the genitive, after the substantive as above, or before the
substantive like θεοῦ υἱός (Matt. 27:54) *Son of God* which is
rare, or after the article like ἡ τοῦ θεοῦ μακροθυμία (1 Pet. 3:20)
the long suffering of God or after the repeated article for emphasis like ὁ λόγος ὁ τοῦ σταυροῦ (1 Cor. 1:18) *the word that of the Cross.*
If both substantive and genitive are definite, they both have
the article as in 1 Pet. 3:20 above. So Nathanael said to
Jesus Σὺ εἶ ὁ υἱὸς τοῦ θεοῦ (Jo. 1:49) *Thou art the Son of God*
(cf. Peter in Matt. 16:16). This is the law of the correlation
of the article. But Satan only said to Jesus εἰ υἱὸς εἶ τοῦ θεοῦ
(Matt. 4:3, 6) *if thou art Son of God* (or a son of God). Jesus
terms himself υἱὸς τοῦ θεοῦ in Jo. 10:36 when meeting the
criticism of his enemies, elsewhere ὁ υἱὸς τοῦ θεοῦ (Jo. 5:25).
With a proper name the second article is not required as in
Matt. 1:12 τὴν μετοικεσίαν βαβυλῶνος *the removal to Babylon* (already definite as proper name). It is important to note the
force of the one article with attributive genitives like 2 Pet.
1:11 τὴν αἰώνιον βασιλείαν τοῦ κυρίου ἡμῶν καὶ σωτῆρος 'Ιησοῦ
χριστοῦ *the eternal Kingdom of our Lord and Saviour* (the one
article τοῦ pointing at κυρίου καὶ σωτῆρος as one individual
just like ὁ ἀδελφὸς ὑμῶν καὶ συνκοινωνός (Rev. 1:9) *your brother
and companion*). So in 2 Pet. 1:1 ἐν δικαιοσύνῃ τοῦ θεοῦ ἡμῶν
καὶ σωτῆρος 'Ιησοῦ χριστοῦ can only mean grammatically *in
righteousness of our God and Saviour Jesus Christ*. Winer
admits this as the necessary grammar, but for doctrinal reasons draws back. Grammar has nothing primarily to do with
theology. So in Tit. 2:13 τὴν μακαρίαν ἐλπίδα καὶ ἐπιφάνειαν τῆς
δόξης τοῦ μεγάλου θεοῦ καὶ σωτῆρος Χριστοῦ 'Ιησοῦ *the happy hope
and epiphany of our great God and Saviour Christ Jesus.* The
use of ἐπιφάνειαν besides the single article τοῦ points directly
to the second coming of Christ Jesus. Note the correlation
of articles here (τὴν, τῆς, τοῦ). Paul's doctrinal system (Phil.
2:9; Col. 1:15-19; 2:9; Rom. 9:5; Acts 20:28) does not forbid
the necessary force of the single article in Tit. 2:13.

(3) With Adjuncts.

When the adjunct has the article before it, the phrase is, of course, attributive. So in τοῖς ἐν χριστῷ Ἰησοῦ (Rom. 8:1) *those in Christ Jesus*, διὰ τῆς ἀπολυτρώσεως τῆς ἐν Χριστῷ Ἰησοῦ (Rom. 3:24) *by the redemption that is in Christ Jesus*. But if no article comes before it, the adjunct may be predicate like ἐν τῇ σαρκί (Rom. 8:3) which goes with κατέκρινε, not with τὴν ἁμαρτίαν. It is not sin in the flesh of Christ, but the condemnation of sin that took place in the flesh of Christ. But εἰς τὸν θάνατον in Rom. 6:4 goes with διὰ τοῦ βαπτίσματος because of the preceding verse. The tone of voice may decide how one interprets such an adjunct as in 1 Thess. 4:16; Lu. 16:10. The one article may point at several adjuncts (2 Pet. 1:4).

(c) With Predicates.

When the substantive has the article and the adjective has not, the adjective is generally predicate. Thus μεγάλῃ τῇ φωνῇ (Acts 26:24) means *with the voice elevated or loud*, not *with the loud voice*. Heb. 7:24 ἀπαράβατον ἔχει τὴν ἱερωσύνην means *he has the priesthood unchangeable*, not *he has his unchangeable priesthood*. So also in Mk. 3:1 ἐξηραμμένην ἔχων τὴν χεῖρα the meaning is *having the hand withered*. As a rule the article is not used with the predicate noun even if the subject is definite. The article with one and not with the other means that the articular noun is the subject. Thus ὁ θεὸς ἀγάπη ἐστίν can only mean *God is love*, not *love is God*. So in Jo. 1:1 θεὸς ἦν ὁ λόγος the meaning has to be *the Logos was God*, not *God was the Logos*. If the article occurs with both predicate and subject they are interchangeable as in 1 Jo. 3:4 ἡ ἁμαρτία ἐστὶν ἡ ἀνομία *sin is lawlessness* and also *lawlessness is sin* (a needed lesson for our day). If the predicate is well-known or identical with the subject, the article may be employed. So in Jo. 3:10 Σὺ εἶ ὁ διδάσκαλος; *Art thou the teacher?* (the well-known etc). See also Acts 21:38 ὁ Αἰγύπτιος *the (famous) Egyptian*. The old idiom with μέσος survives in μέσης νυκτός (Matt. 25:6) *the middle of the night.* In Matt. 10:16 ἐν μέσῳ λύκων *in the midst of wolves* we see the common use like εἰς μέσον, ἐκ μέσου, κατὰ μέσον almost like a compound preposition. The adjective ἄκρος has no idiomatic use, but τὸ ἄκρον τοῦ δακτύλου (Lu. 16:24) means *the tip of the finger.*

(d) With Proper Names.

A proper name usually requires no article for it is definite already. Just so we do not use the article with home, husband, wife, father, mother, son, daughter, unless there is special reason for doing so. Sometimes we can see the reason for the article as in Acts 19:13 τὸν Ἰησοῦν ὃν Παῦλος κηρύσσει *the Jesus whom Paul preaches* (article with Jesus, not with Paul). But the demon comes back with τὸν Ἰησοῦν γινώσκω καὶ τὸν Παῦλον ἐπίσταμαι *the Jesus I know and the Paul I understand.* But in most instances the use or non-use of the article with proper names seems whimsical to us as in Acts 19:1 τὸν Ἀπολλὼ εἶναι ἐν Κορίνθῳ Παῦλον. The article may be with the word in apposition when not with the proper name as with Ἰωάνης ὁ βαπτιστής (Matt. 3:1) *John the Baptist.*

(e) With Pronouns.

The genitive of personal pronouns may be used where the article is used as τὸν πατέρα μου (Matt. 26:53) *the Father of me* or not used as φίλοι μου (Jo. 15:14) *friends of mine,* δούλους ἑαυτοῦ (Lu. 19:13) *slaves of his own.* The position of the genitive is immaterial as in τῇ αὐτοῦ χάριτι (Rom. 3:24) *by his grace,* τῆς χειρὸς αὐτῆς (Matt. 8:15) *her hand.* The article is used before the possessive pronoun as τῷ σῷ ὀνόματι (Matt. 7:22) *in thy name* unless it is predicate as σά (Lu. 15:31) *thine.* The article often occurs alone instead of the possessive as ἀπενίψατο τὰς χεῖρας (Matt. 27:24) *he washed off the hands (his hands).* We have τὸν δεῖνα once (Matt. 26:18) *so and so.* Ἴδιος outside of ἰδίᾳ and κατ' ἰδίαν usually has the article as οἱ ἴδιοι (Jo. 1:11) *his own people,* but ἰδίοις ὀψωνίοις (1 Cor. 9:7) *at his own charges.*

Τοιοῦτος sometimes is without the article as ἐξουσίαν τοιαύτην (Matt. 9:8) *such authority*, but usually with it as οἱ τοιοῦτοι (Rom. 16:18) *such men*, and once αἱ δυνάμεις τοιαῦται (Mk. 6:2) *such powers*. Once only does the article occur with τοσοῦτος ὁ τοσοῦτος πλοῦτος (Rev. 18:17) *so great wealth*.

The article is used once with ὅδε as εἰς τήνδε τὴν πόλιν (Jas. 4:13) *into this city*. This apparently predicate position of the article as with οὗτος and ἐκεῖνος must not be confused with the usual predicate position of adjectives. It is an awkward construction to the English, but there is a parallel in the French idiom *la république française*. In Homer τοῦτον τὸν ἄναλτον = *this man insatiate that he is*. Probably the articular noun was felt to be in apposition with οὗτος. So it became a fixed idiom as the early inscriptions show. The order is immaterial whether ὁ ἄνθρωπος οὗτος (Lu. 2:25) or οὗτος ὁ ἄνθρωπος (Lu. 14:30). When the article is not used, οὗτος is a real predicate as in ταύτην ἐποίησεν ἀρχὴν τῶν σημείων (Jo. 2:11) *this he did a beginning of the miracles*.

Without the article in the singular πᾶς is "every" as πάντα πειρασμόν (Lu. 4:13) *every temptation*. With abstract substantives this is tantamount to "all" as πᾶσαν χαράν (Jas. 1:2) *all joy*. So also if it is a proper name and so a single object like πᾶσα Ἱεροσόλυμα (Matt. 2:3) *all Jerusalem* (πόλις *city* understood). Since γραφή is sometimes regarded as definite πᾶσα γραφή (2 Tim. 3:16) can be "all Scripture" or "every Scripture." There is a slight, though not material, difference between πᾶσα ἡ πόλις (Matt. 8:34) *all the city* (as a whole) and ὁ πᾶς νόμος (Gal. 5:14) *the entire law* (as an entity). The order can be either πάντας τοὺς ἀρχιερεῖς (Matt. 2:4) *all the chief priests* or τὰς πόλεις πάσας (Matt. 9:35) *the cities all of them*. πᾶς ὁ ἀκούων (Matt. 7:26) is parallel with πᾶς ὅστις ἀκούει (Matt. 7:24). The article with the plural gives the sum total as τὰ πάντα (Col. 1:16) *the all things* (*the universe*). With ἄπας we have either ἄπαντα τὸν λαόν·(Lu. 3:21) *all the people*, τὴν ἐξουσίαν ταύτην ἅπασαν (Lu. 4:6) *this power all of it*, or τὴν ἅπασαν μακροθυμίαν (1 Tim. 1:16) *the whole long suffering*. Ὅλος can be used without the article as ἐνιαυτὸν ὅλον (Acts 11:26) *a whole year* or usually with it as ὅλος ὁ κόσμος (Rom. 1:8) *all the world,* ἡ πόλις ὅλη (Acts 21:30) *the city as a whole.* Ὅλος is predicate in Jo. 9:34 ἐν ἁμαρτίαις σὺ ἐγεννήθης ὅλος *thou was begotten in sins the whole of thee.*

(f) *With the Vocative.*

Here we have an old Greek idiom intensified by the Hebrew and the Aramaic usage in which tongues the vocative regularly has the article. So Ἀββά ὁ πατήρ (Mk. 14:36) *Abba, Father* we have to say in English, the Greek repeating the article from the Aramaic Ἀββά. So also τὸ κοράσιον in Mk. 5:41 merely translates ταλειθά. We cannot reproduce this article in English and can only say *Little Maid.* In Jo. 20:28 ὁ κύριός μου καὶ ὁ θεός μου the form is nominative, but the case is vocative. Jesus receives the words as direct address.

388.   *The Absence of the Article.*

It is a curious bit of inadvertence when grammarians speak of the "omission" of the Greek article in the New Testament. That phrase assumes that the article "should" be there to suit the English or German idiom or the grammarian's own rules about the article. As a matter of fact, there is no obligation on any one to use the Greek article unless he feels the need of it to make something more definite than it is without it. If a word is indefinite, the article is not used as μετὰ γυναικὸς ἐλάλει (Jo. 4:27) *he was talking with a woman.* The Greek article is not the only way to make a thing definite. Proper names are used for this very purpose and ordinarily answer very well, as in πρὸς Βαρνάβας Παῦλος (Acts 15:36) unless too many have the same name. Often a genitive makes a word definite enough as πύλαι ᾅδου (Matt. 16:18) *gates of Hades.* But this is not always the case. So θεοῦ υἱός (Matt. 27:54) can be either *a son of God* or *the Son of God.* When there is only one such object, it is definite without the article like ἥλιος (Matt. 13:6) *sun,* γῆ (Lu. 2:14) *earth,* κόσμος (Gal. 6:14) *world.* This idiom is as true of English as of Greek. Some words are definite from the nature of the case like home, husband, wife, father, mother. Some words are so distinctive that they can be regarded as definite like νόμος (Rom. 2:12) *law*, γραφή (1 Pet. 2:6) *Scripture*. So in 1 Cor. 8:4f. note ἐν κόσμῳ, ἐν οὐρανῷ, ἐπὶ γῆς all definite conceptions. So we say at home, in town, in bed, in church (ἐν ἐκκλησίᾳ 1 Cor. 14:35). Prepositions often help to make a word definite as ἐκ πνεύματος ἁγίου (Matt. 1:21) *of the Holy Spirit*. See 1 Cor. 3:22f. for a long list of definite words without the article. There is no mystery about the use and non-use of the Greek article in the New Testament. It does call for accurate knowledge of the Greek idiom itself if one really wishes to know the meaning of the writers. Most translations treat the Greek article in a careless fashion.

Prof. E. C. Colwell has a suggestive article in the April (1933) *Journal of Biblical Literature* in which he shows that the rule in the New Testament, when the verb occurs, is that definite predicate nouns which follow the verb regularly take the article, but those that precede the verb usually lack the article. So in Jo. 9:12 we have Ἐγώ εἰμι τὸ φῶς τοῦ κόσμου, but in Jo. 9:5 φῶς εἰμι τοῦ κόσμου. There is undoubtedly emphasis when the predicate substantive precedes the verb, but emphasis does not necessarily mean definiteness. So ῥίζα πάντων τῶν κακῶν ἐστιν ἡ φιλαργυρία (I Tim. 6:10) does not have to mean that "the love of money is the root of all evils", but simply "a root of all evils" (of all kinds of evils).

CHAPTER XVII

THE VERB (GENERAL REMARKS)

389. *The Name.*

The word *verbum* (ῥῆμα) is simply Latin for *word* and hence the name includes all other parts of speech. But the verb is the word *par excellence* in the Indo-Germanic tongues and hence deserves the name. As a matter of fact both verbs and nouns have often the same root and it is by no means certain which is the oldest, verb form or the noun form. In isolating languages only position can show which is noun and which is verb, but in inflected tongues nouns have case-endings (inflection) and verbs personal endings (conjugation) so that they are easily distinguished. But in English we use "work" as either verb or substantive. The Greek verb unites the verb root and the pronominal (personal) endings, two of the oldest forms of speech. The noun designates, while the verb asserts—a man that does not see that "has no real bottom to his grammatical science" (Whitney).

390. *Two Ideas in the Verb.*

The two ideas in the verb are *action* (or existence or state) and *affirmation*. The one essential idea in the verb is the *affirmation*. Nouns (substantives and adjectives) express action (existence or state), but they do not make affirmations or assertions. It is by the personal endings that verbs are able to make affirmation. Hence the infinitive (verbal substantive) and the participle (verbal adjective) are not verbs in the full sense. They are hybrids and partake of the nature of both verb and noun (verbal nouns), but miss the main point in the verb (affirmation). It is not essential

PARTICIPLE = PART NOUN, PART VERB

that a verb be transitive. The verb εἰμί *I am* is intransitive and merely affirms existence or state, but it is a verb. Whether a verb is transitive or intransitive turns on the meaning of the verb root, not on voice, tense or mode. The same Greek verb may be now transitive, now intransitive. The Greek verb is far richer in its growth and wealth of meaning than the Latin and can only be compared with the Sanskrit. Least of all can the Greek verb be interpreted by verbs in any of the modern tongues.

391. *Two Types of Verbs.*

See Accidence for discussion of the μι–verbs and the ω–verbs. The μι–verbs are the oldest and originally there were no ω–verbs. Now in modern Greek the μι–verbs have disappeared save in εἶμαι. There were some differences in conjugation between the two types which gradually disappeared as the ω–forms won the victory. As the μι–forms were dropped a variable vowel was added. In the New Testament, like the κοινή, we find, for instance ἀφεῖς (Rev. 2:20) instead of ἀφίης as if from ἀφίω instead of ἀφίημι The first century A. D. is a transition period from the μι– to the ω–forms. Even in the Attic δεικνύω was used side by side with δείκνυμι. In the New Testament we find forms like διδῶ (Rev. 3:9).

392. *The Building of the Verb.*

This is a complicated process and has been discussed under Accidence. The thing to note here is that the Greek verb took the root and on it built the wonderful system for the expression of the various angles of thought. This was done by means of suffixes and endings for tense, voice, and mode. These suffixes and endings make plain the voice, the tense, the mode of each verb form in actual use. It is imperative, therefore, that one be able to recognize at once the voice, tense, mode before he undertakes to translate the verb form. The English translation may confuse one instead of helping one. Take Lu. 16:4, for instance, ἔγνων. This form is the active voice, second aorist tense, indicative mode of γινώσκω *to know*. But we cannot reproduce all this in any correspond-ing English word because of the poverty of the English tenses. This is really a timeless aorist indicative, and the best that we can do in English is to say, "I know what to do" (ἔγνων τί ποιήσω). If we say, *I knew* or *I did know*, we miss the sudden and instantaneous grasp of the Greek aorist ἔγνων. It is like our "I've got it." The Greek verb comes to us as a finished product in each form and it is essential to dissect it by the grammatical microscope in order to put it together again intelligently. To understand the Greek verb one must com-prehend clearly the significance of each of the processes that go to the making of voice, tense, and mode out of the verb root. Without a clear knowledge of the verb one cannot interpret a Greek sentence. Exegesis is impossible and preach-ing is impoverished. There are more sermons in the Greek verb in the New Testament than in all the stones in the hills. Dr. H. H. Harris used to say: "The verb expresses *action* (or state) and *affirms* it of a *subject*. It therefore has *tense*, *mode*, *voice*, *person*, and *number*; expressed by stem, connect-ing vowels, ending." The alphabet of the Greek verb is to know the verb by the form itself instead of by some one's translation of it. Hence it is important that one know well the principal parts of the leading verbs that one may tell at a glance what form confronts him in a given sentence.

393. *Unequal Development.*

It is not known which got started first in the building of the verb, whether voice, tense, or mode. It does not greatly matter that we do not know. Of necessity the development was more or less simultaneous. It is possible that in the beginning there was one voice, one tense, one mode. Prob-ably the indicative is the oldest mode, the active the oldest voice, the second aorist (coinciding with the present stem like ἔ-φη-ν, φη-μί) the oldest tense. But the growth of the verb was unequal in many cases as to voice, tense, and mode.

Some verbs like λύω, were developed fully in all directions. Others made very little progress. These are called defective verbs. That is the development stopped short with them. Other verb roots had to be called in to supplement this failure. This is the explanation of such forms as ὁράω, ὄψομαι, εἶδον, each having a different root. So with φέρω, οἴσω, ἤνεγκον and many more. The Greek verb, in spite of the defective verbs, is far richer than Sanskrit or Latin. The English verb is very poor in comparison and has to use auxiliary verbs for all forms except two like "I sing", "I sang". That is all. The various forms differed in verbs in Greek. Some verbs dropped out entirely, some lost certain forms, some gained others. The grammarian must be a true historian and note the changes as they come. In the κοινή many old verbs make new stems like ἱστάνω from ἵστημι, γρηγορέω from ἐγείρω (ἐγρήγορα).

394. *Aktionsart or Kind of Action.*

Probably before there was a difference in tense development verb roots expressed the three chief ideas of tense (punctiliar action, linear action, state of completion). It is possible that this difference in verb root explains the different roots in defective verbs. Thus ἤνεγκον is punctiliar while φέρω is linear. Ἔχω can mean either punctiliar or linear. So ἥκω has the meaning of *I am come* (a state of completion). We can see this difference in our English. To blink the eye is punctiliar, to live a life is linear. Hence it is not enough to learn the force of voice, tense and mode. The real meaning of the verb root has to be considered. In a broad general way the Greek tenses were developed to make plainer the root idea of verbs so that almost any verb might be used either as punctiliar, linear, or state of completion.

CHAPTER XVIII

THE VOICES

395. *The Function of Voice.*

The word *voice* is *vox*, the speaking part of the verb, and this is not a bad name for the function. Voice and tense deal with the action or state of the verb, while mode deals with the affirmation. Tense deals with the state of the action whether punctiliar, linear, state of completion. Voice relates the action or state to the subject. It does this by the personal endings. Hence the infinitive and participle have voice in only a modified sense as they are without personal endings. The names for the three voices are not felicitous for they all deal with the action and the term "middle" has no particular meaning. The voice has nothing to do with the transitiveness or intransitiveness of the verb. That is a property of the verb root (or stem if compound) with which voice is not concerned. Many verbs in the active and middle are intransitive while some passive verbs are transitive.

396. *Active Voice.*

The active voice represents the subject merely as acting. That is all. It is therefore the commonest of the voices and probably the oldest, though that is not certain. Originally there was no passive, but whether the middle is a variation from the active (μαι a doubling of μι, μαμι) or the active from the middle (μι a shortening of μαι or μαμι) is not clearly known. Probably the matter varied with different verbs, some having the active first, some the middle first, some never having but one. Some verbs have only the active voice in one tense, only the middle or the passive in another. In simple truth many verbs are defective on this point. So with ὁράω, ὄψομαι; ἀκούω, ἀκούσομαι and ἀκούσω; εἰμί, ἔσομαι; φαίνω, φανοῦμαι; γίνομαι, γέγονα; ἔρχομαι, ἦλθον, ἐλήλυθα. Some tenses of the same verb may be transitive while others are intransitive like ἔστην (intransitive second aorist active) while ἔστησα (first aorist active) is transitive, both from ἴστημι. So with ἀπόλλυμι and ἀπόλωλα. Prepositions also play quite a part with the transitiveness of verbs like διαβαίνω (Heb. 11:29). The same verb like κλίνω will be now transitive (Matt. 8:20), now intransitive (Lu. 9:12).

Sometimes the verb in the active voice has a causative sense like the Hebrew Hiphil conjugation. That is true of ἐμαστίγωσεν in Jo. 19:1 where Pilate had Jesus scourged. Instead of the middle voice the reflexive pronoun may occur with the active as in σῶσον σεαυτόν (Mk. 15:30) *save thyself.*

397. *The Middle Voice.*
In the Sanskrit we have a full system of active and middle voices for all the tenses except that the infinitive had no voice at all and the participle only a beginning. It is only in the Sanskrit, Zend, Greek, and Gothic that the middle is kept as a distinct voice. The Latin has remnants of the middle in verbs like *miror, sequor, utor.* The passive had only a beginning in Sanskrit (the *ya* conjugation). In Homer the middle is more common than in later Greek. Originally there was no passive voice, but only active and middle. The middle voice differs from the active in that it calls special attention to the subject while the active merely represents the subject as acting. But the middle voice does not of itself indicate *what* the particular is that is emphasised. Thus it may be the direct middle like ἀπήγξατο (Matt. 27:5) *hanged himself* as told of Judas. A number of such direct middles occur in the New Testament like λουσαμένη (2 Pet. 2:22) *washing herself,* θερμαινόμενος (Mk. 14:54) *warming himself.* Sometimes the reflexive pronoun is added to the middle as in σεαυτὸν παρεχόμενος (Tit. 2:7) *furnishing thyself.* See also ἀρνησάσθω ἑαυτόν

double jeopardy
deceiving himself
philip from jailer = kill himself

(Lu. 9:23) *let him deny himself*. The indirect middle is more common, προσελάβοντο αὐτόν (Acts 18:26) *they took him to themselves*. In Acts 22:16 βάπτισαι καὶ ἀπόλουσαι τὰς ἁμαρτίας σου we have the causative middle with both verbs, one direct (*get thyself baptized*) and the other indirect (*and get thy sins washed away for thyself*) as pictured in the baptism. Each middle voice has to be examined for itself to see the precise shade of idea that is accented by it. The so-called "deponent" middles probably never had the active form at all and so never laid it aside. The intensive force of the middle with such verbs of mental action is not hard to perceive as in αἰσθάνο-μαι (Lu. 9:45). But we are hardly able in English to grasp the point of the middle as distinct from the active in such verbs as γίνομαι (γέγονα), ἔρχομαι (ἦλθον). It is better to confess ignorance than to profess knowledge that is really absent. Gildersleeve called this "dynamic" middle "the drip-pan middle" to catch all that was left of it. The middle voice is distinctly retreating in the New Testament as in the κοινή generally.

398. The Passive Voice. *Willingly being acted upon - (than self)*

The passive voice is a later development. Homer, for instance, has only two future passive forms. Before the passive voice arose the Greek had various devices for the passive idea, some of which survived like the active of some verbs like πάσχω, *I experience*, the use of adverbs with the active like κακῶς ἔχω, *I have it bad*, the impersonal active like αἰτοῦσιν (Lu. 12:20) *they ask*, but the most usual way was the use of the middle forms as passives. In fact, in Greek only two tenses developed separate passive forms (the aorist and future). The other tenses (present, imperfect, perfect, past perfect, future perfect) remained precisely the same as the middle. The active and middle had separate endings all through, while the passive had no separate endings at all, but even in the aorist and future had to borrow the active endings for the aorist and the middle for the future, added to a special suffix for these tenses ($\theta\epsilon$ or ϵ, $\theta\eta\sigma$ or $\eta\sigma$). In Homer the aorist middle ἐσχόμην was used as a passive and this occured even in Attic, as ἐσχέθην was a late development.

<u>The passive presents the subject as acted upon, receiving the action, rather than doing the action.</u> Theoretically, as Gildersleeve observes, the passive ought to be found only from transitive verbs with an accusative object. But the facts are against that theory in the Greek as κατηγορεῖται ὑπὸ τῶν Ἰουδαίων (Acts 22:30) *he is accused by the Jews* shows. In the nature of the case the passive is usually intransitive because the subject is the recipient of the action. But some verbs are transitive even in the passive and retain the accusative of the thing when the accusative of the person becomes the subject as was shown in the discussion of the Accusative Case. Note κατηχημένος τὴν ὁδόν (Acts 18:25) *instructed in the way.* Once the passive got into full swing as a voice in the Greek it began to displace the middle voice. This conflict grew until the passive usurped the functions of the middle even in the two forms of its own (aorist and future). In the modern Greek the passive has nearly put the middle out of business. In the New Testament the process is going on so that ἀπεκρίθην (Mk. 12:28) is the usual form for "he replied" rather than the vanishing ἀπεκρίνατο (Mk. 14:61). Here there is no strictly passive idea at all. See also μὴ φοβηθῆτε αὐτούς (Matt. 10:26) *do not fear them.* The distinctive passive form has come to do the work of the middle. The grammars once treated the middle voice as the interloper and spoke of passive forms used as the middle voice at first. It was precisely the other way. The passive used the forms of the middle and finally usurped the function of the middle also. In English we have no separate forms for the middle voice (only by reflexive pronouns) or for the passive except by auxiliary verbs.

So the force of the voice must be noted according to the actual facts of history and context. In 1 Cor. 13:12 we find three voices of the same verb (γινώσκω *I know*, ἐπιγνώσομαι *I shall fully know for myself*, ἐπεγνώσθην *I was fully known*). Never neglect the voice if you wish to understand the Greek verb.

CHAPTER XIX

THE TENSES

399. *The Name and the Function.*

The name *tense*, French *temps* (Old French *tens*), Latin *tempus*, is a mistake. The Latin word, like French, means *time*. That is not the root idea in the Greek tense. There is no time element in tense except in the indicative mode and there it was a later development and not consistently observed. The one essential idea in the Greek tense is *the kind of action* described. One must dismiss all notion of time if he wishes to understand the Greek verb. Like voice tense deals with the action of the verb, not with the affirmation (mode). But while voice relates the action in various ways to the subject, tense presents the state of the action (the kind of action) without regard to time at all. This fundamental idea of the kind of action involved belongs to all the modes and no other idea does. This is the only general idea in tense.

400. *The Three Kinds of Action Presented by Tense.*

These ideas are *punctiliar* (action stated as a point (•), *linear or durative* (action presented as continuous or repeated, ——————— or ....), *state of completion* (action presented as finally attained after effort ———————• or as the permanent result of the completion •———————). That is to say the state of completion involves both the punctiliar and the linear ideas and naturally was the latest development. Originally, before distinct tenses were developed for these ideas, distinct verb roots existed for them, in particular for the punctiliar and the linear. So there were two types of verb roots, one punctiliar like ἐ–ῑδ–ον one linear like ὁοά–ω. Other

verbs used the same root either as punctiliar or linear like
ἔ–φη–ν which can be either aorist or imperfect. Even the
idea of state of completion was expressed by some verb roots
like ἥκω *I have come.* But tenses were developed so as to
express these three ideas with practically any verb root,
though not carried out to the fullest extent.

The three tenses that were created for the expression of
these ideas are for all the modes.

> Punctiliar Action—the aorist
> Linear Action—the present.
> State of Completion—the perfect.

These names are good except "the present" which should
have been called "the imperfect". There is no time element
at all in the present subjunctive, optative, or imperative.
The idea is always linear with no reference to time. But in
the indicative the notion of time was developed gradually and
that brought confusion to the grammarians in naming the
tenses. It is pretty clear that the second aorist indicative
is older than the present indicative which is built on the
root seen in the second aorist. So λαμβάνω is an expansion
of the root λαβ seen in ἔ–λαβ–ον, λάβ–ω, λάβ–οιμι, λαβ–έ. But
unfortunately in the indicative separate tenses for the three
ideas (punctiliar, linear, state of completion) were only developed in past time (aorist, imperfect, past perfect). In
present time in the indicative the tense called "present" is
either punctiliar or linear so that the indicative has only two
separate tense forms (one both for punctiliar and linear action,
one for state of completion). In future time the indicative
has for the most part only one tense, as the future perfect is
for most verbs non-existent (especially the future perfect
active). But the cross development in the indicative has
brought confusion to people's minds and the name "present"
tense has increased it. It is a pity that the term "imperfect"
was not used for all the tenses of linear action. In the indicative past imperfect, present imperfect, future imperfect; for
the other modes imperfect subjunctive, imperfect optative,

imperfect imperative. That nomenclature would classify the whole subject. But it is probably too late to introduce successfully such a revolution in grammatical terminology. But at any rate it will help one to understand the Greek tenses which is the main thing.

401. Punctiliar Action.

(a) *The Aorist* (ἀόριστος).

This tense has an excellent name which means undefined action. It is presented as punctiliar (point action) whether it is actually linear or a state of completion. It is the normal tense to use in Greek unless there is some special reason to use another. If one desires to emphasize the notion of linear action on the one hand or the state of completion on the other, it is not the tense to use. There is no element of past time in the aorist tense. That notion in the indicative mode is due to the augment and to the secondary endings employed. The same tense-stem runs through all the modes and the verbal nouns (infinitive and participle) and always with the single notion of point action.

But the aorist tense itself is subject to the *Aktionsart* of the verb root. All that the aorist tense does is to *represent* the action as punctiliar. As a matter of fact the action may have involved forty-six years as with οἰκοδομήθη (Jo. 2:20) *was built* or the whole history of the race as in ἐφ᾽ ᾧ πάντες ἥμαρτον (Rom. 5:12) *in that all sinned,* but in these instances the aorist is employed for the simple reason that the thing in each case *is looked at as a whole.* This, in fact, is the usual use of the tense. It is often called the *constative* aorist when it is plain that the action did cover an extended period. The writer uses the aorist because duration is not the point about which he is concerned. The aorist is never used "for" any other tense, but only for itself. No Greek tense is ever used "for" any other tense. But sometimes the action of the verb is clearly *ingressive* as in ἐπτώχευσεν (2 Cor. 8:9) *he became*

poor. Here the aorist is punctiliar, of course, but the emphasis is on the entrance into the action described.   So ἔκλαυσεν
(Lu. 19:41) *he burst into tears,* ἵνα γνῶτε (Jo. 10:38) *that ye may
come to know.*   But the verb root may put emphasis on the
completion of the act and this is called the *effective* aorist as in
πληρῶσαι (Matt. 5:17) *to fulfil,* κλείσας τὴν θύραν (Matt. 6:6)
shutting the door.   So then in the aorist the word idea is to be
combined with the tense idea.

The aorist indicative is very difficult to render into English.
That is not true of the aorist subjunctive, optative, imperative,
infinitive or participle where no time element is involved,
but only the point action.   It is quite possible that the aorist
indicative is older than the present indicative with many verbs
and was really timeless like the aorist in the other modes.
As examples note ἔγνων (Lu. 16:4), ἥμαρτες (1 Cor. 7:28), ὡμοιώθη
(Matt. 18:23) where there is no element of time at all.   The
aorist indicative may occur in connection with other tenses,
but is not used for any of them, only the matter must be looked
at from the Greek point of view.   It is a good study in the
apprehension of the Greek aorist indicative to note its use
in connection with the imperfect (Matt. 25:5), the present
(Mk. 14:41), the present perfect (1 Cor. 15:3-5), the past
perfect (Jo. 6:16 and 17), and even the future (Jo. 13:31 and
32).   The so-called epistolary aorist is merely looking at
the letter from the standpoint of the recipient as in ἔπεμψα
Phil. 2:28).

The aorist subjunctive is normal as in ἁμαρτήσωμεν; (Rom.
6:15) *shall we commit a sin?*   In 2 Tim. 2:5 Paul makes a sharp
distinction between ἀθλῇ (present subjunctive and linear,
habit), and ἀθλήσῃ (aorist subjunctive and punctiliar, single
case).   The aorist is the common tense in the subjunctive
mode.   One striking thing about the use of μή with the aorist
subjunctive in prohibitions is to be observed.   It is used to
forbid one to begin the act (ingressive aorist).   Thus μὴ δῶτε
(Matt. 7:6) *do not begin to give,* while μή and the present
imperative means to cease doing or not to have the habit

as μὴ φοβεῖσθε (Matt. 10:31) *stop being afraid*. The optative
mode uses the aorist tense for single acts like μὴ γένοιτο (Gal.
6:14) *may it not happen*.

The aorist imperative has a note of urgency as in ἐλθάτω
(Matt. 6:10) *let come now*. The distinction between the aorist
imperative ἆρον (Jo. 5:8) *take up now* and περιπάτει (present)
go on walking is illustrated in verse 9 by ἦρε καὶ περιεπάτει
he took up (his bed) and went on walking.

In the infinitive and participle the aorist is simply punctiliar. See the distinction drawn by Luke in Acts 15:37f.
between συμπαραλαβεῖν (aorist) proposal of Barnabas *to take
along* John Mark and συμπαραλαμβάνειν (present infinitive) for
Paul's refusal to have Mark again on his hands. The aorist
participle is either simultaneous as in σπεύσας κατάβηθι (Lu. 19:5)
come down in a hurry or antecedent by suggestion as in ἤγειρεν
αὐτὴν κρατήσας (Mk. 1:31) *taking her by the hand he raised her
up*. The Greek never uses the aorist participle for subsequent
action. No example of that use has ever been shown.

Broadus used to call the Greek "an aorist loving language."
Use the aorist tense in the Greek unless there is a real reason
for some other.

(b) *The Aoristic Present Indicative*.

Since the Greek did not develop two separate tenses in
present time for punctiliar and linear action the same form is
used now for one, now for the other idea. This is a pity, and
yet in English we are in precisely the same predicament.
If we say, "I sing", is that punctiliar or linear? Some verbs
naturally have one idea, some the other. Thus by "I say",
"says he" we naturally mean the punctiliar idea, but by
"I sleep" we mean the linear. To be sure we can use the
participle as the Greek sometimes did to make the linear
idea. But, as a rule, in Greek, as in English, the context
has to decide whether the idea in the present indicative is
punctiliar or linear. No such ambiguity exists in the other

modes. In Lu. 7:8 we have a good example of the aoristic or punctiliar present indicative where πορεύεται follows πορεύθητι and ποιεῖ comes after ποίησον. Sometimes we find the aoristic present indicative in the midst of aorist indicatives as in John 20:5-7. The futuristic present indicative is often aoristic or punctiliar as in τίθημι (Jo. 10:15).

(c) The Aoristic Future Indicative.

The Greek failed also to draw the distinction in tense forms in future time in the indicative. From the nature of the case a future action was gradually regarded as punctiliar. So with καλέσεις (Matt. 1:21) ingressive punctiliar *thou shalt call*, πλησθήσεται (Lu. 1:15) effective punctiliar *shall be filled*.

The future indicative has a still further complication since it is a late development apparently from the aorist subjunctive (Giles, *Comp. Phil.*, pp. 446ff.). As a result the future indicative and the aorist subjunctive do not differ greatly in actual use. The aorist subjunctive is a doubtful assertion in present time (though about the future) while the future indicative is a positive assertion in future time (about the future also). So then the origin of the future indicative tense from the aorist (punctiliar) subjunctive combines with the natural uncertainty of future events to emphasize the punctiliar idea. It is not surprising therefore in the New Testament to find either aorist subjunctive or future indicative used with ἐάν, ἵνα, μή ποτε, etc. Forms like πίομαι (Lu. 17:8) which is from πίω (ἔπιον) illustrate the point about the origin from the aorist subjunctive. Another result is the modal element manifest in the future indicative. Because of this element the future indicative is almost a mode as well as a tense. Like the subjunctive and optative the future indicative may be merely *futuristic* or *predictive* as in ἐντραπήσονται (Matt. 21:37) *they will reverence*, or *volitive* as in καλέσεις (Matt. 1:21) *thou shalt call* where the element of will exists, or *deliberative* as in πρὸς τίνα ἀπελευσόμεθα (Jo. 6:68) *to whom shall we go?*

There is in the New Testament no future in the other modes (subjunctive, optative, imperative). The future infinitive has time only relatively to the principal verb even in indirect discourse and it is rare (only six) in the New Testament as in Heb. 3:18. The future participle has only relative time also and is again rare in the New Testament, though still alive in the papyri. Cf. Acts 8:27.

402. Linear or Durative Action.

(a) *The Present.*

The one tense for linear action in all the modes is the so-called "present" (imperfect, it should be called). In the indicative mode the present tense is sometimes punctiliar action as we have seen. But it may also be purely linear. So we have the vivid descriptive present ἀπολλύμεθα (Matt. 8:25) *we are perishing* and σβέννυνται (Matt. 25:8) *are going out*. The progressive present is seen in δουλεύω σοι (Lu. 15:29) *I have been serving thee*. The iterative or customary present occurs in νηστεύω δὶς τοῦ σαββάτου (Lu. 18:12) *I fast twice during the week*, the inchoative in λιθάζετε (Jo. 10:32) *beginning to stone* or conative in πείθεις (Acts 26:28) *trying to persuade*. The so-called historical or dramatic present is due to a vivid picture in the writer's mind as when θεωροῦσιν (Jo. 6:19) occurs in the midst of aorists and imperfects. It is particularly common in Mark (due to Peter's vivid narrative). There is also a futuristic linear present like ἔχομεν (2 Cor. 5:1). The periphrastic present intensifies the linear idea like πρέπον ἐστίν (Matt. 3:15).

In the subjunctive note in Jo. 10:38 ἵνα γνῶτε καὶ γινώσκητε *that you may come to know and keep on knowing*, where the same verb and mode are used with only the change in tense to justify the repetition. So in ἔχωμεν (Rom. 5:1) *let us keep on having* in contrast with what σχῶμεν (ingressive aorist) would be. It is not an exhortation to make peace (εἰρήνην σχῶμεν), but to enjoy peace (εἰρήνην ἔχωμεν). An example of the rare present optative appears in Acts 17:18 τί ἂν θέλοι; *what would he wish?* The force of the present imperative is plain in χαίρετε (Phil. 4:4) *keep on rejoicing.* With μή in prohibitions the present imperative means either to cease doing what one is doing as in μηκέτι ἁμάρτανε (Jo. 5:14) *no longer go on sinning* or not to have a habit as in μὴ ψεύδεσθε (Col. 3:9) *do not have the habit of lying.* The force of the present infinitive is sharply seen in ἁμαρτάνειν (1 Jo. 3:9) *to go on sinning,* not ἁμαρτεῖν or ἁμαρτῆσαι *to commit a sin.* The use of the present participle for repetition is clearly seen in πωλοῦντες ἔφερον (Acts 4:34) and for a single case in πωλήσας ἤνεγκεν in verse 37.

(b) *The Imperfect.*

In past time of the indicative mode the imperfect always gives the linear idea. The imperfect was only employed in narrative when the durative idea was to be accented. It may be merely descriptive of the process like ἤσθιον (Lu. 17:27) *they were eating,* ἐθεώρει (Mk. 12:41) *he was beholding,* and ἐπνίγοντο (Mk. 5:13) *were being choked* (one after the other) in contrast with Luke's constative aorist ἀπεπνίγη (Lu. 8:33); or repeated action like ἐβαπτίζοντο (Matt. 3:6) *were baptized from time to time;* or customary action like ἀπέλυεν (Mk. 15:6) *he was in the habit of releasing* and ἐζώννυες (Jo. 21:18) *thou used to gird;* or inchoative action like ἐκβολὴν ἐποιοῦντο (Acts 27:18) *they began to make a throwing out;* or attempted (conative) action like ἐκάλουν (Lu. 1:59) *they tried to call* (but sharply interrupted, οὐχί) and διεκώλυεν (Matt. 3:14) *he tried to hinder;* or prolonged action like ἐκάθευδον (Matt. 25:5) *they went on sleeping* (after the aorist ἐνύσταξαν *they nodded*). The imperfect occurs in the midst of aorists and past perfects, but is always true to its picturesque idea like ἤρχοντο and διεγείρετο in Jo. 6:17 and 18 and ὑπῆγον in verse 21. Note in Matt. 9:24 ἀπέθανεν (aorist), καθεύδει (present), κατεγέλων (imperfect). The periphrastic imperfect (the participle with ἦν) intensifies the linear idea as in our English. It is more common in the New Testament because of the Hebrew influence on the Septuagint, though the κοινή shows it also. So ἦν διανεύων (Lu. 1:22) *he was beckoning.* It is a common idiom in Luke.

(c) *The Future Tense.*

Merely *futuristic* are some examples of the linear future indicative like ἐλπιοῦσιν (Matt. 12:21). Others are *volitive* like the legal precepts οὐ φονεύσεις (Matt. 5:21) *thou shalt not kill,* ἀγαπήσεις (Matt. 5:43) *thou shalt love.* The *deliberative linear* future appears in ποσάκις ἁμαρτήσει; (Matt. 18:21) *how often shall one sin?* The periphrastic future is always linear like ἔσεσθε εἰς ἀέρα λαλοῦντες (1 Cor. 14:9) *ye shall be speaking into air* (like the radio!). The periphrastic future was common in the Sanskrit. Already in the New Testament θέλω is used with the subjunctive with or without ἵνα like θέλετε ἀπολύσω; (Matt. 27:17) *do you wish that I release?* But the infinitive is the rule with θέλω in the New Testament. In the modern Greek we have two futures: θὰ λύσω for the punctiliar idea and θὰ λύω for the linear. The use of μέλλω with the infinitive survives in the New Testament as a substitute for the future either with the aorist (Rom. 8:18), the present (Matt. 11:14), or the future (Acts 11:28) infinitive.

403. *State of Completion.*

(a) *The Present Perfect.*

This tense runs through all the modes with the same ideas, though naturally it is most frequent in the indicative. As a matter of fact the perfect optative is obsolete in the New Testament so that in Acts 21:33 Luke has ἐπυνθάνετο τίς εἴη καὶ τί ἐστιν πεποιηκώς *he was inquiring who he was and what he had done* (not even the periphrastic perfect optative). The perfect optative was always rare as was the perfect subjunctive, though εἰδῶ occurs ten times in the New Testament like Matt. 9:6. There are a few periphrastic passive perfect subjunctives as in Lu. 14:8; Jo. 3:27; 16:24. See the periphrastic active subjunctive in 2 Cor. 1:9 and Jas. 5:15. The perfect imperative also is almost non-existent in the New Testament. In Jas. 1:19 ἴστε may be imperative or indicative. There remain ἔρρωσθε (Acts 15:29), πεφίμωσο (Mk. 4:39), and the periphrastic ἔστωσαν περιεζωσμέναι (Lu. 12:35).

But the present perfect indicative is in the full tide of its power as a tense. It has the linear and the punctiliar ideas combined (a state of completion). But sometimes one idea comes first, sometimes the other. Thus in 2 Tim. 4:7 Paul uses three perfects (ἠγώνισμαι, τετέλεκα, τετήρηκα) which follow this graph (————•), the linear plus the punctiliar: "I have fought the good fight, I have finished my course, I have kept the faith." He is at the top of the hill with a backward look at the climb. He has run the race as he glances backward again. Sometimes the graph is the opposite (•————) as in ἐγήγερται (1 Cor. 15:4) where this tense comes between two aorists. Jesus has been raised and is still risen, Paul means. Sometimes it is a line of broken continuity which lies behind with this graph (.............) as in ἀπέσταλκα (2 Cor. 12:17) *I have sent at various times.* Often the dramatic present perfect comes in the midst of aorists and imperfects in a way to challenge attention at once like ἀπελήλυθεν (Jas. 1:24) *he has gone off* (as if James sees him sharply). It used to be said that the present perfect indicative was used with the idea of the aorist indicative, but that is not at all likely till we come to the Byzantine Greek which has broken down under the influence of the Latin. There is no New Testament example that does not yield a good sense as a genuine present perfect. So in Rev. 5:7 ἦλθεν καὶ εἴληφεν *he came and he has taken* (John sees the Lamb grasp the Book). The most difficult example is 2 Cor. 2:13 οὐκ ἔσχηκα ἄνεσιν *I have not had rest.* Here Paul has a vivid realization of the agony of spirit at Troas which still haunts him as he describes it. One needs a vivid historical imagination to reproduce the ideas in the Greek tenses. Without that one is constantly tempted to flatten out the picture into a lifeless monotony. But with proper elasticity of mind one follows the mood of the speaker or writer as he jumps from tense to tense like a song-bird. It depends wholly on the speaker or writer how he will picture a given action whether as punctiliar, linear, or state of completion. There is nothing for the hearer or the reader to do but to go with him as he sings or soars in a sustained flight. No sensible man uses one tense where he means another tense. That would be jargon. Different Greek writers vary greatly in the use of the tenses, some preferring one, some another. In the Sanskrit the perfect increased in use as the aorist decreased. In the Latin the aorist and the present perfect blended and took the same form, like *dixi* (either *I said* or *I have said*), but kept a different sequence of tenses. The Greek loves variety. Uniformity belongs to the professional grammarian, not to the living language. The reduplication is an effort to express completion in the verb stem itself. There is a threefold history of reduplication. It is intensive in the aorist like ἤγαγον, continuous (repetition) in the present like δίδωμι, completed state in the perfect like δέδωκα. The modern Greek has wholly dropped the reduplicated perfect save in the present participle. Instead of it the modern Greeks use ἔχω with the aorist infinitive like ἔχω λύσει. The older Greek has already begun to use ἔχω λύσας (participle). But that is not the idiom in ἔχε με παρῃτημένον (Lu. 14:18) which simply means *hold me excused*. We do not know the origin of the –κα stems with the perfect. The periphrastic perfect indicative occurs also like τί ἐστιν πεποιηκώς (Acts 21:33) *what he has done*, πεπεισμένος ἐστίν (Lu. 20:6) *is persuaded*. Forms like τετήρηκαν (Jo. 17:6) are after the analogy of ἐτήρησαν. The Greek perfect cannot always be adequately translated into the English idiom, but it can be understood in Greek.

The perfect infinitive occurs 47 times, chiefly in indirect discourse like νομίζοντες ἤδη τεθνηκέναι (Acts 14:19). But the perfect object infinitive occurs also like ἀπολελύσθαι ἐδύνατο

⟨Acts 26:32⟩. The perfect participle usually pictures vividly the state like κεκοπιακώς in Jo. 4:6 describing the weary Christ. See also εἶδον πεπτωκότα (Rev. 9:1) and contrast it with ἐθεώρουν πεσόντα (Lu. 10:18). So also note ὁ λαβών in Matt. 25:20 and ὁ εἰληφώς in verse 24.

(b) *The Past Perfect.*

Here we deal only with the indicative. The augment with the past perfect is not always used in the New Testament as was true in Homer. So τεθεμελίωτο (Matt. 7:25) *had been built.* It was never very common in the Greek. The Boeotian had no past perfect. It was a kind of literary luxury like the perfect subjunctive, optative, and imperative, though far more common than those perfects even in the κοινή. In narrative the aorist indicative was used as a matter of course unless one desired to describe the action by the imperfect or to limit it by the past perfect. The past perfect emphasizes completion in past time. It was like sticking a stake in the past and marking the completion up to that point. Naturally the Greeks did not often care to do that, though it could be done and was sometimes done by the past perfect tense. It is interesting to note that, where Matt. 27:18 has ὅτι παρέδωκαν, Mark 15:10 has ὅτι παραδεδώκεισαν. Matthew did not care to preserve the distinction that Mark had made by the use of the past perfect. John uses the past perfect more frequently than the Synoptic Gospels. An interesting example is found in Jo. 6:17 where between two imperfects (ἤρχοντο and διεγείρετο the going of the disciples pictured and the tossing of the sea by the wind) John inserts two past perfects σκοτία ἤδη ἐγεγόνει (darkness had already come) καὶ οὔπω ἐληλύθει 'Ἰησοῦς (and Jesus had not yet come). These two past perfects push the action back to the early stage of the going and the storm. Darkness had come and Jesus had not come, while the storm raged onwards. In modern translations of the New Testament the Greek aorist is often translated as if it were a past perfect, but that should not be done. The aorist did not draw the distinction made by the past perfect. The Greek used the periphrastic past perfect also like ἦσαν ἐληλυθότες (Lu. 5:17), ἦν ἀπολωλώς (Lu. 15:24). But, when the Greek does use the past perfect, one may be sure that the stake in past time has been placed. Note in particular ᾠκοδόμητο (Lu. 4:29), ἐβέβλητο (Lu. 16:20).

(c) *The Future Perfect.*

This was always a rare tense and is nearly extinct in the New Testament. It is not often necessary to express a state of completion in future time. The few examples are confined to the indicative. We have εἰδήσω in Heb. 8:11 (from the Septuagint), but κεκράξονται in Lu. 19:40 Westcott and Hort reject because not supported by Aleph B L. The two ancient Greek forms ἑστήξω and τεθνήξω do not appear in the New Testament. We have only left periphrastic forms like ἔσομαι πεποιθώς (Heb. 2:13, from the Septuagint). There remain only ἔσται δεδεμένον and ἔσται λελυμένον in Matt. 16:19, ἔσται δεδεμένα and ἔσται λελυμένα in Matt. 18:18, and ἔσονται διαμεμερισμένοι in Lu. 12:52. There was never much need for this tense.

CHAPTER XX

THE MODES

404. *The Meaning of Mode.*

Mode (Latin *modus*) deals with the *manner* of the *affirmation*. Voice and tense deal with the *action*, not the affirmation. There is a curious disagreement among grammarians concerning the number of the modes (or moods) in Greek. Some, including Moulton, decline to call the indicative a mode save when it is a *"modus irrealis"* and apply the term only to the *variations* from the indicative as the standard verb. Others, like Gildersleeve with whom I agree on this point, consider the indicative the chief mode and the others "side modes", to use Gildersleeve's phrase. Certainly the ancient Greeks were not concerned with our modern terminology. Some would include the infinitive and participle, though they are obviously not modes, since they are without personal endings or mode suffixes. The infinitive makes no affirmation save by indirection and has no subject. There was an old *injunctive mode* (Brugmann, *Gr. Gr.*, p. 332) which contributed much to the imperative mode before it disappeared. That leaves four modes in the Greek (indicative, subjunctive, optative, imperative). But the subjunctive and the optative are so close kin in idea that Donaldson and Jannaris treat them as one mode. At any rate there are only three ideas separate in the four modes (definite assertion, doubtful assertion, commanding assertion). The modes, like the tenses, deal with the *statement*, not with the facts in the case. Each mode expresses its own idea and one mode is not used "for" another. The imperative was the latest mode to develop and the ideas later expressed by the imperative had to be expressed at first in some other way. Some of these ways continued after the imperative arose, but it is a mistake to call those earlier methods "the imperative." The future indicative, as we have seen, has a modal aspect, and some grammarians even call it a distinct mode which is unnecessary. One other remark is to be made which is that each mode has precisely the same force in subordinate clauses as in independent clauses. There is an element of psychology in the use and in the interpretation of the modes. Each one uses the mode that expresses the mood of his mind at the moment. It is our task to catch that mood. The Greek word for mode (ἔγκλισις) means the delicate *inclining* (from ἐγκλίνω) this way or that. It is, in a word, the tone or temper of the speaker or writer as the intellects, the emotions, the will may be involved.

405. *Definite Assertion by the Indicative.* (ἡ ὁριστικὴ ἔγκλισις). It is the mode of definite assertion. It is not a question whether the statement is true or whether the user believes it to be true. The point is that he *states* it as a fact or true and wishes it to be so received. Most untruths are expressed in the indicative mode. The author does not desire to throw doubt on his statement of an untruth. So the indicative is the normal manner of affirmation unless there is special reason for stating it otherwise (in a doubtful way or in a commanding way). The name *indicative* is not particularly happy and distinctive since all the modes "indicate" the manner of affirmation. But it is the main mode and so has monopolized a word that really applies to all four. The indicative has no mode sign, as have the subjunctive and optative, but the personal endings are added directly to the tense stem, as is true also with the imperative mode. The Greeks used the indicative, the mode *par excellence*, according to the genius of their own language. There is sometimes difficulty in squaring the Greek indicative with any of our modern languages, but that is our weakness, not that of the Greek. It is immaterial whether the indicative is used in question or

declarative statement as we see both in Jo. 11:26f., πιστεύεις τοῦτο; ἐγὼ πεπίστευκα *believest thou this?......I have believed.* The verb may be affirmative (as above) or negative as in Mk. 14:61 οὐκ ἀπεκρίνατο οὐδέν *he answered nothing at all.*

There are some special uses of the indicative mode that call for comment. A present necessity, obligation, propriety, or possibility may be expressed by the imperfect indicative just as our "ought" is really "owed". The obligation still exists and comes over from the past. For this usage note ἔδει in Acts 24:19 where Paul uses it of the Jews from Asia who had made the disturbance in Jerusalem who were not present in Caesarea. But ἔδει in Jo. 4:4 is purely historical narrative. See other illustrations of the idiom in ἀνῆκεν (Col. 3:18), καλὸν ἦν (Matt. 26:24). No ἄν was used in such conclusions of the second class condition, for the idea is plain enough without it. Sometimes it is a feeling of courtesy that leads to the use of the imperfect as in ἐβουλόμην (Acts 25:22) *I was just wishing* or even a shrinking back from a brink as in ηὐχόμην (Rom. 9:3) *I was on the point of praying.* The use of the imperfect and aorist indicative in conditions of the second class is thoroughly idiomatic and will be further discussed under conditional sentences. See Lu. 7:39; Jo. 15:22, 24. See also for impossible wishes as in 2 Cor. 11:1; 1 Cor. 4:8.

The present indicative to us sometimes seems more abrupt than it actually is as in θέλομεν (Jo. 12:21) *we wish.* So in the sharp question in Jo. 11:47 τί ποιοῦμεν; *What are we doing?* not, *What are we to do?*

The special modal use of the future indicative as merely futuristic, volitive, or deliberative has already been discussed under Tense.

406. *Doubtful Assertions by the Subjunctive or the Optative.*

(a)   *The Subjunctive* (ἡ ὑποτακτικὴ ἔγκλισις).

The name is unfortunate, for it means *subjoined* (*subjungo*) and that implies that it is the mode in subordinate clauses which is by no means always true. The mode occurs often in independent clauses and the indicative is very common in subordinate clauses and both the optative and the imperative are so used. The name *conjunctive*, which some grammarians prefer, is really no better. But the point of concern is not the name, but the idea expressed by the mode. It has already been stated that the subjunctive and optative are really variations of the same mode for the same idea of doubtful statement. In the Sanskrit the optative finally displaced the subjunctive save in the imperatival uses. In Latin the subjunctive did service for both modes (past tenses for the optative). In Greek the subjunctive gradually drove out the optative save in future wishes like γένοιτο. The chief difference between the subjunctive and the optative can be conveyed by our words *probability* (*subjunctive*) and *possibility* (*optative*). Both are modes of doubtful assertion, but the optative is more doubtful.

It is not clear what was the original meaning of the subjunctive and the grammarians differ widely. It does not really matter. We do know that in the subjunctive the doubtful statement takes one of three turns (futuristic, volitive, deliberative) whichever was the first to arise. It may be merely futuristic like the future indicative. This is a common idiom in Homer and examples survive in the New Testament in subordinate clauses like ὃ προσενέγκῃ (Heb. 8:3) *which he shall offer*. The futuristic subjunctive is likely also with οὐ μή in Mk. 9:41 and the rhetorical question εἴπῃ in Lu. 11:5.

There is no question about the volitive use of the subjunctive. In the first person no other mode was used outside of ἄφες like ἄφες ἐκβάλω (Matt. 7:4) *let me pluck it out* (really parataxis), ἄφες ἴδωμεν (Matt. 27:49) *let us see*, where ἄφες has

become stereotyped (in modern Greek just ἄs) like a conjunction. We see δεῦρο and δεῦτε also so used as in Acts 7:34
and Mark 12:7. But usually the simple subjunctive is enough
with μή (negative) as in Jo. 19:24 μὴ σχίσωμεν *let us not rend it*
or without as ἔχωμεν (Rom. 5:1) *let us keep on having.* The use
of μή with the second person aorist subjunctive also resisted
the encroachment of the imperative. This prohibition held
the field for prohibitions against beginning an action (ingressive aorist) as in μὴ νομίσητε (Matt. 5:17) *do not begin to think.*
In the third person the same point holds as in 2 Cor. 11:16
except that the aorist imperative did occasionally occur
with μή as in μὴ καταβάτω (Mk. 13:15) *let him not come down.*

The deliberative subjunctive is common enough. In the
direct question it is frequent as in δῶμεν ἢ μὴ δῶμεν; (Mk. 12:15)
shall we give or shall we not give? (*Are we to give or not to give?*)
This problem is put up to Christ as a grave dilemma by the
crafty theological students in Jerusalem. The subjunctive
as the mode of doubtful statement suits precisely. The
indirect question simply retains the deliberative subjunctive
of the direct query. In Matt. 6:31 Jesus asks τί φάγωμεν;
What are we to eat? (*What shall we eat?*) A serious problem
for many housewives who worry unduly over it. But in
verse 25 Jesus had said μὴ μεριμνᾶτε τῇ ψυχῇ ὑμῶν τί φάγητε
stop being anxious (μή and the present imperative) *for your
life* (dative case of personal interest) *what ye are to eat* (deliberative subjunctive retained in the indirect question).

The Greek love of vivid statement, even if doubtful, made
the subjunctive more common than the optative. The subjunctive is more common in Homer than the later Greek
which used the future indicative more than Homer did. The
negative of the subjunctive is μή, but Homer used οὐ with the
futuristic subjunctive.

(b) *The Optative* (ἡ εὐκτικὴ ἔγκλισις).

This name suits well one use of the optative for wishes
concerning the future, but not for the other uses. It is much

more than the wishing mode. The optative, like the subjunctive, deals with the future, a "softened future" (Monro,
Hom. Gr., p. 229), from the standpoint of the past. In the
Sanskrit the optative displaced the subjunctive except in
the first person volitive use, but in Greek the subjunctive
finally drove out the optative. Both languages, like the Latin,
felt the two modes to be unnecessary. There are only 67
examples of the optative in the New Testament of which Luke
has 28 and Paul 31 outside of Eph. 1:17 (δώη Westcott and
Hort). It is not in John, Matthew, or James. It was always
a luxury of the language and was used more by Xenophon
and Plato than other writers. κοινή writers like Strabo and
Polybius use it sparingly. Like the subjunctive the optative
has three uses (the futuristic, volitive, deliberative). The
futuristic use has the negative οὐ and is commonly called the
potential optative. Originally in Homer and the poets this
"mood of the fancy" (Gildersleeve) was used without ἄν.
"It was used to express a future in a milder form" (Moulton,
Prol., p. 197) "and to express a request in a deferential style."
It is probable that in Acts 25:16 πρὶν ἢ ἔχοι καὶ λάβοι we have
the futuristic optative in indirect discourse where the futuristic subjunctive was in the direct. It is certain that in Acts
26:29 εὐξαίμην ἄν (*I could wish*) we have this "softened future"
or potential optative. There are several questions like πῶς
ἂν δυναίμην; (Acts 8:31) *how could I?* and 17:18 τί ἂν θέλοι;
what would he wish? that may be merely futuristic though
the deliberative idea hovers in the background. Clearly
deliberative are the indirect questions in Lu. 1:62 τὸ τί ἂν
θέλοι as to *what he would wish* and τί ἂν ποιήσαιεν (Lu. 6:11)
what they would do where the deliberative optative with ἄν
of the direct question is simply retained in the indirect. The
optative without ἄν in an indirect question for a present
indicative in the direct like τὸ τίς εἴη in Lu. 22:23 is another
matter. But there is no question about the volitive use of
the optative as in μηδεὶς φάγοι (Mk. 11:14) *may no one eat*
and Acts 8:20 where εἴη is used in an imprecation. **The**

most common example is μὴ γένοιτο like Lu. 20:16 *may it not happen* (fourteen of the fifteen examples in Paul's Epistles). This is the only optative that survives in modern Greek, "the coffin of the dead optative" (Clyde, *Greek Syntax*, p. 84).

407. *Commanding Assertion by the Imperative.* (ἡ προστακτικὴ ἔγκλισις).

The imperative was the last of the modes to get started and has followed the optative into oblivion in modern Greek save in the second person (Thumb-Angus, *Handbook of the Modern Greek Vernacular*, p. 154). The forms are a make-shift (sometimes the non-thematic stem like δείκνυ or the mere thematic stem like ἄγε, the infinitive sigmatic aorist like βάπτισαι, remnants of the old injunctive mode like -σο and -τε, the special forms -θι, -σον and -τω). The first person was never developed in the imperative. After the imperative arose the previous devices in its stead continued to be employed like the future indicative σὺ ὄψῃ (Matt. 27:4), the subjunctive like λάχωμεν (Jo. 19:24) and μὴ ἀποστραφῇς (Matt. 5:42), the infinitive like χαίρειν and κλαίειν (Rom. 12:15), the participle like φρονοῦντες (Rom. 12:16). These various alternatives for the imperative are not the imperative and must not be so explained. In the second person plural of the present imperative the form is precisely that of the present indicative and only the context can decide which it is as in Jo. 5:39 ἐραυνᾶτε *ye search* (or *search*), Jo. 14:1 πιστεύετε *ye believe* (or *believe*). There is a periphrastic imperative with the participle like ἴσθι εὐνοῶν (Matt. 5:25) *be reconciled*, ἔστωσαν περιεζωσμέναι (Lu. 12:35) *let them be girded*.

The imperative has various uses that the context makes clear. It may be direct command like ἀγαπᾶτε (Matt. 5:44) *keep on loving*, hortatory like ποιησάτω (Rev. 22:11) *let him do*, entreaty like βοήθησον ἡμῖν (Mk. 9:22) *help us*, permissible like καθεύδετε λοιπὸν καὶ ἀναπαύεσθε (Matt. 26:45) *sleep on now and take your rest*, condition like λύσατε τὸν ναὸν τοῦτον (Jo. 2:19) *destroy this temple*, or τοῦτο ποίει καὶ ζήσῃ (Lu. 10:28) *do this and thou shalt live,* prohibition (a negative command) like μὴ θησαυρίζετε (Matt. 6:19) *stop laying up treasures.*

There may be asyndeton between two imperatives, like ὁρᾶτε βλέπετε (Mk. 8:15) *see to it beware* or even ὁρᾶτε μηδεὶς γινωσκέτω (Matt. 9:30) *see to it let no one know.* The imperative is not common in subordinate clauses, but it does occur ᾧ ἀντίστητε (1 Pet. 5:9) *whom stand against* and εἰς ἣν στῆτε (1 Pet. 5:12) *in which stand.* Sometimes ἵνα and the subjunctive occur without the imperative before it as in ἵνα φοβῆται (Eph. 5:33).

408. *The Use of ἄν with the Modes.*

There is much difficulty in understanding clearly the Greek modal ἄν. It is used with the indicative, subjunctive, or optative, but not with the imperative. It is freely used in Homer with the future indicative and with the subjunctive. Tatian also uses ἄν with the future indicative. It occurs chiefly in dependent clauses. In independent clauses in the New Testament ἄν appears with the indicative like ἐγίνωσκεν ἄν (Lu. 7:39) *he would know* or the optative like τί ἂν θέλοι; (Acts 17:18) *what would he wish?* In dependent clauses ἄν occurs with the indicative like ὅταν (ὅτε + ἄν) ὀψὲ ἐγένετο (Mk. 11:19) *when (or whenever) it became late,* or the subjunctive like ἐὰν (εἰ + ἄν) γαμήσῃς (1 Cor. 7:28) *if you marry* or the optative like τί ἂν θέλοι (Lu. 1:62) *what he would wish.* There is no necessity for ἄν in any clause or mode. It is not even known what ἄν means. Leo Meyer argues that the Greek ἄν is kin to the Gothic *an* and the Latin *an* and originally had two meanings, one "else", the other "in that case rather," Latin and Gothic preserving the first, Greek the second. Note also the old English an = if. Monro holds that the primary use of ἄν and κε in Homer was with definite and particular examples, the indefinite coming later and being secondary. In the New Testament both uses exist, the indefinite more common. The definite use of ἄν appears in Mk. 11:19 above and in Rev. 8:1 ὅταν ἤνοιξεν τὴν σφραγῖδα τὴν ἑβδόμην *when he opened the seventh seal.*   We see the indefinite use in Mk. 6:56 ὅπου ἂν εἰσεπορεύετο *wherever he went.*   Sometimes ἐάν (εἰ + ἄν) was spelt ἄν as in ἄν τινων ἀφῆτε τὰς ἁμαρτίας (Jo. 20:23) *if you forgive the sins of any.*   Still more common in the New Testament is the use of ἐάν = ἄν ignoring the εἰ in composition like ὃς ἐὰν οὖν λύσῃ (Matt. 5:19) *whoever therefore breaks.*   This use of ἐάν for ἄν had quite a vogue during the first century A. D. and for some time afterwards.

CHAPTER XXI

COORDINATE AND SUBORDINATE CLAUSES (CON-JUNCTIONS)

409. *Asyndeton.*

This is lack of connection between words or clauses, the words coming separately. This can be very effective as in the triple repetition of βλέπετε in Phil. 3:2. See also the four verbs (descriptive imperfects) in Lu. 17:27 ἤσθιον, ἔπινον, ἐγάμουν, ἐγαμίζοντο *they were eating, they were drinking, they were marrying, they were being married* (a vivid picture of the time when the flood came). But asyndeton does not always exist for rhetorical effect in the New Testament. The Gospels show it more, for instance, than Romans with its closely knit argument. The literary Attic writers generally avoided it between sentences and even paragraphs, not to say between words. But in the Gospels frequent breaks occur between sentences and paragraphs with no connection as in John 13:21, 22, 23, 24, 25. See two imperatives together without conjunction in Matt. 9:31. In Romans, in particular, Paul follows the ancient custom and connects paragraph with paragraph by various particles. In the Gospels this is not so commonly done. The inner bond is not so closely knit by particles like δέ, καί, τε, ἀλλά, οὐδέ, γάρ, οὖν, ἄρα, ἤ, δή, κτλ.

410. *Conjunctions.*

They are sometimes called *particles* (παραθῆκαι). The conjunctions (*con-jungo*) join together words, clauses, sentences, paragraphs. They are essential to connected thought to avoid a scrappy, disjointed style. It is possible by proper order to present the sequence of thought, but words are not perfect and do not always carry the same content to all minds.

It is better to call these connectives conjunctions than particles for that term has to be used for intensive particles and negative particles or adverbs. They are all adverbs and all particles including prepositions and interrogative particles. The Greek language has a wealth of conjunctions that interpret the relation of words with words, clauses with clauses, paragraphs with paragraphs. Without the use of these conjunctions a balanced and rounded period like Lu. 1:1-4 would not be possible. Broadly speaking there are two kinds of conjunctions (paratactic or coordinating and hypotactic or subordinating).

(a) *Paratactic.*

These coordinating or paratactic conjunctions are of many kinds (copulative, adversative, disjunctive, inferential). A bare skeleton sketch is alone possible here.

The *copulative* list includes τε (four times in Rom. 14:8) which binds together like our "both--and." Luke has τε—καί (Lu. 2:16) and τε—δέ (Acts 19:2). The most common is καί which is more frequent than usual because of the Septuagint translation of the Hebrew *wav* by καί. Note four examples of καί in Jo. 1:14. καί comes at the beginning of sentences more frequently than formerly (Jo. 13:27). καί may mean *also* as in Matt. 8:9 or *even* as in Lu. 10:17. Sometimes καί has an adversative use as will be shown. For καί—καί see Jo. 6:36 and καί γάρ Jo. 4:23. In Matt. 26:15 καί has almost the force of ἵνα. Luke has καί ἐγένετο fifty times. There are three constructions καί ἐγένετο καί (Lu. 5:17), καί ἐγένετο and the verb (Lu. 1:23), καί ἐγένετο and the infinitive (Mk. 2:23. In Lu. 24:4 ἰδού follows the second καί. Another common copulating conjunctive is δέ as in the genealogy in Matt. 1:2-16. 'Αλλά also may be merely copulative as in 2 Cor. 7:11. For ἀλλά in the conclusion of a condition see Rom. 6:5.

The *adversative* list includes δέ as in Matt. 5:21 ἐγὼ δὲ λέγω *but I say* (so also verses 28, 32, 34, 39, 44). See καί δέ in Jo.

6:51. A good example of ἀλλά occurs in Lu. 1:60 οὐχί, ἀλλά. See ἀλλ' ἤ in 2 Cor. 1:13. Πλήν as a conjunction is always adversative as in Lu. 6:24. So is μέντοι (Jo. 4:27), ὅμως (Gal. 3:15), both rare in the New Testament. An exception may be marked by εἰ μή as in Matt. 12:4. It is certain that καί is sometimes used with the notion of "and yet," or "but" as in Lu. 12:24 καὶ ὁ θεὸς τρέφει αὐτούς, and yet God nourishes them. We have οὔτε—καί in Jo. 4:11.

The *disjunctives* are ἤ either singly as in Matt. 5:17 or repeated *either--or* as in Mk. 13:35 (four times), ἤτοι—ἤ (Rom. 6:16,) εἴτε—εἴτε as in 1 Cor. 10:31, οὐδέ—οὐδέ (Rev. 9:4), οὔτε—οὔτε as in Lu. 20:35, μηδέ—μηδέ (Matt. 10:10), μήτε—μήτε as in Matt. 5:34-36. There are, besides, various combinations of the disjunctives. So οὐκ—οὐδέ (Acts 8:21), μή—μηδέ (Jo. 4:15), οὐδέ—οὔτε (Gal. 1:12).

The *inferential* conjunctions are chiefly three. Ἄρα has the notion of correspondence as in Lu. 11:48; Matt. 12:28. Γάρ is the most frequent conjunction. It is composed of γε and ἄρα and may be merely explanatory as in Mk. 5:42 or purely illative as in Matt. 1:21, αὐτὸς γὰρ σώσει for he will save. In Matt. 27:23 τί γὰρ κακὸν ἐποίησεν; Why, what evil did he do? both ideas appear. Οὖν is particularly common in the Gospel of John (200 times). Sometimes it is merely transitional or continuative as in Jo. 12:1, but the illative use is plain in Rom. 5:1. Ἄρα οὖν is common in Paul (Rom. 8:12). But see also τοιγαροῦν (Heb. 12:1), τοίνυν (Lu. 20:25), ἀνθ' ὧν (Lu. 12:3), διό (Rom. 1:24), ὥστε (Matt. 19:6), οὗ χάριν (Lu. 7:47), δι' ἣν αἰτίαν (2 Tim. 1:12).

(b) *Hypotactic.*

Here the conjunctions perform a much more serious purpose. Originally all conjunctions were paratactic without any subordinating clauses. This is the language of childhood always and largely of the vernacular. It is true of portions of the Old Testament. The Sanskrit and the Hebrew are poor in subordinating conjunctions. But it was inevitable that with the development of language some clauses should be subordinated to others. Greek is richer than Latin and English in this respect. There would be the main idea in the principal clause and the other clauses would circle around it in various ways. These subordinate clauses all sustain a case relation to the principal clause as subject of the verb or object of the verb or as adjective describing subject or object or as adverb in a case modifying some part of the principal clause. These subordinate clauses include relative clauses, temporal clauses, local clauses, comparative clauses, final clauses, consecutive clauses, causal clauses, conditional clauses, wishes (some of them), indirect discourse, the infinitive, the participle, all the rest of the discussion of syntax except direct interrogative sentences, wishes (some of them), negative particles, intensive particles, figures of speech. The discussion of the conjunctions employed in these various subordinate clauses can best be made in the chapters that follow. A sample may be given here. Thus ὅτι may introduce a direct quotation (recitative ὅτι) as in Matt. 4:6, an indirect quotation (declarative ὅτι) as in Matt. 2:16, a causal clause as in Lu. 6:20. So ὡς is used in comparative clauses, temporal clauses, indirect discourse, even ὡς ἄν as in Rom. 15:24. We find ὅτε and ὅταν hundreds of times, ἐπεί (Heb. 9:26) and ἐπειδή seldom (Lu. 11:6), ἕως often though ἄχρι and μέχρι seldom, ὅπου often, οὗ fairly so, ὅθεν moderately so. But all this in due season. It should be repeated at this point that voices, tenses, modes have precisely the same force in subordinate clauses as in independent sentences.

The Greek is a highly organized language. It is possible in Greek to express the most delicate shades of an idea by means of voice, tense, mode, cases, prepositions, particles, conjunctions. Often an idea in Greek can be expressed in various ways that are substantially alike, but yet differ in ways that the sensitive Greek mind understands. So the Greek has liberty where the Latin has bonds. The Greek may use coordinating clauses or subordinating clauses with conjunctions, or the infinitive, or the participle. His sentences may be short or long. He may use prepositions freely or not. Only do not accuse a Greek of using one construction for another. Freedom is the glory of the Greek language. Each writer has his own style and flavor.

CHAPTER XXII

RELATIVE CLAUSES

411. *The Purpose of Relative Clauses.*

The relative brings two clauses together by agreement with the antecedent (expressed or unexpressed) in the principal clause. The relative clause thus links the two clauses together by agreement in gender, number, and sometimes case, for discussion of which points (even assimilation and incorporation of antecedent) see chapter XV on *Pronouns*. At first the relative ὅς was demonstrative and so the original relative clause was *paratactic*, not *hypotactic*. It may even be the oldest form of parataxis. But gradually as the true relative sense developed the subordinate clause idea grew.

412. *Kinds of Relative Clauses.*

Each relative clause is itself either adjectival, substantival, adverbial. The true relative is an adjectival pronoun which describes the antecedent. A good example is seen in Λάζαρος ὃν ἤγειρεν ἐκ νεκρῶν Ἰησοῦς (Jo. 12:1) where Lazarus is described as *whom Jesus raised from the dead* (raised him before this feast which he now attended). So in Jo. 11:3 ὃν φιλεῖς ἀσθενεῖ *he whom thou lovest is sick* (the unexpressed antecedent is the subject of ἀσθενεῖ and is described by ὃν φιλεῖ. But like any other adjective the relative clause may be used as a substantive and itself be the subject of the principal verb as in Matt. 10:38 ὃς οὐ λαμβάνει τὸν σταυρὸν αὐτοῦ καὶ ἀκολουθεῖ ὀπίσω μου οὐκ ἔστιν μου ἄξιος *who does not take up his cross and follow after (behind) me is not worthy of me*. The subject of ἔστιν is the ὅς clause. Compare "who steals my purse steals trash". But there is the adverbial use also. So ὡς καὶ ἡμεῖς ἀφήκαμεν *as we also forgave.* Here the relative adverb ὡς is itself an ablative form (ὡτ) and the clause is an adverb of comparison or manner like the associative instrumental case. In simple truth every subordinate clause is itself in a case relation to some word in the principal clause either as substantive, adjective, or adverb.

413. *Most Subordinating Conjunctions Relative in Origin.*

Of these relative conjunctions ὅτι (ὅ + τι) may be declarative and so nominative and subject like οὐχ οἷον ὅτι ἐκπέπτωκεν ὁ λόγος τοῦ θεοῦ *it is not possible that the word of God has failed* where the ὅτι clause is the subject of οὐχ οἷον(ἐστιν) In Jo. 1:34 the ὅτι clause is the accusative, the object of μεμαρτύρηκα. Then again the ὅτι clause may be causal as in Matt. 11:21, but always in a case. So in Latin *quod* may be either relative and declarative or causal and in late Latin *quia* was used in the declarative sense of *quod*. So we can follow the fortunes of the local relative adverb ὅπου, the comparative ὡς, the final ὅπως and even ἵνα, temporal ἕως and ὅτε. It is by means of the relative adverbs that Greek and Latin became so rich in subordinate clauses compared with the poverty of the Sanskrit and the Hebrew. The relative pronouns themselves (ὅς, ὅστις, etc.) came to be used, as we shall see directly, in senses approximating the notions of cause, purpose, result and almost condition.

414. *But the Relative Clause Remains a Relative.*

The relative clause may have the resultant effect of cause, purpose, result, or condition, but it is not true that the relative clause is either of these things. It is just like the participle in this respect and is often practically interchangeable with the articular participle, but after all the two constructions are distinct though parallel. So in Matt. 7:24 we have πᾶς ὅστις ἀκούει and in 7:26 πᾶς ὁ ἀκούων. The two constructions are very similar, but after all one is relative and

the other is participle. It is only confusion to call them
identical. Each has its own syntactical explanation. Precisely so one may note ὁ λαμβάνων in Jo. 13:20 and ὃς λαμβάνει in
Matt. 10:38. The Greek is rich in variety of idiom. We
should not flatten them out. So there is undoubtedly an
argumentative tinge in the use of οἵτινες ἀπεθάνομεν τῇ
ἁμαρτίᾳ (Rom. 6:2), *we the very ones who died to sin*, but that is
not to say that οἵτινες is precisely the same construction as
the conjunction ὅτι, ἐπεί, etc. The Latin so used *qui* and
sometimes *quippe qui* to make it plainer. The same situation exists when purpose is expressed by the relative as in
ὃς κατασκευάσει (Mk. 1:2), a favorite Attic idiom. So also
purpose is manifest with δι᾽ ἧς λατρεύωμεν (Heb. 12:28) *by which
we are to serve*, ὃ προσενέγκῃ (Heb. 8:3) *which he is to offer* (cf.
ὃ προσφέρει in 9:7 *which he offers*). There is practical result
in ἄξιός ἐστιν ᾧ παρέξῃ τοῦτο (Lu. 7:4) *he is worthy to whom thou
wilt do this thing*. See also ὅπου φάγω (Mk. 14:14) and οὐκ
ἔχω ὃ παραθήσω (Lu. 11:6). The relative ὃ here is not ἵνα or
ὅπως, though it is a parallel idiom. Against Goodwin, Burton,
and all others who advocate "conditional relative clauses"
with elaborate schemes and constructions, it is to be said that
the Greek does use the relative clause in a sense parallel to
the conditional clause with εἰ and ἐάν, but, that after all,
it is *only parallel, not identical*. It is to misunderstand the
delicate shade of the Greek idiom to treat one as if it were
the other. In Mk. 4:9 Jesus says ὃς ἔχει ὦτα ἀκούειν ἀκουέτω
let him who has ears to hear hear. But in Mk. 4:23 he puts it
thus εἴ τις ἔχει ὦτα ἀκούειν ἀκουέτω *if any has ears to hear let
him hear*. This is a conditional sentence with εἰ while the
first with ὃς is purely relative. In Matt. 13:9 the phrase
occurs thus ὁ ἔχων ὦτα ἀκουέτω *let the one who has ears hear*.
The articular participle here is parallel idea with the relative
ὃς clause which is very much like the conditional εἰ clause,
but not quite. It is still a relative clause. With the Greek
freedom and variety of idiom a thing can be put several ways
without mere monotonous repetition. So in John 14:13 we

have ὅτι ἂν αἰτήσητε *whatever ye ask* which is followed by ἐάν τι αἰτήσητε *if ye ask anything.* Once again in Mk. 8:34 we have εἴ τις θέλει *if any one wishes,* but in verse 35 ὃς ἐὰν θέλῃ *whoever wishes.* It is superficial to call them identical and "interchangeable." They are parallel and similar, but not identical. They illustrate the Greek variety as we see it in Luke's use of ἐν τῷ with the infinitive when he could have used the participle or ὅτε and a finite verb.

415. *Definite and Indefinite Relative Clauses.*

Every relative clause is either definite or indefinite like the English "who" and "whoever". The definite relative clause describes a particular individual like ἐποίησεν δώδεκα οὓς καὶ ἀποστόλους ὠνόμασεν (Mk. 3:14) *he appointed twelve whom he also named apostles.* The relative describes the twelve. The indefinite relative pictures any one in general without a definite individual in mind like ὃς ἔχει δοθήσεται αὐτῷ (Mk. 4:25) *whoever has it shall be given to him.* With the definite relative the indicative as the mode of definite statement occurs uniformly as in ὁ κύριος ὃς στηρίξει (2 Thess. 3:3) *the Lord who will establish.* The subjunctive as the mode of doubtful statement would not be expected with the definite relative. It is only with the very strong negative οὐ μή that we seem to have it as in εἰσίν τινες τῶν ὧδε ἑστηκότων οἵτινες οὐ μὴ γεύσωνται θανάτου (Matt. 16:28 = Mk. 9:1) *there are some of those that stand here who will not taste death.* But see the subjunctive of purpose in Heb. 8:3 and 12:28. The indicative can be used with the indefinite relative, that is, a positive or definite statement is made about the indefinite pronoun as in ὅσοι ἥψαντο (Matt. 14:36). Besides, ὅς can be either definite or indefinite and the same thing is true of ὅστις which is either indefinite as ὅστις ἔχει (Matt. 13:12) *whoever has* or definite as βασιλεῖ ὅστις ἐποίησεν γάμους (Matt. 22:2) *a king who made a wedding,* γυναῖκες αἵτινες ἠκολούθησαν τῷ Ἰησοῦ (Matt. 27:55) *women who followed Jesus.* The subjunctive is common with the indefinite relative in the New Testament (122 times) like ὅστις τηρήσῃ (Jas. 2:10) *whoever keeps,* ὅστις ἂν ποιήσῃ (Matt. 12:50) *whoever does.*

416. The Use of ἄν in Relative Clauses.

As we have already seen, ἄν makes a clause more definite or more indefinite (usually this). The use of ἄν was rare in Homer with indefinite or general statements, but gradually became more common. Radermacher finds modal ἄν (or ἐάν) decreasing in the κοινή with indicative, subjunctive, or optative in relative, temporal, final, or conditional clauses. In the New Testament with relative clauses the use of ἄν is nearly always indefinite as in ὃς ἂν ὁμολογήσει (Lu. 12:8) *whoever shall confess,* ὃς ἐὰν λύσῃ and ὃς ἂν ποιήσῃ (Matt. 5:19) *whoever breaks* and *whoever does.* There is one example of ἄν with the relative which makes it rather more definite ὅσοι ἂν ἥψαντο (Mk. 6:56) as compared with ὅσοι ἥψαντο in Matt. 14:36. In the temporal clause ὅταν ἤνοιξεν (Rev. 8:1) ἄν may make it more definite. The use of ἄν is common with the future indicative as ὃς δ'ἂν ἀπολέσει (Mk. 8:35) *whoever will lose.* But it occurs with the imperfect indicative like ὅπου ἂν εἰσεπορεύετο (Mk. 6:56) *wherever he went* and the present indicative like ὅπου ἂν ὑπάγει (Rev. 14:4) *wherever he goes.* Ὅσος, like ὅς and ὅστις, may have ἄν or ἐάν as ὅσα ἂν αἰτήσητε (Matt. 21:21) *as many things as (whatever) you ask,* ὅσα ἐὰν θέλητε (Matt. 7:12) *as many things as (whatever) you wish.* The classic idiom οὐδείς ἐστιν ὅς (Mk. 10:29) has no effect on the mode.

417. Negatives in Relative Clauses.

It is usually οὐ with the indicative as ὃς οὐ λαμβάνει (Matt. 10:38) *whoever does not take.* But occasionally with the Indefinite relative μή the subjective negative is used as in ὃ μὴ ὁμολογεῖ (1 Jo. 4:3) *which does not confess,* referring to πᾶν πνεῦμα with a subtle touch in this use of μή. So also ἃ μὴ δεῖ in Tit. 1:11 and ᾧ μὴ πάρεστιν in 2 Pet. 1:9. With the subjunctive the negative is always μή as in ὃς ἂν μὴ ἔχῃ (Lu. 8:18) *whoever does not have,* ἥτις ἂν μὴ ἀκούσῃ (Acts 3:23) *whichever does not hear.*

CHAPTER XXIII

TEMPORAL CLAUSES

418. *The Character of Temporal Clauses.*

"The vague original relative import becomes specialized" (Thompson, *Syntax of Attic Greek*, p. 329) in temporal and local clauses. Like the purely relative clauses the temporal clause may be definite or indefinite, may use the indicative or the subjunctive mode, may have ἄν or not according to the circumstances in each clause. There is a large number of the conjunctions that are employed in temporal clauses (mostly original relative adverbs). They can be grouped in a loose fashion according to the general idea in each. The construction varies with each conjunction. Greek versatility is well illustrated by these conjunctions.

419. *The Notion of When or While.*

(a) Ἐν ᾧ.

This phrase implies χρόνῳ and means "in which time." It is not strictly a conjunction, but it amounts to one with the sense of "while" as ἐν ᾧ ἔρχομαι (Jo. 5:7) *while I am coming*. See also Mk. 2:19; Lu. 19:13. The phrase has other uses also, local in Rom. 2:1; 14:21f., causal in Rom. 8:3.

(b) Ἕως.

This is not the usual sense of ἕως (until), but with the present indicative it is like the Latin *dum* and means *while* as in Mk. 6:45 ἕως αὐτὸς ἀπολύει τὸν ὄχλον *while he himself dismisses the multitude*. The future is sometimes vividly drawn into the present by the use of ἕως and the present indicative like ἕως ἔρχομαι (Jo. 21:22f.) *while I am coming*. So as 1 Tim. 4:13.

Even ἕως ὅτου may be so used as in ἕως ὅτου εἶ μετ' αὐτοῦ (Matt. 5:25) *while* (*so long as*) *thou art with him.*

(c) Ἐπειδή and ἐπάν.

Ἐπεί in the temporal sense has disappeared from the New Testament as a variant in Lu. 7:1 where ἐπειδὴ ἐπλήρωσεν is the correct text *when he had finished.* This is also the only temporal use of ἐπειδή. But ἐπάν *whenever* with the subjunctive occurs three times (Matt. 2:8; Lu. 11:22, 34).

(d) Ἐφ' ὅσον.

This phrase implies χρόνον (time) and means *for so long time as* (*so long as*) as in Matt. 9:15. In Mk. 2:19 we have ὅσον χρόνον and in Rom. 7:1 ἐφ' ὅσον χρόνον ζῇ *for so long time as he lives.* In Heb. 10:37 ὅσον ὅσον (LXX Is. 26:20) is a Hebraism though not unlike papyri examples.

(e) Ἡνίκα.

This pronoun occurs only twice in the New Testament, both about the future. One of them has ἄν and the present subjunctive ἡνίκα ἂν ἀναγινώσκηται Μωϋσῆς (2 Cor. 3:15) *whenever Moses is read.* The other with ἐάν and the aorist subjunctive is also in 2 Cor. 3:16 ἡνίκα ἐὰν ἐπιτρέψῃ *whenever it turns.*

(f) Ὅτε and ὅταν.

These are by far the most frequent temporal conjunctions in the New Testament. Ὅτε (*when*) is freely used with any tense of the indicative like ὅτε ἐτέλεσεν (Matt. 7:28) *when he finished.* Most of the examples present definite past time so that it is rare with the present indicative as in ὅτε ζῇ (Heb. 9:17) *when he lives.* The future indicative with ὅτε is naturally indefinite even when preceded by ὥρα in Jo. 4:21,23. But ὅταν (whenever, indefinite) is equally frequent with the subjunctive, either aorist like ὅταν ἴδητε (Matt. 24:33) *whenever ye see* or present like ὅταν εἰσφέρωσιν (Lu. 12:11) *whenever they bring.* Occasionally the future indicative occurs also like ὅταν δώσουσιν (Rev. 4:9) *whenever they shall give.* But we find occasionally the present indicative like ὅταν στήκετε (Mk. 11:25) *whenever ye stand*. And even the imperfect like ὅταν αὐτὸν ἐθεώρουν (Mk. 3:11) *whenever they beheld him* or the aorist like ὅταν ὀψὲ ἐγένετο (Mk. 11:19) *when it became late* (or *whenever it became late*). In Rev. 8:1 ὅταν ἤνοιξεν it is certain that it means *when he opened* (definite), not *whenever he opened* (indefinite).

(g) Ὡς.

As a temporal conjunction ὡς (*as* or *when*) commonly has the indicative as ὡς ἐπλήσθησαν (Lu. 1:23) *when they were fulfilled*, and ἄν may also be used as ὡς ἂν ἤγεσθε (1 Cor. 12:2) *as ye would be led* (*from time to time*). Here we seem to have the old iterative force of ἄν preserved as in Acts 2:45; 4:35 (Moulton, *Prolegomena*, p. 167). In Mk. 9:21 note πόσος χρόνος ἐστὶν ὡς; *how much time since?* But ὡς appears with the subjunctive also either with ἄν as ὡς ἂν πορεύωμαι (Rom. 15:24) "*when I am on my way*" (present and so durative) and ὡς ἂν ἔλθω (1 Cor. 11:34) *when I arrive* (aorist and so punctiliar) or without ἄν as ὡς καιρὸν ἔχωμεν (Gal. 6:10) *when* (or *as*) *we have opportunity*.

420. *The Notion of Until.*

Here again a variety of conjunctions are employed.

(a) Ἀφ' οὗ.

This phrase calls for χρόνου *from which time* or *since* being the idea as in Lu. 13:7 τρία ἔτη ἀφ' οὗ ἔρχομαι *three years since I have been coming*. The same idea is in Lu. 24:21. But in 13:25 ἀφ' οὗ ἂν ἐγερθῇ the use of the subjunctive with ἄν calls for ἀπὸ τούτου ὅτε as the idea, *from that time when* or "*when once*." Hence it is virtually equal to ἕως (until) in Lu. 13:25.

(b) Ἄχρι

We have in the New Testament ἄχρις only twice (Gal. 3:19; Heb. 3:13). It is more frequently a preposition like ἄχρι καιροῦ (Lu. 4:13) *until an opportunity* than a conjunction.

And the simple conjunction ἄχρι as in ἄχρι τελεσθῇ (Rev. 20:3) *until is finished* is not so frequent as ἄχρι ἧς ἡμέρας εἰσῆλθεν (Lu. 17:27) *until which day* Noah came and ἄχρι οὗ (supply χρόνου *time*) as ἄχρι οὗ πληρωθῶσιν (Lu. 21:24) *until (which time) they be fulfilled.* If an actual historical event is referred to the aorist indicative is used as ἄχρι οὗ ἀνέστη (Acts 7:18) *until there rose up* or the imperfect as ἄχρι οὗ ἡμέρα ἤμελλεν γίνεσθαι (Acts 27:33) *until day was about to come.* The only example of the present indicative is ἄχρις οὗ τὸ σήμερον καλεῖται (Heb. 3:13) *so long as the today is called* where the notion of "until" has practically vanished. The future indicative can be used also as ἄχρι τελεσθήσονται (Rev. 17:17 *until they be finished,* once with ἄν as ἄχρι ἂν ἥξω (Rev. 2:25) *until I come.* But the subjunctive is the usual construction for future time as ἄχρι οὗ θῇ (1 Cor. 15:25) *until he put,* once with ἄν as ἄχρις ἂν ἔλθῃ (Gal. 3:19) *until there come.*

(c) Ἕως.

So also ἕως is more common in the New Testament as preposition like ἕως τοῦ χριστοῦ (Mt. 1:17) *until Christ* than as conjunction. As a conjunction we have ἕως (Matt. 2:13) and ἕως οὗ (Matt. 14:22), and ἕως ὅτου (Matt. 5:25). They are all employed in substantially the same sense (until), χρόνου being understood with ἕως οὗ and ἕως ὅτου. When an actual past event is referred to, the aorist indicative is used as ἕως ἦλθεν (Matt. 24:39) *until there came,* ἕως οὗ ἐζυμώθη (Matt. 13:33) *until was leavened,* ἕως ὅτου ἐφώνησαν (Jo. 9:18) *until they called.* For present time it has the notion of "while" as already indicated as Mk. 6:45 and so also ἕως ὅτου in Matt. 5:25. For the future ἕως has the subjunctive usually with ἄν as ἕως ἂν ἀποδῷς (Matt. 5:26) *until you pay,* but sometimes without as ἕως ἔλθῃ (Matt. 10:23) *until there come.* In Mk. 14:32 ἕως προσεύξωμαι the notion is more *while I pray.* Ἄν does not occur with ἕως οὗ or ἕως ὅτου. In Lu. 13:8 ἕως ὅτου σκάψω *until I dig* and ἕως οὗ ἀναπέμψω *until I send* it is probably the aorist subjunctive though the form is the same as the future indicative. Matt. 14:22 ἕως οὗ ἀπολύσῃ *until he send away* is the parallel passage to Mk. 6:45 ἕως ἀπολύει *while he sends away*.

(d) Μέχρι.

This word is more frequent as a preposition μέχρι τῆς σήμερον (Matt. 11:23) *until today* and occurs only three times as a conjunction (Mk. 13:30; Gal. 4:19; Eph. 4:13). Once (Eph. 4:13) the form is μέχρι and μέχρις οὗ in the other two. In all three examples the aorist subjunctive is used without ἄν. Ἕως kept the field against ἄχρι and μέχρι for "until" and ἕως remains common in the papyri, inscriptions, κοινή writers.

(e) Πρίν.

There are only three examples of πρίν as a conjunction in the New Testament and two of these are in the same sentence (Acts 25:16). In each instance πρὶν ἤ occurs though ἤ is doubtful in Lu. 2:26 πρὶν ἤ ἄν ἴδῃ *until he see* and here ἄν also occurs. In each instance πρὶν ἤ comes after a negative sentence according to classic idiom, a literary touch only in Luke's writings. But in Lu. 22:34 he has ἕως τρὶς ἀπαρνήσῃ after οὐ φωνήσει ἀλέκτωρ where πρίν would be the classic idiom. In Lu. 2:26 the subjunctive is retained after the secondary tense, but in Acts 25:16 the subjunctive is changed to the optative with both verbs so that we have πρὶν ἤ ἔχοι—λάβοι, the only time in the New Testament where the subjunctive (ἔχῃ—λάβῃ) is so changed, another literary touch. Luke alone in the New Testament employs πρίν as a conjunction.

421. *The Infinitive in a Temporal Clause.*

(a) Πρίν.

Eleven times πρίν or πρὶν ἤ occurs with the infinitive in the New Testament. πρίν was originally an adverb, then a preposition with the ablative in Pindar πρὶν ὥρας. = πρὸ ὥρας. Homer used πρίν with the infinitive 81 times. The article

is not used, but the infinitive with πρίν is in the ablative case.
So πρὶν Ἀβραὰμ γενέσθαι (Jo. 8:58) *before Abraham was.* Usu-
ally the examples are in the future with the simple punctiliar
idea and the aorist infinitive as πρὶν ἀποθανεῖν τὸ παιδίον μου
(Jo. 4:49) *before my child die (before dying as to my child).*
Πρὶν ἤ with the aorist infinitive occurs in Mk. 14:30.

(b) Πρὸ τοῦ.

There are nine of these examples like πρὸ τοῦ ὑμᾶς αἰτῆσαι
αὐτόν (Matt. 6:8) *before you ask him (before the asking him as
to you).* The tense is aorist each time except a present in Jo.
17:5. The idea is very much like πρίν and the infinitive.
The inscriptions give examples of πρὸ τοῦ and the infinitive.

(c) Ἐν τῷ.

This idiom is rare in the ancient Greek, but there are 500
examples in the LXX due to translation from the Hebrew
be and the infinitive construct. It is more common in Luke
than anywhere else in the New Testament, due to the influence of the LXX on Luke, the most literary writer in the New
Testament. With the present infinitive ἐν τῷ has the idea
of "while" as ἐν τῷ ἱερατεύειν (Lu. 1:8) *while he was serving
as priest (in the serving as priest as to him).* The aorist infinitive with ἐν τῷ may have the notion of "when" as ἐν τῷ εἰσαγαγεῖν τοὺς γονεῖς τὸ παιδίον Ἰησοῦν *when the parents brought
in the child Jesus (in the bringing in the child Jesus as to the
parents)* in Luke 2:27.

(d) Μετὰ τό.

There are fifteen instances of this idiom. A good example
is μετὰ τὸ παραδοθῆναι τὸν Ἰωάνην (Mk. 1:14) *after John was delivered up (after the being delivered up as to John).* Here again
Luke uses this idiom more than any other writer. For the
use of μετά with the accusative in the sense of "after" see
chapter on Prepositions.

(e) Ἕως τοῦ.

There is only one example of this construction in the New Testament ἕως τοῦ ἐλθεῖν (Acts 8:40) *until he came* (*until the coming as to him*). Here, of course, ἕως is a preposition, not a conjunction. This construction occurs in the LXX.

422. *The Temporal Participle.*

The old Greek writers employed the circumstantial participle with great freedom where the modern Greek prefers temporal conjunctions with the finite verb. The New Testament comes in the midst of the transition period, but any page of the New Testament, especially the Acts of the Apostles, will reveal a rich abundance of this idiom. The temporal participle would either agree in case with the subject, object or other word in the sentence or it would be the genitive absolute, put in a separate construction. In the chapter on the Participle this matter will receive adequate treatment. It is only necessary here to note several matters of importance. The participle does not of itself express time any more than it does cause, condition, or purpose. The participle simply presents the action in a descriptive fashion as an adjective. The imagination must fill out the picture. There is nothing in the participle that indicates the notions of "while", "when", "as", "after", "until". The present participle is merely descriptive and has no time in itself as Ἰακὼβ ἀποθνήσκων εὐλόγησεν *Jacob dying blessed*. The present participle with an imperfect may suggest repeated action as πωλοῦντες ἔφερον (Acts 4:34) *selling they brought* (from time to time). The aorist participle may suggest simultaneous action as σπεύσας κατάβηθι (Lu. 19:5) *come down in a hurry* or antecedent action as πωλήσας ἤνεγκεν (Acts 4:37) *selling he brought* (*having sold he brought*). So εἰσελθών in Mk. 1:21. The aorist participle never gives subsequent action. The Greek does not have that idiom, not even in ἀσπασάμενοι (Acts 25:13) which is simultaneous (effective aorist κατήντησαν).

CHAPTER XXIV

LOCAL CLAUSES

423. *These Conjunctions All Relative Adverbs.*

But they deserve separate treatment. The conjunctions used are ὅθεν, οὗ, ὅπου.

(a) Ὅθεν.

With ὅθεν (*whence*) only the indicative occurs in the New Testament as ὅθεν ἐξῆλθον (Lu. 11:24) *whence I came.* So also ἐξ οὗ (*from which*) occurs in a local sense as ἐν οὐρανοῖς ἐξ οὗ (Phil. 3:20) *in heaven from which.*

(b) Οὗ.

Οὗ (*where*) is more common as οὗ ἦν τὸ παιδίον (Matt. 2:9) *where the child was.* Once we find οὗ ἐὰν with πορεύωμαι (1 Cor. 16:6). So οὗ is used with verbs of motion as of rest as in οὗ ἤμελλεν αὐτὸς ἔρχεσθαι (Lu. 10:1) *whither he himself was about to go.*

(c) Ὅπου.

Ὅπου (*where*) is the usual local conjunction in the New Testament. We find it with verbs of rest as ὅπου ἦν (Mk. 2:4) *where he was* or with verbs of motion as ὅπου ἐγὼ ὑπάγω (Jo. 8:21) *whither I go.* The New Testament does not use ὅποι *whither.* The usual mode is the indicative with a definite antecedent as ἐν βηθανίᾳ ὅπου ἦν ὁ Ἰωάνης (Jo. 1:28) *in Bethany where John was.* Sometimes the iterative (indefinite) use of ἄν occurs with the indicative as ὅπου ἂν εἰσεπορεύετο (Mk. 6:56) *wherever he was going.* This iterative use of ἄν is found also with the present indicative as ὅπου ἂν ὑπάγει

(Rev. 14:4) *wherever he goes.* The subjunctive occurs also without ἄν as ὅπου φάγω (Mk. 14:14 = Lu. 22:11), the deliberative use in the indirect answering to ποῦ φάγω (direct) though it can be explained as merely futuristic. But clearly futuristic is the subjunctive with ἐάν in ὅπου ἐὰν ἀπέρχῃ (Lu. 9:57) *wherever you go.* For the correlative ἐκεῖ with ὅπου see Lu. 12:34 and καί is a virtual correlative in Jo. 17:24. We find ὅπου also in metaphors as Heb. 9:16.

(d) Ἐν ᾧ.

The relative pronoun with a preposition may be used in a local sense. So in a metaphorical sense we find ἐν ᾧ κρίνεις in Rom. 2:1 *in what thing you judge* and 14:21 ἐν ᾧ προσκόπτει *in what thing he stumbles* and 14:22 ἐν ᾧ δοκιμάζει *in what thing he tests.*

CHAPTER XXV

COMPARATIVE CLAUSES

424. *Conjunctions All Relative in Origin*.

Just as with the Temporal and Local Clauses, but they deserve separate treatment.

(a) *Compounds of the Relative with* κατά.

Καθό (κατά, ὅ) occurs only four times and three times with the indicative as καθὸ δεῖ (Rom. 8:26) *according as it is necessary* and so also 1 Pet. 4:13. The one subjunctive example with ἐάν is 2 Cor. 8:12 where both subjunctive and indicative appear side by side with a fine distinction drawn καθὸ ἐὰν ἔχῃ εὐπρόσδεκτος, οὐ καθὸ οὐκ ἔχει *one is acceptable according to what one may have, not according to what he actually does not have*. The only example of καθά (plural) is in Matt. 27:10 καθὰ συνέταξεν *as the Lord commanded*. Καθάπερ (κατά, ἅπερ) occurs seventeen times counting three disputed with καθώς and always with the indicative and it means "according to which very things" (περ added). As an example take καθάπερ γέγραπται(Rom. 3:4) *precisely as it stands written*.

(b) *Ὡς and Its Compounds*.

The various forms of ὡς (*as*) are much the most common in comparative clauses. The uses of ὡς are many. We have already noticed its use as a temporal conjunction as in Lu. 1:23. It occurs once as a final conjunction (Acts 20:24), also with the infinitive twice (Lu. 9:52; Heb. 7:9), in indirect questions with the sense of "how that" as μνήσθητε ὡς ἐλάλησεν (Lu. 24:6) *remember how he spoke*, as exclamatory ὡς ὡραῖοι οἱ πόδες in Rom. 10:15 *how beautiful the feet*, with participles like ὡς μέλλων (Acts 23:20) *as on the point of,* with superlative adverbs like ὡς τάχιστα (Acts 17:15) *as quickly as possible,* and with the sense of "about" as ὡς δισχίλιοι (Mk. 5:13) *about two thousand.* But it is as a comparative conjunction that ὡς has its chief vogue, usually with the indicative expressed as ὡς θέλεις (Matt. 15:28) *as thou wilt* or implied like ὡς οἱ ὑποκριταί (Matt. 6:5) *as the hypocrites.* Occasionally the subjunctive is used like ὡς ἄνθρωπος βάλῃ (Mk. 4:26) *as when* (or *as if*) *a man cast* and also ὡς καιρὸν ἔχωμεν (Gal. 6:10) *as we may have opportunity.* In 1 Thess. 2:7 we have ὡς ἐὰν τροφὸς θάλπῃ *as ever a nurse nourishes.* The correlative οὕτως occurs also with ὡς as in Acts 8:32; 1 Cor. 4:1 and likewise ὡς—καί (Gal. 1:9).

We have in the New Testament ὡσεί (*as if*) without a verb as Matt. 3:16. The indicative occurs with ὥσπερ (intensive περ added to ὡς) as ὥσπερ οἱ ὑποκριταὶ ποιοῦσιν (Matt. 6:2) *as the hypocrites do* or without a verb like ὥσπερ οἱ ἐθνικοί (Matt. 6:7) *as the Gentiles* or with a participle like ὥσπερ φερομένης πνοῆς βιαίας (Acts 2:2) *as of a mighty rushing wind.* Only once do we find ὡσπερεί and without a verb ὡσπερεὶ τῷ ἐκτρώματι (1 Cor. 15:8) *as if to the one born out of time.*

Καθώς (κατά, ὡς, *according as*) is very frequent with the indicative as καθὼς ἠγάπησα ὑμᾶς (Jo. 13:34) *according as I loved you.* It is a late word but it is common in the papyri also. The correlative οὕτως rarely occurs with it, but see Lu. 24:24. Sometimes καθώς shades off toward the causal idea as in Rom. 1:28. Καθώσπερ is found in the New Testament only once καθώσπερ καὶ ᾽Ααρών (Heb. 5:4) save 2 Cor. 3:18 where Westcott and Hort put it in the margin with καθάπερ in the text.

(c) Καθότι.

There are only two examples of καθότι (κατά, ὅτι, *according to what, according as*) as a comparative conjunction, the others being causal. In both the iterative force of ἄν occurs with the indicative (cf. ὅπου ἂν εἰσεπορεύετο Mk. 6:56). They are καθότι ἄν τις χρείαν εἶχεν (Acts 2:45; 4:35) *according as any one had need.* The two examples are identical.

(d) *Ὅσος.*

The classic idiom of the correlative τοσοῦτο—ὅσον occurs only in Hebrews, though a modified form of it appears in Mk. 7:36 without the correlative and without the comparative with ὅσον. Of the six examples in Hebrews one (9:27) has the correlative οὕτως, but no comparative with καθ' ὅσον or with the correlative, while another (7:20f.) has the comparative with the correlative κατὰ τοσοῦτο, but not with the relative καθ' ὅσον (really causal idea, *in as much as*). Another example (3:3) has no correlative, but has the comparative with both clauses including καθ' ὅσον. In 1:4 the full classic idiom appears in τοσούτῳ κρείττων — ὅσῳ διαφορώτερον with the instrumental case each time (*by so much—by as much*). In 8:6 we have ὅσῳ, but no τοσούτῳ though the comparative is in both clauses. In 10:25 we find τοσούτῳ—ὅσῳ, but no comparative after ὅσῳ. It is significant to observe that this literary idiom appears in its full form only in Hebrews, the most likely book for it in the New Testament. In Jo. 6:11 and Rev. 21:16 ὅσον is a relative, not a conjunction. The double ὅσον ὅσον in Heb. 10:37 is from the LXX (Is. 26:20).

CHAPTER XXVI

CAUSAL CLAUSES

425. *Coördinating Conjunctions.*

These are not technically causal clauses in the usual sense, but they are so practically. They are really *paratactic*, as the relative clauses were originally. There is ἄρα (*accordingly*) from ἀραρίσκω which presents a kind of correspondence as ἄρα μάρτυρές ἐστε (Lu. 11:48) *accordingly ye are witnesses.* The chief inferential particle is γάρ (γε +ἄρα) and it is very common in a variety of senses. It may be merely explanatory as ἦσαν γὰρ ἁλιεῖς (Matt. 4:18) *for they were fishermen.* It is hardly illative in Jo. 19:6 or in Acts 16:37 οὐ γάρ, ἀλλά *not much, but.* It is really illative in λογίζομαι γάρ (Rom. 8:18). A good example of the illative use of οὖν is seen in ποιήσατε οὖν καρπόν (Matt. 3:8) *make therefore fruit.* The transitional use of οὖν has already been noticed as in Jo. 18:12.

426. *Subordinating Conjunctions.*

There are many of these all of which have other uses also.

(a) Ὅτι, διότι, καθότι.

Ὅτι is the most frequent causal conjunction. The indicative is the only mode that is employed with ὅτι in the New Testament as in ὅτι πάντα μου μέμνησθε (1 Cor. 11:2) *because ye remember me in all things.* The negative is always οὐ as in ὅτι οὐ πεπίστευκεν (1 Jo. 5:10) *because he has not believed* except in one instance where μή occurs ὅτι μὴ πεπίστευκεν (Jo. 3:18) *because he has not believed* (a supposed case, ὁ μὴ πιστεύων *the not believing one*). It is not easy to reproduce in English the subtle distinction between the subjective negative μή and the flat negative οὐ. In 1 Cor. 10:17 both ὅτι and γάρ occur in the same sentence. Διότι is διά + ὅτι (somewhat like the old English "for that"). It appears in the New Testament only in the Lucan writings, the Pauline Epistles, Hebrews, James, and 1 Peter. See Lu. 1:13 διότι εἰσηκούσθη *for that was heard.* Both declarative ὅτι and causal διότι occur in Phil. 2:26. Καθότι (*because that,* κατά, ὅτι) is also a causal conjunction (five times), though primarily comparative (Acts 2:45; 4:35) as in Acts 2:24 καθότι οὐκ ἦν δυνατόν *because that it was not possible.*

(b) Ἐπεί, ἐπειδή, ἐπειδήπερ.

Ἐπεί (*since*) is not so common as ὅτι, but still fairly often, as in Heb. 5:2. The mode used is always the indicative. The negative is always οὐ as Lu. 1:34 except once (Heb. 9:17) where μή occurs (cf. Jo. 3:18) ἐπεὶ μὴ τότε ἰσχύει *since it is not then of force* (a conceivable case negatived by μή). The classical use of an ellipse with ἐπεί survives in the New Testament as ἐπεὶ οὐκ ἂν ἐπαύσαντο (Heb. 10:2) *since (in that case* or *if that were true) they would not have ceased.* So also Heb. 9:26 and 1 Cor. 5:10. There is ellipsis also with ἐπεὶ τί in 1 Cor. 15:29. Ἐπειδή (ἐπεί + δή) occurs nine times in the New Testament like ἐπειδὴ αἰτοῦσιν (1 Cor. 1:22) *since indeed they ask.* But ἐπειδήπερ (ἐπεί, δή, περ) occurs only in Luke's literary introduction to his Gospel (1:1).

(c) Ὅθεν.

The causal use of ὅθεν (see local also) occurs more often in Hebrews as ὅθεν ὤφειλεν (Heb. 2:17) *wherefore he was under obligation,* ὅθεν κατανοήσατε (3:1) *wherefore consider.* It is argued by some that in Mk. 4:12 (= Lu. 8:10) ἵνα is used in the sense of ὅτι (*because*) since in Matt. 13:13 ὅτι occurs. It is a nice point that is discussed in my chapter on "The Causal Use of Ὅτι" in Case's *Studies in Early Christianity.* The use can only be considered possible, by no means certain.

427. *Relative Pronouns.*

The relative pronoun does not state a cause or reason, but may imply one as ὃν παραδέχεται (Heb. 12:6) *whom he receiveth.*

In particular is this true of ὅστις as οἵτινες ἔρχονται (Matt. 7:15) *the very ones who (inasmuch as they) come*, οἵτινες ἀπεθάνομεν *we who died*. There are a number of prepositions employed with the relative in a causal sense like ἀνθ' ὧν (Lu. 1:20) *in return for which things (because)*, δι' ἣν αἰτίαν (Lu. 8:47) *for which reason*, διό (Heb. 3:10) *because of which (wherefore)*, διόπερ (1 Cor. 8:13) *because of which indeed (wherefore)*, οὗ χάριν (Lu. 7:47) *for the sake of which (wherefore)*, ἐν ᾧ (Rom. 8:3) *in which thing (in that)*, ἐφ' ὅσον (Matt. 25:40, 45) *inasmuch (for so far forth as)*, and even καθ' ὅσον (Heb. 7:20) *inasmuch as*.

428. *The Infinitive with* διὰ τό.

This is a common idiom for giving the cause or reason as in διὰ τὸ εἶναι αὐτόν (Lu. 2:4) *because he was (because of the being as to him)*, the accusative with διά and the articular infinitive, αὐτόν being the accusative of general reference. In Jo. 2:24 we have διὰ τὸ αὐτὸν γικώσκειν *because he knew* and in verse 25 ὅτι οὐ χρείαν εἶχεν *because he had no need*. The two constructions are parallel, but are not identical nor to be explained in the same way. So also in Jas. 4:2 we have διὰ τὸ μὴ αἰτεῖσθαι ὑμᾶς *because you do not ask* and in verse 3 διότι κακῶς αἰτεῖσθε *because you ask in a bad way*.

429. *The Participle.*

The participle does not state the cause or reason, but only implies it. So δίκαιος ὤν (Matt. 1:19) *being a righteous man (because he was a righteous man)*. It is a very common idiom in the New Testament. Often in such cases the particle is added to make plain the alleged reason which may or may not be the true one. So ὡς διασκορπίζων (Lu. 16:1) *as scattering*, ὡς ἀποστρέφοντα τὸν λαόν (Lu. 23:14) *as disturbing the people*. In Acts 2:2 we have ὥσπερ φερομένης πνοῆς βιαίας *as of a mighty wind borne*.

CHAPTER XXVII

FINAL CLAUSES

430. *Pure Final Conjunctions.*

Final and consecutive clauses use the same conjunctions and it is not easy to distinguish them sharply for they shade off into one another. Purpose may be viewed as contemplated result and result as achieved purpose. But the two clauses can be separated in a broad general way. *Finis* is used in Latin for both *aim* and *end* (result) like our *finish*.

(a) Ἵνα.

This is by far the most common conjunction for pure purpose. It is used chiefly with the subjunctive in the aorist or the present tense as in ἵνα γνῶτε καὶ γινώσκητε (Jo. 10:38), where the whole difference is in the two tenses, *that ye may come to know and keep on knowing*, and rarely with the perfect as in ἵνα εἰδῶμεν (1 Cor. 2:12) *that we may know*. The negative is μή as ἵνα μὴ κριθῆτε (Matt. 7:1) *that ye be not judged*. The future indicative also occurs with ἵνα as ἵνα δώσουσιν (Lu. 20:10) *that they may give*, and even the present indicative as ἵνα γινώσκομεν (1 Jo. 5:20) *that we may know*. Sometimes ἵνα is not preceded by any verb like ἵνα ἐπιθῇς (Mk. 5:23) where we either have to supply a verb or look on the ἵνα clause as a virtual imperative idea. It is more probable that in a case like ἄφες ἐκβάλω we have asyndeton and there is no need to supply ἵνα, but we should take it thus: *Allow it, let me pluck out*. So as to βούλεσθε ἀπολύσω; (Jo. 18:39) *Do you wish? Shall I release?*

(b) Ὅπως.

Thucydides, Xenophon, Aristotle preferred ὅπως to ἵνα, but Polybius liked ἵνα. The New Testament uses ἵνα about eight times as often as ὅπως. The future indicative with ὅπως so common in the ancient Greek is nearly gone in the New Testament. It occurs in various manuscripts and is possible in Matt. 2:8 ὅπως προσκυνήσω that I may worship (same form as the aorist subjunctive). It is certain in Rom. 3:4 ὅπως ἂν δικαιωθῇς καὶ νικήσεις that thou mayest be justified and mayest conquer which is quoted from Ps. 51:6. Here νικήσεις is changed from the subjunctive νικήσῃς there. Ἄν occurs here also with ὅπως and three times in Luke's writings (Lu. 2:35; Acts 3:20; 15:17) and as a variant in some passages. The old idiom of ὅπως with the future indicative after verbs of striving does not appear in the New Testament. Ὅπως occurs chiefly in Matthew and Luke's writings. The subjunctive mode is regularly used as ὅπως δοξασθῶσιν (Matt. 6:2) that they may be glorified. The negative is μή as ὅπως μὴ φανῇς (Matt. 6:18) that thou mayest not appear. In Luke 24:20 ὅπως παρέδωκαν αὐτόν how they delivered him it is not final ὅπως, but indirect interrogative (relative) use.

(c) Ὡς.

The only example of ὡς as a final conjunction in the New Testament is in Acts 20:24 ὡς τελειώσω (Westcott and Hort) that I may finish though some manuscripts have τελειῶσαι (infinitive).

(d) Μή, μήποτε, μήπως.

This is a negative purpose and originally μή was used in a paratactic sentence. In Homer μή alone is far more common than ἵνα μή or ὅπως μή, but μή as a final particle died away and ἵνα μή (1 Cor. 1:17) and ὅπως μή (1 Cor. 1:29) are more frequent in the New Testament. Only the subjunctive is used with μή as μὴ εὕρῃ (Mk. 13:36) lest he find, μή τις λογίσηται (2 Cor. 12:6) lest any one reckon.

With μήποτε the notion of time (ποτέ) has disappeared before that of contingency (lest perchance). It occurs with the subjunctive as μήποτε ἀντικαλέσωσίν σε (Lu. 14:12) *lest perchance they invite thee in return.* The future indicative also occurs as μήποτε ἔσται (Mk. 14:2) *lest perchance there shall be.* In 2 Tim. 2:25 μήποτε δώῃ *lest perchance he give* we have the optative after a primary tense, though some manuscripts have δῴη (subjunctive). Μήπως is rare and occurs with the subjunctive as μήπως γένωμαι (1 Cor. 9:27) *lest in any way I become;* cf. 2 Cor. 9:4. It occurs twice with the Attic idiom of the aorist indicative where the purpose is concerning a past event conceived of as unfulfilled. So μήπως ἔδραμον (Gal. 2:2) *lest somehow I had run,* μήπως ἐπείρασεν (1 Th. 3:5) *lest somehow he had tempted.*

431. The Relative Clause.

Usually with the future indicative as οὓς καταστήσομεν (Acts 6:3) *whom we shall appoint,* οἵτινες ἀποδώσουσιν (Matt. 21:41) *who will give back.* But the subjunctive also appears as παρ' ᾧ ξενισθῶμεν (Acts 21:16) *with whom we are to lodge.* So Mk. 14:14; Heb. 8:3; 12:28.

432. The Infinitive.

Votaw counts 211 examples of the infinitive of purpose in the New Testament. We find it by itself (accusative case) like οὐκ ἦλθον καλεῖν (Mk. 2:17) *I came not to call;* with the common τοῦ (genitive) like τοῦ ἀπολέσαι (Matt. 2:13) *to destroy;* εἰς τό and the infinitive (72 examples) like εἰς τὸ εἶναι (Rom. 8:29) *that he might be;* πρὸς τό (12 in all) like πρὸς τὸ θεαθῆναι (Matt. 23:5) *to be seen;* ὥστε like ὥστε ἐκβάλλειν (Matt. 10:1) *so as to cast out;* ὡς like ὡς ἑτοιμάσαι (Lu. 9:52) *so as to make ready* and only one more, ὡς ἔπος εἰπεῖν (Heb. 7:9) *so to speak.* The close parallel between purpose with the infinitive and ἵνα is seen in Matt. 26:17 ἑτοιμάσωμεν φαγεῖν *that we make ready to eat* (for thee) and Mk. 14:12 ἑτοιμάσωμεν ἵνα φάγῃς *that we make ready to eat* (for thee).

433. *The Participle.*

The future participle for purpose is not so common as in the ancient Greek. Some examples do occur like ἐληλύθει προσκυνήσων (Acts 8:27) *had come to worship,* ἔρχεται σώσων (Matt. 27:49) *comes to save.* There are also present participles, with the notion of purpose like ἀπέστειλεν αὐτὸν εὐλογοῦντα ὑμᾶς (Acts 3:26) *sent him blessing (to bless) you.* It is even urged that the aorist participle of simultaneous action may mean purpose like κατήντησαν εἰς καισαρίαν ἀσπασάμενοι (Acts 25:13) where the late manuscripts have the future ἀσπασόμενοι. That is in itself possible, though hardly needed here with this simultaneous aorist participle with the effective aorist κατήντησαν.

CHAPTER XXVIII

CONSECUTIVE CLAUSES

434. *Sub-Final (Subject and Object) Clauses.*

There are a number of clauses that are not pure purpose nor yet pure result, but hover between the two extremes. These are really subject or object clauses like ὅτι declarative clauses though not so obvious at first. The same final conjunctions occur in this idiom as in other idioms also.

(a) Ἵνα.

This is the chief conjunction as in συμφέρει ἵνα ἀπόληται (Matt. 5:29) *it is expedient that it perish* where the ἵνα clause is the subject of συμφέρει. The subjunctive is usual, but the future indicative occurs as ἐρρέθη ἵνα ἀδικήσουσιν (Rev. 9:4) *it was said that they should not hurt.* Some manuscripts have ἵνα γινώσκουσιν in Jo. 17:3. A long list of verbs in the New Testament use ἵνα with the object clause like προσηύχετο ἵνα παρέλθῃ *he was praying that it might pass by.* In Eph. 1:17 ἵνα ὁ θεὸς δῴη *that God would give* we have the optative after a primary tense παύομαι. There are a number of examples of the non-final ἵνα which are in apposition with words in various cases like μείζονα ταύτης (ablative) ἵνα (Jo. 15:13), ἐν τούτῳ (locative) ἵνα (Jo. 15:8), χάριν (accusative) ἵνα (3 Jo. 4), αὕτη (nominative) ἵνα (Jo. 15:12), largely a Johannine idiom. This use of ἵνα finally drove the infinitive out in modern Greek.

(b) Ὅπως.

It no longer appears with the future indicative after verbs of striving. Only the subjunctive occurs with the few examples in the New Testament. There are three after συμβούλιον ἔλαβον (Matt. 12:14; 22:15; Mk. 3:6). The use of ὅπως is found also after several verbs of beseeching like αἰτέομαι (Acts 25:3), δέομαι (Matt. 9:38), ἐρωτάω (Lu. 7:3), παρακαλέω (Matt. 8:34). προσεύχομαι (Acts 8:15).

(c) Μή, μήποτε, μήπως.

Instead of ἵνα μή a few verbs have μή like βλέπετε μή τις ὑμᾶς πλανήσῃ (Matt. 24:4) see to it that no one lead you astray and usually with the subjunctive, though the future indicative appears also like βλέπετε μή τις ἔσται (Col. 2:8) see to it that there shall not be any one. Even the present indicative may occur if the fear is about the present as in σκόπει μὴ τὸ φῶς τὸ ἐν σοὶ σκότος ἐστίν (Lu. 11:35) look whether the light that is in thee is darkness. The present subjunctive occurs in Heb. 12:15 ἐπισκοποῦντες μὴ ἐνοχλῇ keeping an eye that there may not trouble you. Verbs of fearing come in here though the construction is rare and a literary touch like ἐφοβοῦντο τὸν λαὸν μὴ λιθασθῶσιν (Acts 5:26) they feared the people lest they be stoned.

Μήποτε occurs a few times as with the aorist subjunctive μήποτε παραρυῶμεν (Heb. 2:1) lest perchance we flow by after προσέχειν, with the present subjunctive as φοβηθῶμεν μήποτε δοκῇ τις (Heb. 4:1) let us be afraid lest perchance anyone seem. The future indicative occurs also in Heb. 3:12 βλέπετε μήποτε ἔσται look out lest perchance there shall be.

Μήπως occurs with the aorist subjunctive in 1 Cor. 8:9 βλέπετε μήπως γένηται look out lest somehow there come. If the fear is about the present or the past the indicative is used as φοβοῦμαι μήπως εἰκῇ κεκοπίακα (Gal. 4:11) I fear lest somehow I have toiled in vain. But in Lu. 19:21 we have ὅτι after ἐφοβούμην which can be understood as causal. The infinitive after a verb of fearing means to hesitate to do a thing like ἐφοβήθη ἀπελθεῖν (Matt. 2:22) he feared to go away.

(d) The Relative.

A few examples occur like ἄξιος ᾧ παρέξῃ (Lu. 7:4) he is

worthy to whom thou wilt furnish, οὐκ ἔχω ὃ παραθήσω (Lu. 11:6)
I do not have what I shall present.

(e) *The Infinitive.*

This is one of the commonest constructions with the infinitive when it is the subject as in τὸ ζῆν Phil. 1:21 or the object
as τὸ εἶναι (Phil. 2:6). It is very common with verbs like
αἰσχύνομαι as ἐπαιτεῖν αἰσχύνομαι (Lu. 16:3) *I am ashamed to
beg,* etc., the usual object infinitive.

435. *Pure Result.*

(a) Ἵνα.

The use of ἵνα has been sharply disputed, but gradually
modern grammarians have come to admit the actual ecbatic
use of ἵνα in the New Testament like the Latin *ut* and as is
certainly true of modern Greek. In Rom. 11:11 μὴ ἔπταισαν
ἵνα πέσωσιν; Sanday and Headlam argue that here "ἵνα expresses contemplated result." Lightfoot argues also for the
consecutive use of ἵνα in Gal. 5:17; 1 Th. 5:4. Another clear
example is Lu. 1:43 ἵνα ἔλθῃ. See also Jo. 9:2 τίς ἥμαρτεν
ἵνα τυφλὸς γεννηθῇ; *Who did sin so that he was born blind?* Once
admit this use of ἵνα and a number of passages are plainer
like Rev. 13:13; 1 Jo. 1:9; Rev. 9:20.

(b) Ὅτι.

In Matt. 8:27 we have ὅτι = ὥστε with the notion of result:
ποταπός ἐστιν οὗτος ὅτι καὶ οἱ ἄνεμοι καὶ ἡ θάλασσα αὐτῷ ὑπακούουσιν;
Who then is this that both the winds and the sea obey him? So
also Lu. 8:25.

(c) Ὥστε.

In the ancient Greek actual result was expressed by ὥστε
and the indicative, but in the New Testament only two examples of this idiom survive: John 3:16 ὥστε ἔδωκεν *so that he gave,*
and Gal. 2:13 ὥστε συναπήχθη *so that he was led away together
with.* Elsewhere ὥστε in the New Testament is construed

with the infinitive, both for design (the old idiom) like ὥστε κατακρημνίσαι (Lu. 4:29) *so as to hurl down* and for actual result as ὥστε γεμίζεσθαι τὸ πλοῖον (Mk. 4:37) *so that the boat was filling*. At the beginning of a sentence ὥστε means "and so" as in 1 Cor. 5:8.

(d) The Infinitive.

It is here the simple infinitive without ὥστε that has to be considered as well as τοῦ and the infinitive, πρὸς τό and the infinitive. It once seemed clear to me that the infinitive was never so used for result outside of the construction with ὥστε but my view has changed by a closer consideration of the examples in the New Testament. In itself, if ὥστε and the infinitive came to be used for result (as it did), there is no reason why the infinitive without ὥστε should not follow suit. The consecutive idea seems to be found in the simple infinitives ψεύσασθαι in Acts 5:3, ἐπιλαθέσθαι in Heb. 6:10, ἀνοῖξαι in Rev. 5:5, δοῦναι in Rev. 16:9, to go no further. Moulton (*Prolegomena*, pp. 204, 207) calls it "designed result," but that is "result". See also discussion in Robertson's *Grammar of the Greek New Testament in the Light of Historical Research*, pp. 1001-3. The use of τοῦ and the infinitive follows suit. In Lu. 17:1 and Acts 10:25 τοῦ and the infinitive is treated as if nominative instead of genitive and the subject of the verb. A clear case of result appears in τοῦ μὴ εἶναι αὐτήν (Rom. 7:3) *so that she is not*. So also τοῦ ποιεῖν in Acts 7:19. The epexegetic use of τοῦ and the infinitive is common as in Lu. 9:51. With εἰς τό and the infinitive the original idea was aim or purpose as was true of ἵνα, but gradually the consecutive idea grew till not only the sub-final and epexegetic idea came as in 1 Thess. 2:12; 3:10; 4:9; but actual as εἰς τὸ παρακαλέσαι ἡμᾶς Τίτον (2 Cor. 8:6) *so that we exhorted Titus* and probably also Rom. 1:20 εἰς τὸ εἶναι αὐτοὺς ἀναπολογήτους *so that they are without excuse*. This idiom is common in Romans and Hebrews (11:3 εἰς τὸ γεγονέναι). With πρὸς τό and the infinitive there is more doubt. Result is possible in Matt. 5:28 πρὸς τὸ ἐπιθυμῆσαι, but purpose is possible also. Probably "subjective purpose," is all that can be claimed for the πρὸς τό construction.

(e) *The Relative Clause.*

This is a common idiom in the ancient Greek as with the Latin *qui.* There seem to be a few examples in the New Testament like ὅς γε τοῦ ἰδίου οὐκ ἐφείσατο (Rom. 8:32) *who spared not his own son.* See also Matt. 10:26; 24:2.

CHAPTER XXIX

CONDITIONAL SENTENCES

436. *Four Kinds of Conditional Sentences.*

Here the whole sentence is involved, both the condition (protasis) and the conclusion (apodosis), in the fully stated idiom. The scheme of Goodwin for particular and general conditions is rejected as well as his entire terminology because of its unscientific nature. The mode is what determines the type of the Greek conditional sentence. The condition (protasis) that uses the indicative mode is *determined* by that mode, that is to say, the condition is assumed in the *statement*, which is all that the condition deals with, as being either true or untrue, a fact or a non-fact. The indicative mode in the condition always makes *a clear-cut assertion* one way or the other. If the subjunctive or the optative is used in the condition (protasis) *a doubtful statement* is made whatever may be the actual fact or truth in the case. By these modes of doubtful statement the condition puts it *as doubtful* or *undetermined* (not put in a clear-cut way). If the subjunctive is used, there is less doubt than if the optative is used, precisely the difference between these two modes of doubtful statement. So then there are these four kinds of conditions:

(a) *First Class*: *Determined as Fulfilled* (εἰ, sometimes ἐάν, with any tense of the indicative in condition. Any tense of the indicative in the conclusion).

(b) *Second Class*: *Determined as Unfulfilled* (εἰ and only past tenses of the indicative in condition. Only past tenses in the conclusion, usually with ἄν to make clear the kind of condition used).

(c) *Third Class*: *Undetermined with Prospect of Determination* (ἐάν or εἰ with the subjunctive in the condition, usually future or present indicative or imperative in the conclusion, much variety in the form of the conclusion).

(d) *Fourth Class*: *Undetermined with Remote Prospect of Determination* (εἰ with the optative in the condition, ἄν and the optative in the conclusion).

437. *The First Class*: *Determined as Fulfilled.*

This condition is the most common of all and may be called the normal condition unless there is reason for using one of the others. This condition *assumes* the reality of the condition. The indicative mode *states* it as a fact. The *condition* has nothing whatever to do with the actual fact or truth. It is just here that some of the grammars have erred in the failure to distinguish clearly between the *statement* and the *reality*. It is the condition taken at its face value without any insinuations or implications. The context, of course, must determine the actual situation. The indicative mode determines only the statement. The conjunction εἰ is the usual one employed though sometimes ἐάν occurs. It is not the conjunction, but the mode that determines the conditional statement. The conclusion (apodosis) is normally in the indicative, though the imperative or the volitive subjunctive may be employed. Some representative examples will illustrate the various phases of the subject. In Matt. 12:27 εἰ ἐγὼ ἐν βεεζεβοὺλ ἐκβάλλω τὰ δαιμόνια *if I by Beezeboul cast out the demons,* Jesus *assumes* as true the charge of the Pharisees against him, but merely for the sake of argument. The conclusion is a crushing reply οἱ υἱοὶ ὑμῶν ἐν τίνι ἐκβάλλουσιν; *Your sons by whom do they cast them out?* They claimed to have this power. It is the *argumentum ad hominem*. Then in verse 28 Jesus gives the truth by this same first-class condition: εἰ δὲ ἐν πνεύματι θεοῦ ἐγὼ ἐκβάλλω τὰ δαιμόνια *but if by the Spirit of God I cast out the demons,* which Jesus again *assumes* to be true. The conclusion is not a rhetorical question as above, but an obvious logical (ἄρα) result: ἄρα ἔφθασεν ἐφ' ὑμᾶς ἡ βασιλεία τοῦ θεοῦ *then is come to you the Kingdom of God.* Here the timeless aorist indicative ἔφθασεν drives home the conclusion. These two examples illustrate well the first-class condition. In Matt. 26:33 the future indicative appears in both condition and conclusion: εἰ πάντες σκανδαλισθήσονται ἐν σοί, ἐγὼ οὐδέποτε σκανδαλισθήσομαι *if all shall be tripped in thee, I shall never be tripped.* In Lu. 4:3 εἰ εἶ, εἰπέ the imperative is in the conclusion. In Lu. 19:40 ἐὰν σιωπήσουσιν, κράξουσιν we have ἐάν with the future indicative in the condition. In Jo. 15:20 εἰ ἐδίωξαν, διώξουσιν *if they persecuted, they will persecute.* the aorist indicative is in the condition and the future in the conclusion. In Acts 11:17 εἰ ἔδωκεν, τίς ἤμην; we have past tenses in both condition and conclusion. In 1 Thess. 3:8 ζῶμεν ἐὰν στήκετε we find ἐάν and the present indicative in the condition and the conclusion put before the condition. In 1 Cor. 15:16 εἰ οὐκ ἐγείρονται, οὐδὲ ἐγήγερται note the present indicative with the negative οὐ in the condition and the perfect indicative in the conclusion. These examples illustrate the variety and freedom in the first-class conditions.

438. *The Second Class: Determined as Unfulfilled.*

Conditions that use the indicative mode are naturally taken to belong to the first class (determined as fulfilled) unless there is something in the context to indicate otherwise. The condition must be a determined one, if the indicative mode is used, and be assumed as true unless the contrary is plainly implied. Then the *assumption* is that the condition is untrue, though in actual fact it may be true. In neither case does the condition deal with the actual facts. In Luke 7:39 οὗτος εἰ ἦν ὁ προφήτης, ἐγίνωσκεν ἄν *this fellow if he were the prophet (which he is not), he would know (as he does not).* So the Pharisee argues about his guest. He *assumes* two errors about Jesus, one that he does not know, the other that he is not the prophet that he claims to be. He *assumes* and *states* as contrary to the fact and so *untrue* two actual truths for

Jesus did know and was the prophet. The second-class condition uses only the past tenses of the indicative. If the condition has present or future tenses of the indicative, one knows at once that it is a first-class condition. It is a question only when the past tenses of the indicative are used in the condition. In order to decide that problem the Greek adopted a device for the ordinary examples by the use of ἄν in the conclusion (apodosis) which never comes first in the clause. See Lu. 7:39 above. If this condition is about present time, the imperfect tense is employed like Lu. 7:39 again and Matt. 23:30 εἰ ἤμεθα, οὐκ ἂν ἤμεθα. If the condition deals with the past we find usually the aorist indicative in both condition and conclusion as in Matt. 11:21 εἰ ἐγένοντο, πάλαι ἂν μετενόησαν. Sometimes the condition has the imperfect and the conclusion the aorist like εἰ ἠγαπᾶτε, ἐχάρητε ἄν (Jo. 14:28). See the opposite in Heb. 4:8. In Heb. 11:15 the imperfect is used of past time (continuance in past time) εἰ ἐμνημόνευον, εἶχον ἄν. The past perfect occurs in the protasis like Acts 26:32 εἰ μὴ ἐπεκέκλητο and once in the apodosis like 1 Jo. 2:19 εἰ ἦσαν, μεμενήκεισαν ἄν. Sometimes ἄν is repeated in the apodosis like ἐγρηγόρησεν ἂν καὶ οὐκ ἂν εἴασεν (Matt. 24:43). Then again ἄν is not repeated as in ἐγρηγόρησεν ἂν καὶ οὐκ ἀφῆκεν (Lu. 12:39). Sometimes, again, ἄν was not employed because the context made it plain that it is the second-class condition as in Jo. 15:22 εἰ μὴ ἦλθον καὶ ἐλάλησα αὐτοῖς, ἁμαρτίαν οὐκ εἴχοσαν for the very next words make it clear: νῦν δὲ πρόφασιν οὐκ ἔχουσιν but now they have no pretext. So also as to verse 24. In the same way the absence of ἄν with οὐκ εἶχες in Jo. 19:11 still leaves it clear by the following clause that we have a second-class condition. So again verbs of fitness or propriety like καλὸν ἦν (Matt. 26:24) and οὐ καθῆκεν (Acts 22:22), possibility like ἐδύνατο (Acts 26:32), and obligation like ἔδει (Matt. 23:23).

439. *The Third Class: Undetermined, but with Prospect of Determination.*

This condition *states* the condition as a matter of doubt, but with some expectation of realization. Hence the subjunctive is the mode of doubt used, not the optative the mode of still greater doubt. It is undetermined and so does not use the indicative mode, but there is more hope and that marks it off from the optative. We have seen that the future indicative is a development of the aorist subjunctive so that the difference between the first-class condition with εἰ or ἐάν and the future indicative on the one hand and the second-class condition with ἐάν or εἰ and the aorist subjunctive on the other is not very great, though real and a bit subtle. Often we find first and third-class conditions side by side like εἴ τις καλεῖ and ἐάν τις εἴπῃ 1 Cor. 10:27, ἐὰν ᾖ and εἰ–ἐστίν in Acts 5:38 where Gamaliel gives the benefit of the doubt to Christianity by the kind of conditions used. In Jo. 13:17 the Master draws the distinction sharply between the first and third-class conditions: εἰ ταῦτα οἴδατε (first class, assuming that you do know), μακάριοί ἐστε ἐὰν ποιῆτε ταῦτα (third class, doubtful, but with hope, *if you keep on doing these things*). Cf. also Jo. 10:37 where a like distinction is drawn. The so-called present general condition belongs here, a condition of the second class. In the condition usually we have ἐάν and the subjunctive with the present tense like ἐὰν ἔχητε (1 Cor. 4:15) or the aorist (usually) like ἐὰν τηρήσῃ (Jo. 8:51). Sometimes ἄν (shortened ἐάν) occurs in place of ἐάν like ἂν ὑψωθῶ (Jo. 12:32). Even εἰ occurs with the subjunctive like εἰ καταλάβω (Phil. 3:12). There is great freedom and variety in the conclusion which is often the future indicative like δώσει in Jo. 16:23, but it may be the present indicative like ἔχομεν in 2 Cor. 5:1, or even the aorist indicative like ἥμαρτες in 1 Cor. 7:28, or the imperative like ἐρχέσθω in Jo. 7:37. In Jo. 5:19 we find both uses of ἄν (= ἐάν and the modal ἄν with ἅ).

440. *Fourth Class: Undetermined with Remote Prospect of Determination.*

This condition uses the other mode of doubt (the optative) because the prospect of determination is more remote. The two undetermined conditions are thus marked off by the modes of doubt (subjunctive and optative) from the two determined conditions by the mode of positive assertion (the indicative). And they differ also from each other precisely as the optative differs from the subjunctive. The condition is expressed by εἰ and the optative, the conclusion by the optative and modal ἄν. In the English it is not easy to distinguish between the second-class and the fourth-class condition, though the distinction is perfectly clear in the Greek. Unfortunately in the New Testament the disappearance of the optative has left us with only a few torsos of the fourth-class condition. Thus we have the condition εἰ καὶ πάσχοιτε in 1 Pet. 3:14, but not the conclusion. So also we have εἰ θέλοι in 1 Pet. 3:17 and εἰ τύχοι in 1 Cor. 15:37, but no conclusions. There is a conclusion in Acts 24:19 οὓς ἔδει ἐπὶ σοῦ παρεῖναι καὶ κατηγορεῖν, εἴτι ἔχοιεν πρός με *who ought to be present before thee, if they should have aught against me,* though the conclusion belongs to the second class and so it is a mixed condition. There is a touch of indirect discourse in the condition εἰ ἄρα γε ψηλαφήσειαν αὐτὸν καὶ εὕροιεν (Acts 17:27) *if accordingly at least they should feel after him and find him.* So also as to ἐβουλεύοντο εἰ δύναιντο (Acts 27:39) *they were deliberating if they could.* There are several conclusions of the fourth class like εὐξαίμην ἄν (Acts 26:29) *I should wish,* but no protasis with it. So as to τί ἂν θέλοι; (Acts 17:18) *what would he wish?* In τὸ τί ἂν θέλοι (Lu. 1:62) *as to what he would wish,* and τὸ τίς ἂν εἴη (Lu. 9:46) *as to who would be,* the conclusion of the fourth-class condition is simply retained in the indirect question. There is also an apodosis of the fourth class in Acts 8:31 πῶς γὰρ ἂν δυναίμην ἐὰν μήτις ὁδηγήσει με; *for how could I unless some one will guide me?* But here again the condition belongs to the first class and it is a mixed condition. The so-called past general supposition belonged to the fourth-class condition with a mixed conclusion. There is no example of it in the New Testament.

441. *Mixed Conditions.*

Men's minds do not always work according to rules, not even according to the wonderfully fine system of conditional sentences developed by the Greeks. This play and elasticity and variety suit the Greek genius. All that is involved in a mixed condition is that one of the four kinds of conditions is used in the condition and another in the conclusion. If we recognize life in language, this fact should give us no trouble. All that is needed to understand it is a little elasticity in our own minds as we study it. We have already seen in Acts 8:31 a protasis of the first class (ἐὰν ὁδηγήσει) with an apodosis of the fourth (πῶς ἂν δυναίμην). So also in Acts 24:19 we had a conclusion of the second class (ἔδει) with a condition of the fourth (εἴ τι ἔχοιεν). There are others like Lu. 17:6 εἰ ἔχετε, ἐλέγετε ἄν *if you have, you would say,* a first-class condition and second-class conclusion. The marginal reading in Jo. 8:39 presents a like situation. In 1 Cor. 7:28 ἐὰν γήμῃς, οὐχ ἥμαρτες it is not hard to see how the standpoint changes. Contemplation of the probability of marriage (third-class condition) leads at once to reality as the result (first-class conclusion). There may, in fact, be two conditions in the same sentence, one of one class, the other of another, as we saw above in Jo. 13:17. Two conditions of the same class (first) occur in 1 Cor. 9:11.

442. *Elliptical or Implied Conditions.*

The participle is often used when a condition is implied, though not stated, like τελοῦσα (Rom. 2:27) where the participle means simply "fulfilling", not "if it fulfill". See also λαμβανόμενον in 1 Tim. 4:4. So two imperatives together may suggest a condition without stating it like ὀργίζεσθε καὶ μὴ ἁμαρτάνετε (Eph. 4:26) *be angry and sin not,* meaning "if

ye are angry, do not have the habit of sinning". So also
a question may imply a condition as in Matt. 26:15. Then
again the apodosis may be absent with the result of an aposiopesis or elliptical condition as in Lu. 19:42 εἰ ἔγνως καὶ σύ
if thou hadst known even thou. In 2 Thess. 2:3 ἐὰν μὴ ἔλθῃ we
have mere anacoluthon. The abrupt use of εἰ like Hebrew
im in a solemn oath is also elliptical as in εἰ δοθήσεται (Mk.
8:12) *it shall not be given.* So also as to the use of εἰ in direct
questions like εἰ ἀποκαθιστάνεις; *dost thou restore?* (Acts 1:6.) Sometimes the verb is not expressed as with εἰ in Rom. 8:17, εἰ μή
in Matt. 5:13, εἴπερ in Rom. 3:30, ἐκτὸς εἰ μή in 1 Tim. 5:19,
ὡσεί in Matt. 3:16, ὡσπερεί in 1 Cor. 15:8. Here the verb in
the condition is not expressed, but it is still a condition. See
Jo. 14:2 where we have εἰ δὲ μή, εἶπον ἄν *but if it were not true,
I would have told you,* a condition of the second class. We
have already seen that with ἐπεί there is sometimes a suppressed condition with only the apodosis like ἐπεὶ οὐκ ἂν
ἐπαύσαντο (Heb. 10:2). With verbs of wonder we have only
the condition (a kind of indirect discourse) like ἐθαύμασεν
αὐτὸν εἰ ἤδη τέθνηκεν *wondered at him if he was already dead* (Mk.
15:44). See also εἰ εἴη in Acts 20:16, εἰ δύναιντο in Acts 27:39
and εἰ πως εὐοδωθήσομαι in Rom. 1:10.

443. *Concessive Clauses.*

These are simply conditional clauses with the addition of
καί. Καὶ εἰ (or ἐάν) means "even if" (rare in the New Testament) like καὶ ἐὰν κρίνω (Jo. 8:16) *even if I judge.* In εἰ καί
or ἐὰν καί the idea is rather "if also" or "although" like εἰ καὶ
ἐλύπησα (2 Cor. 7:8) *although I did sorrow.* In Lu. 12:38 we
find κἄν—κἄν. We have καίπερ only five times in the New
Testament and with the participle each time like καίπερ ὤν
υἱός (Heb. 5:8) *though a son.* The correct text in Rev. 17:8
καὶ πάρεσται removes the old error καίπερ ἔσται (καίπερ with
the indicative.)

444. *Negatives in Conditional Clauses.*

With the subjunctive in the condition (third class) the negative is μή as in Lu. 13:3. We have no negative with the optative in the protasis of the fourth class. In the first and second-class conditions where the indicative is used, either οὐ or μή occurs. Μή negatives rather the condition itself and the conclusion is nearly always negative also like εἰ μὴ ἦν οὗτος κακὸν ποιῶν, οὐκ ἄν σοι παρεδώκαμεν αὐτόν (Jo. 18:30) *unless this fellow were an evil doer, we would not have handed him over to thee.* When οὐ occurs in the condition, it is either quite emphatic or there is antithesis expressed or a single word is negative like εἰ οὐ φοβοῦμαι (Lu. 18:4), εἰ οὐκ εἰ (Jo. 1:25), εἰ οὐ πιστεύετε (Jo. 5:47), εἰ οὐ ποιῶ (Jo. 10:37). In Matt. 26:42 both οὐ and μή occur in the same sentences εἰ οὐ δύναται τοῦτο παρελθεῖν ἐὰν μὴ πίω *if this cannot pass by except I drink it.* In 1 Cor. 9:2 εἰ ἄλλοις οὐκ εἰμὶ ἀπόστολος means *if I am not an apostle to others* while εἰ μὴ κτλ would be *unless I am an apostle to others,* a different idea here.

CHAPTER XXX

WISHES

445. *Wishes about the Past.*

Most laments concern what might have been in the past. The old Greek idiom εἴθε or εἰ γάρ, a sort of elliptical condition, has disappeared. In its place we find ὄφελον with the aorist indicative as in ὄφελον ἐβασιλεύσατε (1 Cor. 4:8) *would that you had reigned.* Ὄφελον is really ὤφελον, second aorist active indicative of ὀφείλω without augment. In 2 Cor. 12:11 we have ὤφειλον συνίστασθαι *I ought to be commanded*, the imperfect with the present passive infinitive. Herodotus used ὄφελον with the infinitive. Ὄφελον as a conjunction, like the Latin *utinam*, occurs in the LXX like ὄφελον ἀπεθάνομεν (Ex. 16:3) *would that we had died* and in the inscriptions. Achilles Tatius has ὄφελον ἔμεινας *would that thou hadst remained.* This one example with the aorist indicative (1 Cor. 4:8) is the only instance in the New Testament for wishes about the past. There are more polite ways of expressing a wish about the past like the imperfect tense as ἐβουλόμην (Acts 25:22) *I was just wishing*, ἤθελον (Gal. 4:20) *I was wishing*, ηὐχόμην (Rom. 9:3) *I was on the point of praying.* But usually the past tenses of these verbs present deliberate choice as in Matt. 1:19; 2:18.

446. *Wishes about the Present.*

Here again ὄφελον occurs in place of εἴθε or εἰ γάρ in ὄφελον ἦς (Rev. 3:15) *Would that thou wert* and ὄφελον ἀνείχεσθε (2 Cor. 11:1) *would that you did put up with me.* Some of the manuscripts read ὤφελον in 2 Cor. 11:2. The Textus Receptus has ὄφελον εἴης in Rev. 3:15 without any manuscript authority at all. The optative would make it a wish about the future. There is also the present indicative of verbs of wishing like θέλομεν τὸν Ἰησοῦν ἰδεῖν (Jo. 12:21) *we desire to see Jesus,* βούλομαι προσεύχεσθαι τοὺς ἄνδρας *I wish for the men to pray.* (1 Tim. 2:8).

447. *Wishes about the Future.*

Here again ὄφελον and the future indicative occurs once only, ὄφελον ἀποκόψονται (Gal. 5:12) *would that they would cut themselves off.* The usual way to express a wish about the future is the use of the optative without a conjunction. The present optative occurs so once εἴη in Acts 8:20 τὸ ἀργύριόν σου σὺν σοὶ εἴη εἰς ἀπώλειαν *thy money be with thee for destruction.* Usually we find the aorist optative as in 1 Thess. 5:23 αὐτὸς δὲ ὁ θεὸς τῆς εἰρήνης ἁγιάσαι ὑμᾶς *now may the God of peace sanctify you.* The most frequent wish of this type is μὴ γένοιτο (Gal. 6:14) *may it not happen.* This use of the optative in this idiom is the only one that survives in modern Greek. The only optative in Mark's Gospel is μηκέτι ἐκ σοῦ μηδεὶς καρπὸν φάγοι (Mk. 11:14) *may no one any more eat fruit of thee.* Here in the parallel passage Matthew (21:19) has the volitive subjunctive with the double negative οὐ μηκέτι ἐκ σοῦ καρπὸς γένηται *there shall no more come fruit out of thee.* The imperative can also be used in imprecations like ἀνάθεμα ἔστω (Gal. 1:9) *let him be anathema.* The potential optative with ἄν (apodosis of the fourth-class condition) can express a courteous wish about the future like εὐξαίμην ἄν (Acts 26:29) *I could wish.*

CHAPTER XXXI

INTERROGATIVE SENTENCES

448. *Direct Questions.*

Indirect questions are discussed in the chapter on Indirect Discourse. A number of problems arise about interrogative sentences.

(a) *With No Mark of Interrogation.*

This often happens like συνήκατε ταῦτα πάντα; (Matt. 13:51) *did you understand all these things?* Sometimes it is not easy to decide whether a sentence is interrogative or not like μεμέρισται ὁ χριστός (1 Cor. 1:13) *Christ is divided.* Westcott and Hort make it a question in the margin χριστός; *Is Christ divided?* Only the context can make such a matter clear if there is no particle or pronoun.

(b) *The Kind of Answer Expected.*

There may be no indication as in Matt. 13:51 above. Even with ἆρα the question may be colorless as in ἆρά γε γινώσκεις ἃ ἀναγινώσκεις; *Do you indeed know what you are reading?* But if οὐ occurs, the affirmative answer is expected as οὐκ εἰμὶ ἀπόστολος; (1 Cor. 9:1) *Am I not an Apostle?* (*I certainly am*). When μή is used, a negative reply is anticipated as μὴ ἀπώσατο ὁ θεὸς τὸν λαὸν αὐτοῦ; *Did God push away his people?* (*Surely not*). Sometimes a deal of feeling is suggested by μή like the scorn in μὴ καὶ ὑμεῖς πεπλάνησθε; (Jo. 7:47) *have you also been led astray?* Here the *form* requires the answer No, but in reality the rulers felt that Nicodemus had been led astray. So in Jo. 4:29 μήτι οὗτός ἐστιν ὁ χριστός; *Is this the Messiah?* The form expects the negative answer, but the woman with suppressed excitement was keen enough to use it to create interest without raising a sharp issue. In Jo. 6:67 μὴ καὶ ὑμεῖς θέλετε ὑπάγειν; *do you also wish to go away?* Jesus sympathetically assumes that they do not wish to go away and yet the very question cut to their very hearts.

(c) *Pronouns Used.*

The most common is τίς as in τίς ὑπέδειξεν ὑμῖν (Matt. 3:7) *Who suggested to you?* Other words may be added like ἄρα (Matt. 24:45), γάρ (Matt. 9:5), οὖν (Lu. 3:10). In Mk. 15:24 we have the double interrogative τίς τί ἄρῃ *Who is to take what?* Note the predicative use of τοῦτο in Lu. 16:2 τί τοῦτο ἀκούω περὶ σοῦ; *What is this that I hear about thee?* Frequently τί is an adverb in the sense of "why" like τί με λέγεις ἀγαθόν; (Mk. 10:18) *Why callest thou me good?* So also διὰ τί (Matt. 9:11), εἰς τί (Mk. 14:4), τί ὅτι (Lu. 2:49) *how is it that?* There is a certain amount of confusion between the interrogative and the relative pronouns in the New Testament as in the older Greek and in most languages. The relative would seem to suit better in Jas. 3:13 unless, as Westcott and Hort do, a question mark is put after ἐν ὑμῖν and before δειξάτω. In Mk. 1:24 οἶδά σε τίς εἶ we merely have prolepsis of σέ instead of σύ before εἶ. In 1 Tim. 1:7 we find ἃ λέγουσιν and περὶ τίνων διαβεβαιοῦνται. It is possible that we have the relative used as an interrogative in Matt. 26:50 ἑταῖρε, ἐφ' ὃ πάρει *Friend, why are you here?* The difference between the relative and the interrogative is preserved clearly in Jo. 13:24 εἰπὲ τίς ἐστιν περὶ οὗ λέγει *tell who is the one concerning whom he is speaking.* In 2 Tim. 1:12 ᾧ πεπίστευκα we have the relative *him whom I have believed,* not the interrogative. Note ʾτί *what,* not τίνα *whom* in Acts 13:25 τί ἐμὲ ὑπονοεῖτε εἶναι; *What do you consider me to be?* In 1 Pet. 1:11 we have both τίς and ποῖος. For πόσος (Mk. 6:38) and ποταπός (Matt. 8:27) see Chapter on Personal Pronouns.

(d) *Conjunctions and Particles.*

Besides οὐ and μή there is οὐκοῦν = *therefore* as in Jo. 18:37 but if accented οὔκουν = *not therefore.* Ἆρα expresses bewilder-

ment as in Acts 8:30 and Gal. 2:17 while ἄρα (illative) con-
cludes (Lightfoot) a query. So also Lu. 18:8. The use of
εἰ in a direct question is either a Hebraism or an elliptical
condition as in Matt. 12:10; Acts 1:6. Other conjunctions
used in questions (direct and indirect) are πότε (Matt. 25:38),
ἕως πότε (Matt. 17:17), ποῦ (Lu. 8:25), πῶς (Lu. 10:26), πόθεν
(Jo. 3:8), ὅπως (Lu. 24:20), ὅπου (Mk. 14:14), μή ποτε (Lu.
3:15). Probably ὅτι occurs in a direct question in Mk. 2:16;
9:11 and possibly in Acts 11:3.

(e) *Elliptical Phrases.*

In some of these γένηται has dropped out like ἵνα τί (Matt.
9:4), τί ὅτι (Lu. 2:49). In Jo. 14:22 we have τί γέγονεν ὅτι
without an ellipse. Note the condensed idiom in τί ἄρα
Πέτρος ἐγένετο (Acts 12:18) *What accordingly Peter has become.*
Cf. Jo. 21:21 οὗτος δὲ τί; *but this one what?*

(f) *Alternative Questions.*

They are not frequent in the New Testament. In fact
there is only one example and that is an indirect question
πότερον—ἤ (Jo. 7:17) *Whether—or.* It is common to have ἤ
in the second member of the question as in 1 Cor. 9:8. Then
again we find τίς—ἤ as in Matt. 9:5. Sometimes ἤ precedes
τίς and refers to the previous sentence (Matt. 7:9).

(g) *The Modes.*

The indicative is, of course, the most frequent as in σὺ τίς
εἶ; (Jo. 1:19) *Thou who art thou?* So also τί ποιοῦμεν (Jo. 11:47)
what are we doing? But the deliberative subjunctive is common also like δῶμεν ἤ μὴ δῶμεν; (Mk. 12:15) *Shall we give or shall
we not give?* Then the optative with ἄν occurs in the apodosis of the fourth-class condition as in Acts 17:18 τί ἄν θέλοι;
What would he wish? The modes in indirect questions will
be discussed in the chapter on Indirect Discourse.

(h) *Exclamations.*

In the older Greek relative pronouns were largely employed like οἷος, ὁποῖος, ὅσος, like ὡς ὡραῖοι in Rom. 10:15 though occasionally interrogative pronouns occurred as πόσα in Mk. 15:4, πηλίκος in Gal. 6:11, and τί θέλω in Lu. 12:49. Interjections also are common in exclamations like δεῦτε in Matt. 21:38, ἔα in Lu. 4:34, ἴδε in Jo. 1:29, ἰδού in Matt. 17:5, οὐά in Mk. 15:29, οὐαί in Rev. 18:10, ὦ in Matt. 15:28. But ἴδε is still a verb as a rule (Jo. 7:52). Οὐαί may be used also with the dative (Matt. 11:21) or the accusative (Rev. 8:13).

CHAPTER XXXII

INDIRECT DISCOURSE

449. *Direct Discourse (Oratio Recta).*

In the New Testament, as in the Old Testament and in Homer, direct discourse is far more frequent than the indirect. Quotations are usually given directly as in θέλω, καθαρίσθητι (Matt. 8:3) *I will, be thou cleansed.* But sometimes recitative ὅτι occurs which is not to be translated and which serves only to call attention to the quotation like our quotation marks as λέγετε ὅτι βλασφημεῖς (Jo. 10:36) *Ye say, Thou blasphemest.* Sometimes the nominative absolute preserves the precise words like φωνεῖτέ με Ὁ διδάσκαλος καὶ Ὁ κύριος (Jo. 13:13) *Ye call me "The Teacher" and "The Lord".* Thucydides and Livy give prolonged indirect discourse which is often artificial and labored.

450. *Three Kinds of Indirect Discourse (Oratio Obliqua).*

There are three forms of direct discourse that are transferred to the indirect and so become (a) Indirect Assertions, (b) or Indirect Questions, (c) or Indirect Commands. That is to say, an assertion in the direct becomes an indirect assertion, a question in the direct becomes an indirect question, a command in the direct becomes an indirect command. They require separate treatment.

451. *Indirect Assertion.*

Here again there are three ways of turning the direct into the indirect assertion.

(a) *Ὅτι and the Original Modes usually the Indicative.*

This is the usual method in the New Testament like θεωρῶ ὅτι προφήτης εἶ σύ (Jo. 4:19) *I behold that a prophet art thou.*

There is no clear example of ὡς so used though Acts 10:28 (ἐπίστασθε ὡς ἀθέμιτόν ἐστιν ye know how it is unlawful) comes close to it. See also Lu. 24:6. The indicative mode is retained with ὅτι after secondary tenses and is not changed to the optative as in the ancient Greek. The only exception is the πρὶν ἤ clause in Acts 25:16 which is changed from πρὶν ἤ — ἔχῃ — λάβῃ to πρὶν ἤ — ἔχοι — λάβοι after ἀπεκρίθην ὅτι οὐκ ἔστιν, but even here οὐκ ἔστιν is not changed to οὐκ εἴη after ἀπεκρίθην. The sequence of modes is not carried through. As a rule also there is no change of tense with ὅτι as ἐκεῖνοι δὲ ἔδοξαν ὅτι περὶ τῆς κοιμήσεως τοῦ ὕπνου λέγει (Jo. 11:13) but they thought that he was speaking (so we have to say in English) concerning the taking of rest in sleep. The Greek love of vividness retains the same tense (and mode also in the New Testament), though we cannot do it in English. So ἠλπίζομεν ὅτι αὐτός ἐστιν (Lu. 24:21) we were hoping that it was he. Sometimes the aorist represents an aorist in the direct as in Jo. 1:50 ὅτι εἶδον refers to εἶδον in verse 48. So in Mk. 11:24 πιστεύετε ὅτι ἐλάβετε believe that ye received. In Jo. 9:18 the imperfect ἦν was in the direct as well as the aorist ἀνέβλεψεν. But sometimes the tense was changed as in οὐκ ἔγνωσαν ὅτι τὸν πατέρα αὐτοῖς ἔλεγεν (Jo. 8:27) they did not know that he was (had been) speaking to them of the Father. The person of the verb has to be changed if necessary like ἐνόμισαν ὅτι πλεῖον λήμψονται (Matt. 20:10) they thought that they would receive more. In the direct it was, λημψόμεθα we shall receive. But it was not always necessary as in κἀγὼ δέ σοι ὅτι σὺ εἶ Πέτρος but I say to thee that thou art Peter. Here there is no change of person in the verb. A great variety of verbs employ ὅτι in indirect assertion. Some use also the infinitive and some the participle as well. With καταλαμβάνω we have ὅτι in Acts 10:34, but the infinitive in Acts 25:25. It is sometimes doubtful whether ὅτι is declarative or causal as in Acts 22:29. Paul has κοινή support for his use of ὡς ὅτι (how that, as though) in 2 Cor. 5:19; 11:21; 2 Thess. 2:2. Luke's use of καὶ ἐγένετο καί (almost like ὅτι) has been noticed (Lu. 17:11) and without the second καί (Lu. 17:14) and with the infinitive (Lu. 3:21).

(b) *The Infinitive.*

This construction is not so frequent in the New Testament as in the older Greek. It has faded away before the ὅτι clause. Luke alone uses it to any extent, one mark of his literary style. Paul comes next in his use of it. The same remarks about change of person and tense apply to the infinitive. The present infinitive in indirect discourse has to represent the present indicative or the imperfect indicative. So in Lu. 20:6 πεπεισμένος γάρ ἐστιν 'Ιωάνην προφήτην εἶναι the infinitive εἶναι represents ἦν of the direct. In Jo. 21:25 χωρήσειν represents χωρήσει of the direct and τεθνηκέναι in Acts 14:19 represents τέθνηκε of the direct. The oldest idiom was just to use the infinitive with no noun or pronoun like λέγουσαι καὶ ὀπτασίαν ἀγγέλων ἑωρακέναι *saying also that they had seen a vision of angels.* But often the predicate adjective or pronoun appears in the nominative in agreement with the subject of the verb like φάσκοντες εἶναι σοφοί (Rom. 1:22) *alleging that they were wise.* So we translate it into English, but the Greek idiom really is "alleging being wise" with a predicate nominative like ἐμαρτυρήθη εἶναι δίκαιος (Heb. 11:4) *he was testified to be righteous.* See also Rom. 9:3. But this construction with the nominative was only possible when the subject of the principal verb was under discussion like Jas. 1:26 εἴ τις δοκεῖ θρησκὸς εἶναι *if any one thinks that he is religious.* Otherwise the noun or pronoun has to be put in the accusative of general reference, but not as the "subject" of the infinitive, for the infinitive is non-finite without personal endings and cannot have a subject any more than the participle can. It is only modern grammarians who try to explain the Greek and Latin idiom by the translations into modern languages who talk about the subject of the infinitive. The construction of the infinitive in indirect discourse is only one of the ways that the Greek uses. The ὅτι clause gives us little trouble, for it is closely parallel to the direct and to the English or other modern languages. But the infinitive construction is different. What was the subject of the direct clause when rendered by the infinitive construction, if different from the subject of the principal verb, has to be put in the accusative of general reference, a perfectly neat Greek idiom, but miserable English or German. Take Lu. 24:23 λέγουσιν αὐτὸν ζῆν *they affirm being alive as to him*. That is what the infinitive construction means where the ὅτι construction would have λέγουσιν ὅτι ζῇ *they affirm that he is alive*. It is absurd to try to explain one construction by the other. They are wholly different ways of rendering the direct assertion into the indirect. In English we have only the one idiom. We have to say in both cases: *They affirm that he is alive.* But the Greek has its own greater freedom and variety and has no concern whatever about our difficulty in rendering the infinitive idiom into English or German. Sometimes this accusative of general reference occurs where the nominative in apposition with the subject is possible as πέποιθας σεαυτὸν ὁδηγὸν εἶναι τυφλῶν (Rom. 2:19) *thou art confident that thou thyself art a guide for the blind.* Here αὐτὸς ὁδηγὸς would have been perfectly proper. See also Phil. 3:13; Rom. 6:11; Heb. 10:34. The necessity for the accusative of general reference can be seen clearly in the articular infinitive like Lu. 2:27 |ἐν τῷ εἰσαγαγεῖν τοὺς γονεῖς τὸ παιδίον Ἰησοῦν *in the bringing the child Jesus as to the parents (when the parents brought the child Jesus).* Note the three accusatives with τοῦ διδάσκειν (Heb. 5:12). The article has to be preserved in a literal translation. The negative of the infinitive in indirect discourse is μή as in Mk. 12:18 οἵτινες λέγουσιν ἀνάστασιν μὴ εἶναι *who say that there is no resurrection.*

(c) *The Participle.*

According to the ancient idiom verbs of knowing, perceiving, showing, etc., may have the participle in indirect assertion. See ὁρῶ σε ὄντα (Acts 8:23) *I see thee being (I see that thou art*), ἀκούσας ὄντα σιτία εἰς Αἴγυπτον (Acts 7:12) *hearing of food being in Egypt (hearing that food was in Egypt)*. The aorist tense pictures the single act like ἐθεώρουν τὸν Σατανᾶν πεσόντα (Lu. 10:18) *I was beholding Satan fall*, while the perfect gives a state of completion like ἔγνων δύναμιν ἐξεληλυθυῖαν ἀπ' ἐμοῦ (Lu. 8:46) *I felt power gone from me*. 'Ακούω is found with ὅτι, the infinitive, or the participle as are γινώσκω and οἶδα. Θεωρέω occurs with ὅτι or the participle.

452. *Indirect Question.*

(a) *The Person.*

The person often has to be changed. In Matt. 6:31 we have τί φάγωμεν; *What are we to eat?* In the indirect form the first person is changed to the second in Matt. 6:25 μὴ μεριμνᾶτε τί φάγητε *stop being anxious what ye are to eat*. So in Mk. 9:6 οὐ γὰρ ᾔδει τί ἀποκριθῇ *for he did not know what he was to answer*. Τί ἀποκριθῶ (*what am I to answer?*) was the original and so the first person has been changed to the third.

(b) *The Tense.*

Usually the same tense appears in the indirect that was used in the direct as ἐπυνθάνετο ποῦ γεννᾶται (Matt. 2:4) *he began to inquire where he was to be born*, ἐθεώρουν ποῦ τέθειται (Mk. 15:47) *they beheld where he had been laid*. Sometimes there is a change of tense as in Jo. 2:25 αὐτὸς γὰρ ἐγίνωσκεν τί ἦν ἐν τῷ ἀνθρώπῳ *for he knew what was in man*.

(c) *The Mode.*

As a rule the same mode is retained. The indicative remains indicative as in ἦλθον ἰδεῖν τί ἐστιν τὸ γεγονός (Mk. 5:14) *they came to see what it was that had happened*. The subjunctive remains subjunctive like οὐ γὰρ ᾔδει τί ἀποκριθῇ (Mk. 9:6). A subjunctive in an indirect question is always so because it was so in the direct. Indirect discourse in Greek never changes the indicative into the subjunctive. The optative with ἄν remains so as ἐνένευον τὸ τί ἂν θέλοι (Lu. 1:62) like τί ἄν θέλοι; of the direct in Acts 17:18. When the optative with ἄν occurs in an indirect question it was so in the direct question as in Lu. 9:46. In Lu. 3:15 μήποτε αὐτὸς εἴη ὁ χριστὸς *whether he was the Messiah* we have ἐστίν changed to εἴη according to the ancient idiom. So elsewhere Luke followed the ancient idiom and changed an indicative to an optative like ἤρξαντο συνζητεῖν τὸ τίς ἄρα εἴη (Lu. 22:23) *they began to question as to which was*, though in verse 24 he keeps τὸ τίς δοκεῖ (not δοκοίη) *as to who seemed*. In Acts 21:33 both modes occur. So occasionally the subjunctive is changed by Luke to the optative with εἰ as in Acts 17:27 εἰ ἄρα γε ψηλαφήσειαν αὐτὸν καὶ εὕροιεν *if haply they might feel after him and find him*. This conditional clause is like an indirect question in structure. The deliberate subjunctive is usually retained after a secondary clause as in Lu. 5:19. In 2 Tim. 2:25 μήποτε δώῃ (optative) occurs after a primary tense. The indirect deliberate question may be dependent on a verb like ἔχω as ὅπως σχῶ τί γράψω (Acts 25:26) *that I may get what to write*. So also Lu. 9:58 and with ὅπου in Mk. 14:14.

(d) *The Use of the Article.*

Several examples have been noted of Luke's fondness for the article in indirect questions (Lu. 1:62; 22:2, 4, 23, 24). Take 22:2 ἐζήτουν τὸ πῶς ἀνέλωσιν *they were seeking the how to kill him*. The article makes it plain that syntactically the subordinate clause sustains a case relation to the principal clause. Here the indirect question is in the accusative case, the object of the verb ἐζήτουν.

453. *Indirect Command.*

There are three ways of changing a direct command to the indirect. Some find it a bit difficult to catch this idiom.

(a) *The Infinitive.*

This is the most common way and it must be distinguished sharply from the infinitive in indirect assertion. Thus in

Acts 21:21 λέγων μὴ περιτέμνειν αὐτοὺς τὰ τέκνα μηδὲ τοῖς ἔθεσιν περιπατεῖν indirect assertion means *saying that they do not circumcise their children nor walk in the customs,* an expression of opinion on the part of Paul. But that is clearly not the ground of complaint against Paul. The point is that Paul forbade the Jews to circumcise their children. In the direct it was μὴ περιτέμνετε *do not circumcise,* not οὐ περιτέμνουσιν *they do not circumcise.* So also in Acts 21:4 ἔλεγον διὰ τοῦ πνεύματος μὴ ἐπιβαίνειν *they said by the Spirit for him not to go.*

(b) *The Conjunctions* ἵνα *and* ὅπως.

These are used with a finite verb like the sub-final clause. So παρήγγειλεν αὐτοῖς ἵνα μηδὲν αἴρωσιν (Mk. 6:8) *he charged them that they take nothing,* αἰτούμενοι ὅπως μεταπέμψηται αὐτόν (Acts 25:3) *begging that he send after him.*

(c) *The Deliberative Question.*

A direct command like φοβήθητε (Lu. 12:5) may be put in the indirect form by the deliberative subjunctive like ὑποδείξω τίνα φοβηθῆτε (Verse 4) *I will show you whom ye are to fear.*

454. *Mixture.*

Sometimes one part of the sentence will be changed to the indirect and the other part retained in the direct. So in Acts 1:4 παρήγγειλεν αὐτοῖς—περιμένειν τὴν ἐπαγγελίαν τοῦ πατρὸς ἣν ἠκούσατέ μου *he commanded them to wait for the promise of the Father which ye received from me.* Here "which ye received from me" was not changed to the indirect form. See the same thing in Acts 23:22 where the change is also from the indirect to the direct (ἐκλαλῆσαι—ἐνεφάνισας). In the next verse the change is from the direct ('Ετοιμάσατε) to the indirect (παραστῆσαι). In Acts 27:10 there is a mixture of the ὅτι construction with the infinitive (ὅτι—μέλλειν). The subordinate clause as a rule retains the mode and tense as ὅσα ἔχει in Matt. 18:25 after ἐκέλευσεν πραθῆναι and ἕως οὗ ἀπολύσῃ in Matt. 14:22 after ἠνάγκασεν προάγειν. The exception is πρὶν ἢ ἔχοι—λάβοι in Acts 25:16.

CHAPTER XXXIII

THE INFINITIVE

455. *The History of the Infinitive.*

(a) *The Origin of the Infinitive.*

The original forms were either in the locative (–ενι) or the dative case like δοῦναι (δόϝεναι) like the Sanskrit *davane* and meant "for giving." The forms in –αι, –σθαι, –ναι are all in the dative case. These verbal substantives in the Sanskrit had no voice or tense. This original dative idea is preserved in some of the uses of the Greek infinitive with the idea of purpose as τί ἐξήλθατε εἰς τὴν ἔρημον θεάσασθαι; *What went ye out into the wilderness to see?* The old English has it "for to see." So also ἤλθομεν προσκυνῆσαι (Matt. 2:2) *we came to see* (for seeing). In the –ειν(–ενι) form the case is probably locative. In Sanskrit the substantival idea is dominant over the verbal and this is largely true in Homer.

(b) *Disregard of the Case Idea of the Endings.*

Already in Homer the infinitive begins to be used in any case without regard to the form, no longer as a true dative or a true locative. These forms remain, but the infinitive occurs in Homer as the subject or the object of verbs, just as in Matt. 18:8 καλόν σοί ἐστιν εἰσελθεῖν *it is good for thee to enter*, where the locative form εἰσελθεῖν is the subject of καλόν ἐστιν. The infinitive is treated as an indeclinable substantive in a fixed case-form. So in Matt. 5:34 ἐγὼ λέγω ὑμῖν μὴ ὀμόσαι *I say unto you not to swear*, where the dative form ὀμόσαι is the direct object (accusative case) of λέγω. So the infinitive may be in the genitive as ἔλαχε τοῦ θυμιᾶσαι (Lu. 1:9) *he obtained by lot the burning incense*, or the ablative as κατεῖχον αὐτὸν τοῦ πορεύεσθαι (Lu. 4:42) *they tried to hinder him from going*, the instrumental as τῷ μὴ εὑρεῖν με Τίτον (2 Cor. 2:13) *by my not finding Titus*, the locative as ἐν τῷ χρονίζειν ἐν τῷ ναῷ αὐτόν (Lu. 1:21) *in the delaying in the temple as to him*, besides the common dative like ἤλθομεν προσκυνῆσαι (Matt. 2:2).

(c) *The Articular Infinitive.*

Pindar first used the article with the infinitive as the subject of the verb. Homer did not so use it. But the article did not make the infinitive a substantive, as Winer mistakenly said, for it was already that. The use of the article merely made plainer the substantival aspect of the infinitive and treated it like any other substantive, using the article, when needed, to make it definite, not to make it a substantive. Homer, it may be recalled, made very little use of the article with anything. The infinitive is indeclinable and neuter and occurs only in the singular number, but the article with the infinitive is inflected regularly and serves to make plain the case of the infinitive when it is used. So with τὸ θέλειν παράκειταί μοι (Rom. 7:18) *the wishing is present with me* where θέλειν is the subject of παράκειται, as in Phil. 2:6 οὐχ ἡγήσατο τὸ εἶναι ἴσα θεῷ *he did not consider the being equal with God* we have the accusative case made clear, the object of ἡγήσατο. In Heb. 2:15 διὰ παντὸς τοῦ ζῆν we have the pronoun πᾶς as well as the article with ζῆν *through all the living*.

(d) *In the κοινή.*

The articular infinitive is still common, but the infinitive as a whole begins to disappear before ἵνα and ὅτι with finite verbs. The use of ὅτι for declarative clauses (subject and object) began to displace this common use of the infinitive while ἵνα did this also to some extent and in particular expressed the idea of purpose. In the κοινή we find ἵνα with βούλομαι and δύναμαι in Polybius (literary κοινή) just as we have ἵνα with θέλω in the New Testament like ὅσα ἐὰν θέλητε ἵνα ποιῶσιν οἱ ἄνθρωποι (Matt. 7:12) *whatever ye wish that men do to you.* But the use of τοῦ and the infinitive increased considerably. It existed already with the ablative use of the infinitive like ἐκρατοῦντο τοῦ μὴ ἐπιγνῶναι (Lu. 24:16) *they were restrained from recognizing* and with the genitive to express purpose like ζητεῖν τοῦ ἀπολέσαι (Matt. 2:13) *to seek to destroy.* In Lu. 1:76 both ἑτοιμάσαι and τοῦ δοῦναι express purpose. We have seen that τοῦ and the infinitive may even express result as with τοῦ μὴ εἶναι in Rom. 7:3. The use of τοῦ with the infinitive is very common in the LXX because of the Hebrew infinitive construct which it is used to translate. That fact explains part of its frequency in the New Testament. It occurs with substantives like ἐλπὶς τοῦ σώζεσθαι (Acts 27:20) *hope of being saved,* with adjectives like βραδεῖς τοῦ πιστεῦσαι (Lu. 24:25) *slow in believing,* or with verbs like μετεμελήθητε τοῦ πιστεῦσαι (Matt. 21:32) *repented so as to believe.* But the strangest of all is it to find τοῦ with the infinitive used as the subject like ἀνένδεκτόν ἐστιν τοῦ τὰ σκάνδαλα μὴ ἐλθεῖν (Lu. 17:1) *it is impossible for stumbling blocks not to come* (cf. also Acts 10:25). Here τοῦ seems to be regarded as a fixed case-form like the original infinitive forms.

(e) *In the Modern Greek.*

The culmination is reached here where the infinitive has vanished save as an auxiliary verb in a mutilated form like θέλει λύσει. It is otherwise dead outside of the Pontic dialect. So we have seen the rise and the fall of the Greek infinitive.

456. *A Verbal Substantive.*

The infinitive, therefore, is both substantive and verb at the same time. It is a hybrid and has to be looked at from both sides to understand it. It is an indeclinable substantive, but is used in any case in the singular number except the vocative, with or without the article. As a verb it expresses action and governs cases and came to have voice to a certain extent, but without the power to relate the action to the subject, for it has no subject and no personal endings. See εἶπεν δοθῆναι αὐτῇ φαγεῖν (Mk. 5:43) *he bade that something be given her to eat.* It is thus not a mode. There is tense with the three ideas of tense (punctiliar, durative, state of completion). It has no time except in indirect discourse where it represents the direct, as with χωρήσειν (Jo. 21:25) where the future infinitive represents the future indicative and τεθνηκέναι (Acts 14:19) the perfect indicative of the direct. The aorist infinitive is the normal one to use as with γέγραπται παθεῖν τὸν χριστὸν καὶ ἀναστῆναι ἐκ νεκρῶν ἐν τῇ τρίτῃ ἡμέρᾳ καὶ κηρυχθῆναι (Lu. 24:46) *it is written for the Messiah to suffer and to rise from the dead on the third day and be preached* (three aorists). When the present infinitive occurs it is to stress the idea of linear action as in 1 Jo. 3:9 οὐ δύναται ἁμαρτάνειν *he is not able to go on sinning.* When the perfect infinitive occurs the state of completion is accented as ἀπολελύσθαι ἐδύνατο (Acts 26:32) *he could have been set free for good.* Each time both aspects of the infinitive are to be observed (substantival and verbal). The infinitive may sometimes be periphrastic like the verb as ἐν τῷ εἶναι αὐτὸν προσευχόμενον (Lu. 9:18) *in the praying as to him* (while he was praying).

457. Uses of the Infinitive.

Most of these have already been indicated, but a summary is wise.

(a) As Subject or Object of Verbs.

So τὸ ζῆν χριστός (Phil. 1:21) *living is Christ* (subject nominative) and ἐπαιτεῖν αἰσχύνομαι (Lu. 16:3) *I am ashamed to beg* (object). The shadow of ἵνα is over the infinitive, but it survives like δύναται δουλεύειν (Matt. 6:24) *is able to serve.*

(b) The Epexegetical and Appositional Infinitive.

This a common idiom with verbs and nouns like ἀπέχεσθαι in Acts 15:28 in apposition with τῶν ἐπάναγκες, ἐπισκέπτεσθαι in Jas. 1:27 in apposition with θρησκεία, τὸ μὴ τιθέναι in Rom. 14:13 in apposition with τοῦτο, ποιεῖν in Rom. 1:28 epexegetical of παρέδωκεν. So with μνησθῆναι in Lu. 1:54. The infinitive can follow a substantive like ὁρμὴ ὑβρίσαι (Acts 14:5) *a rush to mistreat* or an adjective like ἱκανὸς λῦσαι (Mk. 1:7) *fit to loosen.*

(c) *Purpose and Result.*

Sufficient examples have already been given, but note καταλῦσαι for purpose (Matt. 5:17) *to destroy* and ψεύσασθαι for result (Acts 5:3). The infinitive in Lu. 20:11f προσέθετο πέμψαι is a plain Hebraism and should be so explained. The use of ὥστε with the infinitive for design as in Lu. 4:29 and result as in 1 Thess. 1:8 has been noted in the chapter on Consecutive Clauses. The use of ὡς with the infinitive also occurs twice ὡς ἑτοιμάσαι (Lu. 9:52) *so as to make ready and* ὡς ἔπος εἰπεῖν (Heb. 7:9) *so to speak.* Once also ὡς ἂν ἐκφοβεῖν (2 Cor. 10:9) *as if to frighten.*

(d) *With Prepositions.*

The prepositions found in the New Testament with the articular infinitive (article necessary to show that not preposition in composition with the infinitive) are numerous. An illustration of each follows: ἀντὶ τοῦ λέγειν (Jas. 4:15) *instead of saying,* διὰ τὸ μὴ ἔχειν (Matt. 13:5) *because of not having,* βραδὺς εἰς τὸ λαλῆσαι (Jas. 1:19) *slow for speaking,* ἐν τῷ σπείρειν αὐτόν (Lu. 8:5) *while he was sowing,* ἕνεκεν τοῦ φανερωθῆναι (2 Cor. 7:12) *for the sake of being manifested,* ἐκ τοῦ ἔχειν (2 Cor. 8:11) *out of the having,* ἕως τοῦ ἐλθεῖν (Acts 8:40) *until the coming,* μετὰ τὸ δειπνῆσαι (Lu. 22:20) *after the dining,* πρὸ τοῦ με παθεῖν (Lu. 22:15) *before I suffer,* πρὸς τὸ θεαθῆναι (Matt. 6:1) *with a view to be seen.*

(e) *Absolutely.*

The common absolute infinitive in greetings in letters, so abundant in the papyri, appears in Jas. 1:1 Ἰάκωβος χαίρειν and also in Acts 15:23 χαίρειν *greeting.* Another absolute use of the infinitive is as an imperative like στοιχεῖν in Phil. 3:16

to go on walking (let us walk) and κλαίειν in Rom. 12:15 *to weep* (weep).

(f) *The Negative.*

The negative for the infinitive is μή even in indirect assertion as in Mk. 12:18 οἵτινες λέγουσιν ἀνάστασιν μὴ εἶναι *who say that there is no resurrection.* Sometimes οὐ occurs, but it is the negative of a single phrase for contrast, not the negative of the infinitive. So καὶ οὐ κατὰ τὴν τάξιν ᾿Ααρὼν λέγεσθαι (Heb. 7:11) *and to be called not after the order of Aaron.*

CHAPTER XXXIV

THE PARTICIPLE

458. *Verbals in* −τος *and* −τέος.

These verbals are not exactly participles since they do not have tense and voice. They are made from verb stems, not from tense stems. The verbal in −τος is more like an adjective while that in −τέος is more like a verb. In the New Testament there is only one verbal in −τέος which is impersonal, expresses necessity, and governs the accusative here, οἶνον νέον εἰς ἀσκοὺς καινοὺς βλητέον (Lu. 5:38) *new wine must be put into fresh wine skins.* Homer did not use the −τέος form. The verbal in −τος is very common and is like the Latin −*tus* as γνωτός (*notus*), ἄγνωτος or ἄγνωστος (*ignotus*). It occurs in both the active and the passive sense. In fact, it is neither active nor passive, but it depends on the verb root. So ἀγαπητός means *beloved* (Matt. 3:17), but ζεστός (Rev. 3:15) *boiling* is active. The passive use is much the more frequent.

459. *The History of the Participle.*

(a) *In Homer and Hesiod.*

It is further developed than the infinitive. In the Sanskrit the participle already had tenses. But it was the Greek that developed the participle to its glory and became a participle loving language (Broadus) mainly by preserving the aorist participle which died in the Sanskrit and the Latin. But it was the historians and orators like Herodotus, Thucydides, Xenophon, Plato, and Demosthenes, who brought the participle to its full usage.

(b)　*In the* κοινή.

Writers of the literary κοινή like Polybius, Strabo, and Plutarch preserve the power of the participle, while the vernacular found it a bit clumsy. In the New Testament the more literary writers like Luke and the author of Hebrews use it most while the Epistles (except 1 Peter) and Revelation show it least.

The more literary the participle became, the less it was used in the vernacular. It is not dead in the Modern Greek, like the infinitive, but it is dying. Conjunctions and finite verbs take the place of the circumstantial participle there.

460.　*The Participle a Verbal Adjective.*

(a)　*Both Adjective and Verb.*

Like the infinitive which is a verbal substantive the participle is a verbal adjective. The name participle (*pars, capio*) means to take part, that is to say, the participle participates in both verb and adjective. But the infinitive participates in both verb and substantive and so deserves the name participle, while the participle is just as non-finite as the infinitive. The names are thus not at all distinctive, but we have to use them. Like the infinitive the participle is not a mode and has no personal endings and makes no affirmation. Hence voice does not relate the action to a subject strictly speaking. It has tense and governs cases like the verb. As an adjective it is declined with all genders in the singular and the plural. Every participle is both adjective and verb. Sometimes like other adjectives (τὸ ἀγαθόν for instance) the articular participle is used as a substantive like πώλησόν σου τὰ ὑπάρχοντα (Matt. 19:21) *sell thy belongings.*

(b)　*As an Adjective either Attributive or Predicate.*

Like other adjectives every participle is either attributive or predicate. The articular participle, which is very common, is always attributive like τῇ ὑγιαινούσῃ διδασκαλίᾳ (1 Tim. 1:10)

the healthful teaching. The article occurs with the participle
a few times in Homer. Often the articular participle is the
equivalent of a relative clause, though not in form, like ὁ
κλέπτων (Eph. 4:28) *the one who steals.* We even find πᾶς
ὁ ὀργιζόμενος (Matt. 5:22) *every one who is angry.* Sometimes
the article is repeated with the participle like τὸ ὕδωρ τὸ ζῶν
(Jo. 4:11) *the water the living.* The article may be used with
the participle when not with the substantive as in σοφίαν τὴν ἀποκε-
κρυμμένην (1 Cor. 2:7) *wisdom the hidden.* The participle may be
attributive without the article like ὕδωρ ζῶν (Jo. 4:10) *living
water.* But without the article the participle is most likely
to be predicate like βλέπετε ἐγγίζουσαν τὴν ἡμέραν (Heb. 10:25)
ye behold the day drawing nigh, ἐθεώρουν τὸν Σατανᾶν πεσόντα
(Lu. 10:18) *I beheld Satan fall.* The predicate participle calls
for more discussion than the predicate adjective because of
the verbal force of the participle. There are two kinds of
the predicate participle (1) supplementary or complementary
(2) circumstantial. Special discussion will be given directly to
these two aspects of the predicate participle.

(c) *As a Verb with Voice and Tense.*

Originally the infinitive had "no voice distinction" (Moulton,
Prolegomena, p. 203), but it did come to have it except the
lack of personal endings. So did the participle. The participle is constantly used to help out voice and tense in the
periphrastic forms. So ἔσεσθε μισούμενοι (Matt. 10:22) *ye shall
be hated* for the periphrastic future passive and ἔσεσθε λαλοῦντες
(1 Cor. 14:9) *ye shall be speaking* for the periphrastic future
with middle and active voices combined. But tense is a
more important matter than voice with the participle. The
aorist participle is punctiliar of course, and is either simultaneous like κατήντησαν ἀσπασάμενοι (Acts 25:13) *they came
down saluting* (when they arrived, effective aorist κατήντησαν)
or antecedent by suggestion like πωλήσας ἤνεγκεν (Acts 4:37)
having sold brought (or *sold and brought*). The aorist participle is never used for subsequent action. No such example

has ever been found, not even διῆλθον κωλυθέντες (Acts. 16:6) *they passed through having been hindered.* The articular aorist participle may be used with any tense, even with the future like ὁ ὑπομείνας σωθήσεται (Matt. 10:22) *he that endures shall be saved.* The present participle expresses linear action and can be used with a verb in the past, present, or future. So πωλοῦντες ἔφερον (Acts 4:34) *they selling brought from time to time* (repeated action) and μεριμνῶν δύναται (Matt. 6:27) *being anxious is able.* In Jo. 9:25 by the use of ἄρτι the present participle is made to refer to past time τυφλὸς ὢν ἄρτι βλέπω *being blind (once blind) I now see.* Sometimes the present participle has a future sense of purpose like ἀπέστειλαν καλοῦντες (Mk. 3:31) *they sent calling.* In Matt. 10:22, as already noted, we have the present participle with a future indicative. The perfect participle gives the state of completion like κεκοπιακώς in Jo. 4:6 *worn out.* Note the difference between ὁ εἰληφώς in Matt. 25:24 and ὁ λαβών in verse 20. There is a periphrastic perfect participle in Eph. 4:18 ἐσκοτισμένοι ὄντες *being in a darkened state.* Note the difference between πεπτωκότα in Rev. 9:1, πεσόντα in Lu. 10:18, and πίπτοντες in Mk. 13:25. In Acts 25:10 ἑστώς εἰμι we have a periphrastic present, though perfect in form, for ἑστώς has lost its "perfect" idea. The future participle is rare in the New Testament. It was never developed in the Boeotian dialect. It is articular in τὸ ἐσόμενον (Lu. 22:49) *that which was to be.* The future participle has only relative time and occurs with the idea of purpose after a past tense like ἐληλύθει προσκυνήσων (Acts 8:27) *he had come to worship.*

461. *The Supplementary Participle.*

This use of the predicate participle serves to complete the idea of the principal verb which would not otherwise be clear. It thus differs sharply from the circumstantial participle which is a sort of loose *addendum* to the sentence. The supplementary participle is nothing like so common in the New Testament as the circumstantial.

(a) *The Periphrastic Conjugation.*

This idiom is common, rather more so in the vernacular than in the literary Attic, and in the New Testament an increase due also to the influence of the LXX and the Aramaic fondness for the idiom. Luke, in particular, is fond of it, as ἦν ˙διδάσκων (Lu. 13:10) *he was teaching,* ἦν συνκύπτουσα καὶ μὴ δυναμένη ἀνακύψαι (verse 11) *she was bending together and not able to bend back.* In Lu. 23:12 we even have προϋπῆρχον ὄντες *they had been before.* The idiom in ἔχε με παρῃτημένον (Lu. 14:18) *hold me excused* is rather different, though a predicate supplementary use of the participle.

(b) *In Distinction from the Infinitive.*

Some verbs use either the infinitive or the participle but with a different idea. The infinitive connects the action with the verb like ἐπαιτεῖν αἰσχύνομαι (Lu. 16:3) *I am ashamed to beg* (and so can not do it), while ἐπαιτῶν αἰσχύνομαι would connect the action with the individual and would mean *begging I am ashamed* (and so shall stop it). The same thing is true of παύομαι which occurs only with the participle (or absolutely) as οὐκ ἐπαύοντο διδάσκοντες (Acts 5:42) *they did not cease teaching* (which they were actually doing). In 1 Cor. 13:8 παύσονται is used absolutely. The ablative infinitive occurs with καταπαύω as in Acts 14:18 κατέπαυσαν τοῦ μὴ θύειν *they ceased from offering sacrifice.* Ἄρχομαι occurs only with the infinitive as in Matt. 4:17 ἤρξατο κηρύσσειν *he began to preach* or absolutely as in Lu. 24:27 ἀρξάμενος *beginning.* In Matt. 11:1 we have ἐτέλεσεν ὁ Ἰησοῦς διατάσσων *Jesus finished commanding.* A good illustration of the supplementary participle occurs in ἵνα φανῶσιν νηστεύοντες *that they may appear to be fasting.* In the New Testament τυγχάνω and φθάνω do not occur with the infinitive or the participle. However προφθάνω does have the ancient idiom once as προέφθασεν λέγων (Matt. 17:25) *spake first,* where the principal idea is in the participle. But the infinitive occurs in Mk. 14:8 προέλαβεν μυρίσαι *she anointed beforehand.* Once also we find ἔλαθον ξενίσαντες (Heb. 13:2) *entertained unawares*, the old idiom with λανθάνω. There is a distinct decrease in this use of the supplementary participle in the New Testament.

(c) *In Indirect Discourse.*

This idiom has already been noted in the chapter on Indirect Discourse. Here the participle as an adjective agrees with the substantive or pronoun and completes the idea. The predicate supplementary participle is plain enough where no idea of indirect discourse is involved like τῶν τὰ αἰσθητήρια γεγυμνασμένα ἐχόντων *those who have the perceptions exercised*. This participle is like a predicate accusative (or whatever the case may be). So γινώσκετε Τιμόθεον ἀπολελυμένον (Heb. 13:23) *know Timothy set free* (*as one set free*, that Timothy is set free, we say in English), ὃ ὁμολογεῖ 'Ιησοῦν χριστὸν ἐν σαρκὶ ἐληλυθότα *which confesses Jesus Christ come in the flesh* (that Jesus Christ has come in the flesh, we say). See the difference in idea between the participle with ἀκούω in 2 Thess. 3:11 ἀκούομεν γάρ τινας περιπατοῦντας ἐν ὑμῖν ἀτάκτως *for we hear of some walking disorderly among you* and the infinitive with ἀκούω in Jo. 12:18 ἤκουσαν τοῦτο αὐτὸν πεποιηκέναι τὸ σημεῖον *they heard that he had done this sign.*

(d) *The Hebraistic Intensifying Participle.*

This is an effort in the LXX to reproduce the Hebrew infinitive absolute εὐλογῶν εὐλογήσω (Heb. 6:14 quoted from LXX, Gen. 22:17). One may compare θανάτῳ τελευτάτω (Matt. 15:4) *let him die the death,* another effort to translate the same Hebrew idiom.

462. *The Circumstantial Participle.*

This use of the participle is practically an additional clause like a subordinate clause with a conjunction. But the addition is made in a free manner without the sharp precision of the conjunctions. The point of contact may be with the subject, object, or any substantive or pronoun in the principal clause, or an entirely independent construction.

(a) Varieties of the Circumstantial Participle.

In fact there are no varieties, but the loose way in which the participle is added allows much liberty in the resultant idea. The participle does not mean time, manner, purpose, or anything of the kind. The context alone can indicate those shades of resultant meaning. For convenience we may note examples. In Jo. 16:8 note the so-called *temporal* participle ἐλθὼν ἐκεῖνος ἐλέγξει *he coming will rebuke*. *Manner* may be illustrated by Matt. 19:22 ἀπῆλθεν λυπούμενος *he went away grieved*. *Means* is indicated in Matt. 6:27 τίς μεριμνῶν δύναται; *Who by being anxious is able?* The idea of *cause* is in Col. 1:4 εὐχαριστοῦμεν ἀκούσαντες *we give thanks having heard*. *Occasion* is suggested in Lu. 4:28 ἐπλήσθησαν θυμοῦ ἀκούοντες *they were filled with wrath on hearing*. The notion of *purpose* appears in Acts 8:27 ἐληλύθει προσκυνήσων *he had come to worship*. *Condition* is suggested in Rom. 2:27 κρινεῖ ἡ ἀκροβυστία τελοῦσα *the uncircumcision will judge fulfilling* (if it fulfill). *Concession* is the idea in Heb. 5:8 καίπερ ὢν υἱός *though a son*. The range and freedom of the Greek participle is thus seen clearly.

(b) The Genitive Absolute.

In Latin it is the ablative absolute (or locative or instrumental). The Sanskrit uses the locative and modern Greek the nominative. This Greek idiom is either genitive absolute or ablative absolute. Usually the substantive or pronoun is one not occurring in the principal clause like Acts 12:18 γενομένης ἡμέρας *day having come*. Sometimes the genitive absolute occurs where there is a noun or pronoun in the sentence for it to agree with as αὐτοῦ ἐνθυμηθέντος—ἐφάνη αὐτῷ where the participle could have been ἐνθυμηθέντι in agreement with αὐτῷ. Then again the genitive absolute may occur without a noun or pronoun like ἐλθόντος καὶ κρούσαντος (Lu. 12:36) where it is plain that Peter is meant. In Matt. 1:18

the genitive absolute actually occurs where the participle could have been in the nominative. On the other hand in Rev. 2:26 ὁ τηρῶν δώσω αὐτῷ there is anacoluthon with the nominative absolute of the participle.

(c) *The Accusative Absolute.*

Τυχόν (1 Cor. 16:6) is an instance, though used as an adverb perhaps, from τυχών. In Acts 2:29 ἐστίν is to be supplied with ἐξόν as it occurs with δέον in Acts 19:36 and so ἐξὸν ἦν in Matt. 12:4. But we probably have the accusative absolute in Acts 26:3 γνώστην ὄντα σε *thee being an expert*, though ἐπὶ σοῦ comes just before.

(d) *Adjuncts with the Participle.*

These do not alter the real force of the participle at all, but simply sharpen the point a bit. So εἰσελθοῦσα εὐθύς (Mk. 6:25) *coming in straightway*, ἅμα ἐλπίζων (Acts 24:26) *at the same time hoping*, καίπερ ὤν (Heb. 5:8) *although being*, ὡς διασκορπίζων (Lu. 16:1) *as squandering* (where ὡς gives the *alleged* reason whether true or false), ὥσπερ φερομένης πνοῆς βιαίας (Acts 2:2) *as if a rushing wind borne*, σύ ποτε ἐπιστρέψας (Lu. 22:32) *thou once having turned, etc.*

(e) *The Independent Participle.*

The nominative absolute (*nominativus pendens*) we have just seen in Rev. 2:26, an anacoluthon. But there are instances where the participle stands alone in the midst of imperatives as if an 'imperative like ἀποστυγοῦντες τὸ πονηρόν, κολλώμενοι τῷ ἀγαθῷ (Rom. 12:9) *abhorring the evil, cleaving to the good*, and also like φρονοῦντες in verse 16. This idiom occurs in the ancient Greek, in the papyri, and in the inscriptions.

463. *Negatives.*

As a rule it is μή as μὴ εὑρόντες (Acts 17:6) *not finding*. In the older Greek οὐ was the usual negative with the participle save in conditional or concessive clauses. But in the κοινή, as the papyri show, it is the other way. Οὐ does not occur except where there is a strong negation or for contrast. In Matt. 22:11 we find οὐκ ἐνδεδυμένον ἔνδυμα γάμου *not clothed with a wedding garment* (an actual case), while in verse 12 we have μὴ ἔχων ἔνδυμα γάμου *not having a wedding garment* (the hypothetical argument). In 1 Pet. 1:8 note the distinction between οὐκ ἰδόντες *not having seen* (actual case) and μὴ ὁρῶντες *not seeing,* (conceived case).

CHAPTER XXXV

NEGATIVE PARTICLES

464. *The History of the Negative Particles.*

(a) *Simple and Compound.*

Greek has two negatives that are used simply (οὐ, μή) or in various compounds (οὐδέ, οὔτε, οὐδείς, οὐθείς, οὐκέτι, οὔποτε, etc., and so for compounds of μή, μηδέ, etc.). Latin has three negatives (*non, ne, haud*). The Sanskrit has *na* and *ma*. Greek did not use *na* (*ne*) and Latin did not use μή (*ma*). *Haud* and οὐ are probably the same word (cf. Zend *ava*). In the Boeotian dialect οὐ never was employed. In Homer indeed μή was freely used with the indicative and οὐ sometimes with the subjunctive. The history of οὐ and μή has been the constant increase of the use of μή. In the modern Greek δέν (for οὐδέν) is only used with the indicative. Perhaps the earliest use of μή was to express prohibition. For the form οὐθέν see 1 Cor. 13:2; Acts 19:27.

(b) *Objective* οὐ *and Subjective* μή.

In general the New Testament uses the negative οὐ and μή in accordance with the idiom of the earlier Greek. The distinction is well observed between the outright negation by οὐ and the subtle and subjective μή. In the Sanskrit the same distinction existed between *na* and *ma*. In English we have to depend on the tone of voice for the difference, but we all know the difference between "no" and "no". Οὐ is direct, positive, categorical, definite; μή is doubtful, indirect, indefinite, hypothetical. Μή is a negative with "a string tied to it." If a girl should say οὐ to a proposal of marriage (especially οὐχί) there would be little hope. But μή would leave room for another trial. The bluntness of οὐ in its strengthened form οὐχί is well shown in Luke 1:60. On the other hand μή in Jo. 4:29 (μήτι οὗτός ἐστιν ὁ χριστός;) but dimly conceals the woman's real conviction about Jesus.

465. *With the Imperative.*

With the imperative therefore μή is the logical, even the necessary, negative as μή μοι κόπους πάρεχε (Lu. 11:7). This is uniform except where parenthetic clauses or sharp contrast is brought out (cf. infinitive). In 1 Pet. 3:3 after ἔστω, οὐχ is set over against ἀλλ'. So also in 1 Pet. 2:18 (implied imperative) we have οὐ μόνον . . . . ἀλλὰ καί. But in Jas. 1:22 μή μόνον is read. In 1 Cor. 5:10 οὐ πάντως is a parenthetical expansion of μὴ συναναμίγνυσθαι So in 2 Tim. 2:14 as to ἐπ' οὐδὲν χρήσιμον and μὴ λογομαχεῖν. In Matt. 5:37 οὒ οὒ is the predicate of ἔστω and with the accented form instead of οὐ. In Rev. 22:9 (ὅρα μή) μή is a conjunction used without the verb. Cf. our "lookout."

466. *With the Subjunctive.*

With the subjunctive μή is also naturally the negative. But in Homer, before the subjunctive was sharply differentiated from the future indicative οὐ was sometimes employed with the subjunctive. The truth seems to be that μή displaced οὐ with the subjunctive, just as it did finally with the participle. Let μὴ δῶμεν (Mk. 12:15) serve as an example. Cf. Jo. 11:50. Οὐ, however, is used with the subjunctive, when μή is a conjunction, for the sake of distinction. So φοβοῦμαι μή πως ἐλθὼν οὐχ οἵους θέλω εὕρω ὑμᾶς (2 Cor. 12:20). So also the marginal reading of WH in Matt. 25:9 (μήποτε οὐκ ἀρκέσῃ), but the text has μήποτε οὐ μή.

467. *With the Optative.*

With the optative both οὐ and μή appear in the older Greek, οὐ in the conclusion of the fourth-class condition, elsewhere μή. As a matter of fact the optative in the New Testament

has no negative save in the case of wishes where it is always
μή. So μὴ γένοιτο (Rom. 3:4).

468. *With the Infinitive.*

The negative of the infinitive in the New Testament is μή,
even in indirect assertion (Mk. 12:18, μὴ εἶναι), save in fixed
phrases, repeated negatives, or when single words are negatived. In Mk. 7:24 οὐ is used much like the ancient idiom in
indirect assertion, οὐδένα ἤθελεν γνῶναι. In Rom. 15:20 οὐχ
ὅπου ὠνομάσθη χριστός is a parenthetic clause with εὐαγγελίζεσθαι.
So καὶ οὐ after δουλεύειν (Rom. 7:6). Usually we have οὐ
μόνον with the infinitive as in Jo. 11:52 with ἀποθνήσκειν. For
the peculiar position of οὐ μόνον see Rom. 4:12, 16. The New
Testament does not use μὴ οὐ with the infinitive, but simply
μή. So with a verb of hindering, μόλις κατέπαυσαν τοὺς
ὄχλους τοῦ μὴ θύειν αὐτοῖς (Acts 14:18). But μή (redundant μή)
is not necessary in this use of the infinitive as ἐνεκοπτόμην
τὰ πολλὰ τοῦ ἐλθεῖν (Rom. 15:22). When the principal verb
of hindering is negative, the simple infinitive is used as in μὴ
κωλύετε αὐτὰ ἐλθεῖν (Matt. 19:14) or μή may be employed as
μήτι τὸ ὕδωρ δύναται κωλῦσαί τις τοῦ μὴ βαπτισθῆναι; (Acts 10:47).
Note τοῦ sometimes. In 1 Cor. 14:39 observe τὸ λαλεῖν μὴ
κωλύετε. In Acts 4:20 both negatives retain their value, οὐ
δυνάμεθα γὰρ . . . . . . μὴ λαλεῖν.

469. *With the Participle.*

With participles μή is commonly used contrary to ancient
custom, but not contrary to the undefined action of the participle; for instance, Matthew has μή with the participle 18
times and οὐ 2, Luke has μή 28 times and οὐ 2, John has μή 11
and οὐ 1. See the difference between οὐ with the participle
and μή with the participle in 1 Pet. 1:8, οὐκ ἰδόντες and μὴ
ὁρῶντες, one a definite case, the other a general statement.
With the article and the participle μή is also the usual construction as τὰ μὴ διώκοντα (Rom. 9:30), but οὐ appears for a strong
negative as in τὴν οὐκ ἠγαπημένην (Rom. 9:25). Cf. τὸν οὐ λαόν

in the same verse. Cf. ὁ οὐκ ὤν (Jo. 10:12). In the modern Greek μή alone is used with the participle.

470. *With the Indicative.*

With the indicative the matter is much more complicated. In the modern Greek δέν is confined to the indicative, and μή is used elsewhere. But the New Testament still uses μή a good deal with the indicative, though less than in the older Greek. A study of the various aspects of the indicative must therefore be made.

(a) *In Ordinary Declarative Sentences (Simple or Compound).*

The negative of the indicative is οὐ. This is in direct harmony with the idea of the mode. So ὁ πιστεύων εἰς αὐτὸν οὐ κρίνεται (Jo. 3:18).

(b) *In Causal Sentences.*

So likewise οὐ is always found unless the reason is subjective or regarded as specially speculative. The only example of ὅτι μή in the New Testament is in Jo. 3:18, ὁ μὴ πιστεύων ἤδη ὅτι μὴ πεπίστευκεν. With this compare 1 Jo. 5:10 where ὅτι οὐ πεπίστευκεν is read, the usual idiom. Cf. also Heb. 9:17 ἐπεὶ μὴ τότε ἰσχύει, which may, however, be a question.

(c) *Conditional Sentences.*

They usually had εἰ μή and εἰ οὐ rarely in the older Greek. In conditions of the second class (determined as unfulfilled) εἰ μή is uniform even in the New Testament (as εἰ μὴ ἦν etc., Jo. 9:33) except in Mk. 14:21 (Matt. 26:24) where we find εἰ οὐ. Here εἰ οὐκ ἐγεννήθη brings out strongly the force of οὐ. But in first-class conditions (determined as fulfilled), leaving out the elliptical use of εἰ μή (Mk. 9:9) and εἰ μὴ δέ, εἰ οὐ is much more frequent in the New Testament than εἰ μή. In the older Greek εἰ οὐ was used when a single word was negatived or there was sharp contrast. Such examples occur in the New Testament as εἴ τις πνεῦμα χριστοῦ οὐκ ἔχει (Rom. 8:9), εἰ γὰρ ὁ θεὸς . . . . . οὐκ ἐφείσατο (Rom. 11:21). So εἰ καὶ τὸν φοβοῦμαι οὐδὲ ἄνθρωπον ἐντρέπομαι (Lu. 18:4). Cf. Jas. 1:23 (καὶ οὐ ποιητής), 1 Cor. 9:2 (εἰ οὐκ εἰμί). Cf. Jo. 1:25.

(d) In Relative Sentences.

With the indicative οὐ is the usual negative as ὃς οὐ λαμβάνει (Matt. 10:38). But a few examples of μή appear in indefinite relative sentences as ἃ μὴ δεῖ (Tit. 1:11), ᾧ μὴ πάρεστιν ταῦτα (2 Pet. 1:9). So also the text of 1 Jo. 4:3 (WH), ὃ μὴ ὁμολογεῖ (marg. ὃ λύει). Cf. ὃς οὐκ ἔστιν (1 Jo. 4:6).

(e) With Expressions of Purpose.

Here μή is the usual negative as ἵνα μὴ φυσιοῦσθε (1 Cor. 4:6), σκόπει μή ἔστιν (Lu. 11:35), βλέπετε μήποτε ἔσται (Heb. 3:12).

(f) With Verbs of Fearing.

Οὐ is the negative after μή, but no example occurs in the New Testament save 2 Cor. 12:20 where μὴ . . . . . . οὐ is found with the subjunctive. In Greek as in Latin ne μή follows the verb of fearing for the positive idea.

(g) In Questions.

Μή expects the answer "no" as Mk. 14:19 (μήτι ἐγώ;), while οὐ requires the answer "yes" as Lu. 17:17 (οὐχ οἱ δέκα ἐκαθαρίσθησαν;). In 1 Cor. 9:8 we have both in different parts of the same question, μὴ κατὰ ἄνθρωπον ταῦτα λαλῶ, ἢ καὶ ὁ νόμος ταῦτα οὐ λέγει; cf. also μή ἀπώσατο; (Rom. 11:1) and οὐκ ἀπώσατο (Rom. 11:2). Sometimes οὐ μή is found in questions as οὐ μὴ πίω αὐτό; (Jo. 18:11) where the answer is in accordance with οὐ. The negatives do not, of course, express the wide range of feeling and emotion in different situations. In a question like μὴ οὐκ ἔχομεν; (1 Cor. 9:4) μή is the negative of the question and οὐκ of ἔχομεν.

(h) *In Prohibitions.*

When the indicative is used in prohibitions οὐ occurs as in οὐκ ἐπιορκήσεις (Matt. 5:33) or οὐ μή as in οὐ μὴ ἔσται (Matt. 16:22).

(i) *In Indirect Discourse.*

Where the indicative is used, the negative of the direct is retained as πῶς οὐ νοεῖτε ὅτι οὐ περὶ ἄρτων εἶπον ὑμῖν; (Matt. 16:11). Burton (*Moods and Tenses*, p. 181) properly notes the redundant οὐ after the verb "deny," ὁ ἀρνούμενος ὅτι Ἰησοῦς οὐκ ἔστιν (1 Jo. 2:22). Cf. French *ne.*

(j) *The Succession of Negatives.*

In Greek this merely strengthens the first negative if the second is a compound form like οὐδέ, μηδείς etc. This use (just like the old English idiom that survives here and there) is not remarkably frequent, yet a number of examples occur as οὐκ ἔφαγεν οὐδέν (Lu. 4:2), μηδενὶ μηδὲν ὀφείλετε (Rom. 13:8). Even three or more negatives may be found as οὗ οὐκ ἦν οὐδεὶς οὔπω κείμενος (Lu. 23:53), οὐκέτι οὐ μὴ πίω (Mk. 14:25). But sometimes τις follows οὐ as οὐχ ἁρπάσει τις (Jo. 10:28). Cf. 1 Thess. 1:8. But when the second negative is a single negative, it retains its force. So οὐ παρὰ τοῦτο οὐκ ἔστιν ἐκ τοῦ σώματος (1 Cor. 12:15); οὐκ ἔχομεν ἐξουσίαν μὴ ἐργάζεσθαι; (1 Cor. 9:6); μὴ οὐκ ἤκουσαν (Rom. 10:18); ὁ μὴ πιστεύων ἤδη κέκριται ὅτι μὴ πεπίστευκεν (Jo. 3:18). Cf. οὐδὲν γάρ ἐστιν κεκαλυμμένον ὃ οὐκ ἀποκαλυφθήσεται (Matt. 10:26), and οὐ μὴ ἀφεθῇ ὧδε—ὃς οὐ καταλυθήσεται (Matt. 24:2). See 1 Cor. 6:9 (οὐ . . . . . οὐ). Cf. also μήποτε οὐ μή (or μήποτε οὐ, mg.) in Matt. 25:9. In Matt. 13:29 Οὔ, μήποτε ἐκριζώσητε each negative has its full force. Cf. μή, μή ποτε (Mk. 14:2). Cf. Mk. 12:24 for οὐ μή in question and μή with participle.

(k) *The Use of οὐ μή.*

The usual construction is with the subjunctive as in οὐ μὴ ἀφεθῇ above (Matt. 24:2). The future indicative is read in οὐ μὴ ἔσται σοι τοῦτο (Matt. 16:22) and is doubtless the correct text in οὐ μὴ τιμήσει (Matt. 15:6) and a few other places (Matt. 26:35; Mk. 14:31). No satisfactory explanation of the origin of this use of οὐ μή has been found. They do not neutralize each other, but each retains its force as in μὴ οὐ in questions (Rom. 10:18). So οὐ μή in questions (Lu. 18:7, οὐ μὴ ποιήσῃ;). Does this use throw any light on the problem? Probably originally each negative had its own force.

(1)   *The Redundant Negative.*

So in 1 Jo. 2:22 (see above) and Lu. 24:16 (ἐκρατοῦντο τοῦ μὴ ἐπιγνῶναι) after a verb of hindering (a negative conception). This appears stranger to us now than it would have done some generations ago before we dropped the repeated and double negatives in English. Compare Shakespeare on this point. Compare this vulgar sentence "Hain't nobody seen nothing of never a hat nowhere about here?" Cf. οὐ μή σε ἀνῶ οὐδ᾽ οὐ μή σε ἐγκαταλίπω (Heb. 13:5).

(m)   *The Emphatic Negative.*

The form οὐχί adds fresh point to the negative οὐ, especially when contrasted with ἀλλά as in Luke 1:60. The position of the negative may also give new emphasis as μὴ πολλοὶ διδάσκαλοι γίνεσθε (Jas. 3:1). In Rom. 3:9 οὐ πάντως means "by no means", but in 1 Cor. 15:51 (πάντες οὐ κοιμηθησόμεθα) οὐ goes with the verb. In Heb. 11:3 μὴ goes with the participle, not the infinitive. Litotes is not infrequent in the New Testament as οὐ μετὰ πολλάς (Acts 1:5) = μετὰ ὀλίγας ἡμέρας. Cf. Lu. 15:13.

(n)   *In Contrasts.*

For οὐχ ὅτι ...... ἀλλά see Jo. 7:22. For οὐχ ἵνα.... ἀλλά see Jo. 6:38. For ἀλλ᾽ οὐκ in the apodosis of a condition see Mk. 14:29. For οὐ μόνον οὐ ...... ἀλλὰ καί see Rom. 5:3. See Jo. 4:11 οὔτε.... καί. For οὐδέ ...... οὔτε see Rev. 5:3, and οὐδείς ..... οὔτε (Rev. 5:4). For οὐδέ ...... οὐδέ see Rev. 9:4. For μηδέ ...... μηδέ see Matt. 10:9. For μήτε ..... μήτε see Acts 27:20. For οὔτε ..... οὔτε see Matt. 12:32. For μηδέ ..... ἀλλά see 1 Pet. 5:2.

As is usual in ancient Greek, καὶ οὐ (Col. 2:8,19), not καὶ μή, follows affirmative clauses.

CHAPTER XXXVI

INTENSIVE PARTICLES

471. *Decreasing Use in the New Testament.*

(a) *Vague Application of the Term.*

The term particle has never been satisfactorily determined. In one sense the word can be applied to all adverbs, prepositions, conjunctions, interjections. They belong to the development of the sentence from simple to complex. In general particles belong to the effort of the language to relate words with words, clause with clause, sentence with sentence, paragraph with paragraph. They are the hinges of speech on which the thought turns, delicate turns of expression, *nuances* of thought that are often untranslatable. They often have an obscure origin.

(b) *Intensive Particles Marks of Emotion.*

The Greeks not simply had fine shades of thought and emotion, but they often expressed them by the intensive particles that are difficult to translate. In modern languages such emphasis depends chiefly on the voice and manner of the speaker or the sensitiveness of the reader to bring it out. Compare a German's use of his hands in speaking and a Frenchman shrugging his shoulders. There is less of this expression than in the older Greek, but still some of it. See, for instance, ἀλλὰ μὲν οὖν γε καί in Phil. 3:8 and εἰ πως ἤδη ποτέ (Rom. 1:10).

472. *The Chief Intensive Particles in the New Testament.*

(a) Γέ (*enclitic*) — *at least.*

It is of doubtful etymology. In the Boeotian, Doric, and

Eleatic dialects it is γά. It may correspond to the k in the Gothic mi-k and German mi-ch (cf. Greek ἐμέ–γε). The Sanskrit gha was used in the same way. It adds nothing to the meaning of the word with which it is used, but serves to intensify the idea. It may minify it as in Jo. 4:2 καίτοι γε and yet indeed (by way of exception) or it may magnify the idea as in Rom. 8:32 ὅς γε τοῦ ἰδίου υἱοῦ οὐκ ἐφείσατο who at least spared not his own son (went as far as this). It occurs 33 times in the New Testament and usually occurs with some other particle like ἀλλά γε (1 Cor. 9:2), ἄρα γε (Matt. 7:20), ἆρά γε (Acts 8:30), εἰ γε (Col. 1:23), εἰ δὲ μή γε (Matt. 6:1), καί γε (Acts 17:27), καίτοι γε (Jo. 4:2), μενοῦν γε (Rom. 10:18), μήτι γε (1 Cor. 6:3), ὄφελόν γε (1 Cor. 4:8) with a touch of irony. As a matter of fact γάρ is compounded of γε and ἄρα, though it is usually an inferential conjunction. Yet it is little more than an intensive particle in Matt. 27:23 τί γὰρ κακὸν ἐποίησεν; Why, what evil did he do?

(b) Δή =surely.

It is possibly a shortened form of ἤδη. In the New Testament the six examples are postpositive, though not enclitic. There is a note of urgency in δή as in διέλθωμεν δή (Lu. 2:15) let us go now and also δοξάσατε δὴ τὸν θεὸν ἐν τῷ σώματι ὑμῶν (1 Cor. 6:20) glorify now then God in your body. So also Acts 13:2. It may be kin to δέ which is much like δή in Lu. 1:76 καὶ σὺ δέ. Once we have δή που (Heb. 2:16), but δή ποτε (Jo. 5:4) has dropped out of the critical text.

(c) Εἰ μήν = assuredly, ναί = verily, νή = by.

We have εἰ μήν in the critical text of Heb. 6:14 rather than ἦ μήν. This odd idiom occurs in the LXX (Ezek. 33:27), in the papyri, and inscriptions. It is mere itacism for ἦ μήν. It is an asseverative particle. The affirmative particle ναί occurs some thirty times in the New Testament, simply as yes (Matt. 13:51), or verily (Matt. 11:9), in contrast with οὐ (Matt. 5:37). The article is used with it in 2 Cor. 1:17.

It occurs in respectful address ναί, κύριε (Jo. 11:27) *Yea, Lord.*
It occurs with ἀμήν in Rev. 1:7. Νή is a peculiarity of the Attic
dialect (possible variation of ναί) and occurs only once in the
New Testament in a strong affirmation νὴ τὴν ὑμετέραν καύ-
χησιν (1 Cor. 15:31) *by the glorying in you* (objective use of
ὑμετέραν). Μά does not occur in the New Testament.

(d) Μέν = *indeed.*

This word is a weakened form of μήν (*surely*). The Doric
used μάν. It is postpositive, but not enclitic. Μέν is far
the most common of the intensive particles in the New Testament, though still less frequent than in the older Greek. The
original use was by itself, μέν *solitarium,* which survives in
the New Testament with no thought of a corresponding δέ.
It is common thus in the Acts (1:1, 18; 3:13, 21; 5:41, etc.).
See also 2 Cor. 11:4. When there is contrast with δέ, ἀλλά,
the contrast may be slight as in Matt. 25:14 ff. or decided as
in 1 Cor. 1:12; Matt. 3:11. Μενοῦν occurs once (Lu. 11:28)
and μενοῦνγε three times (Rom. 9:20; 10:18; Phil. 3:8) and
μέντοι eight times as Jo. 4:27.

(e) Πέρ (*enclitic*) = *thoroughly.*

It is probably a shortened form of περί (more exactly πέρι)
and so means *thoroughly.* It is *extensive* as well as *intensive.*
Westcott and Hort have dropped περ with ὅν in Mk. 15:6.
Elsewhere we have it only with διόπερ (1 Cor. 8:13; 10:14)
and with conjunctions as ἐάνπερ (Heb. 3:14), εἴπερ (Rom. 8:9),
ἐπειδήπερ (Lu. 1:1), ἤπερ (Jo. 12:43, but margin of Westcott
and Hort ὑπέρ), καθάπερ (seventeen times like Rom. 3:4, all
in Paul save Heb. 4:2), καθώσπερ (Heb. 5:4), καίπερ (Heb. 12:17),
ὥσπερ (36 times as Matt. 6:2), ὡσπερεί once only (1 Cor. 15:8).
The idea is uniformly the same "thoroughly."

(f) Τοί = *on this account (or thou then).*

It is of uncertain origin. Brugmann considers it the ethical
dative σοί (τοί) = *thou then.* Others think it the locative

case of the demonstrative τῷ = *on this account*. It does not occur alone in the New Testament, but only combined with other particles as ἤτοι once (Rom. 6:16), καίτοι twice (Acts 14:17; Heb. 4:3), καίτοιγε once (Jo. 4:2), μέντοι eight times (as Jo. 4:27), τοιγαροῦν twice (1 Thess. 4:8; Heb. 12:1), τοίνυν three times (Lu. 20:25; 1 Cor. 9:26; Heb. 13:13).

CHAPTER XXXVII

FIGURES OF SPEECH

473. *Lapse in Mental Processes.*

The human mind does not work methodically according to the rules of any language or of any grammar. Speech is the expression of thought and the thought jumps the track or slips a cog now and then and speech betrays the process of the mind. These rhetorical peculiarities belong to all languages and to all stages of the Greek tongue. It is not strange, therefore, that we should find such lapses, interruptions, sudden changes embalmed in the Greek New Testament. These rhetorical figures are particularly frequent in popular speech and in the language of passion as in 2 Cor. 7:5-12; 8:18-21; Rom. 5:12, 18-21. Paul shows such emotion at times that one can almost hear his heart beat as his language struggles for expression as in Gal. 4:15-20; 6:11-16.

474. *New Testament Examples.*

No one of the New Testament writers has an artificial style or writes according to the rhythmical rules of the rhetoricians. There is no striving for effect, not even in the Epistle to the Hebrews, in spite of the contention of Blass on that point. But the writers of the New Testament have natural spontaneity and at times have the real eloquence of passion, not the labored oratory of the schools. Hence we turn to the New Testament, not to judge them by artificial rules of rhetoric, but to find illustrations of the natural flexibility of men with real earnestness and power of speech.

(a) *Allegory.*

Paul uses the term (ἀλληγορούμενα) in Gal. 4:24 for his interpretation of the two covenants, but does not let allegory run away with him as it did with Philo and many a preacher since his day. So Jesus used the allegory of the Prodigal Son (Lu. 15) and of the Good Shepherd (Jo. 10) as a speaking parable.

(b) *Alliteration.*

Paul shows a fondness for initial alliteration in Rom. 1:29 and 30 πονηρίᾳ πλεονεξίᾳ, φθόνου φόνου, ἀπειθεῖς ἀσυνέτους ἀσυνθέτους ἀστόργους ἀνελεήμονας.

(c) *Anacoluthon.*

There are numerous examples, some simple like the suspended nominative ὁ νικῶν ποιήσω αὐτόν (Rev. 3:12), some more complicated like γράψαντες (Acts 15:23) which does not agree with either ἀποστόλοις or ἐκλεξαμένους in verse 22.

(d) *Annominatio.*

This figure is where the sense and the sound are alike as in Πέτρος and πέτρα in Matt. 16:18, γινώσκεις ἃ ἀναγινώσκεις; (Acts 8:30), μηδὲν ἐργαζομένους ἀλλὰ περιεργαζομένους (2 Thess. 3:11).

(e) *Aposiopesis.*

This figure is seen in Lu. 19:42 εἰ ἔγνως ἐν τῇ ἡμέρᾳ ταύτῃ καὶ σὺ τὰ πρὸς εἰρήνην *if thou hadst known even thou in this day the things pertaining to peace!* The sudden breaking off is very effective. So also Acts 23:9.

(f) *Brachylogy.*

In modern languages we use the parenthesis. See the inserted words (τότε λέγει κτλ.) in the sentence in Matt. 9:6. In Acts 1:1 ἤρξατο implies καὶ διετέλει.

(g) *Chiasm.*

This reverted parallelism is seen in Philemon 5 where ἀγάπην and πίστιν are reversed in the relative clause with εἰς τὸν κύριον Ἰησοῦν καὶ εἰς τοὺς ἁγίους.

(h) *Climax.*

Repetition is natural in emotion as in Lu. 8:24 ἐπιστάτα, ἐπιστάτα *Master, Master*, σταύρωσον, σταύρωσον (Jo. 19:6) *Crucify, crucify,* and the two hours of shouting in Acts 19:34.

(i) *Ellipsis.*

The commonest is the ellipsis of the copula like εἰσίν in Matt. 5:3 μακάριοι οἱ πτωχοὶ τῷ πνεύματι *happy the poor in spirit.* So of τινές before τῶν μαθητῶν (Acts 21:16) *some of the disciples.*

(j) *Hyperbaton.*

This is where a word seems to be in the wrong place, especially adverbs as in 1 Cor. 14:7 ὅμως might come in more smoothly before ἐάν. So in Rom. 4:12 the repetition of the article makes οὐ μόνον seem out of place. Prolepsis of the subject is common as in Matt. 6:28.

(k) *Hyperbole.*

This is a species of exaggeration that is understood and not to be taken literally, as in Jo. 21:25 about τὸν κόσμον. So also Matt. 13:32.

(l) *Irony.*

See the high scorn in the words of Jesus in Matt. 23:32 to the Pharisees. Without understanding this figure Jesus is made to commend the Pharisees for setting aside the word of God by the use of καλῶς in Mk. 7:9.

(m) *Litotes.*

Luke is fond of this figure of negative statement in Acts as 1:5 οὐ μετὰ πολλὰς ταύτας ἡμέρας *not after many days hence — after not many days hence.* So also 14:28 χρόνον οὐκ ὀλίγον *time no little.*

(n) *Meiosis.*

This is an understatement, the opposite of hyperbole, less than the full value, as in 1 Cor. 2:4 οὐκ ἐν πιθοῖς σοφίας λόγοις *not in persuasive words of wisdom.* Here Paul has in mind the sophists and professional spouters of wisdom in Corinth and Athens, but this self-depreciation is a form of *meiosis* and has to be discounted.

(o) *Metaphor.*

Most words are originally pictures and so metaphors like ὁ ποιμὴν ὁ καλός (Jo. 10:11) *the Good Shepherd*. The *simile* is just a bit more formal with the use of ὅμοιος *like* as in Matt. 13:52. *Parables* are just special forms of the metaphor or simile. The greatest parables of all time are those of Jesus.

(p) *Parallelism.*

The Hebrew Old Testament is full of this figure, especially in the Psalms. It is a striking feature of Hebrew poetry, to put a thing in two ways and to repeat one part of it. We have it in the New Testament in Lu. 1:42 to 2:32. There is perfection of form in 1 Cor. 13 and 15. It appears also in the early Christian hymn in 1 Tim. 3:16.

(q) *Paronomasia.*

This may be the repetition of the same word stem like κακοὺς κακῶς (Matt. 21:41) or for similar sounds with different sense like λιμοὶ καὶ λοιμοί (Lu. 21:11). The ancients did not have our prejudice against such "puns" as in ἔμαθεν ἀφ'ὧν ἔπαθεν (Heb. 5:8) *he learned from what he suffered.*

(r) *Pleonasm.*

Repetition is sometimes for effect as in ὑμᾶς .... ὑμᾶς (Col. 2:13). Sometimes it is due to vernacular idioms like ἧς .... αὐτῆς (Mk. 7:25) after the Hebrew idiom and the papyri. So μᾶλλον κρεῖσσον (Phil. 1:23) *more better* is a vernacular idiom seen often in Shakespeare (double comparative). The redundant negative (1 Jo. 2:22) is not a linguistic vice. Vivid details help the picture as in Acts 15:23 γράψαντες διὰ χειρὸς αὐτῶν *writing by their hand.*

(s) *The Rhetorical Question.*

In such a question as in Heb. 2:2-4 no answer is expressed or is necessary. The question answers itself clearly enough.

(t) *Zeugma.*

Zeugma puts together words that do not properly belong together as in 1 Cor. 3:2 γάλα ὑμᾶς ἐπότισα, οὐ βρῶμα *I gave you milk to drink, not solid food.* So also Lu. 1:64 ἀνεῴχθη τὸ στόμα αὐτοῦ παραχρῆμα καὶ ἡ γλῶσσα αὐτοῦ *his mouth was opened and his tongue.*

475. *The Apocalypse.*

In Revelation there are grammatical lapses due to various reasons. Some are on purpose as in the case of ἀπὸ ὁ ὤν (Rev. 1:4) to accent the unchangeableness of God. Note also in the same sentence ὁ ἦν. Others are due to the vividness of conception in the book as καὶ ἦλθεν καὶ εἴληφεν (Rev. 5:7). Cf. also Rev. 10:8-10. This mixing of tenses is common also in Mark. The use of cases without regular accord is found elsewhere, but is more common in Revelation. So τῆς καινῆς Ἰερουσαλήμ, ἡ καταβαίνουσα (Rev. 3:12). The visions add to the excitement and confusion. Cf. nominative and accusative in Rev. 4:1, 4. It is possible that the book may have been dictated and probably like 2 Peter lacked careful critical revision. But these non-literary traits, some of which appear in the non-literary papyri, do not prove the author an ignoramus. It is remarkable that in Acts 4:13 both Peter and John are termed by the Sanhedrin ἀγράμματοι καὶ ἰδιῶται *unlettered and private men.* They were not school-men, but yet were men of power.

INDEX OF NEW TESTAMENT REFERENCES

(Order of Westcott and Hort)

By Rev. C. J. Allen, Ph.D.

(References are to sections unless p. is added for page)

MATTHEW

MARK

JOHN

ACTS

1 CORINTHIANS

2 CORINTHIANS

GALATIANS

EPHESIANS

PHILIPPIANS

HEBREWS

1 TIMOTHY

1 TIM.	SECTION	1 TIM.	SECTION
1:6	344 (e)	4:4	442
1:7	381, 448 (c)	4:13	419 (b)
1:10	460 (b)	5:13	208 c
1:16	387 (e)	5:19	111, 442
2:8	446	5:21	368
2:9	196	5:22	320
3:1	343 (l) *bis*	6:5	342 (j), 344 (e)
3:16	330, 349, 380, 474 (p)	6:9	332
4:1	344 (e)		

2 TIMOTHY

2 TIM.	SECTION	2 TIM.	SECTION
1:6	356	3:13	176 C c
1:12	410 (a), 448 (c)	3:16	387 (e)
2:5	401 (a)	4:7	403 (a)
2:14	465	4:10	349
2:25	452 (c)	4:21	368
2:35	430 (d)		

TITUS

TITUS	SECTION	TITUS	SECTION
1:11	417, 470 (d)	2:13	387 (b) (2) *bis*
1:12	208 c	2:14	371
2:7	397	3:13	162 c

PHILEMON

PHILE.	SECTION	PHILE.	SECTION
5	474 (g)	20	320, 343 (l)
16	342 (o)		

REVELATION

REV.	SECTION	REV.	SECTION
1:4	328, 379 *bis*, 380, 385, 475	2:7	302
1:7	472 (c)	2:12	387 (b) (1)
1:8	380, 385	2:14	342 (c)
1:9	323, 387 (b) (2)	2:16	347 (d)
1:13	174 b, 209 e	2:17	344 (e)
1:18	176 C d	2:20	302, 320, 391
2:3	304	2:25	320, 420 (b)
2:4	301, 304, 320	2:26	462 (b), 462 (e)

GREEK INDEX

The numbers refer to the sections of the Grammar, except those numbers which have p. before them and mean that reference is made to pages. The verbs included in the list under Principal Parts of some Important Verbs (Chapt. IX) are generally not cited in the Index.

ἄμφω p. 252.

ἄν use of 408, 416, 418, 436 (b), (d), 438, 440, 441

ἄν = ἐάν 439.

–αν– decl. of stems in 189 d.

–αν 3 pl. pers. end. 292 c N.

ἀνά with acc. p. 224, p. 237, 356.

ἀνάβα imp. p 165.

ἀνάγαιον form 162 f.

ἀνεῖλαν 301.

ἄνευ with abl. p. 233, p. 250.

ἀνεῦραν 301

ἀνέῳξα aug. 274 N. 2 and 3.

ἀνήρ stem of 106 b; voc. 147, 172 a (b), dat. pl. 184 a; decl. of 185.

ἄνθρωπος decl. of 160.

–ανο/ε tense suffix 287.

–ανος adj. in 176.

–αντ– adj. in 211 Ca.

–αντ part. in 214 A.

ἀντί case of 352 (b); with gen. p. 227, p 229, 357.

ἄντικρυς with gen. p. 229, p. 250.

ἀντίον with dat. p 244.

ἀντίπερα with abl. p. 250.

ἄνω comp. 234, 216 d.

ἀνώγεων form 162 f.

ἀξίως with gen. 339 (c), p. 229.

ἅπαξ adv. 231; with gen. p 227.

ἅπας decl. 211 C a N.

ἀπάτωρ end. 213.

ἀπέναντι with abl. p. 233, p. 250.

ἄπιστος decl. of 207.

ἁπλοῦς decl. of 209b; distrib. 239.

ἀπό with abl. 358, p. 233.

ἀποθανοῦμαι voice 303.

ἀπόλλυμι meaning 396.

Ἀπολλώνιος 312.

Ἀπολλώς 312; decl. of 162 c.

ἀπολῶ form. 303.

ἀπόλωλα meaning 396.

ἄρα infer. conj. p. 317, 425, 448 (d).

ἆρα use of 448 (b) and (d).

ἀραβών 42 b.

Ἄραψ decl. of 176 A and N.

ἀργός end. 208 c.

ἀργυρᾶ decl. of 209 a.

ἀργυροῦς decl. of 209 b.

ἀρήν decl. of 187 c, 188 c.

ἀρνίον use 188 c.

–αριον subst. in p. 175.

–αρος adj. in p. 177.

ἀρούρης gen. 154 c.

ἅρπαξ end. 213, 332.

ἀρραβών spell. 42 b.

ἄρρην form 56 b.

ἄρσην form 56 b, 212 B a.

ἀρχι– prefix p. 180.

ἄρχων decl. of 178.

ἅς form p. 164.

–ας of acc. pl. 140.

–ας, –ης decl. of subst. in 156.

–ασ– decl. of neut. stems in 179-180, 191.

ἀσεβῆν acc. 212 A b.

ἀσθένεια decl. of 154.

ἀσθενής comp. 216.

ἀστήρ form 184 b; decl. of 186 A.

ἄστυ 169.

–αται 3 pl. pers. end. 293 e.

ἄτερ with abl. p. 234, p. 250.

–ατο 3 pl. pers. end. 293 e.

ᾱυ decl. of stems in 201.

αὐτόματος end. 208 c.

αὐτός decl. of 220; use p. 265.

αὐτοῦ adv. p. 226.

ἀφ' οὗ use of 420 (a).

ἀφεῖνται form 304.

ἀφεῖς form 302, 391.

ἀφελπίζοντες spell. 33 b.

ἀφελῶ tense 303.

ἄφες mode p. 164.

ἀφέωνται form 11, 304.

ἀφῆκες form 301, 304.

ἀφηλπικώς spell. 33 b.

ἀφίδω spell. 33b

ἀφίημι conj. pres. system 260;
aor. act. and midd. 257 A.
ἀφίουσιν form 302.
ἀφίω p. 125, 302, 391.
ἄφρων decl. of 212 B b.
ἄχρι with gen. p. 229, p. 250; use
p. 318, 420 (b).

β pronun. of 41 b (1)
β decl. of stems in 176 A.
βάαλ gend. of 118 d.
βαθύς decl. of 211 A a.
βάπτισαι p. 164.
βάπτισον p. 164.
βαρύς decl. of 211 A a.
βασιλεύς decl. of 201 B.
βάτος, gender 163 A.
βελτίων comp. 217 a.
βλάπτω with two acc. p. 219.
βλητέον with acc. p. 221.
βορρᾶς decl. of 156 B.
βοῦς decl. of 201 C.
βουστροφηδόν 28 f.

γ pronun. of 41 b (1).
γ decl. of stems in 176 B.
γάλα decl. of 169, 182 d.
γάρ infer. conj. 329, p. 317; use 425.
γαστήρ decl. of 185 e.
γε encl. 102 A d; use 472 (a).
γέμω with gen. and acc. p. 230.
γένος decl. 169.
γεύω with gen. and acc. p. 230.
γῆ decl. 157.
γῆρας decl. 179 a, 191.
γίγνομαι 47, 60 b.
γιγνώσκω 60 b.
γίνομαι conj. 2 perf. act. 268 A;
voices of 396; meaning 397.
γινώσκω conj. of aor. act. 257 A.
γλυκύς decl. of 211 A a.
γλῶσσα decl. of 154.
γνωρίζω form. 253 d N.

γογγύζω redup. 280 b.
γόης decl. of 176 C c.
γόνυ decl. of 182 c.
γρηγορέω form of 393.
γυνή decl. of 176 B b.

δ pronun. of 41 b (1).
δ decl. of stems in 176 C.
−δα− subst. in p. 175.
δαίμων voc. of 172 b (a).
δάκρυ decl. of 200 c.
δάκρυον 163 B b, 200 c.
δέ copul. conj. 329, 410 (a); advers.
329, 410 (a).
δέδωκα action of p. 303.
δείκνυμι conj. of pres. system 259.
δεικνύς decl. of 214 G.
δεῖνα pron. 226 a; use 379.
δεῖπνον gender 163 A.
δέομαι conj. of pres. system 266 (d)
δένδρα form 142.
δεσμός gender 163 A.
δεῦρο use p. 310.
δεῦτε use p. 310, 448 (h).
δευτεραῖος meaning 240.
δή use 472 (b).
δηλῶν decl. of 214 D N.
Δημοσθένην form 174 b.
δημοσίᾳ case of 231, p. 240.
διά with acc. p. 224, p. 242, p. 359;
with gen. 359.
διὰ τό with inf. 428.
διδάσκω with two acc. p. 219.
διδούς decl. of 214 F.
δίδωμι conj. of pres. system 259;
aor. act. and midd. 257 A; action
of p. 303.
διό use p. 317, 427.
διότι use 426 (a).
διπλοῦς decl. of 209 a and b;
multip. 239.
δίς with gen. p. 227.
δοῖ form 306.

−δον suffix 232.
δούς decl. of 214 F N.
δυεῖν form 111.
δύναιτο form p. 162.
δύνασαι form 293 b N.
δύνῃ form 293 b N.
δύνηται form 306.
δύνωμαι form 306.
δύο decl. of 236 b.
δυσ− prefix p. 180.
δυσί(ν) form 111.
δύω form 111.
δυῶν form 111.
δωρεάν adv. p. 222, 231; case of 348.
δῶρον decl. of 160.

ε aug. 273-4.
ε in vowel-grad. 47, 298 a.
−ε tense suffix 287.
ἔα use 448 (h).
ἐάν use 329, 436 (a) and (c), 437, 439, 441.
ἐὰν καί use 443.
ἑαυτοῦ decl. of 221.
ἐάω 299.
Ἑβραϊστί 232.
ἐγγύς comp. 234; with gen. p. 229, p. 250; with dat. p. 244, p. 250.
ἐγείρω conj. aor. pass. p. 121.
ἔγνων form 301.
ἐγρήγορα redupl. 283 A.
ἐγώ decl. of 220.
ἐγών form 342 (a).
ἐδίδουν form 302.
ἐδολιοῦσαν form 302.
ἔδομαι tense 306.
ἐθέλω form 51 b.
ἐθέλωμι mode p. 162.
ἔθνος decl. of 192.
ει sound of 41 a.
ει genuine diphth. 32 a; spurious 28 a, 32 a, 49 a, 53.
ει in vowel-grad. 47, 298 b.

ει stems in 124; decl. of stems 197-201 D.
εἰ cond., particle 329; use 436 (a)— (d) 437-442, 448 (d).
εἰ γάρ use 445, 446.
εἰ καί use 443.
εἰ μή use 442.
εἰ μήν use 472 (c).
−εια subst. in p. 173.
εἶδαν form 301.
εἰδήσουσιν form 270.
εἰδήσω use 304, p. 305.
εἶδον action of 400.
εἰδώς decl. 215 b.
εἴθε use 445-6.
εἶμαι 16.
εἰμί enclitic forms 102 A c; conj. of pres. system 261; conj. of fut. 267 D, p. 137; voices 396; use 390.
εἶμι conj. of pres. system 261; use 303.
−ειν loc. end. 455 (a).
−εῖν accent of infinit. 272 A a (2).
εἶνε (εἶναι) p. 166.
−εῖον subst. in p. 174.
εἶπα, εἶπας, etc. form 257 B N, 301.
εἰπέ accent p. 164, 272 A b.
εἶπον form 301.
εἰπόν accent 272.
εἰς with acc. p. 224, p. 238, p. 242-3, p. 361.
εἰς τό use with infinit. 435 (d).
εἷς decl. of 236 a; use 314, 384.
εἴτε disjunct. conj. 329; εἴτε—εἴτε p. 317.
εἶχαν form 16.
εἴχοσαν form 11, 302.
ἐκ (ἐξ) 80, 101A; with abl. p. 234, 362.
ἑκατονταπλασίων multipl. 239.
ἐκεῖ adv. 231, 349;
ἐκεῖθεν 232.
ἐκεῖνος decl. 225 b; use p. 269.

ἐκκλησία 17.
ἐκλεκτός end. 208c.
ἔκρινα form 301.
ἐκσῶσαι spell. 39.
ἐκτός with abl. p. 234, p. 250.
ἐκχεῶ form 303.
ἐλάσσων comp. 217 a.
ἐλάττων spell. 56 a.
ἐλάχιστος comp. 217 a.
ἐλαχιστότερος comp. 217 b.
ἔλεξα form 301.
ἔλεος gender 163 B b; decl. of 192.
Ἕλλην decl. of 189.
Ἑλληνιστί adv. 232.
ἐλπίδι breathing 33b.
ἐλπιοῦσιν form 303.
ἐλπίς decl. of 176 C.
ἐμαυτοῦ decl. of 221.
ἐμός poss. pron. 222, p. 266.
ἔμπροσθεν with abl. p. 234, 250.
ἐν (ἐνί) case of p. 237; with loc.
  p. 237-8, p. 242, 345 (b), 360.
ἐν τῷ use with inf. 421 (c).
ἐν ᾧ use 419 (a), 423 (d).
−εν− decl. of stems in 187-8.
−εν decl. of adj. with stems in 212B.
−εν end. of inf. 296 b (1).
−εναι end. of inf. 296 a (2).
ἔναντι with gen. p. 229, p. 250.
ἐναντίον with gen. p. 227, p. 229,
  p. 250; with dat. p. 244.
ἐνδιδύσκω with two acc. p. 219.
ἕνεκα, ἕνεκεν, εἵνεκεν, with gen.
  p. 227, p. 229, p. 250.
−ενι loc. end. 455 (a).
−εντ decl. of partic. with stems in
  214 B.
ἐντός with gen. p. 227, p. 229, p. 250.
ἐνώπιον with gen. p. 230, p. 250.
ἐξέδετο form 301.
ἐξέδοτο form 301.
ἐξῆς adv. 231.
ἔξω 62 b.

ἔξω comp. 216 d; with abl. p. 234,
  p. 250.
ἔξωθεν with abl. p. 234, p. 250.
ἐξῶσαι spell. 39.
−εο− decl. of stems in 161.
−εος adj. in p. 176; decl. of masc. 209
ἐπάν use 419 (c).
ἐπάνω with gen. p. 230, p. 250.
ἐπεί use p. 318, 426 (b), 442.
ἐπειδή use p. 318, 419 (c), 426 (b).
ἐπειδήπερ use p. 426 (b).
ἐπέκεινα with abl. p. 234, p. 250.
ἔπειτα 349.
ἔπεσα and ἔπεσον 301.
ἐπί case of 253 (b); with acc. p. 224,
  363; with gen. p. 227, p. 230, 363;
  with loc. p. 237, 363; with dat.
  p. 244, 363.
ἐπιλανθάνομαι with gen. and acc.
  p. 230.
ἐπισχερώ case of 130.
ἔρημος form 208 b.
Ἑρμῆς decl. 157.
ἔρχομαι voices 396; meaning 397.
−ες (nom. −εσ) subst. in p. 173-4.
−εσ decl. of neut. subst. with stems
  in 192.
−ες masc. proper names with stems
  in 194.
−εσ decl. of adj. stems in 212 A.
−ες nom. pl. case-end. 135.
−εσσι loc. pl. case-end. 139.
ἐστάλην form p. 167.
ἔστην form 301; meaning 396.
ἔστησα meaning 396.
ἐστήξω form 304, p. 305.
ἔστι(ν) accent 102F.
ἐστί (ἐντί) p. 166.
ἐστώς accent 98c; decl. p. 138, 215 c.
ἔσω with gen. p. 230, p. 250.
ἕτερος decl. 226; meaning p. 267.
ἐτίθουν form 302.

−ι loc. case-end. 129.

ι (consonant) 31, 36; between vowels 31 a; changes due to 67-70; with ν and ρ 49 d; stems in 125; verb suffix p. 178-80; in pres. tense stem 317 (f) (1).

−ια subst. in p. 174.

−ιακος adj. in p. 175.

−ιδ (nom. −ις) nouns in p. 175.

ἴδε use 448 (h).

ἰδίᾳ case of p. 240.

−ίδιον subst. in p. 175.

ἰδού use 448 (h).

−ιη− mode suffix 288 b, 307.

−ίημι conj. of pres. system 260.

'Ιησοῦς decl. of 202.

−ικός adj. in p. 175-6.

ἴλεως 162 b.

−ιμος adj. in.

−ιν− decl. of stems in 189 c.

ἵνα case of p. 240; use 430 (a), 434 (a), 435 (a), 453 (b).

−ινος adj. in p. 176.

−ιο/ε tense suffix 287.

−ιο(ο) gen. case-end. 126.

−ιον dim. in 118 c; subst. in p. 174

−ιος adj. in p. 175.

ἴσασι form 304.

−ισκος subst. in p. 175.

ἰστάνω form 393.

ἵστημι conj. of aor. act. 257 A; conj. of present system 259.

ἰχθύς decl. of 200.

−ιων, −ιστος comp. of adj. 217.

κ decl. of stems in 176 B.

−κα tense suffix 287.

κἀγώ crasis 55, 99.

καί copul. conj. 329, 410 (a); advers. use p. 317.

καί εἰ (or ἐάν) use 443.

καίπερ use 443, 462 (d).

καθ' ὅσον use 427.

καθάπερ use 424 (a).

κάθημαι conj. of pres. system 262.

καθό use 424 (a).

καθότι use 424 (c), 426 (a).

καθώς use 424 (b).

καθώσπερ use 424 (b).

κἀκεῖ crasis 55.

κἀκεῖνος crasis 55.

κακός comp. 217 a.

καλός decl. of 206 A.

κἀμέ crasis 55.

κἄν crasis 55.

κατά with acc. p. 224; with gen. p. 230; with gen., abl., acc. p. 364.

κατέναντι with gen. p. 230, p. 250.

κατενώπιον with gen. p. 230, p. 251.

κάτω, κατώτερος 216 d; comp. 234 N.

κεῖμαι conj. of pres. system 262.

κεκράξονται form 270, 304, p. 305.

κέρας decl. 180 N.

κερδηθήσωνται form p. 162.

κιθών spell. 74.

−κις adv. end. 232.

κλαίω form 67 c N.

κλείς decl. 176 C c.

κορβᾶν form 203.

−κος adj. in p. 175.

κόσμιος end. 208 b.

κούμ 25.

κράτιστος comp. 217 a.

κρέας forms of 179 a, 191.

κρείσσων comp. 217 a.

κρίνω conj. of fut. act. and midd. 267 A, 267 B.

κρυφῇ case of p. 240.

κυκλόθεν with gen. p. 251.

κύκλῳ case of 348; with gen. p. 230, p. 251.

κυριότης decl. of 176 C.

κύων decl. of 187 c; 188 b.

Κῶς, acc. Κῶ 162 e.

λ sonant 40a; variation 75; decl. of
    stems in 183.
λαβέ accent 272 A b.
λαβοῦ accent 272 A b.
λάθρα case of 130, 231.
λαῖλαψ decl. of 176 A.
λαμβάνω conj. of aor. act. and midd.
    257 B; root of p. 294.
λαμπάς decl. of 176 C a.
λελυκώς decl. of 215.
λελυμένος decl. of 206 C b.
λεών stem and decl. 168, 177.
λεώς form 162 a.
λιμός gender 163 A.
λίψ decl. 176 A N.
–λος adj. in 176.
λυόμενος decl. of 206 C a.
Λύστρα form 163 B b.
λύω conj. of perf. act. p. 139; midd.
    and pass. 269 (a); conj. of fut.
    perf. pass. p. 142; conj. of present
    system 263 B (a); conj. of fut.
    act. 267 A; of fut. midd. 267B;
    of pass. 267 C.
λύων decl. of 214 C a.

μ sonant 40 c; stops before 59.
μαθητής decl. of 156 A.
–μαι pers. end. 290 B, 293 a.
μακάριος comp. 216.
μάλα comp. 234.
μᾶλλον, μάλιστα 218.
μάστιξ decl. 166.
–ματ– decl. of stems in 179, 180;
    subst. in p. 173.
μάρτυρ decl. of 186 B.
μάχαιρα decl. of 154.
μέγας decl. of 211 B b; comp. 217.
μεγιστάν decl. 189 d.
μειζότερος 217 b.
μείζων decl. of 212 C.
μέλας decl. of 211 B a, 189 d.
μέλι stem of 169, 182 e.

μέλισσα, μελιττα 70 N.
μέν use of 472 (d).
–μεν– decl. of stems in 187, 188.
–μεν pers. end. 290.
–μεν inf. end. 296 b (2).
–μενο– end. of partic. 297 c.
μέντοι advers. conj. 410 (a).
μένω conj. of aor. act. 258.
–μες pers. end. 290.
μέσης with gen. p. 227.
μέσον with gen. p. 230, p. 251.
μετά case of p. 240; with acc. p. 224,
    365; with gen. p. 227, p. 230, 365;
    with art. inf. 421 (d).
μεταξύ with gen. p. 230; with abl.
    p. 251.
μέχρι with gen. p. 230, p. 251; use
    of p. 318, 420 (d).
μή use of p. 300, 417, 430 (d), 434 (c),
    444, 448 (b), 457 (f), 463, 464
    (a)–(j) and (l)–(n).

μή ποτε use 448 (d).
μηδέ use 464 (a) and (n).
μηδέ—μηδέ disjunc. conj. p. 317.
μηδείς use 383.
μήν decl. 189 a—b.
–μην pers. end. 293 a.
–μην in vowel-grad. 47 N.
μήποτε use of 430 (d), 434 (c).
μήπως use of 430 (d), 434 (c).
μήτε use 464 (n); disjunct. conj. p.
    317.
μήτηρ decl. of 185.
μήτι use of 448 (b).
–μι pers. end. 290, 291a.
μικρός comp. 216, 217a.
μνᾶ decl. 157.
μοίρης form 154 c.
–μον– decl. of stems in 187-8.
–μος subst. in p. 173; adj. in p. 176.
μρ(> μβρ) medial 76.

μώλωψ decl. 176 *A* N.
−μων in vowel-grad. 47N.

ν consonants before 60, 61; in comp.
 61 d N; sonant 40 d.
ν movable 78.
−ν acc. case-end. 132.
−ν voc. case-end. 134.
−ν 1 sing. pers. end. 290 A, 292 a;
 3 pl. pers. end. 290 A, 292 C.
−ν− stems in 125; decl. of stems in
 187-189; decl. of adj. with stems
 in 211 B.
ν pres. tense suffix 317 (f) (2).
−να pres. tense suffix 287.
ναί use of 472 (c).
−ναι end. of inf. 296 a (1); accent
 272 A a (1).
−ναι dat. case-end. 455 (a).
ναῦς forms 201 A a.
νεανίας decl. of 156 A.
νέος uncontr. 209 c.
νεωκόρος form 162 b.
νεώς form and decl. 162 a.
νή use of 472 (c).
νη− prefix p. 180.
νῆσις adj. of one end. 213.
νίκη var. 163 B b.
νικοῦντι form 302.
νῖκος var. 163 B. b.
νιπτήρ decl. 186 A c.
−νο/ε pres. tense theme 287.
νόμος decl. of 160.
−νος adj. in p. 176.
νοῦς decl. 201 C b.
νρ(<νδρ) medial 76.
−νς acc. pl. case-end. 141.
−νσι 3 pl. pers. end. 290, 291 d.
−ντ− decl. of stems in 177-8; decl. of
 adj. with stems in 211 C; end. of
 participle 297 a; decl. of participle with stems in 214.
−νται 3 pl. pers. end. 293 e.

−ντι pers. end. 290.
−ντο 3 pl. pers. end. 293 f.
−ντων 3 pl. pers.-end 294 A c.
−νυ pres. tense suffix 287.
νύξ decl. 175.

ξύν 370.

ο in vowel-grad. 47, 298 a.
ο stems in 123, 124; decl. of stems
 in 158, 159.
−ο in form. of subst. 315 (a).
ὁ, ἡ, τό decl. of 224; use 379, 385-7.
ο/ε thematic vowel 254 a, 255,, 287,
 288, 306.
ὄγδοος decl. 209 c.
ὅδε decl. 225 c; use of 379.
ὀδυνᾶσαι form 293 b N; p. 166.
ὁδός decl. of 160.
ὀδούς form and decl. 168, 178 N.
ὅθεν use of p. 318, 423 (a), 426 (c).
οι sound of 41 a; in vowel-grad. 47,
 298 b.
−οι decl. of stems in 201 D.
−οι in opt. 272 B.
οἶδα conj. of 268 *A*.
οἴκοι case of 129, 231, 345 (b),
 347 (a).
οἴκῳ case of 347 (a).
οἷος use of p. 269, p. 270-1, 448 (h).
−οις inst. pl. case-end. 139-140.
ὀλίγος breathing 33 b.
ὄλωλα 283 A.
ὁμοθυμαδόν 232.
ὁμολογουμένως adv. 330.
ὅμως advers. conj. 410 (a).
−ον− decl. of stems in 187-8.
−ον decl. of subst. in 158-9.
−ον decl. of adj .with stems in 212 C.
ὄναρ forms 181 C.
−οντ− decl. of adj. with stems in
 211 C b; of participles with stems
 in 214 C-F.

ὄντως case of 348.
ὀξύρριν form 189 c.
ὀξύς decl. of 211 A a.
–oo decl. of stems in 161.
–oos decl. of adj. with masc. in 209.
ὄπισθεν with abl. p. 234, p. 251.
ὀπίσω with abl. p. 234.
ὁποῖος use of 227 b, p. 269-71, 448 (h).
ὅπου case of p. 226, 348; use p. 318, 423 (c), 448 (d).
ὅπως use of 430 (f), 434 (b), 448 (d), 453 (b).
ὁράω defective in voice 396; action of 400.
ὀρέων uncontr. gen. 192 b.
ὀρκίζω with two acc. p. 219.
ὄρνεον form 161 b.
ὄρνιξ form 176 B c and C b.
ὄρνις form 161 b, 176 C b.
–os decl. of subst. in 158-9.
–os adj. in p. 176; decl. of adj. with masc. in 206-8.
–os gen. case-end. 126.
–oσ subst. with stems in 196; decl. of neut. subst. with stems in 192.
ὅς, ἥ, ὅ decl. of 227; use of 380, 412-17, 427, 431, 434 (d), 435 (e).
ὃς δέ use 379.
ὃς ἐάν 19.
ὃς μέν use 379.
ὅσγε 227 b.
ὅσιος form 208 b.
ὅσος use of 422 (d), 448 (h).
ὅστις decl. of 228; use of p. 270, 413-16, 427, 431.
ὀστοῦν decl. 161 and b.
ὀσφύς decl. of 200.
ὅταν use of p. 318, 419 (f).
ὅτε use of 329, p. 318, 419 (f)
ὅτι use of 329, p. 222, p. 318, 412, 426 (a), 435 (b), 448 (d), 451 (a).
ὅτου form 228 a.

ου genuine diphth. 32 a; spurious 32a, 49c, 53.
ου in vowel-grad. 47, 298 c.
οὐ (οὐκ, οὐχ) use of 417, 444, 448 (b), 457 (f), 463, 464 (a)—(j) and (l)—(n).
οὐ μή use of 464 (k).
–ου decl. of stems in 201 A—C.
οὗ adv. p. 226; use of p. 318, 423 (b).
οὐαί case of p. 244; with dat. p. 244; use of 448 (h).
οὐδέ disjunct. conj. 464 (a); οὐδέ— οὐδέ p. 317.
οὐδείς decl. 236 N; use of 383, 464 (a) and (n).
οὐθείς use of 383, 464 (a).
οὐκέτι use of 464 (a).
οὔκουν use of 448 (d).
οὐκοῦν use of 448 (d).
οὖν infer. conj. 329, p. 317, 425.
οὔποτε use 464 (a).
οὐράνιος genders 208 b.
οὖς decl. 182 b; accent of gen. pl. 175 N.
–ous of acc. pl. 140.
οὔτε disjunct. conj. 329, 464 (a) and (n); οὔτε—οὔτε p. 317.
οὗτος decl. of 225 a; use 379.
οὕτως use of 348.
οὐχί 322.
ὄφελον use of 445-7.
ὄφις decl. 198c.
ὀψέ with abl. p. 251.

π decl. of stems in 176 A.
παῖς stem and form 124, 172 b (a), 172 c, 175 N.
πάλαι case p. 244, 345 (c).
πανοικεί(–ί) case 231, p. 240.
πανπληθεί case of p. 240.
πανταχοῦ adv. p. 226.
πάντη(–ῃ) case 231, p. 240.

ῥήτωρ decl. of 186 *A*; voc. 172 b (a).
–ρος adj. in p. 177.
ρρ origin 56 b; after augment 274
    N. 4; breathing with 33 a.
ρσ origin 56 b.
'Ρωμαϊστί 232.

σ initial 65-6; disappearance of 64;
    consonants before 62; before con-
    sonants 63.
–s case end. 124, 126.
–s pers. end. 290, 291 b.
–s final in adv. 79.
–σ– stems in 125; decl. of stems in
    190-6.
–σα tense suffix 287.
σάββασιν form 163 B b.
–σαι pers. end. 293 b.
σάλπιγξ decl. of 176 *B*.
–σαν pers. end. 290, 290 C.
σάρξ decl. of 176 *B*.
–σθα pers. end. 290.
–σθαι inf. end. 296 a (4); dat. end.
    455 (a).
–σθε pers. end. 293 d.
–σθων pers. end. 294 B b.
–σθωσαν pers. end. 294 B b.
–σι loc. pl. case-end. 138-9.
–σι pers. end. 290, 291 b, c.
–σια subst. in p. 173.
σιδηροῦς decl. 209 b.
σίναπι decl. of 198.
–σις subst. in p. 173.
–σκ– verb suffix 287, 180, 317 (f) (3)
σκόλοψ decl. 176 *A* N.
–σο pers. end. 293c, 294 B a.
–σο/ε tense suffix 287.
σός poss. pron. 222.
σπείρης form 11, 154 c.
σσ var. with ττ 56 a.
–σσι loc. pl. case-end. 139.

στάδιον 163 A.
στάς decl. 178 N.
στάχυς decl. of 200.
στεῖρα form 208 b.
στέλλω conj. of perf. act. p. 139.
–στι adv. end. 232.
στίμι decl. 198 d.
σύ decl. of 220.
συγγενῆν form 174 b.
συκῆ decl. 157.
Συμεών 203.
σύν with asso.-inst. p. 241-2, 370.
συνειδυίης form 154 c.
–συνη subst. in p. 174.
συνίημι conj. of pres. 260.
συνίουσιν form 302.
σχές p. 164, 294 A a.
σῶμα decl. of 180.
σωτήρ decl. of 186*A*.

τ decl. of stems in 176 C.
τ verb suffix p. 180, 287, 317 (f) (4).
ταλειθά 25, 341 (c).
τάσσω conj. of perf. midd. and pass.
    269 (c).
ταυτά crasis 55.
τάχα case of p. 238, p. 240, 348.
ταχύ case of 231, 348.
ταχύς decl. 211 *A* a.
τε copul. conj. 329, 410 (a).
–τε pers. end. 290.
τέθνηκα redup. of 71 a.
τεθνήξω form 304, p. 305.
–τέος verbals in p. 177, 458.
τέρας decl. 180 N.
–τερος, –τατος comp. of adj. p. 177,
    216.
τέσσαρες decl. of 236 d; var. in
    acc. 11, 174 e.
τεταρταῖος adj. 240.
τετραπλοῦς decl. 209 b.
τετέλεσμαι 271 d.

τηλικοῦτος demon. pron. 225 d; use of 269.

–τηρ subst. on p. 173; decl. of subst. in 184-186; vowel-grad. in 47 N.

–τήριον subst. in p. 174.

–της subst. in p. 173, p. 174.

–τι pers. end. 290, 291 c.

τιθείς decl. of 214 B.

τίθημι conj. of aor. act. and midd. 257 A; conj. of pres. system 259.

–τικος adj. in p. 176.

τίκτω form 74.

τιμᾶν (τιμᾷν) 52 f.

τιμάω conj. of pres. system 264 (b).

τιμιώτατος 216 c.

τιμῶν decl. of 214 E.

τίς, τί decl. of 229; use of 381, 448 (c), (e), (h).

τὶς, τὶ encl. 102 A; decl. of 230; use 382.

τίς—ἤ use 448 (f).

–τις subst. in p. 173.

τοί use of 472 (f).

τοιγαροῦν infer. conj. p. 317.

τοίνυν use of p. 317.

τοιόσδε demon. pron. 225 d; use p. 269.

τοιοῦτος demon. pron. 225 d; use p. 269.

–τος verbals in p. 177, 458.

τοσοῦτος demon. pron. 225 d.

τοὐναντίον crasis 55.

τοὔνομα crasis 55.

τρεῖς decl. of 236 c.

τρέπω conj. of 2 aor. pass. p. 119; conj. of fut. pass. 267 C.

–τρια subst. in p. 173.

τρίβω conj. of perf. midd. and pass. 269 (b).

τριήρην form 174 b.

τ–τρον subst. in p. 174.

τ(σσ) 56a.

–τω pers. end. 294 A a.

–τωρ subst. in p. 173; decl. of subst. in 184, 186 A; vowel-grad. in 47 N.

–τωσαν pers end. 294 A e.

υ (consonant) between vowels 31 b.

υ in vowel-grad. 47, 298 c.

υ stems in 123-4; decl. of stems in 199-201C; decl. of adj. with stems in 211 A.

ὑγιῆν form 174 b.

ὕδωρ decl. 181 a.

–υϝ decl. of stems in 200.

ὑμέτερος poss. pron. 222;.use p. 266.

–υντ decl. of part. with stems in 214 G.

ὑπέρ adv. 352; with acc. p. 224; with abl. p. 234, 371.

ὑπεράνω with abl. p. 234, p. 251.

ὑπερέκεινα with abl. p. 234, p. 251.

ὑπερεκπερισσοῦ with abl. p. 234, p. 251.

ὑπήκοος form 209 c.

ὑπό with acc. p. 224, 372; with abl. p. 234, 372.

ὑποκάτω with abl. p. 234, p. 251.

φ decl. of stems in 176 A.

φάγεσαι form p. 166, 293 b. N.

φάγομαι 303.

φαίνω voices of 396.

φέρω action of 394; tenses of 393.

φημί encl. forms of 102 A c; conj. of pres. system 261.

φιλῶν decl. of 214 D.

φράτερσιν, φράτορσιν 186 A a.

φρέαρ decl. 181 a, b.

φρήν 173 b N.

φωνή decl. of 154.

φῶς decl. 175 N., 182.

φωστήρ decl. 186 A c.

χ decl. of stems in 176 B.

χαίρειν abs. p. 164.

INDEX OF SUBJECTS

The references are to the sections unless p. is added when it will be to the page.